In the literature on the Dutch Revolt – indeed, in the scholarship on revolution as a whole – the experience of the leading textile and trading center of Lille stands out as singular. Although affected by powerful economic, political, and religious currents that provoked rebellion in many other cities, it was renowned for adhering to the existing order. In this comprehensive study, Robert S. DuPlessis draws on a wide range of primary sources to illuminate the processes of selective adaptation that by the 1560s had endowed Lille with a structural tendency to stability.

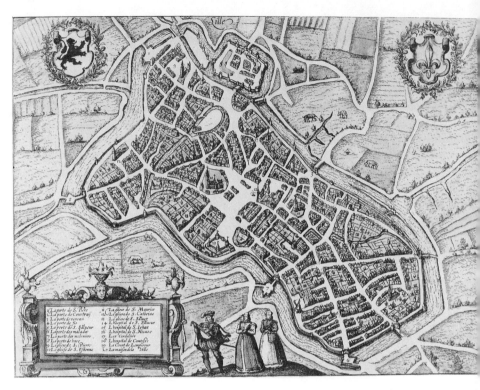

The City of Lille. Engraving from the sixteenth century. Lille, Musée de l'Hospice Comtesse.

CAMBRIDGE STUDIES IN EARLY MODERN HISTORY

Editors

J. H. ELLIOTT   OLWEN HUFTON
H. G. KOENIGSBERGER

Lille and the Dutch Revolt

CAMBRIDGE STUDIES IN EARLY MODERN HISTORY

Edited by *Professor J. H. Elliott, Regius Professor of Modern History,*
Oxford University; Professor Olwen Hufton, Harvard University;
Professor H. G. Koenigsberger

The idea of an "early modern" period of European history from the fifteenth to the late eighteenth century is now widely accepted among historians. The purpose of the Cambridge Studies in Early Modern History is to publish monographs and studies which will illuminate the character of the period as a whole, and in particular focus attention on a dominant theme within it, the interplay of continuity and change as they are represented by the continuity of medieval ideas, political and social organization, and by the impact of new ideas, new methods and new demands on the traditional structures.

The Old World and the New, 1492–1650
J. H. ELLIOTT

The Army of Flanders and the Spanish Road, 1567–1659: The Logistics of Spanish Victory and Defeat in the Low Countries Wars
GEOFFREY PARKER

Gunpowder and Galleys: Changing Technology and Mediterranean Warfare at Sea in the Sixteenth Century
JOHN FRANCIS GUILMARTIN JR

The State, War and Peace: Spanish Political Thought in the Renaissance 1516–1559
J. A. FERNÁNDEZ-SANTAMARIA

Calvinist Preaching and Iconoclasm in the Netherlands 1544–1569
PHYLLIS MACK CREW

Altopascio: A Study in Tuscan Rural Society 1587–1784
FRANK MCARDLE

The Kingdom of Valencia in the Seventeenth Century
JAMES CASEY

Filippo Strozzi and the Medici: Favor and Finance in Sixteenth-Century Florence and Rome
MELISSA MERIAM BULLARD

Rouen during the Wars of Religion
PHILIP BENEDICT

Neostoicism and the Early Modern State
GERHARD OESTREICH

The Emperor and his Chancellor: A Study of the Imperial Chancellery under Gattinara
JOHN M. HEADLEY

The Military Organization of a Renaissance State: Venice c. 1400 to 1617
M. E. MALLETT AND J. R. HALE

Prussian Society and the German Order: An Aristocratic Corporation in Crisis c. 1410 to 1466
MICHAEL BURLEIGH

Richelieu and Olivares
J. H. ELLIOTT

Other titles in this series are on page following the Index.

Lille and the Dutch Revolt

Urban Stability in an Era of Revolution 1500–1582

ROBERT S. DUPLESSIS

Swarthmore College

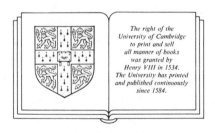

The right of the
University of Cambridge
to print and sell
all manner of books
was granted by
Henry VIII in 1534.
The University has printed
and published continuously
since 1584.

CAMBRIDGE UNIVERSITY PRESS

Cambridge

New York   Port Chester   Melbourne   Sydney

Published by the Press Syndicate of the University of Cambridge
The Pitt Building, Trumpington Street, Cambridge CB2 1RP
40 West 20th Street, New York, NY 10011, USA
10 Stamford Road, Oakleigh, Melbourne 3166, Australia

© Cambridge University Press 1991

First published 1991

Printed in the United States of America

Publication of this book was aided by a grant from Swarthmore College

Library of Congress Cataloging-in-Publication Data
DuPlessis. Robert S.
Lille and the Dutch Revolt : urban stability in an era of
revolution, 1500–1582 / Robert S. DuPlessis.
p.   cm. – (Cambridge studies in early modern history)
ISBN 0-521-39415-5
1. Lille (France) – History.   2. Netherlands – History – Wars of
Independence, 1556–1648 – Influence.   I. Title.   II. Series.
DC801.L687D86   1991
944'.28 – dc20   90-41556
CIP

British Library Cataloguing in Publication Data
DuPlessis, Robert S.
Lille and the Dutch Revolt : Urban Stability in an era of
revolution 1500–1582. – (Cambridge studies in early
modern history)
1. France. Lille. Social Conditions, history
I. Title
944.28

ISBN 0-521-39415-5 hardback

For my mother and father

Contents

List of illustrations and tables   *page* ix
Acknowledgments   xi
Notes on dates, money, and citations   xiii
Abbreviations   xiv

Introduction: Cities and the Dutch Revolt   1

Part One: Forces of revolt and stabilizing structures

1. Magistrat, city, and central state   17
2. "Substantial merchants conducting important trade"   50
3. "Cloth of every type and price"   85
4. Impoverishment and intervention   119
5. Piety and the parameters of reform   158
    Epilogue: Stress and stability   195

Part Two: Revolution and stability

6. A city's "fine duty": Lille in the iconoclastic fury,
    1566–1567   203
7. "Trampling and oppression": Lille under Alba and
    Requesens, 1567–1576   233
8. From "common cause" to "special league": Lille between
    Estates-General and reconciliation, 1576–1582   256

Conclusion: Stability in revolution   307

Contents

Appendixes

A. The population of Lille in the sixteenth century   321
B. Marriage portions in sixteenth-century Lille (1544–1600)   324
C. Assessments for Hundredth Penny tax, 1569   326
D. Immigration to Lille of families
   of sixteenth-century merchants   327
E. The wealth of leading commercial families in Lille
   during the sixteenth century   330
F. Sources for the standard of living: problems and
   attempted solutions   340
G. Monetary payments disbursed by Lille's Common
   Fund, 1536–1582   349

Note on primary sources   351
Index   357

List of illustrations and tables

Figures

1.1.	The Magistrat of Lille	*page* 18
3.1.	Draperie sealed in Lille, 1517–65	87
3.2.	Output of Lille's sayetteurs, 1495–1565	92
3.3.	Output of changéants and velveteens by Lille's bourgetteurs, 1541–65	95
4.1.	Grain prices and wage rates in Lille, 1501–65	125
4.2.	Grain prices and economic activity in Lille, 1501–65	131

Plates

1.	The Halle Echevinale	7
2.	The Château de Courtrai	8
3.	The Palais Rihour	9
4.	The Collegiate Church of St. Pierre	160

Maps

1.	Lille in the early sixteenth century	4
2.	Walloon Flanders in the sixteenth century	6

Tables

1.1.	Distribution of officeholding in Lille's Magistrat by family, 1541–65	26

Illustrations and tables

1.2. Total terms in office of Lillois serving in the Magistrat, 1541–65   27

1.3. Lille's aides and loans to the central government, 1501–65   42

1.4. Receipts by Lille's municipal treasury, 1501–65   43

2.1. Loans by Lille's merchants to governmental institutions, 1537–62   67

2.2. Marriages between merchant and artisan families in Lille, 1544–60   69

2.3. Frequency of trade at or with Antwerp by Lillois during the sixteenth century   72

2.4. The estate of Jean de Bertault, 1574   77

4.1. The evolution of indexes of prices, rents, and wages in Lille, 1501–65   121

4.2. Price and wage indexes in Lille, 1556–7 through 1566–7   129

4.3. Percentage of annual income needed to purchase grain for family of four or five persons in sixteenth-century Lille   133

4.4. Major sources of revenue of Lille's Common Fund, 1536–65   146

4.5. Leading expenditures of Lille's Common Fund, 1536–65   147

4.6. Loaves of bread distributed by Lille's Common Fund, 1537–66   149

4.7. Receipts and disbursements of Lille's Common Fund by parish, 1536–65   150

4.8. Indexes of Common Fund outlays, grain prices, and employment in Lille, 1561–6   154

5.1. Occupations of Lillois who were prosecuted or emigrated due to their religious beliefs, 1544–66   184

6.1. Indexes of cash and bread distributions by Lille's Common Fund, January–December 1565 and 1566 compared   224

7.1. Indexes of textile output in Lille, 1566–76   239

7.2. Indexes of Common Fund outlays, grain prices, wages, and employment in Lille, 1566–76   240

8.1. Indexes of textile output in Lille, 1576–82   261

8.2. Indexes of Common Fund outlays, grain prices, wages, and employment in Lille, 1576–82   263

F.1. Estimated budgets of urban wage earners in preindustrial Europe   346

Acknowledgments

In the course of the many years spent on this study, I have accumulated numerous scholarly and personal debts. I am extremely grateful to the Foreign Area Fellowship Program (now unhappily no longer in existence) for originally supporting research for this project, and to Swarthmore College for grants that allowed further archival work in France and Belgium, the construction of the figures, and time for rewriting. Of the many librarians and archivists who have so generously assisted me, I would like to give special thanks to Serge Fremaux of the municipal archives of Lille, who in addition to friendly aid *sur place* has subsequently answered queries by mail; and to Lois Peterson and Minda Hart of the interlibrary loan service of McCabe Library, Swarthmore College, for obtaining innumerable books and articles. The influence of many scholars is, I hope, evident and acknowledged throughout the book. I would like to thank Hugo Soly in particular for many helpful suggestions and comments, as well as (along with Rina Lis) generous hospitality. Martha Howell aided me in clarifying some ideas. My greatest scholarly, and large personal, obligations are to Wim Smit, under whose direction a much earlier (and rather different) version was prepared as a doctoral dissertation. Since that time he has patiently read and reread countless drafts of the manuscript, never failing to offer timely advice. J. H. Elliott and H. G. Koenigsberger performed a signal service by forcing me to rewrite the text substantially. Over the years, Monique Lecomte has obtained photocopies of many articles and essays that were not available in American libraries and provided warm hospitality on several of my visits to Lille. Using computer skills far in advance of mine, Nick Jackiw rapidly and carefully produced the maps. John Boccio generously offered his time and computer expertise to produce the figures, and Mary

Hasbrouck helped me revise them. Eleanor Bennett typed drafts of many of the chapters and deserves my special gratitude for putting the tables in presentable form. Amid her own very heavy scholarly and family responsibilities my wife Rachel helped me see the manuscript through over the long haul and provided an attentive critical reading of the final version. Our daughter Koré's eagerness to celebrate the final submission of the work helped hasten it to completion. I dedicate the book to my parents, for their love and support and, more specifically, for initially awakening my interest in history.

Notes on dates, money, and citations

Dates. Up to the beginning of 1576, the year started at Lille on Easter; after that point, the city switched to the Gregorian calendar, in which January 1 is the first day of the year. In this book, all dates have been changed to the Gregorian or new style.

Money. Two kinds of money are referred to in this book. (1) The parisis system, originally established by the French kings. It included the livre parisis (abbreviated in the tables and notes of this book simply as liv.), a money of account. Each livre was divided into 20 sols (s.) or 240 deniers (d.). Thus 1 sol was worth 12 deniers. (2) The system based on the florin (fl.), a money of account worth 2 livres parisis. A florin was divided into 20 patars (or 40 gros of Flanders) and 240 deniers tournois. The livre de gros, which contained 240 gros, was worth six florins or twelve livres parisis.

Citations. All citations not in English have been left as found in the archival or printed documents. Diacritical marks have not been added to names of individuals (e.g., Gerard has not been modernized to Gérard, nor Helie to Hélie). All translations are mine.

Abbreviations

AASL	Archives de l'aide sociale de Lille in AML
ADN	Archives départementales du Nord (France)
AEN	Archives de l'Etat à Namur (Belgium)
AESC	*Annales: économies, sociétés, civilisations*
AET	Archives de l'Etat à Tournai (Belgium)
Aff. gén.	Affaires générales in AML
AGR	Archives Générales du Royaume (Brussels)
AH	Archives hospitalières in ADN
AML	Archives municipales de Lille
BCHDN	*Bulletin de la Commission Historique du Département du Nord*
BCRHB	*Bulletin de la Commission royale d'histoire de la Belgique*
BML	Bibliothèque municipale de Lille
BN	Bibliothèque nationale (Paris)
BSEPC	*Bulletin de la Société d'Etudes de la Province de Cambrai*
BSHPF	*Bulletin de la Société de l'Histoire du protestantisme français*
C.	Carton in Aff. gén.
CFMP	*Correspondance française de Marguerite de Parme*
CG	*Correspondance du Cardinal de Granvelle*
	Correspondance de Marguerite d'Autriche, duchesse de Parme, avec Philippe II
CMA	*Correspondance de Marguerite d'Autriche, duchesse de Parme, avec Philippe II*
CP, ed. Gachard	*Correspondance de Philippe II*
CP, ed. Lefèvre	*Correspondance de Philippe II, deuxième partie*

Abbreviations

CS	*Correspondance secrète de Jean Sarrazin*
d.	dossier in Aff. gén. or denier (see note on money)
EA	Papiers d'Etat et d'Audience in AGR
fl.	florin(s) (see note on money)
liv.	livre(s) parisis (see note on money)
MSSAAL	*Mémoires de la Société des sciences, de l'agriculture et des arts de Lille*
PP	*Past and Present*
RB	Archives of the Raad van Beroerte (Council of Troubles) in AGR
RBPH	*Revue Belge de Philosophie et d'Histoire*
RSG	*Resolutiën der Staten-Generaal*
RN	*Revue du Nord*
s.	sol (see note on money)
SA	Stadsarchief Antwerpen (Belgium)
Tab.	Tabellion in ADN
VSWG	*Vierteljahrschrift für Sozial- und Wirtschaftsgeschichte*

INTRODUCTION

Cities and the Dutch Revolt

> Looking at the Netherlands as a whole, they appear a veritable
> land of towns.[1]

With the possible exception of parts of Tuscany and Lombardy, no other
area of sixteenth-century Europe could boast such a high proportion of
city dwellers nor so vibrant and diverse an urban civilization as the Low
Countries.[2] Although never constituting sovereign republics like those
found in medieval and Renaissance Italy, cities formed the most developed political entities in the Netherlands. Armed with extensive privileges, they enjoyed considerable power over the urban populace in addition to a significant degree of autonomy from the Habsburg state, whose
central institutions were as yet but weakly developed.[3] Cities dominated
the representative estates of the core provinces of Flanders, Brabant,
and Holland and had a powerful voice even in more rural areas. Because
the Estates-General was little more than a meeting of delegates from the
provincial bodies, the towns also carried a great deal of weight in national politics.

Antwerp was the greatest commercial and financial center of the age,
"the outstanding cosmopolitan town of the century."[4] Amsterdam, chief
among a host of lively ports in Holland and Zeeland, was coming to

---

[1] Pieter Geyl, *The Revolt of the Netherlands*, 2nd ed. (London, 1958), pp. 44–5.

[2] According to the most recent estimate, in 1550 some 19.5% of the population of the present-day
Netherlands and Belgium lived in towns of at least 10,000 inhabitants. The corresponding figure
for northern Italy was 15.1%; for Europe as a whole, 6.3%. See Jan de Vries, *European Urbanization 1500–1800* (Cambridge, Mass., 1984), table 3.7, p. 39 and passim.

[3] Cf. J. W. Smit, "The Netherlands Revolution," in *Preconditions of Revolution in Early Modern
Europe*, ed. Robert Forster and Jack P. Greene (Baltimore, 1970), p. 28: "The real loci of power
were the noble dynasties and the towns."

[4] J. A. Van Houtte, *An Economic History of the Low Countries 800–1800* (New York, 1977), p. 183.

I

predominate in the important Baltic trade. Woolen textiles and luxury crafts brought renewed prosperity to many other cities. Towns were also home to a flourishing humanist culture, propagated by numerous printing presses and by chambers of rhetoric, uniquely Netherlands institutions that sponsored public literary contests and dramatic presentations. Particularly in the southern provinces, cities teemed with great cathedrals, parish churches, and religious houses. Yet already by the 1520s, Lutherans were to be found in many towns, and other reforming movements later proselytized and organized there with great success.

The grievances and aspirations of the aristocracy contributed importantly to the outbreak of the Dutch Revolt in 1566, and nobles remained central to the military operations mounted over the next eighty years. But as Tibor Wittman has noted, "the Netherlands Revolution was above all an urban phenomenon."[5] Cities were the principal foyers of rebellion and cities experienced the most radical changes.[6] Urban centers were the sites of sustained popular mobilization and they repeatedly underwent violent political and religious struggles. Not surprisingly, then, Spanish military and diplomatic efforts focused on subjugating towns, although they met with only partial success. A combination of force and guile did result in the reconquest of an area corresponding to much of present-day Belgium. But in the republic that emerged in the northern provinces, cities reigned supreme in nearly every aspect of economic, social, political, and intellectual life.

This book is intended as a contribution to our understanding of urban behavior during this momentous upheaval. My focus is the city of Lille, now in northern France but in the sixteenth century the chief town of one of the seventeen provinces that composed the Habsburg Netherlands.[7] A local study can usefully illuminate the causes, course, and outcome of the revolt for two related reasons. First, a sturdy particularism characterized life in the early modern Low Countries, and nowhere more visibly than in the cities, marked as they were by distinctive

---

[5] Tibor Wittman, *Les Gueux dans les "bonnes villes" de Flandre (1577–1584)* (Budapest, 1969), p. 239.

[6] The events described in this book form part of what is most often called the *Dutch Revolt*, although in the Netherlands the term *Eighty Years' War* is commonly employed, and recently some scholars have begun to refer to the *Netherlands Revolution*. Each tag carries with it a distinctive interpretation and set of ideological presumptions, although these are rarely made explicit.

[7] From west to east and south to north, the provinces were Artois, Cambrai, Hainaut, Namur, Flanders, Walloon or French Flanders, Tournai and the Tournésis, Brabant, Mechelen, Zeeland, Holland, Utrecht, Gelderland, Overijssel, Drenthe, Friesland, and Groningen and the Ommelanden.

political regimes, economic activities, social structures, and cultural configurations. Second, as recent scholarship has argued, the Dutch Revolt ought to be considered not a single phenomenon with unitary origins and a common development, but a congeries of multiple rebellions. These rebellions converged at times but sprang from diverse causes, pursued distinct objectives and often followed divergent paths.[8]

In his *Description of All the Low Countries,* published in 1567, the Italian merchant and long-time Antwerp resident Lodovico Guicciardini praised Lille as "a beautiful and rich city." Filled with handsome civil and religious edifices, it was inhabited by "great nobility," "a large number of great merchants," and "many industrious artisans."[9] Home to the provincial administration, and customary meeting place for the provincial Estates, Lille was, in Guicciardini's words, "the chief [town] and capital of all Flanders known as Walloon."[10]

The town that Guicciardini celebrated covered about a hundred hectares at a spot where the Deûle River, flowing roughly north toward its confluence with the Lys some fifteen kilometers downstream, divided into a number of channels. The small islands thus created gave the city that arose on them no later than the eleventh century its name. As Lille grew, the branches of the Deûle were canalized, and additional canals

---

[8] Cf. J. W. Smit, "The Present Position of Studies Regarding the Revolt of the Netherlands," in *Britain and the Netherlands,* ed. J. S. Bromley and E. H. Kossman (London, 1960), p. 28: "There were a number of revolts, representing the interests and the ideals of various social, economical and ideological groups: revolts which sometimes run parallel, sometimes conflict with one another, and at other times coalesce into a single movement."

[9] The quotations in this section are my translations from the French version, Lodovico Guicciardini, *Description de tout le Païs-Bas autrement dict la Germanie Inférieure, ou Basse-Allemaigne* (Antwerp, 1567), pp. 330–3.

[10] Originally part of the country of Flanders – Lille was important enough to sit as one of the five "members" of the Flemish Estates from 1180 to 1304 – the Walloon section had been detached during the early fourteenth-century Franco-Flemish wars and administered directly by the French crown between 1304 and 1369. Upon its cession to Burgundian control, the area retained its political autonomy and was endowed with a governorship and Estates. An asymmetrical rectangle 25 to 40 km. wide, the province stretched some 60 km. from the Lys valley north of Lille – where from Armentières to Halluin villages producing woolen cloth crowded the riverbanks – to a swampy farming district south of Douai. Situated approximately in the middle of the present Département du Nord, it was bordered by the Lys River on the northwest toward Flanders and on the south by the Scarpe, tributary to the Scheldt (in French, Escaut). The irregular boundary with Artois on the west lacked distinguishing natural features, as did the eastern border with the Tournésis. Including enclaves on the east bank of the Scheldt north of Tournai, along with a few settlements south of Douai (other provinces likewise had enclaves of their own inside Walloon Flanders), the province measured about 1,450 sq. km., thus occupying only 2% to 3% of the total land area of the Netherlands. But its mid-sixteenth-century population of 140,000 to 150,000, living in some 190 hamlets, villages, and towns, constituted 7 or 7.5% of the 2 million inhabitants of the seventeen provinces.

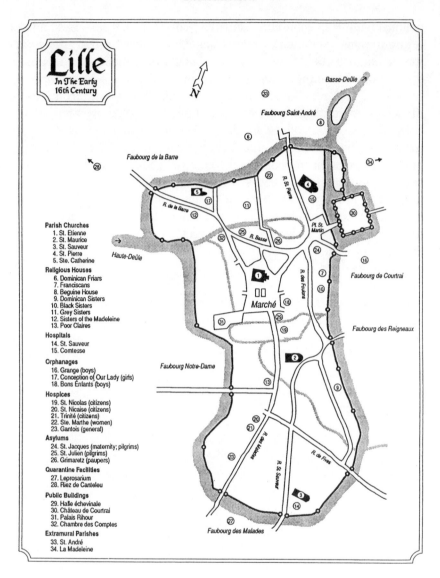

Lille
In The Early
16th Century

Basse-Deûle

Faubourg Saint-André

Faubourg de la Barre

R. St. Pierre

Pt. St. Martin

R. de la Barre

R. Basse

Haute-Deûle

R. des Fullons

Faubourg de Courtrai

Marché

Faubourg des Reigneaux

Faubourg Notre-Dame

R. des Malades

R. St. Sauveur

R. de Fives

Faubourg des Malades

Parish Churches
1. St. Etienne
2. St. Maurice
3. St. Sauveur
4. St. Pierre
5. Ste. Catherine

Religious Houses
6. Dominican Friars
7. Franciscans
8. Beguine House
9. Dominican Sisters
10. Black Sisters
11. Grey Sisters
12. Sisters of the Madeleine
13. Poor Claires

Hospitals
14. St. Sauveur
15. Comtesse

Orphanages
16. Grange (boys)
17. Conception of Our Lady (girls)
18. Bons Enfants (boys)

Hospices
19. St. Nicolas (citizens)
20. St. Nicaise (citizens)
21. Trinité (citizens)
22. Ste. Marthe (women)
23. Gantois (general)

Asylums
24. St. Jacques (maternity; pilgrims)
25. St. Julien (pilgrims)
26. Grimaretz (paupers)

Quarantine Facilities
27. Leprosarium
28. Riez de Canteleu

Public Buildings
29. Halle échevinale
30. Château de Courtrai
31. Palais Rihour
32. Chambre des Comptes

Extramural Parishes
33. St. André
34. La Madeleine

Map 1. Lille in the early sixteenth century

dug, bringing boats up to busy quays where their cargoes were unloaded for sale or transshipment, providing water for a host of industrial uses from mills to tanneries, and irrigating the moats that entirely surrounded the town walls (see Map 1).

With at least 30,000 residents in the mid-sixteenth century,[11] Lille likely ranked among the half-dozen largest cities in the Netherlands.[12] Five varied parishes lay within its walls. St. Etienne, the largest with some 1,100 houses in the 1560s, was home to Lille's richest merchants as well as many professionals and prosperous artisans. Located in the center of town on the western side of the *Marché*, it faced the seat of municipal authority, the Halle échevinale. In a late sixteenth-century drawing (Plate 1), this asymmetrical building awaits its forthcoming demolition huddled next to the handsome mannerist New Hall (1594) that took its place. On the second floor of the old Halle is the *bretesque*, a bay window with a pointed roof, from the windows of which all city ordinances and regulations were read and thereby officially published. Towering above the Halle is an ungainly belfry, where the town clock and bells hung. These were rung to mark the beginning and end of the workday, and also to summon citizens in an emergency. At the right side of the drawing can be seen the wooden houses with high gables that predominated in Lille well into the eighteenth century, whereas at the left, next to the New Hall, stands a brick building with stepped gables, still a rarity in sixteenth-century domestic architecture.

To the east of the Marché was the parish of St. Maurice (1,060 houses), Lille's most occupationally diverse, and at the very east of the city lay the parish of St. Sauveur, with 1,030 houses lived in mainly by textile artisans. The parish of St. Pierre, housed in the collegiate church of the same name, included 300 houses in the northwestern corner of the city, whereas to the southwest was Ste. Catherine (400 houses), fully incorporated within Lille as recently as 1415 and home to many artisans, a significant proportion of whom seem to have been Flemish-speaking immigrants. As Map 1 shows, numerous religious congregations, hospitals, hospices, asylums, and orphanages were scattered throughout the city. Several institutions were also situated outside the walls – the Do-

---

[11] See Appendix A.

[12] In the mid-sixteenth century Antwerp counted about 90,000 inhabitants, Ghent perhaps 50,000, Brussels 40,000, and Bruges 35,000. Amsterdam was approximately the same size as my calculation for Lille, while Utrecht, Mechelen, and Tournai (each with 25,000) and 's Hertogenbosch (23,000) were slightly smaller. See de Vries, *European Urbanization*, pp. 271–2, 292–4.

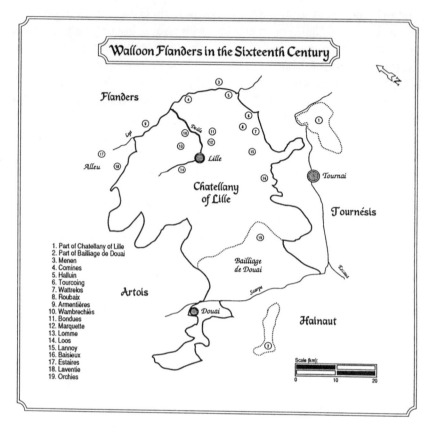

Map 2. Walloon Flanders in the sixteenth century

minican monastery, the Beguine house, an orphanage, the Riez de Canteleu where some citizens chose to lodge in makeshift barracks during
epidemics, and the citizens' leper house, which lent its name to the
faubourg des Malades, the suburb that had grown up around it. Other
suburbs crowded near many of the city gates. Finally, there were two
small extramural parishes, St. André and La Madeleine, both of which
had predominantly poor and laboring populations.

As Guicciardini noted, Lille could boast some fine public buildings.
Unfortunately, only a very few have survived, and these are truncated
and much altered. Contemporary views, however, help recreate them.
Before the revolt, a traveler coming from Flanders would initially have

Plate 1. The Halle Echevinale. Drawing from the late sixteenth century. Lille, Musée de l'Hospice Comtesse.

spied the imposing mass of the many-towered Château de Courtrai, built about 1298 by King Philip the Fair of France (Plate 2). Sitting on a separate islet, and surrounded entirely by its own massive fortifications, the castle – or rather, the garrison within – became a source of friction during the Dutch Revolt. Resentful of repeated incidents between soldiers and townspeople, and fearful that the troops might pour out one night and – as happened elsewhere – perpetrate a massacre, in 1577 the municipal government gladly paid handsomely for the right to demolish the citadel.

A more recent addition to the city was the Palais Rihour (Plate 3), which lay south of the Marché, across the city from the Château de Courtrai. This sizable brick and stone building was erected between 1453 and 1473 for Philip the Good, duke of Burgundy and count of Flanders, who spent much time in Lille, his favorite city. As Brussels increasingly became the permanent seat of Netherlands government, however, his successors visited the palace less and less. In the sixteenth century, it fell into disuse, save the largest wing, on the right side of the

7

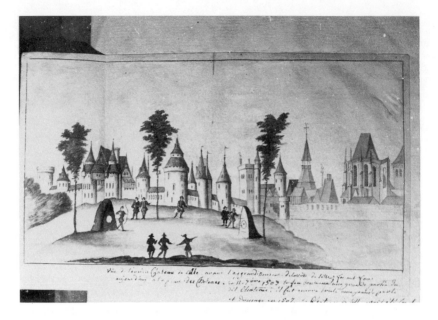

Plate 2. The Château de Courtrai. At the right, the choir of the Collegiate Church of St. Pierre. Copy of a late fifteenth-century miniature. Lille, Musée de l'Hospice Comtesse.

picture. This housed the Gouvernance, where the governor of Walloon Flanders lived and the members of his staff had their offices. If no longer a favorite princely residence, however, Lille remained the seat of an important Chambre des Comptes that handled royal revenues for nearly half the Netherlands.[13] Since 1413, the chamber had been located in an old *hôtel* at the end of the rue Esquermoise, thus contributing to the spatial dispersion of the institutions of the central government.

"Because," Guicciardini reported, "of the commerce and industries that are practiced there," Lille "is considered the principal city of these Low Countries behind Antwerp and Amsterdam." Its merchants dealt in dyestuffs, grain, cattle, and many other items from Walloon Flanders, which the *Description* characterized as "both good and beautiful," blessed with fertile soil and "fair and ample" pastures, if "hardly of great extent (see Map 2)." But their fortunes were made by extensive and broad-based

---

[13] Walloon and Flemish Flanders, Artois, Hainaut, Tournai and the Tournésis, Namur, and Mechelen all were subject to the Chamber of Accounts at Lille.

Plate 3. The Palais Rihour. Christoph Butkens, *Supplément aux trophées tants sacrés que profanes du duché de Brabant*, 2 vols. (The Hague, 1726), vol. 1, facing p. 24. University of Michigan Library).

international trade in grain, wine, cloth, and much more besides, conducted largely through Antwerp. Hundreds of artisans, ranging from painters to pastry cooks, from glovemakers to goldsmiths, plied their trades in Lille. Every other craft paled, however, in comparison with textiles – tapestries for a prince or the Medici, expensive wool *draps* for civic officers and wealthy churchmen, but most of all a continuing profusion of cheap woolens and mixed stuffs dispatched in enormous quantities to nearly every corner of Europe and on to Spanish America.

As we shall see, the trade and textiles of Lille generally prospered up to and through the period of the revolt, and they continued to grow, often dramatically, until the early seventeenth century. After that point, to be sure, the city's economy felt the effects of growing rural and foreign competition, rising mercantilist barriers, and disruption due to annexation by France in 1667. Yet all across the eighteenth century, Lille

9

remained a leading woolen-cloth center, and it subsequently transformed itself into a great cotton and linen producer. The primacy of textiles has waned in recent years, but as late as 1970 spinning, weaving, and associated trades formed the largest single sector of the urban economy in terms of employment, and the Lille-Roubaix-Tourcoing conurbation boasted the strongest concentration of textile activity in Western Europe.

For a number of historiographical reasons, Lille ought to be of considerable interest to the student of the Dutch Revolt. In his early twentieth-century *Histoire de Belgique,* still the paradigmatic account, Henri Pirenne argued that explosive strains in Netherlands urban society, generated by profound changes during the reigns of Charles V (1506–55) and his son and heir Philip II (1555–98), ultimately if unwittingly produced rebellion. In their efforts to build a centralized state, the Habsburg rulers frequently intervened in local political quarrels, refashioned urban magistracies, and enhanced the authority of the prince's administrative and judicial officials. Thus, despite consistently deployed obstructionist tactics, municipal institutions lost ground to a dynamic, progressive, and increasingly powerful centralized regime. At the same time, the crown's infringement of jealously guarded civic liberties and its growing financial demands bred intensifying conflict between sovereign and cities. The process of state formation also endowed urban elites, like their noble and ecclesiastical counterparts, with a national consciousness. As a result, Pirenne believed, they proved able to put aside the localism that had bedeviled all previous revolts and rise in unity against the alien, authoritarian dynasty superimposed upon, but increasingly estranged from, the nation it was bringing into existence.

Cities were also, according to Pirenne, marked decisively by the impressive economic growth that animated the sixteenth-century Netherlands. The emergence of capitalist trade and industry – most notably in the woolen textiles of the southern provinces – bred both entrepreneurs who sought power and status commensurate with their new wealth, and a proletariat experiencing downward social mobility. The price revolution that had begun around 1500 sharpened the effects of the social changes that had resulted from the expansion of capitalism. Entrepreneurs, merchants, and speculators of every ilk benefited from inflation, but rentiers and particularly the ever-expanding mass of wage earners faced a declining standard of living.

Calvinism first emerged in the areas strongly marked by this transformation, Pirenne argued; in his words, the new religion spread "in the wake of capitalism." Its novelty and radicalism appealed to parvenu businessmen who had few links to traditional values, whereas to workers it promised both a better life in the future and desperately needed charity in the present. The new faith channeled elite and popular protest into a massive assault simultaneously on the orthodox church, established government, and traditional social order. Thanks to superb organization and disciplined leaders with an unswerving commitment to radical political and religious change, Calvinism provided both the ideology and the resources necessary for revolution.[14]

Pirenne cited Lille as standing at the forefront of economic change: it was, he declared, a prominent foyer of *"grande industrie"* and home to "capitalists" and "proletarians."[15] Along with Antwerp, Valenciennes, and cities in Holland, he claimed, sixteenth-century Lille was "adapting to the new conditions of the times," thereby attaining an "astonishing prosperity."[16] Consequently, in Pirenne's view, the city was also a major Calvinist center.[17] Yet although Lille fit well Pirenne's definition of a center of rebellion, it became renowned instead for stability, security, and adhesion to the existing order.

Despite the problem that Lille thus presented to his interpretation, Pirenne never tried to account for the city's distinctive history during the revolt. The original impetus for this study, therefore, was the desire to comprehend and explain Lille's anomalous behavior: not merely the city's failure to act as Pirenne's model predicts but its stability amid revolutionary conditions.

I take stability to need explanation because I do not consider it the "natural" condition of society, a state of equilibrium toward which a

14 See Henri Pirenne, *Histoire de Belgique*, 7 vols. (Brussels, 1922–32), esp. vol. 3, books II and III, and vol. 4. The quotation is from 3:436.
15 Ibid., 3:435. Cf. ibid., 3:285, where Pirenne stressed the proletarianization of workers in Lille as in other urban and rural centers, especially in textile regions. In another passage (ibid., 3:245), however, Pirenne's position seems ambiguous. In the text, he wrote that Lille, Tournai, and Valenciennes were undergoing capitalist development similar to that occurring in the rural centers of Hondschoote and Armentières. But in n. 2 he maintained that the survival of trade corporations in Lille, "as altered as they were, prevented the birth of an industry as tightly subject to capital as that in the countryside." It is not clear from the latter comment whether he considered Lille's industrial structure to have been *sui generis* or to have resembled that of the other cities.
16 Ibid., 3:188.
17 Ibid., 3:435.

society tends if left to itself. On the contrary, I regard conflict and change to be permanent attributes of every society, due to asymmetrical relations of production, unequal distributions of power, and discrepant religious commitments, intellectual concerns, and cultural traditions. Instability is, then, as normal as stability: Because stability and instability are constituent elements of human society, neither is ever entirely lacking from any given historical situation.[18]

For the purposes of this study, I use the term *stability* to mean the absence of significant collective action – issuing in iconoclasm, coup, or radical regime – that could have overturned the religious or political order of sixteenth-century Lille. Stability did not preclude conflict, adjustment, and accommodation. It did, however, entail the perpetuation of current structures of domination and subordination, belief and practice. As I shall show, stability was never achieved once and for all but involved a continuous process of stabilization. Further, stability was attained not by implementing a predetermined program but by responding to specific conditions, situations, and demands as they arose in urban society. Thus the process of stabilization in sixteenth-century Lille is best discerned by examining actions taken at the time, although occasionally comments by contemporaries help clarify the premises and goals guiding some measures.

This book analyzes both circumstances generating instability in Lille and means by which stabilization was nevertheless accomplished. Part I investigates critical aspects of the city's development between about 1500 and the spring of 1566, the eve of the first phase of insurrection ushered in by aristocratic maneuvering and increasingly public Protestant activity. Each chapter focuses on factors commonly identified as causes of the revolt and on the responses they evoked in Lille. Because existing power relations endowed the city government with primary responsibility for, and a keen interest in, stability, the actions of the municipal ruling class loom large in this book. If stability is to survive without lapsing into outright coercion, however, it must win broad assent. Hence Part One also attends to the reasons why important sectors of the urban populace subscribed to, or even called for, official intervention. Throughout Chap-

---

[18] For some general considerations, see F. E. Dessauer, *Stability* (New York, 1949). Historians of Venice have traditionally dealt with stability; apart from them, however, scholars of early modern Europe are just beginning to consider the topic at length. For two stimulating recent accounts, see James Casey, *The Kingdom of Valencia in the Seventeenth Century* (Cambridge, 1979), and Theodore Rabb, *The Struggle for Stability in Early Modern Europe* (New York, 1975).

ters 1–5, Pirenne's interpretations as well as modifications suggested by other historians are considered in light of the evidence from Lille. In general, the first part examines, in Charles Tilly's terms,[19] the interests and resources that facilitated or impeded mobilization for collective action.

Part Two considers Lille between 1566 and 1582, a time of pronounced and prolonged political conflict throughout the Netherlands. Several recent accounts have emphasized political and military measures, notably those proposed or carried out by the provincial governor, that frustrated destabilizing collective action.[20] Chapters 6–8 suggest that such steps were viable only because of the prior development of structures promoting stabilization and their further elaboration during the revolt.

Local studies permit analyses that can capture the complexity of historical phenomena. This is a notable advantage to students of the Dutch Revolt, because in the "land of towns" political and economic integration was rudimentary and cities were therefore quite diverse. Yet for all the intensity and clarity of vision that can result, a narrow focus creates problems of its own. Peculiar attributes of a given situation may loom so large as to conceal more widespread patterns and processes; at the same time, important events or trends may be absent from a specific locality or from surviving sources. Thus local studies can remain highly specific and idiosyncratic, even antiquarian, thereby complicating generalization. Furthermore, existing studies of cities in the Low Countries concentrate either on political narrative in which motive, tactics, violence, and other essentially conjunctural and ideological matters predominate, or on the slow evolution of social and economic structures in isolation from politics and *histoire événementielle*.

The first two parts of this book attempt to avoid these pitfalls both by comparing circumstances in Lille with those prevailing in other towns and (especially in Part Two) by integrating political, social, and economic analysis. Because all Netherlands cities reacted in some way to Habsburg financial demands, efforts at political centralization, and religious policy, the conclusion attempts systematic comparisons. Drawing upon the scholarship of collective action, it contrasts conditions in Lille that

---

[19] See Charles Tilly, *From Mobilization to Revolution* (Reading, Mass., 1978).
[20] Cf. Solange Deyon and Alain Lottin, *Les casseurs de l'été 1566* (Paris, 1981), and *Histoire de Lille*, vol. 2, ed. Louis Trenard (Toulouse, 1982).

discouraged mobilization of opposition groups with conditions in other cities of the Netherlands that proved conducive to coups and revolutions. Finally, it suggests revisions in existing interpretations of the revolt, attending particularly to relations between social and economic change and political convulsion.

A wide variety of quantitative and qualitative data is drawn upon in the course of this case study of urban stability. Yet although we shall encounter a number of forceful and influential people, on the whole the extant sources do not permit us to gain much insight into the character or motivation of specific individuals. Indeed, even portraits of prominent sixteenth-century Lillois seem not to exist. Doubtless this lacuna eliminates some of the color from our story. It would be of great interest to know more about, say, the members of the great de Fourmestraux merchant clan – leading pastel importers, alleged grain hoarders, important political figures, and reputed Calvinists. Again, one would like to uncover the truth about the town pensionary Antoine Muyssart. On the basis of surviving materials, as we shall see, he can be understood either as a devoted guardian of Lille's interests in the turbulent late 1570s or as an accomplice of radicals allied with William of Orange.

Whatever the dramatic loss entailed, however, the dearth of personal information does not, in my view, distort the story narrated in this book. For I shall argue that stability was achieved in Lille not by actions taken by individuals but by the interaction of cohesive groups. My account emphasizes structures and collectivities – not because they rigidly determined the behavior of the people who composed them, but because they were the means through which human agency was expressed. Our investigation of the roots of stability properly begins, then, by examining the urban political class and the institutional framework within which it operated.

PART ONE

Forces of revolt and stabilizing structures

1

Magistrat, city, and central state

I

According to the civic myth of origin current in early modern Lille, its municipal government had been founded by an *amitié* or free association of citizens. In the remote past, these men had joined together under the leadership of the *rewart* (or *respector amicitiae*) and had solemnly sworn to aid and protect one another. As the living embodiment of the enduring vitality of this ancient pact, the rewart marched first in all public processions and annually took the oath of office in the name of the incoming Magistrat or *Loi*.[1] Though in part correct, recent scholarship suggests, this mythic account is incomplete. It now appears that the Magistrat emerged in the early thirteenth century when representatives of the burgher commune, probably founded in the later eleventh century, amalgamated with judges originally instituted by the Flemish counts sometime after 1100.[2] The earliest surviving written charter, imposed by Countess Jeanne of Flanders in 1235, codified customs and privileges already current and systematized the municipal administration in a collegiate form. This constitution was to be embellished as the magistrates assumed new responsibilities, but it did not essentially change until the French Revolution.[3]

Figure 1.1 outlines the membership of the city government.[4] The

---

[1] Ed. Van Hende, *Lille et ses institutions communales de 620 à 1804* (Lille, 1888), p. 63.

[2] Alain Derville, "Trois siècles décisifs: l'expansion d'une région et la naissance d'une cité-mère (XIe-XIIIe siècles)," in *Histoire d'une métropole*, ed. Louis Trenard (Toulouse, 1977), pp. 115–17.

[3] Gérard Sivéry, "Quelques aspects des institutions lilloises au Moyen Age," in *Histoire de Lille*, ed. Louis Trenard, 2 vols. (Lille and Toulouse, 1970, 1982), 1:288.

[4] For a discussion of civil servants, see Albert Croquez, *Histoire de Lille*, 2 vols. (Lille, 1935–9), 1:73–4. A third pensionary was hired in 1565. The civil servants hired their own staff as needed.

Conclave (33 members who made policy by majority vote)
   Rewart
   Aldermanic bench (12 *échevins*, one of them designated mayor)
   Council (4 *voir-jurés*, 8 *jurés*)
   Prud'hommes (8)*
Nonvoting organs
   Apaiseurs (5)
   Gard'orphènes (5)
Civil servants
   Conseillers-pensionnaires (2 pensionaries: advisors and head admin-
      istrators)
   Procureur-syndic (1: town attorney)
   Clerks (2: 1 for civil affairs, 1 for criminal)
   Treasurer

* The prud'hommes, referred to simply as the *huit-hommes* in most contemporary documents, participated in deliberations informally from the early
  fifteenth century, by right after 1467.

Figure 1.1. The Magistrat of Lille

aldermanic bench wielded primary authority in the city due to its distinctive electoral, administrative, and judicial competences. Aldermen
alone were consulted in the selection of their successors; in addition,
they named the rewart, *voir-jurés*, and *gard-orphènes*. The *échevins* were
responsible for nearly every aspect of the day-to-day direction of municipal affairs, from security to chimney inspections, from festivals to toll
collections. The small municipal bureaucracy gave some assistance, but
most tasks were performed by about two dozen committees composed
largely of aldermen.[5] The bench also enjoyed extensive legal jurisdiction
over Lille and its outskirts (*banlieue*). It heard appeals from sentences
handed down by the tribunals of the *apaiseurs*, gard'orphènes, and textile
crafts,[6] and formed the court of first instance in nearly all other urban
civil and criminal cases. Treason, sedition, and counterfeiting were not
within the échevins' purview, however, and royal officials and the clergy

---

[5] For slightly different lists of these committees, see AML, Reg. 430, fols. 129v–33v (1580), and
   BML, MS. 597, unnumbered fols. between rosters of the Magistrats for 1607 and 1608.
[6] The members of the cloth-industry tribunals, who were simultaneously the directors of their
   respective crafts, were all aldermanic appointees. See Paul Maufroid, *Essai sur l'échevinage de Lille*
   (Paris, 1911), p. 135, and my discussion in Chapter 3.

were exempt from their jurisdiction. But they did claim the right to try all litigation involving Lille's citizens anywhere in the province of Walloon Flanders.[7]

Voir-jurés and *jurés* aided the aldermen with every aspect of municipal affairs save the judicial,[8] but the remaining officials had more specialized duties. Beyond his ceremonial function, the rewart was commander in chief of the civic militia, whereas the *huit-hommes* supervised financial accounts and helped the aldermen set municipal tax quotas.[9] Apaiseurs arbitrated quarrels among townspeople or, if their efforts failed, proceeded against them in their special tribunal presided by the rewart.[10] Gard'orphènes managed the property of bourgeois orphans up to the age of majority (eighteen years for boys, fifteen for girls).[11]

Every October, the town attorney formally requested the sovereign, in his role as count of Flanders, to name four commissioners for the selection of the new Magistrat or *renouvellement de la Loi*. Customarily reappointed year after year, the commissioners usually included the governor of Walloon Flanders or his proxy the lieutenant governor, the *châtelain* of the castellany of Lille, a *maître* from the Chambre des Comptes, and a leading nobleman of the province.[12] The 1235 charter obliged the four to confer with the parish priests of St. Etienne, St. Sauveur, St. Maurice, and St. Pierre, as well as with the aldermen leaving office, but formally it was their sole responsibility to choose new aldermen and invest them with office on All Saints' Day. Following this ceremony, the new échevinage first elected one of its number to be the mayor who presided over meetings, then appointed the rewart and voir-jurés. Next, the seventeen men chosen so far picked the jurés. Presumably because as clergy they were both independent of the Magistrat and knowledgeable about individuals' qualifications, the four pastors pre-

---

7 Jacques Foucart, *Une institution baillivale française en Flandre. La Gouvernance du souverain bailliage de Lille-Douai-Orchies, Mortagne et Tournaisis* (Lille, 1937), pp. 146–7 and chap. VII.

8 Croquez, *Histoire de Lille*, 1:119–21. Voir-jurés were also occasionally called upon to complete the terms of aldermen or rewarts who died while in office. Other positions were left vacant until the next election.

9 Actual collection and disbursement of monies were, however, handled by the treasurer and his staff. Van Hende, *Lille et ses institutions communales*, pp. 63–4.

10 Ibid., p. 64. Unfortunately, none of the records has survived.

11 *Gard'orphènes*, common throughout the southern Low Countries, were not mentioned in Lille's charter of 1235 but had come into existence there before 1320 and were admitted to the Magistrat before 1364. See Lucien Marchant, *Les gard'orphènes à Lille* (Paris and Lille, 1902).

12 BML, MS. 597, lists their names and positions each year just prior to the Magistrat they helped select.

viously consulted named the huit-hommes and the apaiseurs. Finally, the aldermen designated the gard'orphènes.[13]

Eligibility for office was determined primarily by gender and juridical status. Only *bourgeois* – those males, currently or previously married, who belonged to the corporate group of the citizenry – could aspire to a place in the municipal government.[14] All women and all *manans* and *habitans* (the nonbourgeois residents of the town) were excluded *de jure*. Bourgeois status might be inherited or bought. A son born when his father was a citizen acquired the status *par relief* by paying a small fee during the year following his marriage.[15] Citizenship *par achat*, available to other men, required the applicant to have lived and paid taxes in Lille for at least three years, present a valid baptismal certificate, pay several fees, and be accepted by the aldermanic bench at one of its meetings on the first Thursday of the month.[16]

Between 5 and 10 percent of Lille's entire population – one-fifth to two-fifths of all adult males – were citizens.[17] Not all were eligible to serve in the Magistrat in a given year, however. Those who had been

---

13 Van Hende, *Lille et ses institutions communales*, pp. 63–4.

14 Besides eligibility for civic office, bourgeoisie conferred a number of rights and duties. Citizens and their families were to be judged only by their peers, the aldermen, and they were supposed to be exempt from arrest by another jurisdiction unless the échevinage gave its express consent. If any official apprehended a burgher and refused to deliver him to the aldermen, the urban militia, led by the rewart, was obliged to rescue him. Citizens also claimed immunity from arrest for debt on Sundays and holy days, totaling nearly a quarter of the year. Particularly important, the property of a bourgeois condemned to death, even for heresy, was not to be confiscated. This privilege, as we shall see in section II of this chapter, led to major disputes between central and municipal governments during the sixteenth century. Further, bourgeoisie gave exemption from some taxes, including seigneurial levies, and entry to the barracks set up in the Riez de Canteleu, a meadow west of town that served as a retreat from contagious diseases. In return for these privileges, burghers were obligated to defend the city by serving up to forty days a year in the militia, performing watch duty whenever summoned by the aldermen (alternately, one could send a servant or hire a substitute), and rushing to aid any fellow citizen when rallied by the special *cloche du ban* in the Halle that only the aldermen could order rung. [Théodore Leuridan], "La bourgeoisie de Lille," *BSEPC* 24 (1924):10, 15–18, 20–4, 26–7.

15 Ibid., pp. 12–14. There was no retroactivity for sons whose father obtained bourgeoisie after the children's birth. Illegitimate sons of citizens could accede to the status, though other bastards could not.

16 Ibid., p. 9; AML, Aff. gén., C. 410, d. 17.

17 Based on tax receipts, Arlette Dal, "La bourgeoisie à Lille, de 1565 à 1792, étude juridique et statistique" (Mémoire de Maîtrise, Université de Lille III, 1971), pp. 76–7, 241, has calculated that an average of some 1,900 citizens were alive during any given year in the late 1560s. Croquez, *Histoire de Lille*, 2:61–3, claims that there were 2,000 bourgeois in 1566. Using information from registers enumerating the new bourgeois admitted each year (AML, Reg. 955–7) and lists of citizenship oaths sworn before the Magistrat (AML, Reg. 276–7), I reach a higher estimate, that between 2,500 and 3,000 bourgeois were alive at any point during the mid-sixteenth century. See Appendix A for Lille's population.

convicted of crimes, who had become insolvent, or who resided even temporarily in territory exempt from aldermanic jurisdiction were disenfranchised until their situation was regularized by échevinal dispensation or the return of affluence.[18] Also disqualified were bourgeois who engaged in lawsuits against the town.[19] Citizens practicing certain professions were likewise excluded: usurers, bailiffs, various officials of the provincial government, all municipal employees, farmers of taxes and monopolies granted by the Magistrat, and lawyers pleading cases before the aldermen.[20]

Kinship also served to rule out, temporarily, some otherwise qualified citizens. The rewart, mayor, and aldermen were forbidden to be fathers, sons, brothers, fathers-in-law, sons-in-law, brothers-in-law, uncles-in-law, nephews-in-law, or cousins-german-in-law to any new or retiring aldermen. Voir-jurés could not be similarly related to the incoming rewart, mayor, or aldermen. The huit-hommes, too, were bound by the same nepotism rules, though only with reference to their replacements.[21] Finally, although there was no limit on the total number of times an individual could serve in the government, or on movement among positions, several offices mandated delays between terms. A man might be named alderman only every third year, huit-hommes could be appointed for two consecutive terms but then were forced to take one off, and a year had to elapse between each apaiseur's term.[22]

Despite all these restrictions, the number of bourgeois available at any one time to serve in some position in the Magistrat was quite large, no fewer than a thousand men and probably many more. The citizen body was also heterogeneous in composition, containing numerous long-distance merchants, lawyers, physicians, and even an occasional *chevalier*, although artisans of all types predominated.[23] Hence the potential political class was broad in size and background.

---

18 There are few records of such cases, but see BML, MS. 597, year 1570 (Jean de Ferlin) and year 1590 (Sebastien le Prevost).

19 Ibid., years 1557 (Adrien Henniart), 1563 (Guillaume Lachier), 1569 (Jean Lachier).

20 For the regulations, see ibid., pp. 67–70 at end of MS.

21 Ibid., pp. 71–9 at end of MS. The remaining officials were not subject to prohibitions of this kind.

22 The rewart, councillors and gard'orphènes were allowed to serve an unlimited number of terms without interruption. Ibid., p. 73 at end of MS. A last rule specified that mayors and rewarts be natives of Lille, though this was occasionally violated; see AML, Reg. 15,885, fols. 22v–3, 9 March 1563.

23 For occupations, see AML, Reg. 276–7, 955–7. Before 1565, newly admitted citizens were not required to list their professions, so no statistical precision is possible before that date, but

Notwithstanding the diversity of the citizenry, analysis of the 238 men selected for the Magistrat between 1541 and 1565 demonstrates that the actual ruling group was a homogeneous oligarchy dominated by merchants, though containing a significant admixture of men holding seigneurial titles and of professionals.[24] In a typical year during this quarter century, Lille's municipal government was composed of twenty-three merchants, five or six men referred to as seigneurs, three lawyers, two or three physicians, two artisans, one *rentier*, one administrator, and four or five men whose occupations cannot be determined.

Besides filling a majority of the forty-three seats on the entire Loi, merchants usually boasted an absolute majority, or close to it, on each individual organ of government save the rewartship, which was the bailiwick of seigneurs. In all likelihood, moreover, merchant ascendance was even more pronounced than the available information discloses, because Lillois often continued to devote themselves to commercial ventures after purchasing or inheriting feudal holdings conferring more prestigious titles. Pierre Dupont, for example, was listed as a merchant during his first three years on the Loi (1553, 1554, 1557), but from 1558 to his retirement in 1569, he was entered as seigneur of Mons-en-Baroeul, although he remained a busy trader all the while.[25]

The great majority of the merchants named to the Magistrat were active in long-distance commerce, usually through Antwerp. Granted, the intensity of political participation varied significantly among Lille's merchants. Many men successfully combined political and commercial careers. During the 1540s and 1550s, for example, Arnold de Smerpont was busy making his fortune as a merchant, yet he was also appointed three out of every five years to municipal office. Conversely, service on the council in 1545 did not prevent him from being a leading importer of Bordeaux wine.[26]

slightly later figures given by Dal, "Bourgeoisie à Lille," p. 273, indicate that between half and three-quarters of all new citizens were artisans and shopkeepers, with textile makers alone accounting for nearly 50% of the total.

[24] Analysis of the occupations of members of the Magistrat can begin no earlier than 1540, the date at which such information is routinely listed in the registers. Data from the chief source, BML, MS. 597, have been supplemented by information from the following: AML, Reg. 414–19, 948; AH Comtesse, Reg. 4443–532; AASL, Reg. J 558–80; AML, Reg. 15,434–5bis; ADN, Tab. 1146–8, 2828, 3308, 3851–5, 3857–9, 4165, 4168, 4237, 4250; and Coornaert, *Français à Anvers*.

[25] See BML, MS. 597, under years mentioned; for some of his commercial contracts, see AML, Reg. 15,435bis.

[26] See Jan Craeybeckx, *Un grand commerce d'importation. Les vins de France aux anciens Pays-Bas (XIIIe–XVIe siècle)* (Paris, 1958), p. 245, and my Chapter 2, section III, and Appendix E.

Other merchants seem to have placed business interests ahead of office holding. The Dragon, Gobau, Masquelier, and other families prominent in the Antwerp trade never had a single member selected for so much as a justiceship of the peace, whereas men from such distinguished mercantile families as the Baillet, du Gardin (du Jardin), Levasseur, and Desmuliers spent only a few terms in the Magistrat. On occasion, too, merchants found that the demands of business interrupted their political service. Adrien Henniart, for instance, was alderman in 1557 and gard'orphène in 1558 before being sent to Narva when Czar Ivan IV began to welcome foreign merchants to Russia. But after his return several years later, Henniart was selected for the Loi eleven more times.[27]

The political careers of one group of Lillois suggest that some leading merchants were left off the Magistrat, chosen for only a few terms, or placed disproportionately in minor jobs because they were known or suspected Protestants. According to a report on merchants trading at or with Antwerp, drawn up in 1566 by a secret agent working for the regent Margaret of Parma, the Lille Calvinists included the Delobel, Castellain, de Has, Delecluse, Dupont, Coene, du Bosquiel, Desbucquois, and le Moisne families, along with some of the de Fourmestraux, the children of François Fasse, the household of Hubert Deliot, Jean de Hollande (also known as Jean de Bertault), and perhaps the Mahieu family.[28] Although not all the allegations can be confirmed, we do know that some members of the Delobel, Deliot, Dupont, and de Fourmestraux families were indeed Protestants.[29]

Of those on the list, no de Has or Delecluse sat in Lille's municipal government during the sixteenth century, nor did Jean de Hollande or the children of François Fasse, though François himself did. Men from several other named families were seldom appointed even though they lived long after their final term in office, and all had numerous additional kin who were never put in the municipal government despite being important merchants. Of the le Moisne, for example, only Antoine was chosen and for just one term; two Deliot were selected for one term

---

[27] For his service in the Magistrat, see BML, MS. 597; for his presence in Narva, see Chapter 2, section I.

[28] For the denunciation, see Léon Van der Essen, "Les progrès du luthéranisme et du calvinisme dans le monde commercial d'Anvers et l'espionnage politique du marchand Philippe Dauxy, agent secret de Marguerite de Parme, en 1566–1567," *VSWG* 12 (1914) :217, 223 n. 6.

[29] See Chapter 5, section III.

each, another for five; four Delobel men were chosen one to four times, nearly all in minor posts; and Jaspart Coene was named alderman but once. The de Fourmestraux and Castellain, who had members frequently selected at other times during the sixteenth century, all but disappeared from the Magistrat in the 1560s, when Protestant agitation and the reaction to it were at their height.

One or two individuals from the remaining families were appointed many times but others were ignored, even though they too were outstanding merchants. Thus Pierre Dupont was selected fifteen times between 1553 and 1569, but Jean and Guillaume never; Jean Desbucquois six times (1560–8), Pierre not once. Gerard and Nicolas du Bosquiel both served multiple terms while Mahieu was never tapped; Toussaint Mahieu died in office, yet Gerard and Nicolas never held even the lowliest position. Admittedly, the fact that these families were not wholly barred from the Magistrat makes it impossible to state definitively that Protestantism, real or alleged, rather than business commitments (with the correlate of frequent travels or residence at Antwerp or elsewhere), personal choice, or unsuitability kept them out. On balance, however, the evidence strongly implies that a careful process of exclusion allotted reputed or known adherents to Reformed religion a distinctly smaller share of political power than their economic prominence would seem to have warranted.

Men calling themselves seigneurs, who formed the second sizable group in the Magistrat, were of two types. The majority were commoners who had recently given up their previous profession or, like the Pierre Dupont mentioned previously, continued to exercise it even though preferring to use an honorific. A minority could boast patents of nobility. Even the most distinguished of these men belonged, however, not to important families with vast landholdings and highly placed relatives throughout the Netherlands but, like Jacques Ronsee and his son François, seigneurs of Rabecque, to the gentry of Walloon Flanders.

Other minor nobles were descendants of Lillois who, after making fortunes in commerce and banking, had entered the prince's service and eventually been rewarded with titles. By the sixteenth century, at least one of these men enjoyed a long noble lineage. Jacques de Tenremonde, seigneur of Blanche Maille and vicomte of Merignies, an officeholder twelve times from 1548 to 1562, traced his ancestry back to a money changer who had become lieutenant governor of Flanders and ennobled in 1391.[30] But most titles were of considerably more recent vintage. The Dommessent, seigneurs of Boisgrenier, for example, had been granted nobility in 1527 in return for faithful service by two family members who had been lieutenant governors of the province. The de Preudhomme, seigneurs of Coisne, had received their title in 1530, when Pierre, mayor of Lille, was honored for assisting Emperor Charles V on embassies to Gelderland.[31] Besides lacking the personal prestige to overawe their commoner colleagues or to act as the nucleus of a landed faction, such men constituted a tiny proportion of the ruling class. On the average, only one noble was appointed each year, and he was usually granted the rewartship, the most honorable but by no means the most powerful post.

The last major category of magistrates consisted of professionals. Some were physicians, others practicing lawyers. Yet others were employed as councillors or auditors at the Chamber of Accounts or, more frequently, headed a charitable institution such as an orphanage. Significantly, many of the professionals who served multiple terms were linked by birth or marriage to merchants.

Artisans were greatly underrepresented in the Magistrat as compared with their numbers in the bourgeoisie as a whole. Even if all officials whose occupation cannot be determined turned out to be craftsmen or shopkeepers – which is not likely to have been the case[32] – only about 15 percent of Lille's political leadership could then be said to have come from the strata that supplied the bulk of the citizenry. Proportionately, most artisans were designated apaiseurs and fewest held positions as aldermen or councillors. Equally important, all but a handful remained in the Magistrat for three years or fewer, making it difficult for them to enjoy the kind of influence that derived from protracted service. What is more, the artisans appointed to municipal government came overwhelmingly from a small number of trades that were both capital inten-

---

[30] See Pierre Feuchère, "La bourgeoisie lilloise au moyen âge," *AESC* 4 (1949) :421–30; Gérard Sivéry, "Histoire économique et sociale," in *Histoire de Lille*, 1:263–4; Robert Marquant, *La vie économique à Lille sous Philippe le Bon* (Paris, 1940), pp. 35–6.

[31] Cf. also the Hangouart, who paid 1,000 liv. for their patent in 1550. J. Le Roux, *Recueil de la Noblesse de Bourgogne, Limbourg . . . Flandres, etc. enregistrée à la Chambre des Comptes du Roi commençant en l'an 1424 & continué jusques à l'an 1714* (Lille and Brussels, 1715), pp. 28, 30, 32–3, 38–40, 48–9, 52; BML, MS. Godefroy 112, passim.

[32] It might seem logical to expect that men whose professions were not listed in the Magistrat register had less prestigious artisanal jobs, but it turned out that many of those whose occupations I was able to find in other sources were merchants.

Table 1.1. *Distribution of office holding
in Lille's Magistrat by family, 1541–65*

No. of men per family in office	No. of families	% of all families	No. of terms served (entire career)	% of all terms served (entire career)
1	102	66.23	658	36.47
2	31	20.13	481	26.66
3	15	9.74	423	23.45
4–6	6	3.90	242	13.41
Total	154	100.00	1,804	99.99

Source: BML, MS. 597.

sive and involved significant commercial activity. Textile craftsmen were virtually excluded; at best, one held a seat every third year.

Thanks to their wealth, business interests, and family relations, the dyers, apothecaries, and goldsmiths who were chosen for the Loi had less in common with the majority of artisans than with their merchant colleagues. The apothecary Jean le Mesre, for example, alderman in 1542 and 1548 and councillor in 1543, provided his daughter Jeanne with a dowry suitable for a merchant's child, including 600 livres in cash, land worth an equivalent amount, and 200 livres for wedding expenses.[33] Some magistrates listed as artisans were in fact better known as merchants; others had personal connections, whether by marriage or by birth, to the merchants with whom they associated in government.

Being an international merchant, seigneur, or practitioner of one of the liberal professions was, then, something of a *de facto* requirement for admission to the Magistrat. Table 1.1 demonstrates, however, that family affiliation was extremely important in determining which individuals from among those made eligible in this way would actually be selected.

Analyzing the small minority of families that was nearly continuously represented in municipal government once again emphasizes merchant ascendancy in the ruling class. Five of the six dynasties placing four or

[33] AML, Reg. 15,435, 11 September 1550. Cf. the 900 liv. of rentes purchased in 1555 and 1557 by the goldsmith Jean Thiebreghien (apaiseur in 1556 and 1559); AML, Reg. 16,289, fols. 70v–110; Reg. 16,291, fols. 65–86. See also Appendix B.

Table 1.2. *Total terms in office of Lillois serving in the Magistrat, 1541–65*

No. of terms (career)	No. of men	No. of men as % of total	Cumulative %	No. of terms as % of total	Cumulative %
1	62	26.05	26.05	3.04	3.44
2–4	73	30.67	56.72	11.97	15.41
5–7	24	10.08	66.80	7.87	23.28
8–15	41	17.23	84.03	25.83	49.11
16–34	38	15.97	100.00	50.89	100.00

Source: BML, MS. 597.

more men in the Loi were leaders in long-distance trade (the Castellain, de Fourmestraux, du Bosquiel, Fremault, and Mahieu), whereas the remaining clan, the de Preudhomme, had recently entered the provincial nobility. Of the families that could boast three members on the Magistrat during this quarter century, six were composed wholly of merchants, three others contained both merchants and lawyers, one had merchants as well as a rich apothecary, and one more included both merchants and seigneurs. Many of these leading political families were, moreover, linked by marriage. Intermarriage not only served to reinforce ties among those practicing the same occupation, but also crossed professional lines, bringing greater unity to the group as a whole.[34]

Each of the men appointed to Lille's municipal government between 1541 and 1565 served an average of 7.58 terms during his entire political career.[35] But as Table 1.2 discloses, the mean conceals significant disparities. Clearly, power was very unequally shared among citizens. More than half the appointees (those serving one to four terms) received less than a sixth of the positions; conversely, more than half the offices were occupied by less than a sixth of those selected (those named sixteen or more times). This lopsided apportionment of seats meant not only

---

34 The records, mainly notations in BML, MS. 597, are not sufficiently complete to permit quantitative rigor regarding intermarriage.

35 Many of the magistrates discussed here began to sit in the Loi before 1541, and many continued in office after 1565. Hence individuals served as many as thirty-four terms, even though the period in question totaled only twenty-five years.

that the large majority of officials occupied a minority of seats, but also that each year an average of fewer than eight posts – less than a fifth of the total – was filled by men new to the municipal government.[36] Further contributing to the concentration of power in the Magistrat was the fact that seventy-four men, nearly one-third of the total, never sat on the aldermanic bench or the council but were relegated to the less powerful specialized bodies. Most were individuals who lacked significant family and professional connections. They were apparently considered of sufficient stature to deserve inclusion in the Loi, but only in subordinate roles and for just a few terms.[37]

As virtually no summaries of Magistrat meetings have survived, there is no basis for making a qualitative judgment as to which individuals dominated politics in Lille. But reviewing patterns of office holding reveals the existence of an inner circle, consisting of men chosen for eight or more terms, at least half of which were spent on the aldermanic bench or in the council. The fifty-seven individuals constituting this group were chosen so repeatedly between 1541 and 1565 (serving an average of nineteen of the twenty-five possible terms) that although only a quarter of the officials they occupied 60 percent of all positions and nearly four-fifths of council seats. Among them were to be found members of all six leading political dynasties as well as representatives of twelve of the fifteen families that placed three men in the Loi during this period. Just as individual members of these families sat for term after term, moreover, many families were represented for decades. Thus Guillaume Castellain was appointed twenty-one times between 1521 and 1546; his relative Mathieu held office on twenty occasions from 1537 to 1564, and Mahieu's son Jean, the third person from this family to belong to the inner circle, was selected for nine terms between 1574 and 1585. And at least sixteen of the group's thirty-one marriages listed in the official register linked men of the inner circle to women from other families represented therein.

Occupationally, this inner circle corresponded closely to the composition of the Magistrat as a whole. Merchants formed slightly over half the

---

[36] The precise mean was 7.72 new men a year. The sole period of notable deviation from the average was 1557–60, when an average of 10 new men per year entered the government in order to replace people killed in an epidemic.

[37] Of the 74, 40 served only once, while the average number of terms of the entire group was a low 2.30.

group, while seigneurs constituted the next largest segment, followed by lawyers, physicians, administrators, and rentiers. Only two artisans – an apothecary and a goldsmith – were included, so that artisanal representation in the political elite was even slighter than in the entire Loi, although just as skewed to the more prosperous trades. Evidence dating from 1562 suggests, moreover, that the members of the inner circle were marginally wealthier than the men who held office for shorter periods of time. In that year, a forced loan was imposed on more than three hundred Lillois to buy grain for the poor. All thirty current or past inner circle members then alive contributed an average of 55.83 florins. Among the remaining donors were eighty-two other men who presently sat on the Magistrat or had been named at least once to it. Fifty-seven of them gave a mean of 50.96 florins; the remaining twenty-five provided nothing.[38]

Although no single career pattern prevailed, the appointments received by two individuals indicate how offices were distributed among men of the inner circle. In particular, it is clear that these men constantly rotated among the aldermanic bench, council, and (to a lesser extent) college of huit-hommes, and that they infrequently served as apaiseurs or gard'orphènes. Antoine Cauwet, perhaps a merchant before 1553, when he began to be listed as seigneur of le Molinel, held office during nine of the thirteen years between 1546 and 15 October 1559, when he died just two weeks before the end of a term as échevin. His first post was on the aldermanic bench, where he subsequently sat every fourth year (1550, 1554, 1558); in between, he served as huit-homme in 1549 and councillor in 1551, 1553, 1556, and 1557.

The offices held by Nicolas du Bosquiel, member of one of Lille's greatest merchant families, who after 1563 was also referred to as seigneur of le Berghe, show that a similar configuration obtained among those serving the longest. His thirty-three-term career, which started in 1545, included thirteen years as alderman, five of them as mayor. With two exceptions, he reappeared on the échevinage every third year – as often, that is, as the rules permitted. When not on the bench, he was chosen eighteen times as councillor, once as a huit-homme, and once as a gard'orphène. Between his initial appointment and his retirement on 1

---

[38] The overall mean was 44.35 fl. Calculated from information in Alain Lottin, "Une liste des riches lillois soumis à un emprunt forcé en 1562," *RN* 60 (1978) :68–72, and BML, MS. 597.

November 1584, he was left off the municipal government just six times, and he served without interruption during the entire quarter century 1545–69.

Limiting consecutive terms, prohibiting simultaneous office holding by close relatives, and annually selecting officials with the involvement of prominent noncitizens all helped prevent the formation of a strictly hereditary patriciate in Lille. But these procedures did little to inhibit the growth of an oligarchic inner circle, composed of men who were repeatedly selected for the critical positions and were able to stay in the Magistrat nearly continuously by moving from position to position. The council in particular functioned as a place to which political leaders transferred upon completing terms as aldermen. The members of the inner circle, who spent 31.5 percent of their terms as échevins, were named councillors for 60.7 percent of their remaining years in municipal government. As an added bonus, the council provided a bedrock of experience and continuity to the Magistrat. On the average, fewer than one councillor per year had never before held some office, by far the lowest proportion of all bodies.[39] Furthermore, individuals from the inner circle frequently sat for two consecutive terms, so the council showed much the smallest fraction of men lacking previous experience in the job.[40]

Lille's municipal regime thus constituted what Wittman has termed a narrow "ruling stratum." Although a diverse citizenry was available for appointment to office, the Loi was uniformly monopolized by merchants, seigneurs, and professionals of similar wealth and status, who often intermarried to boot. Such men brought to the task of government a community of interests that was knit still closer by constant interaction during the many years in which they repeatedly occupied key offices. Regular admission of new men into both Magistrat and inner circle did not alter the social composition of this ruling class, because upward political mobility was largely reserved for those engaging in a few select occupations and boasting the requisite personal relationships. Yet in

[39] The precise figure was 0.64 councillors new to the Magistrat each year (5.3%), compared with 0.68 orphans' guardians (13.6%), 2.4 aldermen (including mayors) (20%), 1.4 justices of the peace (28%), 2.28 huit-hommes (28.5%), and 0.36 rewarts (36%). Calculated from BML, MS. 597.

[40] Each year, on average, 3.08 of 12 councillors (25.7%) were serving in that post for the first time, compared with 4.6 aldermen (38.3%), 2.13 gard'orphènes (42.5%), 3.76 huit-hommes (47%), 3.25 apaiseurs (65%), and 0.72 rewarts (72%). Calculated from BML, MS. 597.

contrast to the situation that, according to Wittman, existed in other Flemish cities,[41] Lille's political class did not form a patriciate largely cut off from commerce and industry. On the contrary, merchants continually and directly controlled municipal politics, despite the complications introduced by religion, business commitments, and the inclusion of new men. Thus city government in Lille could remain in close touch with the central concerns of the dominant stratum in urban society.

For all that it was directed by a restricted oligarchy, moreover, Lille challenges Smit's assertion that in the towns of the sixteenth-century Netherlands "we find factions everywhere struggling for political power."[42] Popular movements throughout the thirteenth century had culminated in brief victories between 1297 and 1305.[43] Yet the craft guilds had failed to maintain any institutional representation in Lille's city government, so one of the most potent agents of party strife in urban magistracies was missing. Disputes within the Magistrat may also have been forestalled by the apparent policy of barring known Protestants. Structural features such as the rotation of officials, which permitted a large segment of the oligarchy to hold powerful positions at some time in their careers, likewise tended to curb factionalism.

Equally important, the brief tenure of most officeholders ensured that there was a constant flow of new blood into Lille's Magistrat.[44] Even the inner circle included a majority of men who did not belong to the leading clans. At the same time, new political dynasties like the Bave and le Mesre, whose members were destined for repeated service during the later sixteenth and seventeenth centuries, were established in the 1541–65 period. Thus the possibility that influential individuals or families might be excluded from what they considered their rightful share of political power – a potent source of resentment and even upheaval in other towns[45] – was minimized, the more so because the Loi contained representatives of the dominant social groups. Finally, Lille's artisanal economy characterized by small producers, the formation of which is traced in the third chapter, foreclosed the appearance of a substantial group of industrial entrepreneurs that similarly might have demanded

---

[41] Wittman, *Les gueux dans les "bonnes villes" de Flandre,* pp. 93–5.
[42] Smit, "Netherlands Revolution," p. 29; for a brief description of these struggles, see ibid., pp. 29–31.
[43] Derville, "Trois siècles décisifs," pp. 126–8.
[44] The 181 men not in the inner circle served an average of only 4.01 terms each.
[45] Cf. Smit, "Netherlands Revolution," pp. 30–1.

political power commensurate with its economic strength. A number of converging factors, in short, reduced the likelihood of internal factionalism and challenges from outside the political class that might have unsettled or even paralyzed urban governance and provided an excuse for interference by the central state.

II

The structure and cohesion of the Magistrat were critical in creating an environment favorable to the maintenance of civic autonomy. But what happened in practice? Did Lille's municipal government retain real power under Charles V? Or does its history support Pirenne's contention that initiatives taken by the central regime eroded civic authority?

Its relations with craft guilds, its establishment and governance of a municipal welfare system, and its role in religious affairs all suggest that the Magistrat not only held its own but actually expanded its power in this period. Artisan corporations, to begin with, had long been firmly subject to the city government. Not only did the aldermen ratify all craft statutes, but in some instances they appointed guild leaders or even participated in administering corporate rules.[46] In the case of the new light-woolens weaving guilds, which rapidly became the largest and most important in Lille, the Magistrat's ascendancy was considerably extended, since by law aldermen themselves formed a third or even a half of the councils that directed these corporations.[47] Across the first two-thirds of the sixteenth century, moreover, the aldermen regularly occupied seats allotted to representatives of other groups, thereby appropriating the lion's share of positions on the textile councils. Significantly, those selected were drawn almost without exception from the inner circle of the Magistrat.[48] As we shall see in later chapters, the city fathers made excellent use of their opportunities for close involvement in the affairs of these trades.

The organization of a municipal charity system also helped enhance

[46] See AML, Reg. 16,002–3, passim.

[47] Maurice Vanhaeck, *Histoire de la sayetterie à Lille*, 2 vols. (Lille, 1910), 1:116–20, 2:28, doc. 5 (the sayetteurs' guild was directed by two say-cloth merchants, two masters, and two aldermen); and AML, Aff. gén., C. 1160, d. 5 (before 1543, the bourgetteurs' corporation was run by two aldermen, one merchant and one master; after that date, another master replaced the merchant).

[48] These conclusions are based on cross tabulations of the lists for the Vingtaine of sayetterie given in AML, Reg. 429–30, with BML, MS. 597. No lists survive for the Siège of bourgetterie, but as we have seen the government was guaranteed at least half the seats there.

the magistrates' authority over urban society. The "Common Fund for the Poor," established in 1527 and elaborated across the next several decades, promoted identification and policing of the persons of the needy. Welfare recipients became the objects of a new ideology and apparatus of domination as well as the beneficiaries of a more efficient method of material assistance.[49] Like the light-woolens industry, the Common Fund was controlled by the core of the ruling class. The great majority of the *ministres généraux* who managed it consisted of past and present aldermen and councillors, the bulk coming from the most prominent political families and their close allies. Even more lopsidedly than the Magistrat itself, the Common Fund was the preserve of merchants, who normally constituted three-quarters of the ministres généraux. In this respect, ironically, practice in Catholic Lille resembled that in Calvinist Geneva, where the central charitable institution (known as the Hôpital Général) was directed by the body of "prosperous merchants who governed the state."[50] Just as they remained in the municipal government for extended periods of time, moreover, the men named to the Common Fund served for long periods, the norm being a decade.[51] In this way, too, Lille smacks of Geneva. The commissioners of the Hôpital Général in the "Protestant Rome" were so repeatedly reelected that over time their body unofficially turned into a committee of the city government.[52]

Parish commissions, which operated Lille's fund on a daily basis, served both to associate the interests and goodwill of the neighborhood notables appointed to them with those of the governing oligarchy and to provide the Magistrat with frequent reports on the poor.[53] A mixture of centralized and decentralized administration thus permitted the municipal government to assume important new responsibilities without having to broaden the oligarchy's membership and thereby dilute its cohesion.

[49] For a detailed discussion of the founding and functioning of the Common Fund, see Chapter 4, section III.

[50] Robert Kingdon, "Social Welfare in Calvin's Geneva," *American Historical Review* 76 (1971) :53.

[51] These calculations are based on cross tabulations of the lists of commissioners printed at the beginning of each Common Fund account (AASL, Reg. J 558–80) with BML, MS. 597.

[52] Kingdon, "Social Welfare in Calvin's Geneva," p. 56. A variation on the theme was played at Lyon, where the eight commissioners of the Aumône Générale, originally designated by the magistrates, soon resorted to cooptation and became independent of the communal authorities. See John-Pierre Gutton, *La société et les pauvres. L'exemple de la généralité de Lyon, 1534–1789* (Paris, 1971), p. 275.

[53] For more detail, see Robert DuPlessis, "Charité municipale et autorité publique au XVIème siècle: l'exemple de Lille," *RN* 59 (1977):197.

The Loi had long enjoyed a great deal of influence over religious life in Lille, a situation facilitated, as Alain Lottin has suggested, by the lack of a resident bishop.[54] Not only did the aldermen sponsor and subsidize processions and other public religious manifestations, but they regulated a wide variety of matters touching the faith, from the ringing of church bells to the establishment of new institutions. In addition, the Magistrat affected parochial affairs by appointing churchwardens (*marguilliers*), who had charge of everything save administration of the sacraments. The wardens maintained the church fabric, ornaments, and linens; supervised the parish charities; distributed places in the cemeteries; and gave permission for burial inside the church, the erection of monuments, or the carving of inscriptions. They also managed lay-endowed foundations supporting the observance of the canonical hours and even chose the priests (*horistes*) who chanted the seven canonical hours. However, the Loi reserved to itself the right of disciplining and on occasion expelling horistes, as well as correcting unruly chaplains and cantors. Only curés were subject to episcopal jurisdiction. Furthermore, the city fathers presided over the annual meetings of the various parochial organizations and were supposed to review their financial statements.[55]

Decisions handed down by the central government in the reign of Charles V strengthened the Loi's power at the expense of the church. Rejecting the appeal of a dismissed horiste, the Council of Flanders in 1523 emphatically confirmed the Magistrat's administrative power over parishes.[56] A few years later, the city government secured the right to try violators of the imperial placards against heresy.[57] In 1535, to give a final illustration, the chapter of the collegiate church of St. Pierre was forced, after much resistance, to share one of its most cherished prerogatives and permit the aldermen to open Latin schools.[58]

Continuing divisions within the light-cloth industry, unresolved problems of begging and poor relief, the fact that the chapter was authorized to supervise the teachers and subject matter in the municipal Latin schools – all this and much else testifies that the Magistrat's control of

---

[54] Alain Lottin, *Lille, citadelle de la Contre Réforme? (1598–1668)* (Dunkerque, 1984), p. 59.

[55] Ibid., pp. 62–7; Henri Platelle, "La vie religieuse à Lille," in *Histoire de Lille*, 1:395–6. For a more detailed discussion of disorderly parish clergy in the mid-sixteenth century, see Chapter 5, section I.

[56] ADN, Reg. B 19,456, fol. 176.

[57] For a more extended discussion of heresy cases, see Chapter 5, section II.

[58] See Chapter 5, section I.

the city had very real limits. It is clear, nonetheless, that the municipal government used formal and informal means alike to consolidate power in its hands during the early sixteenth century. On many – probably most – occasions, the magistrates took the initiative. Their establishment of an innovative structure for the new drapery took place apart from any directives from the imperial government. Their foundation of the Common Fund predated and indeed contributed to the promulgation of Charles V's 1531 decree mandating similar systems throughout the Netherlands. And their determination to set up lay-controlled schools, though paralleling developments in other cities, did not result from any policy decreed by Brussels. Yet whatever its origins, the growth of the Loi's power was at least condoned and at times actively assisted by the central state.

The enhancement of the Magistrat's authority over Lillois raises questions about the validity of the Pirennean view of urban political decline. But that interpretation also rests on the belief that a more assertive regime in Brussels was curbing municipal power. In order to assess that judgment, relations between local and princely governments must be scrutinized. The period between the mid-1550s and mid-1560s merits particular attention, since many historians have seen Philip's reign as the time when urban leaders became severely disaffected with the regime in Brussels.

The Magistrat's relations with the chief princely officials and bureaucracies located in Lille are a good place to begin. Now even before the sixteenth century, the provost, the sovereign's representative for judicial affairs, had become in effect a functionary of the municipal courts, making arrests, prosecuting cases, and carrying out aldermanic sentences.[59] When codifying procedures for apprehending and releasing suspects in 1532, moreover, the Loi sharply restricted the provost's access to the conclave, further curbing his authority. Margaret of Parma subsequently ordered the provost admitted whenever matters of public order were discussed, but he was forbidden entry when actual deliberations were in process.[60] Although the provost retained some rights, in short, his subordination to the municipality was confirmed.

---

[59] Croquez, *Histoire de Lille*, 1:46, 139, 2:148–9.
[60] AML, Reg. 15,884, fols. 194v–6, 2 March 1532 (reiterated 15 October 1541); Reg. 15,885, fols. 30v–1v, 16 December 1562, for Margaret's ruling. The latter document is printed in Maufroid, *Echevinage de Lille*, doc. lxx, pp. 217–19.

Considering its strategic role in the state apparatus and the expertise of its staff, it might be anticipated that the Chamber of Accounts intervened decisively in urban politics. The actual situation was quite different. Admittedly, the chamber was consulted regarding economic and fiscal matters. Perhaps contacts of this sort, or the fact that many of the city's pensionaries had previously been employed by the chamber, prompted Wittman's contention that the institution "created numerous bonds between her [Lille] and the king."[61] Yet since most of the chamber's personnel came from outside Walloon Flanders, only a few were eligible to serve in the Magistrat, and only a tiny minority ever did.[62] Furthermore, the chamber's increasing work load – recall that it was responsible for princely finances in seven provinces – left it little time to carry out its assigned tasks, let alone extend its competence. By 1556, the chamber had fallen so far behind in auditing Lille's financial registers – one of the means Pirenne cited as enabling the central government to dominate urban magistracies – that seven annual volumes had not been checked, and five never were. At the aldermen's behest, Brussels turned the job over to the electoral commissioners, a decision that if anything emancipated city finances from the oversight of the central government or indeed – given most commissioners' lack of expertise and their other duties – anyone else's.[63]

Like *stadthouders* elsewhere in the Low Countries, the governor of Walloon Flanders combined in his person military, administrative, and judicial leadership of the province, making him the single most powerful government official.[64] In addition to their assigned tasks, moreover, governors came from the high nobility and thus might be expected to have enjoyed de facto prestige and authority. Adrien de Croy, count of Roeulx, who filled the position between 1533 and his death in 1553, was the son of a knight of the Golden Fleece who had been Charles V's chamberlain, and Adrien himself was raised with the emperor and became one of his closest advisors.[65] His successor from 1554 to 1563,

---

[61] Wittman, *Les gueux dans les "bonnes villes" de Flandre*, p. 243.

[62] For a list of some of the men who worked in the Chambre from 1559 to the late sixteenth century, see BN, Fonds français, MS. 2809, fols. 73v–7v. Less than a half-dozen masters and councillors from the Chambre can be identified among those selected for the Loi between 1541 and 1565; see BML, MS. 597. For a brief historical account, see Sivéry, "Institutions lilloises," pp. 277–9.

[63] For the decision, see BML, MS. 597, pp. 33–4 at end of volume.

[64] See Foucart, *Souverain bailliage*, and Sivéry, "Institutions lilloises," pp. 279–84.

[65] *Biographie nationale* (Brussels, 1866–), vol. IV, cols. 533–5.

Jean de Montmorency, seigneur of Courrières, came from one of the leading families of the Netherlands.[66]

For several reasons, however, the governors did not play much of a role in prerevolt Lille. Walloon Flanders, too small to have its own council or court of appeals,[67] was not the focus of attention of men who simultaneously held more influential posts. Croy, for instance, was concurrently governor of Artois (since 1524) and Flanders (from 1539).[68] More crippling, the governorship was vacant from the death of Montmorency in early August 1563 to the arrival of Maximilien Vilain, baron of Rassenghien, on 1 June 1566, so provincial administration had ground to a virtual standstill by November 1564.[69] Worse still, the first lieutenant governor Denis de le Cambe, seigneur of la Haye, who was temporarily in charge in the interim, was suspected of favoring Protestantism and therefore not vigorously enforcing edicts against heresy.[70]

This evidence hardly suggests that the local and provincial agents of the central state were expanding their authority at the expense of the Magistrat's. Nor do decisions taken in Brussels bespeak a clear policy of curbing municipal jurisdiction. To be sure, the aldermen were overruled on occasion, as in 1534, when Charles decreed that Lille's drap weavers could make novel types of cloth and ordered a reluctant Magistrat to set up inspection procedures.[71] Ordinarily, however, the city fathers' ver-

---

66 The most complete list of governors is found in Edmond Poullet, *Les gouverneurs de province dans les anciens Pays-Bas catholiques* (Brussels, 1873), pp. 179–80; see also ibid., pp. 12–13.

67 See letter of Margaret of Parma to Philip II, 30 November 1564, *CMA*, 3:503–4, in which she notes that in Walloon Flanders the governor and his first lieutenant "tiegnent illecques le lieu du conseil provincial." Appeals were taken to the Council of Flanders, sitting in Ghent.

68 See *Biographie nationale*, vol. IV, cols. 535–7; Foucart, *Souverain bailliage*, pp. 86, 127–9.

69 The hiatus was caused by the stubbornly pursued claims of four prominent nobles: Egmont, who maintained that Philip had promised him the governorship; Aerschot, on the basis of his wife's important seigneuries located in the province at Halluin and Comines; Hoogstraten (Antoine de Lalaing); and Hachicourt (Philippe de Montmorency, *chef des finances* at Brussels). See Margaret to Philip, 12 August 1563, *CMA*, 3:64–5; same to same, 30 November 1564, ibid., pp. 503–4. For marriage ties among Egmont, Hoogstraten, and Hachicourt, see Geoffrey Parker, *The Dutch Revolt* (Ithaca, 1977), p. 271.

70 Although no solid evidence against de la Haye was found, Margaret of Parma requested that henceforth only those men known to be firm Catholics be appointed lieutenants and that they be required to swear an oath of orthodoxy; letter of 15 September 1563, *CMA*, 3:114. Upon de la Haye's death, Baude Cuvillon, *avocat fiscal* at the Gouvernance, was given the job largely because he was a fervent Catholic who could lead the fight against the heresy pullulating throughout the castellany; Margaret to Philip, 8 October 1564, ibid., pp. 441–2.

71 Vanhaeck, *Sayetterie à Lille*, 2:48–9, doc. 14. It should be mentioned that Charles' decision explicitly permitted the Magistrat to modify his directive or not to comply at all if it should determine, after consultation with the Chambre des Comptes, drapers, and other knowledgeable townspeople, that such a step would be best for *le bien publique* of Lille. This stipulation underlines the sovereign's reluctance to act in opposition to the local authorities.

dicts and prerogatives were upheld by the sovereign and his courts.[72] Again, what the Magistrat took to be urban monopolies were overridden at times, most prominently in 1535 and 1547, when residents of several nearby villages won permission to weave certain types of cheap cloth.[73] But the central regime was more likely to come down on the side of the city's purported rights: These very decisions, for instance, reserved the manufacture of says, the light woolens most in demand at the time, to the city alone.[74] Lille would, of course, have preferred to prevent all rural textile production. But unlike medieval Ghent and Bruges, which marched their urban militias out to smash looms in the countryside, Lille could not hope to make regional economic policy on its own. So if the city did not achieve all that it wished, it did get a large measure of satisfaction by appealing to Brussels.

Implementing the central government's religious policy did, however, generate grave conflicts between sovereign and Magistrat, for it infringed the Loi's authority and the city's privileges. As early as 1529, Lille joined other towns to protest an imperial decree that put heresy prosecutions in the hands of two members of the Council of Flanders. The edict violated a 1522 compact that confirmed the Magistrat's jurisdiction over all crimes committed in the town, save by princely officials or by clergy, and all cases involving Lille's citizens no matter where in the province they transpired – imperial matters of sovereignty alone excepted. On the face of it, the 1529 complaint resulted in victory for the cities, whose magistrates recovered the right to proceed against heretics as long as they followed guidelines laid down subsequently.[75]

The decision failed, however, to resolve competing interpretations of a long-contentious matter – the disposition of the property of individuals convicted of committing lese majesty. Thus it opened the door to more serious controversies that went beyond the initial issue. Brussels

---

72 For just two examples, see AML, Reg. 15,884, fols. 114–15 and 145–6v, enforcing clerical contributions to a forced loan and prohibitions on tanning in exempt enclaves.
73 Vanhaeck, *Sayetterie à Lille*, 1:272–3; and Chapter 3.
74 See Vanhaeck, *Sayetterie à Lille*, 2:45–6, doc. 12, and 1:271. Cf. AML, Reg. 15,884, fols. 148–9, 218v–19, for other decrees similarly favorable to urban pretensions.
75 The text of the 1522 agreement is printed in *Privilèges et chartes de franchises de la Flandre*, ed. Georges Espinas, Charles Verlinden, and Jean Buntinx, 2 vols. (Brussels, 1959–61), 2:73–7, no. 230. The compact had been substantially sustained after a struggle with the bishop of Tournai in 1526–7; see Chapter 5, section II; Maufroid, *Echevinage de Lille*, p. 102 and no. lxvi, pp. 213–15; Charles-Louis Frossard, *L'Eglise sous la Croix pendant la domination espagnole. Chronique de l'église réformée de Lille* (Paris and Lille, 1857), pp. 11, 155–63 (text of the 1529 law).

insisted that the goods of heretics, whose crime government jurists defined as a form of treason, be forfeit. Yet the privilege of nonconfiscation was well established in the city's law and custom. By its terms, no property of any citizen found guilty of any offense, no matter where perpetrated, was ever to be forfeit, nor that of anyone arrested in Lille, citizen or not.[76] It was, moreover, a liberty of central importance to a commercial town and perhaps even more so in the eyes of a predominantly mercantile oligarchy.

For a decade and a half following the 1529 controversy, the central government did not insist on confiscation in the few heresy cases prosecuted. But a bitter dispute broke out in 1545, when Brussels expropriated the property of four men who had fled Lille after the arrest of a prominent Protestant preacher. The aldermen's remonstrance to the Great Council at Mechelen was summarily rejected, and in 1549 a new imperial edict called again for confiscation without exception, although Lille apparently refused to publish the decree.[77]

Once again, the issue receded into the background, only to resurface dramatically in May 1564 when Paul Chevalier, a leading Calvinist preacher, was seized in Lille. Based on the fact that its sergeants had captured the minister, the Gouvernance claimed the right to condemn and execute him; in accordance with imperial law his property was to be expropriated as well. The aldermen, however, sought jurisdiction on the grounds that Chevalier had been taken in Lille and that prosecution of heretics was not among the cases reserved to the Gouvernance in earlier accords. Nor did the Magistrat agree to confiscation. What with appeals, counterappeals, and negotiations, the affair dragged on into mid-November, when Gouvernance officials ran out of patience and resolved to proceed on their own with a trial and punishment. But their move was defiantly parried by the Magistrat, which ordered the sworn companies of crossbowmen, harquebusiers, and longbowmen not to help keep order at the execution, as was their custom.

---

[76] For comtal decisions dating from 1418, 1430, and 1477 that had forbidden either the inquisition or any secular authority to seize the property even of heretics, see Paul Fredericq, *Corpus documentorum inquisitionis haereticae pravitatis neerlandicae*, 5 vols. (Ghent, 1889–1906), 1:281–2, 315–18 (docs. 253 and 278); 3:55–6, 76–80, 121–2 (docs. 46–7, 62, 89).

[77] See Jules Houdoy, "Chapitres de l'histoire de Lille . . . . Le privilège de non-confiscation . . . ," *MSSAAL* third ser. 10 (1872):92; Marie-Paule Willems-Closset, "Le protestantisme à Lille jusqu'à la veille de la révolution des Pays-Bas (1521–1565)," *RN* 52 (1970):202; and Chapter 4, section I.

The newly appointed lieutenant governor Baude Cuvillon had deployed the military confraternities to assist his handful of sergeants in heading off any "uproar" (*tumulte*) when another preacher had been burned at the stake just a few days earlier. Again fearing the worst, he pleaded with the regent to nullify the aldermen's directive.[78] Evidently sharing his apprehensions, Margaret of Parma commanded the militia companies to aid Cuvillon, pending a decision on the merits of Lille's complaint. "In a time as hard" as the present, she wrote, any weakness on the part of the constituted authorities might embolden *le peuple* to "rise up against the law."[79]

Margaret referred the dispute to her Privy Council for adjudication, and the aldermen sent the companies to the execution. But they remained adamant in their claims, storming out of the sentencing when Cuvillon decreed the prisoner's property forfeit wherever seizure was allowed.[80] The Magistrat protested vehemently again in early 1565, when the Gouvernance prosecuted two citizens of Lille for holding conventicles and two others for public scandal.[81] The city's asserted rights were, however, destined to be upheld only in part. While confirming Lille's privilege of nonconfiscation, the Privy Council's verdict on the issues raised in this case gave the governor jurisdiction over all violations of imperial heresy placards.[82] So far as can be told, this decision did not weaken the Magistrat's commitment to prosecuting Protestants, which continued vigorously right up until April 1566, when the regent essentially suspended heresy hunting.[83] Still, a declaration by the provincial Estates of Walloon Flanders dating from June 1566 suggests that the fate of these municipal rights and privileges remained a sore point on the eve of the revolt. The statement demanded that arrests and searches by royal officials be prohibited unless local magistrates had

---

[78] Cuvillon to Margaret of Parma, 19 November 1564, printed in Léon Halkin and Gérard Moreau, "Le procès de Paul Chevalier à Lille et à Tournai en 1564," *BCRHB* 131 (1965):55–7.

[79] Letter of 26 November 1564, printed ibid., pp. 59–60. Margaret noted that commotion had already attended Protestant martyrdoms elsewhere.

[80] See ibid., pp. 23, 62 (sentence from Gouvernance records). Despite their histrionics, the aldermen seem to have won, because Cuvillon only called for confiscation *ès lieux où confiscation a lieu*, which was of course not the case in Lille.

[81] AML, Reg. 16,980, fols. 102v–3, 104.

[82] See Halkin and Moreau, "Procès de Chevalier," p. 22 n. 1, and for the full text of the decision, AML, Reg. 15,885, fols. 108–8v, 16 February 1566.

[83] See Chapter 5, section II.

given permission and were present, and that privileges of nonconfiscation be reaffirmed without exception.[84]

Many historians consider fiscal policy to have been another leading bone of contention before the revolt. In their accounts, Habsburg international ambitions led to increasing financial demands that generated strong resentments among populace and political elites alike. Generally contained by Charles V, the conflict is held to have flared into the open under his heir when the regime's fragile structure of taxes and loans foundered. Did the situation in Lille conform to this dismal picture? Was the financial burden pressing ever more heavily on townspeople? Did it engender significant conflicts that alienated local from central authorities?

Table 1.3 displays the fiscal effects of imperial policy. It demonstrates that the conquest of eight provinces between 1521 and 1543, hostilities in the Baltic during the 1530s, and especially repeated warfare with France (1521–9, 1536–7, 1542–4, and 1551–9) required Lille to pay ever higher *aides* (subsidies) and loans for almost four decades. Admittedly, the last column on the right in Table 1.3 indicates that in constant monetary units the growth in the city's obligations was far less dramatic than when expressed in current units. To people at the time, however, the apparent increase must have been striking. What is more, the rising demands coming from Brussels occurred in an economic environment marked by chronic inflation, lagging wages, and, from the early 1560s, uncertain job prospects.[85]

Only the period from 1544 to 1551 provided some respite. But it was quickly followed by renewed fighting and the largest subventions of all. In the mid-1550s, just at the beginning of Philip's reign, frequent aides were supplemented by two loans of 200,000 livres each. Peace, resulting initially (1557) from financial exhaustion but ratified by the treaty of Cateau-Cambrésis in April 1559, did not lead to lower taxes. On the contrary, aides reached their highest level of the century in the years 1561–5. To be sure, loans fell to zero, as the crown's unmanageable

---

[84] The document is printed in Verheyden, "Chronique de Gaiffier," pp. 68–72. Although signed by the seigneurs representing the four castelries of Walloon Flanders, as well as by Lille's pensionary, it bears the unmistakable stamp of the city's Magistrat, as was typical in the provincial Estates. See section III.

[85] See Chapter 4, sections I–II.

Table 1.3. *Lille's aides and loans to the central government, 1501–65*

Period	Aides	Loans	Total	Total adjusted for inflation[a]
	Annual mean (livres)			
1501–10	6,344.38	0	6,344.38	7,377.19
1511–20[b]	6,766.07	0	6,766.07	6,766.07
1521–30	13,118.70	0	13,118.70	8,630.72
1531–40[b]	11,653.69	10,402.83	22,056.52	13,207.50
1541–50	13,132.51	2,145.45	15,277.96	7,998.93
1551–60	15,138.15	40,000.00[c]	55,138.15	21,793.74
1561–5	22,935.34	0	22,935.34	7,748.43

[a] The inflation adjustment is calculated on the basis of the wheat price index (base = 1511–20 mean), for which see Table 4.1.
[b] The account books for 1518 and 1539 are missing.
[c] Besides two loans of 200,000 livres apiece in 1555 and 1557, financed by the sale of rentes by the city government, individuals in Lille and the castellany also directly lent the crown at least another 160,290 livres during this decade; AML, Aff. gén., Pièces 146/2765–7; Reg. 15,885, fols. 3–16v.
Sources: AML, Reg. 16,237–99, 895; Reg. 15,885, fols. 1–3, 19–21v.

debt (nearly 9.4 million florins in 1557) provoked a temporary suspension of both the remittance of interest and the repayment of principal, thereby choking off the government's access to most borrowers. But this maneuver only meant that financial needs now had to be met substantially by taxes: a nine-year grant voted by the Estates-General in 1558, as well as triennial aides agreed to in 1560 and 1563.[86]

Like most urban magistrates,[87] Lille's aldermen chose to pay these sums by raising sales and other indirect taxes (levies on beer and wine

---

86 For the debt, see P. A. Meilink, "Notulen en Generaal Advies van de Staten Generaal van 1557/58," *Bijdragen en Mededeelingen van het Historisch Genootschap* 55 (1934):274–5, 358–9; Pirenne, *Histoire de Belgique*, 3:386. According to Parker, *Dutch Revolt*, p. 39, "the Spanish government's short-term debt in 1556 stood at 7,000,000 ducats (14,000,000 florins [28 million liv.]), seven times the crown's annual revenue. There was no way of repaying this sum, and the interest payments absorbed almost all available revenues." For a summary account of the aides and other forms of central-state taxation, see Jan Craeybeckx, "Aperçu sur l'histoire des impôts en Flandre et au Brabant au cours du XVIe siècle," *RN* 29 (1947):87–108, esp. 90–6.
87 Cf. Smit, "Netherlands Revolution," p. 34.

Table 1.4. *Receipts by Lille's municipal treasury, 1501–65*

Period	Mean receipts per year (livres)		
	Sales and indirect taxes	Sales of annuities	Reimbursements
1501–10	22,037.29	5,714.37	5,448.67
1511–20ᵃ	27,852.51	8,701.63	9,502.62
1521–30	32,037.05	6,314.68	10,862.90
1531–40ᵃ	37,739.81	17,358.13	19,725.97
1541–50	44,448.18	5,716.12	7,985.01
1551–60	46,334.44	68,962.30	4,885.21
1561–5	50,625.00	22,096.80	0

ᵃAccounts for 1518 and 1539 are lacking.
Sources: AML, Reg. 16,237–99, 895.

constituted by far the biggest component, contributing up to three-quarters of the total) and selling *rentes* or annuities (similar to bearer bonds).

Table 1.4 emphasizes that tax income (the bedrock of municipal finance, habitually supplying 55 to 60 percent of all receipts) grew steadily across the first two-thirds of the sixteenth century. Not only were new levies imposed, but demographic and economic expansion brought about a rising volume of transactions.[88] Sales of annuities, however, varied greatly, directly reflecting the changing level of the central government's financial demands (compare Table 1.3 with Table 1.4). Hence the 1550s was the period of maximum rente sales – a total of 471,000 livres in 1555 and 1557 alone – while important quantities were also sold in the early 1560s.

Within limits, the interest due on annuities could be paid from other sources of income, notably taxes. During the first half of the sixteenth century crown revenues were also regularly assigned to the municipal treasury to reimburse the city for previous grants. These transfers in-

---

88 The letters-patent signed by Charles V and Philip II, copies of which are in AML, Reg. 15,884–6, mention the taxes to be levied to pay for the aides.

cluded seigneurial dues, a share of the 25 percent of sales taxes normally reserved for the sovereign, and portions of aides. The right-hand column of Table 1.4 shows that such reimbursements grew progressively through the 1530s but then dropped sharply; in fact, they never amounted to more than 5,000 livres a year after 1544. The earliest cuts can be traced to the central government's reduced requirements for money during most of the 1540s: Less money needed to be paid back. But the crown's failure to resume anything but minimal remittances, despite the return of large aides and loans in the 1550s, and despite explicit pledges of quick reimbursement by Charles V and Philip II,[89] testifies to its mounting financial crisis.

Combined with the heavy current sales of annuities, the near-cessation of transfers badly encumbered Lille's municipal treasury after mid-century. Interest payments on rentes, which had gradually risen from an annual average of 18,133 livres in 1501–10 to 24,840 livres in 1541–50, shot up to a yearly mean of 56,918 livres between 1555 and 1561.[90] Already in the late 1550s shopkeepers began protesting that taxes imposed to pay Lille's share of the aides were hurting business.[91] It seems likely, too, that Lillois who had purchased annuities or lent money to the princely government were not pleased either by the suspension of interest payments in 1557 or by the eventual forced conversion of loans into bonds carrying lower rates.

By the early 1560s, the fiscal crisis of the central state was taking its toll on municipal finances. In 1562, Lille could no longer keep up interest payments on the annuities it had sold. Although the sum of 72,000 livres was borrowed from the provincial Estates, most of it had to be used for other purposes, leaving only 24,860 livres for rentiers, a far cry from the 61,751 livres disbursed the previous year. When long-promised transfers of crown revenue once again failed to materialize in 1563, and the Estates could lend just 6,000 livres, the city was forced to

---

[89] See AML, Reg. 15,885, fols. 19–21v, 25 August 1554 and fols. 1–3, 3 April 1557. On the latter occasion, Philip promised to repay Lille's loan of 200,000 liv. no later than the following 1 February, "notwithstanding any other concerns that might arise, no matter what they be." Cf. AML, Reg. 16,291 (1557), fol. 65, when Philip promised that rentes sold by Lille would be reimbursed by means of deductions from aides over the next eight years.

[90] No figures are available for 1551–4 (AML, Reg. 16,285–8); for 1555–61, see ibid., Reg. 16,289–95.

[91] Without denying the petitioners' allegation, both the provincial Estates and the regent confessed that the need for revenue was too pressing to discontinue a 2% surcharge on retail transactions, the specific focus of disgruntlement. AML, Reg. 15,885, fols. 88–8v, 94.

acknowledge that it could neither repay the loans nor remit the interest due the owners of annuities. By early 1564, the town's creditors were threatening to arrest Lillois to spur action on their claims for nearly 65,000 livres.

At this point, the aldermen petitioned Margaret of Parma for immediate assistance. In response, the crown offered a few palliatives – 1,000 livres from the income of the comtal domain, permission to divert a portion of the next aide, authorization to levy a few new taxes in the future. Reflecting its own delicate financial condition, however, Brussels turned aside Lille's demands for substantial aid with expressions of sympathy and a confession that Lille would have to continue to hold off its creditors by any means possible.[92] Simply to satisfy existing claims, the town was forced to impose additional taxes and apply them to groups usually exempt. Although successful in terms of revenue, this expedient angered half a dozen past and present members of the Magistrat. Joining with fellow "knights, noblemen, and squires," they appealed to the Council of Flanders to uphold their purported immunity "from time immemorial" from paying taxes on wine, beer, grain, and other foodstuffs.[93]

Lille was fortunate to be spared some of the issues that embittered relationships between Philip II and his subjects in other towns. The city suffered neither the depredations of troops made idle by a truce in October 1558 but not paid off and dismissed until nearly a year later, nor the presence of a garrison of Spanish soldiers.[94] The scheme for new bishoprics also affected Lille very little. Nevertheless, financial difficulties and conflicts over heresy prosecutions and the privilege of nonconfiscation ripened for many years, they erupted as points of serious contention between Magistrat and central government in the decade prior to the onset of the revolt, and they strained the fabric of the civic polity in the 1560s. These circumstances would seem to support historians

[92] AML, Aff. gén., Pièce 147/2771, 12 February 1564.
[93] For the new taxes, see AML, Reg. 15,885, fols. 25–7; for the nobles' suit, see ibid., fols. 53v–4v. The outcome is unknown.
[94] In a request for funds to the provincial Estates, dated 24 May 1559, Philip II admitted that the troops were causing many problems; AML, Reg. 15,885, fols. 89–90v. Two months later, the Magistrat of Douai begged its counterpart in Lille to pay its share of aides at once so that the troublesome soldiers could be discharged (AML, Aff. gén., Pièce 129/2381). For the dispute over the Spanish garrisons, settled only when Philip agreed to repatriate them in 1561, see Parker, *Dutch Revolt*, p. 46.

who argue that the kinds of problems usually resolved amicably under Charles V were transformed into qualitatively different antagonisms under his successor. Similarly, Brussels's determined pursuit of its religious policies evidently pulled the aldermen between cooperation with the central state and defense of civic privileges.

Under Philip II, the Magistrat was clearly concerned about encroachments on municipal autonomy and exhibited signs of disaffection with the regime. Yet it would be misleading to exaggerate the novelty, extent, or duration of disputes between Brussels and Lille or to underestimate the substantial areas of consensus between them. The city had a particularly strong incentive to keep on good terms with the central government so that its claims to regional textile-weaving monopolies could be secured or even extended.[95] It may well be as a result of such considerations, in fact, that the aldermen never balked at trying to fulfill the crown's financial needs. Moreover, by the 1560s whatever disagreements over the content of heresy hunting may once have existed lay in the past. Even when (as at the time of the 1564 trial) the Loi provocatively staked claims at odds with the central state's, in the end it bowed to Brussels's dictates. For its part, the crown usually countenanced measures that enhanced the Magistrat's power within the city and strengthened Lille's predominance within the castellany. Political negotiation certainly intensified after midcentury, but this should not be interpreted to mean that relations between city and sovereign had reached the breaking point.

III

What role did particularism as compared with national attachments play in sustaining or disturbing relations between central and municipal governments? Studying the representative institutions in which Lille participated affords some insight, for they both shaped and reflected the consciousness of the ruling strata of the Netherlands. Unfortunately, the relevant archives of the Estates of Lille, Douai, and Orchies, the provincial Estates of Walloon Flanders, begin in 1566. Hence it is difficult to judge whether the body served to perpetuate or even to reinvigorate localism before that time. Still, by the 1550s it had established some

---

95 See Chapter 3, section II.

permanent administrative machinery, including a financial bureau headed by a "collector of aides."[96] This elaboration of the Estates' structure
might be taken to exemplify the growing "regional political integration"
that, according to Smit, hampered national unification.[97]

Given the city's paramount position within the Estates, any such integration could scarcely fail to advance Lille's affairs. The assembly, which
routinely met in the aldermen's chamber in Lille's city hall, was supposed to comprise representatives from the towns of Lille, Douai, and
Orchies, as well as the bailiffs (*seigneurs hauts-justiciers*) of the four administrative divisions of the castellany. But in practice it was Lille's
aldermen, councillors, and huit-hommes, attending each meeting en
masse, who directed proceedings. They received the crown's requests
for aides, the major business of the Estates; prepared responses; and
presented them to the bailiffs for ratification.[98] Deputies from Douai
and Orchies were not necessarily invited to participate, yet these cities
were bound by any decisions taken.[99] Not surprisingly, then, the Estates
proved sympathetic to Lille, as evidenced by the loan of 72,000 livres in
1562 when the town's ability to repay must already have been open to
question, as well as the 6,000 livres lent the next year, when Lille had in
effect suspended payment on its debts.

The provincial Estates, in short, helped voice and defend Lille's particular interests. At the same time, developments stimulated by Habsburg financial needs probably endowed the assembly with an increasingly significant political function. Certainly its activity in the late

---

[96] See AML, Aff. gén., Pièces 129/2377 and 129/2388.

[97] Smit, "Netherlands Revolution," p. 36.

[98] Anatole de Melun, "Histoire des Etats de Lille," *MSSAAL* 2nd ser. 7 (1860):242-3, 252-4;
ibid., 3rd ser. 1 (1864):267; AML, Reg. 277, fol. 9. The seigneuries were the baronies of
Phalempin (comprising roughly the southeastern part of Walloon Flanders north of the bailliage
of Douai) and Cysoing (the northeastern portion), the *terre* of Wavrin (the southwestern section),
and the seigneurie of Comines (the northwestern castellany). The seigneur of Phalempin was
also bailiff of Lille; he administered areas around the city but enjoyed no authority within it.
Delegates of the nobility and clergy were convoked by the governor after the Estates had voted
an aide and were obliged to make a contribution.

[99] The small financial contributions owed (according to a traditional allocative formula) by Douai
(one-third of what Lille paid, or 7.41% of the total) and Orchies (one-eleventh of Douai or
0.67%), probably explain why they were not regularly summoned. Lille owed two-ninths
(22.22%), the rest of the castellany 69.7%; Jules Houdoy, *L'impôt sur le revenu au XVIe siècle. Les
Etats de Lille et le duc d'Albe* (Lille, 1872), p. 3 n. 1. Purely in terms of population, this division was
not exploitative. With some 30,000 inhabitants, Lille was home to about a fifth of the province's
residents, while Douai had 10,000 to 12,000 inhabitants and Orchies perhaps 1,000 to 2,000.
See Introduction and Appendix A.

1560s and early 1570s, when it coordinated a successful campaign of resistance to tax proposals, betrays some familiarity with techniques of political management and mobilization that could only have been learned in the prerevolt period.[100] This incident illustrates the maturing of an institutional structure and practices that could champion municipal as well as provincial concerns once the revolt was underway. Yet there is no evidence that the Estates exacerbated tensions between city and regime in prior years. The emergency loans made to Lille in 1562–3 suggest, in fact, that the Magistrat, this time by recourse to the Estates, wished to work with, not against, Brussels if at all possible.

Members of Lille's Magistrat also attended most meetings of the Estates-General, which Pirenne considered the focus of a developing anti-Habsburg national consciousness that eventually turned against the dynasty that had formed it. Lillois normally constituted a substantial proportion or even majority of the provincial representatives, and they typically determined the positions taken by the entire delegation.[101] Attendance did not, however, signify leadership: Neither city nor province ever played a weighty part in the Estates-General.[102] Significantly, Lille showed little interest in the critical gathering of 1557–8, which demonstrated "a momentary but nevertheless surprising unity of action against the prince." The city sent but two delegates who intervened mainly to reduce the tax assessment of their province and town, though in the end they agreed to pay a larger proportion than before.[103] In sum, on the central as on the regional level, Lille's substantive involvement with representative institutions seems not to have inspired sentiments counterposing nation to ruler. The Magistrat's consent to

---

[100] For this resistance, see Chapter 7, section II.

[101] Robert Wellens, *Les Etats Généraux des Pays-Bas des origines à la fin du règne de Philippe le Beau (1464–1506)* (Heule, 1974), pp. 357–8.

[102] One of the reasons for Walloon Flanders's inconsequential role is suggested by its share of total Netherlands aides: 2.9% in 1473 and 1505, 3.3% in 1540–8. These proportions pale in comparison with those of Flanders (25.4% at the former dates, 33.8% at the latter) or Brabant (21.7% and 28.8% respectively). See N. Maddens, *De Beden in Het Graafschap Vlaanderen tijdens de regering van Keizer Karel V (1515–1550)* (Heule, 1978), pp. 7–8, 10–11.

[103] For the quotation, see Smit, "Netherlands Revolution," p. 35. At the meetings in 1555, when Charles abdicated in favor of Philip, Lille had six representatives, Douai and Orchies four each, and the castellany six. Two years later, the castellany was represented by three men and Douai by one. See John Gilissen, "Les Etats-Généraux des pays de par deça (1464–1632)," *Standen en Landen* 33 (1965):286, 289. For Lille's contributions to the discussions, see Meilink, "Notulen en Generaal Advies van de Staten Generaal van 1557/58," pp. 275, 291, 297, 305–6, 350–9. In the original request, Walloon Flanders was asked for a sum equaling about 5.1% of the total, but in the end the province paid one twenty-fourth (4.2%).

higher aide payments, as well as its low profile in the Estates-General, suggests that if anything the urban ruling class felt more attachment to Philip than to the assembly.

Informal signs of developing national awareness are similarly difficult to discern. The towns consulted on political and economic matters remained the same ones – Tournai, Valenciennes, Arras, and occasionally Ghent or Bruges – whose advice had been sought in the Middle Ages. Despite increasing commercial relations, the cities of Brabant and Holland, not to mention those in other provinces of the Low Countries, had yet to enter the aldermen's relevant mental universe. Nor do we find civic ritual or language expressing a notion of the *patrie*. The processions that mentioned the fatherland in calling for the return of peace were a product of the revolt, not a sign of national feeling that helped bring it on. At least on the part of Lille's political elite, there is nothing to suggest any indigenous movement groping toward nationhood in developing antagonism to the dynasty.

IV

Doubtless Lille's magistrates were not pleased with the Habsburgs' growing financial difficulties nor with the tax burden thereby created. At times, too, they rejected the judicial claims of princely government. Still, they proved repeatedly prepared to cooperate with that government. This willingness did not result from divisions within the Loi or diminished municipal autonomy in consequence of imperial policies. Instead, it rested upon an absence of factionalism combined with secure local hegemony and a knowledge of the benefits – especially concerning the city's vital textile trades – that cooperation could yield. Friction was manifestly growing during the reign of Philip II, but up to the eve of the revolt the aldermen still sought to defend the interests of their city and class while fulfilling Brussels's demands.

2

~~~~~~

"Substantial merchants conducting important trade"

After two crisis-ridden centuries, historians agree, the Netherlands economy experienced pronounced growth during the first half of the sixteenth century. The character and extent of structural transformation, and the relation of economic change to the coming of the Dutch Revolt are, however, matters of debate. As the site of vigorously expanding long-distance trade and textile crafts, Lille is an excellent place to test conflicting interpretations. Did the city participate in a transition to capitalism and the social changes consequent upon it? Or did continuity characterize its social and economic development? How did social and economic factors contribute to or counteract the onset of rebellion?

I

Topography favored the development of commerce at Lille. Located on the Deûle, major tributary of the Lys, which in turn feeds into the Scheldt, the city enjoyed direct river access to rich grain-producing regions, countless textile villages and towns, and – what proved crucial in the sixteenth century – the great international port of Antwerp. Furthermore, an abrupt drop of several meters in the level of the Deûle that necessitated the transshipment of waterborne cargoes stimulated warehousing and transport activities at Lille. So did its position on the geological frontier between the hard chalk of the Mélantois (northern extension of the gently rolling Artois plateau) and the wet sands and clays of the Flemish plain, since this made Lille a logical place for changing teams and transferring goods coming overland.[1]

[1] Raoul Blanchard, *La Flandre: étude géographique de la plaine flamande en France, Belgique et Hollande* (Lille, 1906), esp. p. 437; Pierre Bruyelle, "Facteurs physiques du développement," in *Histoire de Lille*, 1:27–34, 46–52.

"Substantial merchants"

Over the years, natural transport arteries had been improved and extended. Before the mid-thirteenth century, the municipal government constructed locks at the confluence of the Deûle and the Lys and, beginning in 1271, canalized the Upper Deûle. A dense network of routes converging at Lille also evolved during the Middle Ages: the chief arteries between Flanders and France, the main highway between Calais and Cologne, roads to Brussels via Tournai and Oudenaarde, to Valenciennes, and to La Bassée, among others.[2]

During the Middle Ages, when Lille served as the chief market town for a region encompassing Walloon Flanders and portions of neighboring Artois,[3] some of its merchants are known to have ventured as far as Italy.[4] But like their colleagues from other Flemish cities, most functioned as intermediaries between local producers and consumers and the foreign traders – particularly Italians and Frenchmen – who gathered at the great fairs of Champagne and Flanders, including one held in Lille for a month each year.[5] Lillois were most active in the twelfth and thirteenth centuries, selling textiles, dyestuffs, hops, and grain, while buying wine from France and raw wool from England.[6]

Widespread famine, plague, and warfare disrupted commerce across Europe during much of the fourteenth and fifteenth centuries. Increasing competition in the cloth trade, much of it from aggressive English producers, caused additional difficulties for the Low Countries. Lille's access to customary markets was further complicated by a series of

---

2 Derville, "Trois siècles décisifs," pp. 104–6; Michel Mollat, *Le commerce maritime normand à la fin du Moyen Age* (Paris, 1952), pp. 286–7; Henri Laurent, *Un grand commerce d'exportation au Moyen Age. La draperie des Pays-Bas en France et dans les pays méditerranéens (XIIe–XIVe siècles)* (Paris, 1935), pp. 246–7.

3 Sivéry, "Histoire économique et sociale," p. 244.

4 *Medieval Trade in the Mediterranean World*, ed. Roberto Lopez and Irving Raymond (New York, 1955), doc. 160, pp. 324–5 (1222); Renée Doehaerd, *Les relations commerciales entre Gênes, la Belgique et l'Outremont d'après les archives notariales de Gênes, aux XIIe et XIIIe siècles*, 3 vols. (Brussels and Rome, 1941), 1:156; 2:67, 185 (docs. 138, 363). For travels elsewhere, see Mollat, *Commerce maritime normand*, pp. 182 n. 27, 322; Craeybeckx, *Vins de France aux anciens Pays-Bas*, p. 66; Laurent, *Draperie des Pays-Bas*, pp. 131, 133; T. H. Lloyd, *The English Wool Trade in the Middle Ages* (Cambridge, 1977), p. 9.

5 Simone Poignant, *La foire de Lille. Contribution à l'étude des foires flamandes au Moyen Age* (Lille, 1932); Laurent, *Draperie des Pays-Bas*, esp. pp. 94, 98, 100, 104, 237, 269, 272 n. 10; Elizabeth Chapin, *Les villes des foires de Champagne des origines au début du XIVe siècle* (Paris, 1937), pp. 96, 110 n. 21, 140; Sivéry, "Histoire économique et sociale," pp. 162–3, 169–70.

6 Derville, "Trois siècles décisifs," pp. 101, 110–11; Marquant, *Vie économique à Lille sous Philippe le Bon*, p. 165; Brigitte Sory, "Le commerce des vins 'français' dans le ville de Lille aux XIVe et XVe siècles," *Mémoires de la Fédération des Sociétés historiques et archéologiques de Paris et de l'Ile de France* 10 (1959):7–19; Lloyd, *English Wool Trade*, pp. 9–14.

untoward events. The opening of sea routes between Italy and the Netherlands, as well as political troubles in France, provoked the permanent decay of the fairs through which so much of the city's trade had traditionally been funneled, and Walloon Flanders was put under direct French rule between 1304 and 1369.[7] Yet even in this dark period Lille maintained its superiority in regional commerce, and French wine and traffic with central Europe continued to provide some vitality to its long-distance trade.[8]

Already before 1500, moreover, the presence of foreign merchants at Lille and of Lillois abroad heralded an upturn that in the course of the sixteenth century was destined to raise the city's commerce far above any previous level. Urban demographic and industrial growth, fueled especially by a prolonged textile boom, were important factors in Lille's commercial progress.[9] The city's hinterland was also undergoing pronounced expansion. From 1505 to the 1540s the number of hearths in Walloon Flanders grew nearly 30 percent, and the increase reached almost 60 percent in the northern part of the province where rapidly developing cloth manufactures were concentrated.[10] Throughout this area and the larger industrialized zone that stretched across western and southern Flanders, northern Artois, and into Hainaut, Lille's merchants often played critical and lucrative roles as intermediaries between rural producers and Antwerp. Not only did they provide access to the international market, but they channeled specie to villages where credit instruments like the bill of exchange were as yet rarely used for settling accounts.[11]

From their city's hinterland Lille's traders also obtained industrial raw materials, including wool, thread, flax, madder, woad, and hides.[12] Al-

---

[7] F. Bourquelot, *Etude sur les foires de Champagne aux XIIe, XIIIe et XIVe siècles*, 2 vols. (Paris, 1865), 1:301–17; Sivéry, "Histoire économique et sociale," pp. 209–15, 243–52.

[8] Alain Derville, "De 1300 à 1500: de grands malheurs ou de petits bonheurs?" in *Histoire d'une métropole*, p. 155; Hektor Ammann, *Die wirtschaftliche Stellung der Reichsstadt Nürnberg im Spätmittelalter* (Nuremberg, 1970), p. 138.

[9] For Lille's population, see Appendix A. For tax receipts, see AML, Reg. 895, 16, 237–89.

[10] For rural population, see ADN, Reg. B 3762–3.

[11] For trade in rural cloth and the provision of financial services, see Emile Coornaert, *Les Français et le commerce international à Anvers, fin du XVe–XVIe siècle*, 2 vols. (Paris, 1961), 1:158, 164, 173, 207, 2:202. It should be emphasized, however, that many villages and small towns had produced cloth for centuries, during which time they had developed their own direct commercial contacts with Antwerp.

[12] Coornaert, *Français à Anvers*, 1:157–8, 183; AML, Reg. 15, 434.

though Douai was the main market in the Low Countries for domestically grown grain, Lillois distributed some local wheat. More important, Lille became the site of one of the foremost livestock auctions in the Netherlands. Even in the early seventeenth century, when its peak had passed, two thousand or more head of cattle, sheep, and horses changed hands there each Wednesday.[13]

Besides this intense regional trade, the merchants of sixteenth-century Lille actively engaged in long-distance commerce with nearly every corner of Europe. In exchange for woolen cloth, their main export item, they handled wine, wool, and salt from Spain and Portugal; alum (used as mordant in dyeing), spices, silks, and other luxury goods from Italy; wool and tin from England. The Baltic area sent primary goods such as fur, wool, and increasing amounts of grain, whereas iron, brass wire, Rhine wine, and cheap wool were obtained from the German states. France remained a major commercial partner. Besides wine, which as before was the leading import, Lille traded grain from regions just across the border, which also became suppliers of wool. Salt was bought on the Atlantic coast; woad at Bordeaux and (up until the 1560s) Toulouse. Finally, Lillois bought and sold wool, metals, cloth, bark for tanning and currying, butter and cheese, beer, salt, fish, and much else besides from the other provinces of the Netherlands.[14]

The French wine trade nicely illustrates the increasing direct involvement of Lille's merchants in foreign trade during the sixteenth century. Before that time, Lillois had obtained nearly all their wine from brokers in Bruges, Rouen, and Paris, or from Frenchmen, Venetians, and Lombards who brought it to Lille.[15] But in the 1520s they began to bypass these middlemen and purchase large quantities directly from the producing regions. In 1522, for instance, Jean Cornette had 1,400 to 1,500 casks of wine dispatched from Burgundy. Fragmentary records also disclose that vintners from Lille acquired substantial amounts of wine in

[13] Jacques Godard, "Contribution à l'étude de l'histoire du commerce des grains à Douai du XIVe au XVIe siècle," *RN* 27 (1944):171–205; Robert DuPlessis, "Urban Stability in the Netherlands Revolution. A Comparative Study of Lille and Douai" (Ph.d. diss., Columbia University, 1974), pp. 126–44; Jean Buzelin, *Gallo-Flandria sacra et profana* (Douai, 1625), p. 14.

[14] Coornaert, *Français à Anvers*, 1:158, 168 n. 8, 197, 2:113 n. 1; Gilles Caster, *Le commerce du pastel et de l'épicerie à Toulouse de 1450 environ à 1561* (Toulouse, 1962).

[15] Mollat, *Commerce maritime normand*, pp. 182 n. 27, 322; Craeybeckx, *Vins de France aux anciens Pays-Bas*, p. 66; Sory, "Commerce des vins 'français'," p. 17.

Auxerre in 1541. Pierre Vigneron bought 955 hogsheads (*muids*); Allard "Donnez" (probably Drumez), 717 hogsheads; Helie Desplancques, 303; and Jacques de Vendeville, 137.[16]

Most Burgundian and Auxerrois wine was sent overland to the Netherlands. Yet despite their home city's inland location, Lille's merchants captured a large share of the swiftly growing seaborne trade from western France. Much of this business originated at Bordeaux. From about 1540, however, Lillois also began to work regularly through La Rochelle. Boats were chartered there to carry wine to the Netherlands' staple port of Middelburg, where Lille merchants had established representatives. In 1559, for example, Pierre Delesalle (Deledalle) received wine for Jean de Has, in 1563 and 1564 for Jacques de Vendeville, in the latter year for the company of Pierre Sallengre and Bauduin Herreng, in 1564 and 1565 for Georges Fremault and Nicolas Barge.[17] Rochelais often served as Lillois' agents in this trade, as in 1563, when a local man sent 450 casks to the partners Jean and Nicolas de Fourmestraux and Antoine de Thieffries.[18] After midcentury, however, Lillois like other foreign merchants increasingly traveled to La Rochelle either as factors for their fellows at home or to take personal charge of their own business.[19] Of the thirty-five northerners registered there between April 1563 and March 1565, eight were from Lille, as against seven from Hamburg, five from Amsterdam, four from Middelburg, and two each from Antwerp and Ghent.[20]

As this example suggests, Lille's sixteenth-century merchants voyaged more widely than their medieval predecessors. They became particularly well known in commercial centers throughout the southern Low Countries. In the northern provinces they concentrated on such major ports

---

[16] Roger Dion, *Histoire de la vigne et du vin en France des origines au XIXe siècle* (Paris, 1959), pp. 236, 240, 289, 344; Etienne Trocmé and Marcel Delafosse, *Le commerce rochelais de la fin du XVe siècle au début du XVIIe* (Paris, 1952), pp. 74–7, 78 n. 17; Craeybeckx, *Vins de France aux anciens Pays-Bas*, pp. 76, 213, 222, 225, 242, 244–9, 255, 265–6, 275; Sory, "Commerce des vins 'français,' " p. 9 n. 1. Each cask from Burgundy held 100 liters, each hogshead from Auxerre 205–300.

[17] *Documents pour servir à l'histoire du commerce des Pays-Bas avec la France jusqu'à 1585. Tome I. Actes notariés de la Rochelle 1423–1585*, ed. M. A. Drost (The Hague, 1984), docs. 110, 133, 193, 195, 199, 200, 240 (pp. 87–8, 109–10, 167–8, 169–70, 173, 174, 212–13).

[18] As each of these casks contained 900 liters, the shipments totalled 405,000 liters; Trocmé and Delafosse, *Commerce rochelais*, pp. 74–8 (on the latter page, the names of the Lillois are given as de Fornestraulx and de Trufferie).

[19] See *Documents du commerce des Pays-Bas avec la France*, docs. 113–14, 118–20, 133, 135, 169, 187, 193, 195, 199–200, 205–6, 240 (pp. 91–2, 95–7, 109–10, 112–13, 142–3, 160, 167–8, 169–70, 173–4, 179–81, 212–13).

[20] Craeybeckx, *Vins de France aux anciens Pays-Bas*, p. 275. Only Ghent and Lille were not seaports.

as Amsterdam, focus of the expanding Baltic grain trade; Dordrecht, transshipment point for goods coming down the Rhine; and Middelburg. However, they also visited smaller towns such as Flushing, Alkmaar, and Delft.[21] Beyond their traditional destinations in France – Paris and the Champagne fairs – they now showed up in the wine regions; the English Channel ports; Rouen, Nantes, and Toulouse; and in Lyon, used for contact with Italy, where Lillois still rarely went. On occasion they traveled to Savoy and Lorraine, as well as to the Iberian peninsula.[22] Despite the unmistakable superiority of Hollanders in the Baltic trade, merchants from Lille started to appear in Lübeck, Bremen, Stockholm, Copenhagen, Danzig, and Reval by midcentury.[23] They also were found in Worms and Cologne, gateways to the Rhineland; at the celebrated fairs of Frankfurt; and in other central European trading centers, such as Leipzig, Erfurt, and Nuremberg. This contact was facilitated after Lille merchants who may have been Protestants settled in several cities, notably Frankfurt, starting in the 1550s.[24]

Its merchants' peregrinations notwithstanding, by far the greatest part of Lille's commerce was conducted through Antwerp, "the metropole of Western Europe."[25] So strong was its orientation to Antwerp, in fact, that Lille does not appear on a roster of the ten leading overland export centers in the sixteenth-century Netherlands. Its absence is the more striking because the list mentions the nearby towns of Arras (a distant second far behind Antwerp), Valenciennes (third), and Douai (tenth), none of which approached Lille's overall commercial importance.[26] By

---

21 For a summary of Lillois' Netherlands trade, see Coornaert, *Français à Anvers*, 1:165.
22 Ibid., 1:157–8, 165–7, 183, 213, 243; Craeybeckx, *Vins de France aux anciens Pays-Bas*, pp. 217, 238–9; Caster, *Commerce de pastel*, pp. 171–89; Richard Gascon, *Grand commerce et vie urbaine au XVIe siècle. Lyon et ses marchands (environs de 1520–environs de 1580)*, 2 vols. (The Hague, 1971), 1:123–4; AML, Reg. 15, 434–5.
23 Coornaert, *Français à Anvers*, 1:168; *Niederländische Akten und Urkunden zur Geschichte der Hanse und zur deutschen seёgeschichte*, ed. Rudolf Häpke, 2 vols. (Munich and Leipzig, 1913–23), 2:144, doc. 369.
24 Coornaert, *Français à Anvers*, 1:158, 167–8; Ammann, *Wirtschaftliche Stellung der Reichsstadt Nürnberg*, p. 138; Hermann Kellenbenz, "Wirtschaftsgeschichte Kölns im 16. und beginnenden 17. Jahrhundert," in *Zwei Jahrtausende Kölner Wirtschaft*, 2 vols. (Cologne, 1975), 1:383, 391; Alexander Dietz, *Frankfurter Handelsgeschichte*, 4 vols. (Frankfurt, 1910–25), 2:14, 18, 20, 33, 62, 268.
25 The quotation is from the chapter heading in Herman Van der Wee, *The Growth of the Antwerp Market and the European Economy (14th–16th Century)*, 3 vols. (The Hague, 1963), vol. 2, part I, chap. V.
26 See Wilfrid Brulez, "De Handel," in Genootschap voor Antwerpse Geschiedenis, *Antwerpen in de XVIde eeuw* (Antwerp, 1975), p. 120.

way of Antwerp, Lillois were able to conduct business with distant places they never visited, like the New World or Asia Minor, or very rarely went to, such as Italy and England. However, the true measure of the Brabant port's significance for Lille lies in the fact that many of its merchants' countless transactions with Germany, France, the other provinces of the Netherlands – even with cities as close as Tournai and Courtrai – were concluded in Antwerp, rather than in the hometown of either buyer or seller.[27]

Although the effects of Antwerp's growth were felt in nearly every corner of the Low Countries – which formed, as Pirenne so rightly expressed it, Antwerp's economic "suburbs"[28] – Lillois seem to have benefited more than most. A larger number of merchants from Lille than from any other Netherlands city are known to have traded at or through Antwerp: four hundred between the late fifteenth and late sixteenth centuries, three-quarters of them in the years from 1540 to 1580 when Antwerp was at its zenith.[29] Pioneers like Simon Bouvy had entered the Antwerp trade as early as 1445, and at least one family, the du Bosquiel, had the acumen to link its destiny with Antwerp's from 1463, thereby laying the foundation of the fortune that would propel it to commercial and political prominence in sixteenth-century Lille. But like their fellows from other cities, Lillois began to appear on the banks of the Scheldt in significant numbers only after 1510, becoming especially numerous from the mid-1540s.[30]

Admittedly, Antwerp alone handled three-quarters of all Netherlands exports, and Amsterdam had the lion's share of the Low Countries' vital grain imports. But by the 1560s the success of Lille's merchants in gaining control of a large part of the flourishing textile and raw material trade of the southern Netherlands, along with a diversified long-distance commerce, had made their city an "authentic regional capital." More than that, it was one of the foremost commercial centers in west-

---

[27] Coornaert, *Français à Anvers*, 1:166, 169, 312, and passim; Renée Doehaerd, *Etudes anversoises. Documents sur le commerce international à Anvers*, 3 vols. (Paris, 1962–3), 3:208, doc. 3647.

[28] Pirenne, *Histoire de Belgique*, 3:267.

[29] On the rise of Antwerp, see J. A. Van Houtte, "La genèse du grand marché international d'Anvers à la fin du Moyen Age," *RBPH* 19 (1940):87–126, and especially Van der Wee, *Growth of the Antwerp Market*. For the figures cited in the text, see Coornaert, *Français à Anvers*, 1:160–1, 358–62. Based on the vagaries of the survival of documents, they are doubtless much below the true figures, as Coornaert notes, but there is no way of calculating the extent of error.

[30] For the periods of most intense activity at Antwerp by Lillois, see Coornaert, *Français à Anvers*, fig. "Nombre de marchands" at the end of vol. 2.

ern Europe, behind the top dozen or so but nearly on a par with Rouen, a city more than twice its size.[31]

II

Some innovations in business methods accompanied the emergence of this increasingly active merchant class. One of the most important was the use of representatives abroad, which allowed Lillois to conduct more diversified, regular, and well-informed trade throughout Europe. Agents might be itinerant: Denis Baillet was engaged in 1544 to travel "far and near, by sea and by land," to attend to the *negotiation et marchandise* of the three men who hired him.[32] When more stable representation was needed, foreign merchants might serve as correspondents, just as Lillois handled goods and settled accounts for Londoners, Genoese, Toulousains, or Germans.[33] Some important merchants even had permanent resident agents, almost branch managers, in cities with which they carried on intense trade. Factors were especially numerous in Antwerp – where Lillois owned compounds consisting of a warehouse, office, and dwelling[34] – but they were also found at Bordeaux, La Rochelle, Toulouse, Lisbon, Seville, even Narva and Moscow.[35]

In Lille, as elsewhere, agents' stipends and terms of employment varied from employer to employer, even from year to year.[36] Some were paid salaries, others received commissions. When Denis Baillet received his peripatetic appointment, for example, he was promised 150 florins spread over four years. Jean Castellain's factor, on the contrary, worked on a consignment basis, taking 1.5 percent of the value both of goods he sold at his employer's behest and those he sent to Castellain, a 0.25

---

[31] Goris, *Colonies marchandes mériodionales à Anvers*, pp. 330–4; Coornaert, *Français à Anvers*, 1:157 (for the quotation). Philip Benedict, *Rouen during the Wars of Religion* (Cambridge, 1981), p. 3, estimates Rouen's population at between 71,000 and 78,000 around the mid-sixteenth century.

[32] AML, Reg. 15,434, fols. 165v–6v. Cf. Pierre Jeannin, "Les relations économiques des villes de la Baltic avec Anvers au XVIe siècle," *VSWG* 43 (1956):328, for Jean le Moisne's work in the Baltic for Charles Delescluse.

[33] See Coornaert, *Français à Anvers*, 1:164–5, 2:73, 290–1, doc. VI; ADN, Tab. 4165; AML, Reg. 15,435, fols. 56v–7.

[34] SA, Not. 2073, fols. 56v–7v; Coornaert, *Français à Anvers*, 1:167 n. 1.

[35] Coornaert, *Français à Anvers*, 1:165 n. 5, 169; n. 17 above; and Artur Attman, *The Russian and Polish Markets in International Trade 1500–1650* (Göteborg, 1973), pp. 26–7, 73, 77.

[36] See the general comments in Van Houtte, *Economic History of the Low Countries*, pp. 208–9, and in Barry Supple, "The Nature of Enterprise," in *The Cambridge Economic History of Europe*, 7 vols. (Cambridge, 1941–78), 5:409.

percent fee for money changing consequent upon these transactions, and 0.25 percent for money that he remitted to Castellain upon the latter's demand.[37]

By the terms of the contract just cited, Denis Baillet was forbidden either to trade for his personal account or, unless so directed, to do business for merchants other than those who had hired him. But other contracts allowed agents to work for more than one merchant or partnership and also to conduct some trade on their own, perhaps to parlay an initially small capital into economic autonomy.[38] By 1559, in fact, Baillet himself simultaneously represented the de Fourmestraux and the Delobel of Lille, the van den Hove of Antwerp and Middelburg, and a number of men from Cambrai, among others. He was so busy that he employed at least one assistant.[39]

The partnership, which enabled merchants to broaden their contacts and procure additional capital, was another new way of doing business diffused in northern Europe during the sixteenth century.[40] Lillois, it seems, were more willing to form commercial associations than were their colleagues from other cities. Only with fellow townspeople, however, did partnerships prove durable, as the companies that Lille's merchants established with foreign traders proved ephemeral even by the standards of the time.[41]

Practice in Lille confirms the generalization that the company was usually grounded in the family.[42] Often it was the members of a nuclear family who formed a commercial house. Women – as far as can be determined, these were always widows – were frequently included. Hence we find, for example, not only the collaboration of Jean de le Dalle with his father in the wine business, but also Marie de Fourmestraux, spouse of the late Jean Delobel, working with her son Jacques.[43] At least among the great international traders, merchant

---

37 AML, Reg. 15,434, fols. 165v–6v; Coornaert, *Français à Anvers*, 2:73 n. 3. Cf. SA, Not. 2073, fols. 56v–7v.
38 Cf. Supple, "Nature of Enterprise," p. 409.
39 Craeybeckx, *Vins de France aux anciens Pays-Bas*, pp. 237, 242–3, 255. Cf. Coornaert, *Français à Anvers*, 2:73 n. 1, 75–6.
40 J. N. Ball, *Merchants and Merchandise. The Expansion of Trade in Europe 1550–1630* (New York, 1977), p. 125.
41 Coornaert, *Français à Anvers*, 1:160, 167, 213, 224, 2:47.
42 See Supple, "Nature of Enterprise," p. 410.
43 Craeybeckx, *Vins de France aux anciens Pays-Bas*, pp. 247, 249 n. 205; AML, Reg. 15,885, fols. 3–16v; cf. Coornaert, *Français à Anvers*, 2:68–9.

companies might also be composed of men and women from the extended family, both those of the same generation and more senior or junior partners.[44]

Partnerships likewise drew on more than a single Lille family or lineage; frequently, though by no means inevitably, these business relationships were cemented by ties of marriage.[45] Sizable groupings were not unknown: in 1542, Collard, Jacques, Nicolas junior, and Gilles de Fourmestraux, together with Jeanne Dupont (widow of Pierre de Fourmestraux and mother of at least two of the men just named), Guillaume Dancoisne, Antoine de Thieffries, and Robert du Bosquiel "united together as regards merchandise."[46] It appears, however, that the majority of companies involved only two to four individuals, such as Helie Desplancques and Jacques Delobel, who were partners in the buying and selling of French wine; or Gerard Mahieu, Jean Dubois, and Pierre Dupont, colleagues in 1565.[47]

Irrespective of size or personal ties among partners, many firms were temporary, established to conduct one specific transaction, finance a single trip, or do business for a limited period of time.[48] They did not, moreover, necessarily have exclusive claims upon the activity or capital of the partners. Thus merchants might form several companies at once, each with different collaborators, or at the same time trade both as individuals and as part of a group. Helie Desplancques and several Delobel men, for instance, who organized a firm in 1545, also continued to market wine on their own.[49] In addition, Lille's merchants continually formed, dissolved, and reestablished commercial companies. So Jacques Delobel, who worked with Helie Desplancques in 1545, four years later shipped goods from St. Malo in conjunction with Hughes Delobel and in 1559 collaborated with Jacques van den Hove.[50]

Amid all this transience, there were some signs of more permanent associations. In particular, a nucleus of partners could provide a degree of continuity to successive ventures. In 1542, Nicolas and Jacques de

---

44 *Histoire de Lille*, 2:60; cf. Coornaert, *Français à Anvers*, 2:43.
45 For intermarriage within the merchant elite, see my discussion in section III.
46 Henri Fremaux, *Histoire généalogique de la famille De Fourmestraux* (Lille, 1907), p. 199 n. 3.
47 Coornaert, *Français à Anvers*, 1:163, 165, 358. Cf. Fremaux, *De Fourmestraux*, p. 198; *Histoire de Lille*, 2:60.
48 See, for example, AML, Reg. 15,434, fols. 165v–6v.
49 Coornaert, *Français à Anvers*, 2:45 n. 2; cf. ibid., p. 46 n. 4.
50 Ibid., p. 43; AML, Reg. 15,435, fols. 56v–7. According to Coornaert, *Français à Anvers*, 2:46 n. 4, Delobel was involved in four or five different firms within the space of fifteen years.

Fourmestraux and Antoine de Thieffries were included in the eight-person partnership already mentioned; in 1544, these three men put together their own company; by the mid-1550s, if not earlier, a concern grouping Nicolas de Fourmestraux and Antoine de Thieffries with Jean de Fourmestraux had come into existence; and these three men were part of an eighteen-partner association dating from 1565.[51] Some companies, moreover, enjoyed great longevity in their original form. The brothers Thomas and Louis du Retz associated with a few close friends to do business with Spain and France in 1529, the house not dissolving until 1559, when the two founders died.[52] Companies ordinarily terminated automatically upon the decease of any of the original partners. Yet they might continue across generations if children succeeded their parents, as Jean junior and Alexandre Gobau replaced their father in the firm of Jean Gobau and Etienne Denis after his death or retirement in 1560.[53]

Already by the mid-sixteenth century, then, merchant companies were common in Lille. Some overspilled kinship boundaries and spanned generations. Others were willing to hire people from outside the family to serve as agents,[54] suggesting that the notion of the firm as an entity separate from the individual trader or merchant family was beginning to emerge. Lillois also took advantage of several other up-to-date business practices, including the bill of exchange and a degree of geographical specialization.[55]

The modern aspects of commerce in sixteenth-century Lille stand out in comparison with early seventeenth-century Amiens, a textile and commercial city of about the same size. In Amiens, merchant companies were "excessively rare," those few that did exist remained almost exclusively confined to family members, and bills of exchange were seldom employed.[56] Yet at the same time that Lillois proved receptive to some

---

[51] Fremaux, *De Fourmestraux*, p. 199 n. 3; AML, Reg. 15,434, fols. 165v–6v; AML, Reg. 15,885, fol. 4; *Histoire de Lille*, 2:60. The company of eighteen people also included the widows of two individuals from the eight-person venture.

[52] Coornaert, *Français à Anvers*, 2:41. Cf. ibid., 1:165–6, for a business relationship lasting from 1540 to at least 1566.

[53] Ibid., 2:46 and n. 4; ibid., p. 43, for other examples.

[54] For instance, Jean Bigot and Jean de Meullebroucq represented the partnership of de le Dalle and Mulier in Lisbon for several years; Craeybeckx, *Vins de France aux anciens Pays-Bas*, p. 255.

[55] Coornaert, *Français à Anvers*, 1:158, 169 n. 4; 2:33.

[56] Pierre Deyon, *Amiens, capitale provinciale. Etude sur la société urbaine au 17e siècle* (Paris and The Hague, 1967), pp. 98–101.

advanced practices, they clung to many long-standing modes of business organization and technique favored by the great majority of their contemporaries.[57] Individual trading and short-term associations among members of a single family retained their popularity. Merchants of all types and stature still frequently accompanied goods to destinations far across Europe or traveled long distances to buy directly from producers. Even the largest traders sold retail as well as wholesale, and those who concentrated their efforts on particular commodities were few in number and generally minor in scale of operation.[58]

Old-fashioned, too, was the continued use of cash in sizable transactions despite the risks involved. As late as 1580, Albin Villain, agent of Martin Muette and Nicolas Tesson, was carrying 1,760 florins to buy cloth at Hondschoote when he was waylaid outside Armentières by roving soldiers.[59] Turnover of capital could be very slow, too, because payment for goods was stretched out for as long as six years. And even in the later sixteenth century some merchants still resorted to barter to settle accounts.[60]

Finally, Lille's trading community appears to have been as sluggish as others in the Netherlands to adopt the new means of financial record keeping developed in Renaissance Italy. This inertia persisted despite the diffusion of Italian methods both informally and through the publication of works such as Jan Ympyn's *Nieuwe Instructie* (1543), a close copy of Luca Pacioli's famous treatise on accounting, and a French-language handbook on the subject brought out in 1562 by François Flory, a Lillois working at Antwerp.[61] The three sixteenth-century account books that have survived in Lille consist of little more than lists of receipts and payments. Entries are not classified, personal and business terms are indiscriminately jumbled together, and settlement is routinely noted simply by striking out the record of the original transaction. The only hints of a more modern spirit are to be found in the posting of

[57] Cf. Coornaert, *Français à Anvers*, 2:31–43; Van Houtte, *Economic History of the Low Countries*, pp. 206–9.

[58] See Coornaert, *Français à Anvers*, 2:18–19, 32–3. Cf. Ball, *Merchants and Merchandise*, pp. 23–4.

[59] ADN, Tab. 3308, fols. 124–5v.

[60] Coornaert, *Français à Anvers*, 2:64; ADN, Tab. 1146, no. 64, fol. 25v.

[61] For Italian developments, see Michael Chatfield, *A History of Accounting Thought* (Hinsdale, Ill., 1974), chap. 3, and Lopez and Raymond, *Medieval Trade in the Mediterranean*, chap. 22. Regarding Ympyn's work and the slow acceptance of accounting in the Netherlands, see Ball, *Merchants and Merchandise*, pp. 25–7. For Flory, who also taught accounting, see Coornaert, *Français à Anvers*, 2:50 n. 4, and Van der Wee, *Growth of the Antwerp Market*, 2:331.

debits and credits on separate pages and the preponderance of Arabic numbers rather than Roman numerals.[62]

It is clear, in short, that Lille's commercial structure was only partially transformed. Some evidence of progressive attitudes and behavior can be found, for some merchants routinely used agents, formed larger and more durable companies, and availed themselves of more flexible means of transferring money. Its spirit of initiative also distinguished the group as a whole from both its predecessors and many contemporaries. But there is also much that bespeaks hesitation, because Lille's commercial community neglected numerous innovations, including insurance, discounting, and modern methods of bookkeeping.

It would be mistaken to conclude, however, that the merchants of Lille were indifferent to opportunities for growth. Rather, they showed themselves concerned less with intensive growth (achieving a higher rate of profit through improvements in technique) than with extensive growth (raising aggregate profits by trading more goods in more places). Hence they adopted ways of doing business – in particular, the employment of factors and the formation of partnerships – that by augmenting personnel and capital widened access to the developing world market. By selectively appropriating innovation, Lille's merchants built substantial and sustained commercial relations with important trading centers all across the Continent. As a result, they could successfully exploit rising European and overseas demand while securing the material resources that underlay their political and social domination of urban life.

III

Very few of Lille's sixteenth-century merchants had a commercial pedigree stretching back to the great days of the city's medieval commerce. Like their peers elsewhere, most old families that had survived the perils of mortality had quit trade, acquired urban bonds, land, ecclesiastical preferment and princely office, and ascended into the robe – even, now and then, the sword – nobility. Those whose ancestors had been at the

---

[62] AML, Reg. 6524 (late sixteenth century; mostly Roman numerals); Reg. 6525 (largely Arabic numbers in accounts running from 1542 to 1580); Reg. 15,634 (only Arabic numbers in accounts from 1582 to 1607).

forefront of the city's trade in the high Middle Ages had long since withdrawn from the world of business. Instead, they were landed seigneurs, prominent officials in the provincial government and Chambre des Comptes, councillors to the Burgundian dukes and their Habsburg successors, canons, and abbots.[63]

The history of the Hangouart family illustrates the process. Descendants of leading cloth traders and bankers in the thirteenth and fourteenth centuries, Hangouart men subsequently acquired numerous seigneuries and moved into the upper ranks of officialdom and the clergy. Already in the fifteenth century one had been appointed provost of Lille and then provincial lieutenant governor, and in the sixteenth century family members gained even greater renown. Wallerand, chaplain to Charles V and Philip II, was also canon and dean of the collegiate church of St. Pierre at Lille, provost of both St. Barthélemi at Béthune and St. Amé at Douai, and chancellor and rector of the university of Douai in its early years. His three brothers held equally distinguished positions in the secular world. Rogier, sieur of Créquillon and of Cobrieux, was a *maître ordinaire* in the Chambre des Comptes; Philippe served as imperial tax collector for Lille and its castellany as well as councillor to Charles V and Philip II; Guillaume was councillor, then president of the Council of Artois. Their sons included both robe and sword nobles, while their daughters either married such men or entered high positions in religious orders.[64]

Because of the nearly complete metamorphosis of the earlier commercial class, the revival of trade that began in the later fifteenth century not only led to an expansion of Lille's mercantile community as a whole but ensured that it would be composed largely of new men. A few of these did come from families that had long been in the city. This group included the Denis, whose progenitors had originally acquired citizenship at the end of the thirteenth century; the du Bosquiel (in Lille from at least 1302); the Bave, du Bus, and Dancoisne, whose forebears

63 Feuchère, "Bourgeoisie lilloise au moyen âge," pp. 421–30; Derville, "De 1300 à 1500," pp. 143, 147–52, 155.
64 Sivéry, "Histoire économique et sociale," pp. 263–4; Paul Denis du Péage, *Receuil de généalogies lilloises*, 4 vols. (Lille, 1906–8), 3:1187–98; Le Roux, *Recueil de la Noblesse*, pp. 48–9; BML, MS. Godefroy 112, fols. 21v–2. For the equally revealing histories of the Fremault and de Preudhomme, see Feuchère, "Bourgeoisie lilloise au moyen âge," pp. 424–5 n. 5; Henri Fremaux, "Histoire généalogique de la famille Fremault (1200–1538)," *BCHDN* 27 (1909):1–61; Le Roux, *Recueil de la Noblesse*, p. 40; BML, MS. Godefroy 112, fols. 19–19v.

had immigrated in the fourteenth century.[65] But Appendix D shows that many merchant families in sixteenth-century Lille were more recent immigrants. A steady flow of outsiders to the city starting about 1420 accelerated toward the turn of the century and, most likely due to the opportunities created by sustained commercial growth, did not falter until after about 1560. Even when the pace slackened thereafter, newcomers periodically settled in the city.

The de Smerpont had been prominent landowners if not nobles in Artois, and Guillaume Drumez, cloth merchant born ca. 1450, was the natural son of Oste de Croix, sieur of Drumez.[66] Apart from them, however, the founders of Lille's mercantile families were of plebeian extraction. Some had been merchants before moving to Lille, like the Poulle of Houplines, Jean de la Chapelle of Tournai, or the van der Leure from Courtrai.[67] But most individuals took up trade subsequent to their arrival, so that geographical movement engendered occupational change and, frequently, upward social mobility. Peasant ancestry appears to have been quite common. The brothers Mathieu and Nicolas de Fourmestraux, founders of the premier merchant clan in sixteenth-century Lille, were the sons of a *laboureur;* the earliest known de Vendeville, progenitor of another leading family, was a *cultivateur;* and doubtless among those who hailed from villages there were many other children of farmers.[68] Artisans also contributed to the formation of Lille's mercantile community. Hugues de Thieffries, father of Jacques, cloth merchant, was himself a light-cloth weaver; Nicolas Tesson's father was a brewer at St. Omer.[69]

A large and extremely heterogeneous group of townspeople, characterized by wide disparities of activity and wealth, engaged in commerce during the sixteenth century.[70] On the fringes of the mercantile community were men like the goldsmith Allard Desmaistres, who sold a few

---

[65] Denis du Péage, *Recueil de généalogies lilloises,* 4:1419; 3:1149–59, 1169–70; 1:14, 37; idem, "Mélanges généalogiques," *BSEPC* 15 (1910):78; 16 (1911):135.

[66] Denis du Péage, "Mélanges généalogiques," *BSEPC* 19 (1914):72–3; idem, *Familles de Flandre* (Bruges, 1951), p. 73.

[67] Denis du Péage, *Recueil de généalogies lilloises,* 1:131–2; Fremaux, *De Fourmestraux,* pp. 257, 262.

[68] Fremaux, *De Fourmestraux,* pp. 194–6, 207. See also Denis du Péage, *Recueil de généalogies lilloises,* 2:623.

[69] Denis du Péage, "Mélanges généalogiques," *BSEPC* 17 (1912):232; idem, *Recueil de généalogies lilloises,* 2:600.

[70] This "democratization of international trade" was not limited to Lille; see Van der Wee, *Growth of the Antwerp Market,* 2:321, and Wilfrid Brulez, "L'Exportation des Pays-Bas vers l'Italie par voie de terre au milieu du XVIe siècle," *AESC* 14 (1959):471–2.

rasières of grain on the side.[71] Straddling the border between industry and commerce, though more regularly involved in trade, were merchant-artisans whose commercial dealings were a direct outgrowth of the crafts they practiced. By exploiting contacts forged with merchants who stayed at his inn in Lille, for instance, Jean Renault could conduct business through Antwerp, while Jean Pollet marketed textiles he finished in his fulling mill.[72]

Trade enabled a few merchant-artisans (usually those in capital-intensive crafts) to become affluent and prominent members of local society. When Marie, daughter of the merchant-tanner Lievin Laigniel, was married in 1550, she received a dowry consisting of 2,500 livres in cash and annuities worth 500 livres in principal, a settlement comparable with what the daughter of a comfortable full-time merchant could expect.[73] Antoine de Flandres, a dyer who also had wide-ranging commercial interests throughout Europe, furnishes another example of a prosperous merchant-artisan. He contributed 240 livres each to forced loans in 1552 and 1556–7, and 50 florins in 1562. De Flandres also paid the thirteenth highest assessment of the 247 surviving for the "Hundredth Penny," a 1 percent tax on capital assets, including real estate, collected in 1569.[74] When in 1574 his son Jean married Michelle, daughter of the merchant Antoine de Sailly, de Flandres provided a marriage portion worth 14,000 livres (8,000 in cash and annuities with a principal valued at 6,000), fifth largest of the approximately three hundred dowries that have survived from the sixteenth century.[75]

Over and above the occasional traders and the merchant-artisans were the many Lillois whose primary occupation was commerce. Within this stratum were to be found the richest individual Lillois; as a group, too, full-time merchants were more prosperous than their fellow townspeople. Returns for the Hundredth Penny show that merchants paid the highest mean and median tax. As reported in Appendix C, the records also reveal that on the average merchants owed three times as much as

[71] AML, Reg. 15,435, fols. 73v–4.
[72] Coornaert, *Français à Anvers*, 2:50 n. 8; ADN, Tab. 1149, no. 48, fols. 54–5. Cf. ADN, Tab. 1146, no. 25, fols. 179–9v.
[73] AML, Reg. 15,435, 8 May 1550. For comparisons, see Appendix B.
[74] AML, Pièce 146/2765–7; Reg. 15,885, fol. 13; Lottin, "Liste des riches lillois," pp. 68–72; AML, Reg. 966. For the Hundredth Penny, see Appendix C. On de Flandres's widespread commercial activities, see Coornaert, *Français à Anvers*, 2:54.
[75] ADN, Tab. 3852, 6 March 1574 (n.s.). The bridge brought a dowry of 9,000 liv.

shopkeepers and artisans in capital-intensive trades, at least five times as much as the most prosperous weavers, and nearly one and a half times as much as nobles and seigneurs.

All full-time merchants were not equally wealthy, however; a distinct hierarchy prevailed among them. Their assessments for the Hundredth Penny, ranging from 1.1 to 142.5 livres, represented the extreme figures for the half of the city for which documentation has survived.[76] Again, while some merchants' children received dowries worth over 10,000 livres, many had to be content with much less (Appendix B). For instance, to the marriage between Catherine du Bus and Gilles Casteckre, daughter and son of merchants, the bride brought 1,800 livres in cash, the groom 1,000 livres and six years of rental income from a house on the Fishmarket in Lille.[77] Monies turned over to the municipal and central governments in forced loans, summarized in Table 2.1, also disclose the widely varying resources of Lille's merchants, while at the same time pointing up their greater average wealth as compared with that of other townspeople.

Many, perhaps even the majority, of Lille's merchants seem to have had resources corresponding to those of the more prosperous artisans and merchant-artisans. Appendix B indicates that children from the lower ranks of the merchant class and the upper strata of the artisanate received similar dowries. In the forced loan of 1562, to take another example, 40 percent of the merchants and 50 percent of the artisans contributed 24 to 40 florins; a total of 93 percent of the former and 100 percent of the latter subscribed 50 florins or less.[78] For their part, the Hundredth Penny rolls reveal that there were more merchants than artisans of middling affluence. Slightly more than one-quarter (28 percent, to be exact) of the merchants paid 4.9 livres or less and another fourth was charged between 5.0 and 9.9 livres; 76 percent of artisans fell into the first category, and only 20 percent into the second.[79] Not only,

---

76 Data exist for the parishes of Ste. Catherine, two quarters and a small fragment of a third from St. Etienne, and St. Pierre. There is nothing for St. Sauveur, the cloth makers' parish, or for St. Maurice. St. André and La Madeleine may not have been included as they lay outside the city walls.

77 ADN, Tab. 3852. The value of the rental income is not stated in the contract.

78 The absolute numbers of merchants and artisans were, however, quite different: 68 traders and 7 craftsmen put in the sum of 50 fl., while another 52 and 7 respectively gave between 24 and 40 fl. See Lottin, "Liste des riches lillois," pp. 68–72. I have identified most of those listed from a great variety of sources.

79 For artisans in capital-intensive trades alone, the figures were 58% and 34% respectively.

Table 2.1. *Loans by Lille's merchants to governmental institutions, 1537–62*
(all amounts in livres)

Date and nature of loan	Source	Range of merchant contributions	Mean of merchant contributions	Range of all contributions	Mean of all contributions
1537: to Lille's municipal government to rebuild town's fortifications (N = 250)	AML, Reg. 902, fols. 86v–92v	12–400	181	8–2,000	99
1543: to Charles V for troops to fight the French (N = 141)	AML, Reg. 15,884, fols. 223v–6	40–1,200	419	40–2,000	230
1552: to Charles V for troops to fight the French (N = 150)	AML, Aff. gén., Pièce 146/2765–7	200–2,000	465	200–6,000	423
1556–7: to Charles V for troops to fight the French (N = 261)	AML, Reg. 15,885, fols. 3–16v	100–4,000	771	100–4,000	434
1562: to municipal government to buy grain to distribute to the poor (N = 302)	AML, Reg. 15,923, fols. 24–8v; printed in Lottin, "Liste des riches lillois," pp. 68–72	50–300	87	40–300	88

moreover, did these groups enjoy comparable means, but at times they felt enough social solidarity to intermarry, as Table 2.2 indicates.

The numerous small and medium merchants were the wide base on which Lille's commercial vigor was built, for they ceaselessly traded an impressive variety of goods throughout the Low Countries and northern France. But those renowned in the sixteenth century and ever since were the great international traders, men – and a handful of women – who bought several thousand bales of pastel or shipped hundreds of casks of wine at a time. Among the Lillois within this elite, some powerful individuals stood out on their own. Julien le Febvre, for example, supplied over 40 percent of the French wine consumed in Antwerp in 1550, owned two houses there, and basked in the friendship of many influential merchants.[80] It was, however, the members of some two dozen families who predominated: the Baillet, Coene, Dancoisne, Delannoy, Drumez, Dubois, Dupont, Fasse, de Has, Henniart, Levasseur, le Moisne, Poulle, de Thieffries, de Vendeville, and, at the very apex, a select group of extremely large, rich, and powerful clans, including the du Bosquiel, Castellain, Deliot, Delobel, de Fourmestraux, van der Leure, Mahieu, and de Smerpont (or Semerpont).[81]

Although the scope of their operations rarely rivaled those of the famous German and Italian houses, some of these Lillois did rank among the leading Netherlands merchants of the era.[82] In the terrible "hunger year" of 1565–6, when the de Fourmestraux, Delobel, Mahieu, and van der Leure allegedly raised 700,000 florins for an attempt to corner the Netherlands grain market, the Antwerp municipal government characterized them as constituting "some of the leading and richest offices [*comptoirs*] and companies of merchants here in the Netherlands."[83] On their side, the de Smerpont and de Vendeville were important figures in the La Rochelle and Bordeaux wine trade, able on occasion to fill whole ships exclusively with their own goods.[84] In just the first two weeks in October 1559, for example, Jacques de Vendeville's agent chartered three small ships in La Rochelle to carry thirty-five, thirty-four, and thirty-nine casks of wine to Middelburg. De Ven-

---

[80] Craeybeckx, *Vins de France aux anciens Pays-Bas*, pp. 222, 225, 265–6.
[81] See ibid., pp. 245, 249 n. 205; and Coornaert, *Français à Anvers*, 1:160, and the "Liste provisoire" at the end of vol. 2.
[82] Coornaert, "Le commerce de Lille par Anvers au XVIe siècle," *RN* 29 (1947):247–8.
[83] For the statement, see Coornaert, *Français à Anvers*, 1:162.
[84] Ibid., 2:64, 228; Craeybeckx, *Vins de France aux anciens Pays-Bas*, p. 245.

Table 2.2. *Marriages between merchant and artisan families in Lille, 1544–60*

Date of contract	Source	Groom			Bride		
		Name and occupation[a]	Father's name and occupation[a]	Marriage portion[b]	Name	Father's name and occupation	Marriage portion[b]
5 June 1544	AML, Reg. 15,434	Lievin Laigniel, tanner	Nicaise	Unspecified	Jeanne de la Chapelle	Jacques, merchant	1,000 fl. (2,000 liv.)
9 November 1544	Ibid.	Mahieu Wicart	Pierre, merchant	600 fl. (1,200 liv.)	Marguerite Carlier	Georges, dyer	600 fl. (1,200 liv.)
8 May 1550	AML, Reg. 15,435	Pol de le Barre, merchant	Guillaume	Unspecified	Marie Laigniel	Lievin, tanner	1,250 fl.; 250 fl. annuities (3,000 liv.)
11 September 1550	Ibid.	Antoine Despretz, merchant	Charles	750 fl. (1,500 liv.)	Jeanne le Mesre	Jean, merchant apothecary	0.7 ha. land, worth 300 fl.; 300 fl.; 100 fl. for wedding (1,400 liv.)
19 June 1560	AML, Reg. 15,435bis	Jean Lempereur, goldsmith	Cornille, goldsmith	30 fl.; 0.7 ha. land with buildings in Phalempin; one-half of 0.25 ha. land; one-half of house in Lille; one-fourth of 2 houses in Lille	Catherine de le Fortrie	Jean, merchant	999 liv.; 200 liv. annuities; 2.1 ha. land in Sequedin, worth 1,218 liv. (2,417 liv.)
19 June 1560	Ibid.	Jean Vanderlinde, fine-cloth retailer	Jean	Unspecified	Marie de le Fortrie	Jean, merchant	1,183 liv.; house worth 1,115 liv.; 200 liv. annuities (2,494 liv.)

[a] Where determinable.
[b] Details as provided in the contract. Land measurements are converted to modern equivalents (ha. = hectares); annuity principal, when not specified, is figured by multiplying annual income by 16, since "denier 16" (6.25%) was the most common interest rate. Amounts in parentheses are total values of dowries in livres, when this can be calculated.

deville himself, when in La Rochelle four years later, hired a two-hundred-cask vessel to make the same trip.[85]

Most prominent of all were the de Fourmestraux, at least thirteen of whom traded at or with Antwerp between 1531 and 1587.[86] Probably the best-known member of this family was Nicolas, a vintner of note as well as one of the chief importers of pastel from Bordeaux to the Netherlands from 1545 to at least 1556.[87] De Fourmestraux or their representatives were stationed in Bruges, Amsterdam, Haarlem, Delft, Rouen, La Rochelle, Toulouse, and Lyon; and they dealt on a regular basis with the principal Italian firms in Antwerp and Lyon, not to mention leading merchants in London, Dublin, and throughout Germany. Around 1560, several kinsmen established a partnership with "one of the most powerful merchants" of Antwerp, Pauwels van Dale, and cooperated with the well-known Toulousain pastel trader Pierre Assézat.[88]

Some of their gains were said to be ill-gotten. Charges of attempted grain monopoly leveled against the Antwerp de Fourmestraux in 1565–6 have already been mentioned. During that same year, the de Fourmestraux firm in Amsterdam was guilty of withholding large amounts of wheat from the market in anticipation of worsening shortages and higher prices, or so the sheriff of the city asserted when he seized 180 lasts (about 15,300 bushels).[89] So wealthy were the de Fourmestraux that the loss of 60,000 livres worth of merchandise to English privateers in a single twelve-month period did not bankrupt them, and the Protestant branches of the family could subscribe 100,000 livres to an abortive project for securing religious freedom from Philip II.[90]

---

85 *Documents du commerce des Pays-Bas avec la France,* docs. 118–20, 133 (pp. 95–7, 109–10).

86 Coornaert, *Français à Anvers,* 1:360. Cf. ibid., 1:160: The de Fourmestraux "raised themselves very close to the greatest international traders."

87 Craeybeckx, *Vins de France aux anciens Pays-Bas,* pp. 237–9, 244.

88 Coornaert, *Français à Anvers,* 1:160. In September 1565, van Dale's overstuffed grain warehouse in Antwerp literally burst apart, triggering a riot; see Charles Verlinden, Jan Craeybeckx, and Etienne Scholliers, "Price and Wage Movements in Belgium in the Sixteenth Century," in *Economy and Society in Early Modern Europe,* ed. Peter Burke (New York, 1972), p. 67. On Assézat and the Toulouse woad trade, see Caster, *Commerce de pastel,* pp. 171–89, and the summary in Ball, *Merchants and Merchandise,* pp. 166–9.

89 James Tracy, "Habsburg Grain Policy and Amsterdam Politics: The Career of Sheriff Willem Dirkszoon Baerdes, 1542–1566," *The Sixteenth Century Journal* 14 (1983):318. Perhaps it was to finance speculation of this sort that, according to information forwarded to Spanish authorities, the de Fourmestraux had borrowed a large amount of money on the Antwerp Bourse in December 1565; see Granvelle to Gonçalo Perez, 9 February 1566, in *CG,* 1:110.

90 Coornaert, *Français à Anvers,* 1:160. The losses occurred in 1557–8. The proposal for religious freedom, which involved raising a total of 3 million fl. to be paid to Philip, was advanced on 27

In their origins, these people did not differ noticeably from the mass of small and middling merchants. As Appendix D indicates, the great commercial families, like the lesser, had settled in Lille all across the fifteenth and early sixteenth centuries. Socially, too, the leading merchants had genealogies as motley as the rest. They were descended perhaps from nobles (de Smerpont) and definitely from peasants (de Vendeville and de Fourmestraux), artisans (Dancoisne, de Thieffries, and Baillet), and immigrant traders (Coene and Poulle). A handful of foreign merchants always lived in early modern Lille, and during the 1580s and 1590s a small colony of Spanish traders grew up. Some of its members acquired citizenship and one was even selected, albeit briefly, to sit in the city government.[91] But perhaps because Lille never became a trading or financial center of the very first order, no powerful stratum of rich Germans, Italians, or other foreigners settled there. In sharp contrast to Bruges or Antwerp – though very much like Amsterdam[92] – the top merchants in Lille were men from the Low Countries; men who came, in fact, very largely from Walloon Flanders and contiguous areas.

What set these men apart from the bulk of merchants was a potent combination of far-flung commercial interests, considerable wealth, and a dense web of family and business relationships. Some evidence of the extensive contacts of Lille's mercantile community has already been put forward, and the impressive direct trade between Lille and cities throughout Europe noted. Still, because of the centrality of Antwerp to international trade during most of the sixteenth century, the amount of contact with the Brabant port is a convenient index of the breadth and intensity of the business carried on by long-distance merchants. Table 2.3 attests to the much keener dealings of Lille's commercial elite at Antwerp compared to those of the majority of merchants.[93]

Data concerning the wealth of the principal merchants are very incomplete but enough exist to show that many ranked among the richest men in Lille. Etienne Denis, for example, who was active in the Antwerp trade between 1545 and 1575, was obliged to contribute 50 florins in the

October 1566 to the Antwerp magistrates; see Léon Van der Essen, "Episodes de l'histoire religieuse et commerciale d'Anvers dans la seconde moitié du XVIe siècle," *BCRHB* 80 (1911):349–50, n. 3.
91 See Fremaux, *De Fourmestraux*, p. 210; AML, Reg. 15,888, fols. 178–9; BML, MS. 597, years 1584 and 1585.
92 Van Houtte, *Economic History of the Low Countries*, p. 186.
93 The table is based on information in Coornaert, *Français à Anvers*, 2:358–62.

Table 2.3. *Frequency of trade at or with Antwerp by Lillois during the sixteenth century*

	Total people	Total families	Total cita- tions	Mean per person	Cita- tions per family	Mean No. of merchants per family
All Lillois	382	235	637	1.67	2.71	1.63
Leading merchant families	100	23	242	2.42	10.52	4.35
Nonelite merchant families	282	212	395	1.40	1.86	1.33

forced loan of 1562 and pay the ninth highest Hundredth Penny levy (30.5 livres) listed in the surviving records. In addition, he presented his son Jean with a marriage portion made up of both a manor containing twelve hectares of garden, meadow, and arable, and a fief of another ten hectares.[94]

That fortunes of this order were common among members of Lille's commercial elite is suggested by the information about a dozen leading families assembled in Appendix E. Locally, resources of the magnitude shown in that appendix could be matched by a few nobles and government officials. But as Appendixes B and C indicate, on the whole merchants had greater wealth than members of other occupational and social groups.

For all the continuity of leading families across generations illustrated in Appendix E, the merchant elite of sixteenth-century Lille did not constitute a closed clique. As we have seen, immigration constantly infused new blood, while expanding opportunities promoted a great deal of social mobility. At the same time, however, a complex network of business and personal relationships endowed Lille's trading community with a notable degree of cohesion. A remarkable example of the commercial links that could be forged among the top lineages was the company formed in 1542, cited previously, that joined together de Four-

[94] Lottin, "Liste des riches lillois," pp. 68–72; AML, Reg. 966 (first quarter of St. Etienne); Denis du Péage, *Recueil de généalogies lilloises*, 4:1425–6, 1435–8.

mestraux, Dancoisne, de Thieffries, and du Bosquiel. But even a random sample of smaller and more typical partnerships illuminates with equal clarity the degree to which the elite was bound together by means of merchant ventures. Suffice it to cite just two: the trading firm organized around 1550 by Jacques de Thieffries, Antoine le Moisne, Jean de Smerpont, and Jean Drumez; and the partnership constituted in 1565 among Jean Dubois, Pierre Dupont, and Gerard Mahieu.[95]

These commercial associations were, moreover, frequently cemented by intermarriage. In the 1542 company just referred to, at least two of the partners were sons-in-law of de Fourmestraux men. Guillaume Dancoisne was married to Collard's daughter Michelle, and Nicolas de Fourmestraux was the father of Antoine de Thieffries's wife Marguerite.[96] Similarly, Antoine de Thieffries repeatedly joined in other trading ventures with his father-in-law during the 1540s and 1550s.[97]

Even when trading partnerships are not known to have been reinforced by wedlock, a high rate of intermarriage obtained among the chief merchant families. This fact becomes apparent if only one generation is examined. The wealthy merchant Jean Levasseur, for instance, had three wives – Jeanne de Has, Jeanne Deliot, and Marie de Fourmestraux – while his brother Jacques was married to Catherine Mahieu.[98] Tracing marital alliances over several generations yields even more striking evidence of the extent of elite intermarriage. In the course of the sixteenth century, the various branches of the de Fourmestraux were affines of at least half of the other principal merchant families and through them were distantly related to most of the rest. Although this clan was exceptionally large, a similar pattern emerges from study of the reasonably complete genealogies that have been assembled for the de Thieffries, Dancoisne, Drumez, Castellain, du Bosquiel, and de Vendeville.[99]

95 Fremaux, *De Fourmestraux*, p. 198 n. 1; *Histoire de Lille*, 2:60.
96 Denis du Péage, "Mélanges généalogiques," *BSEPC* 16 (1911):137; *BSEPC* 17 (1912):233. Robert du Bosquiel was probably also an in-law; see idem, *Recueil de généalogies lilloises*, 3:1158–9.
97 Fremaux, *De Fourmestraux*, p. 199 n. 3; AML, Reg. 15,434, 12 December 1544; AML, Reg. 15,885, fol. 4; ADN, Tab. 1149, no. 33, fols. 23v–4.
98 BML, MS. 597, years 1561, 1565.
99 Fremaux, *De Fourmestraux*, passim. Two or more alliances took place between the de Fourmestraux and the Delobel, du Bosquiel, Dupont, de Has, and Mahieu during the sixteenth century. For the other genealogies, see Denis du Péage, "Mélanges généalogiques," *BSEPC* 17 (1912):232–3; *Familles de Flandre*, pp. 74–8; *Recueil de généalogies lilloises*, 3:920–1, 1158–9; ibid., 2:623–7.

It would be tedious to review the alliances forged by all of these families, and impossible to analyze them statistically owing to gaps in the record. But synopsis of the marriages contracted by the Dancoisne illustrates the scope of intermarriage among leading mercantile clans. The men of this family wed women from at least the Delobel, de Fourmestraux, Coene, and Dupont families, while female members of the clan are known to have found spouses among the Baillet (twice), de Smerpont, Delobel, and de Thieffries.[100]

In their conjugal policies, then, the great international merchants exhibited strong group solidarity. They did not, however, disdain ties with new families. As a matter of fact, the entry of newcomers into Lille's commercial elite was often ratified by marriage with members of already established clans. After their arrival in the course of the sixteenth century, for example, the de Vendeville wed Mahieu, Bernard, Fasse, Castellain, and Baillet, while Coene married Dupont, Dancoisne, and de Fourmestraux.[101] Yet endogamy within the merchant community did not preclude marriage with other members of the municipal ruling class; rather, it served to create the core of a wider political unity.[102]

As we have seen, the merchant class of Lille bought and sold great quantities of textiles, wine, grain, metals, dyestuffs, salt, and a myriad of other goods. In pursuit of commercial gain they crowded the Antwerp Bourse, traveled widely and stayed in close touch with agents scattered throughout Europe, sent cloth to Indians in the highlands of Peru, and purchased rye cultivated by serfs in Poland. But commerce was not their sole source of income, any more than it was for their fellows throughout sixteenth-century Europe.[103]

For one thing, they invested widely in real estate. Many traders bought commercial and residential property. They owned sandpits in the suburb of La Madeleine, dyestuff mills in the surrounding countryside, breweries, workshops, and storage cellars in the city. In addition, they purchased numerous houses in every section of Lille, renting them to

---

100 Denis du Péage, "Mélanges généalogiques," *BSEPC* 16 (1911):135–9.
101 AML, Reg. 15,435bis, 13 October 1560; Denis du Péage, *Recueil de généalogies lilloises*, 3:623, 626.
102 See Chapter 1.
103 Cf. Ball, *Merchants and Merchandise*, p. 124.

fellow merchants, professionals, government officials, and artisans.[104] But most of all, merchants acquired land throughout the rich farming areas around Lille. Although not disdaining other land, a sizable number sought properties endowing its owner with a seigneurial title. If few followed the example of the wealthy Guillaume Deliot, who purchased more than half a dozen fiefs and seigneuries totaling well over a hundred hectares, possession of feudal land was unremarkable even among less prominent men.[105]

Lille's merchants also bought annuities, particularly the so-called *rente à constitution.* In annuities of this sort, the debtor received a lump sum in return for granting the creditor a periodic payment derived from the income from a specific source, usually a piece of property.[106] Rentes of this type were acquired most commonly from peasants and to a lesser extent from craftsmen, though also from members of the nobility or even merchants. An individual annuity might have a principal of more than 1,000 livres, but for the most part merchants seem to have restricted their purchases to rentes worth between 100 and 600 livres. Such annuities seem mainly to have been bought as long-term investments. On occasion, however, debtors redeemed them within a few years, suggesting that some were sold in order to cover deficits in current income.[107]

In contrast to their enthusiasm for annuities on individuals, Lille's merchants were normally reluctant to buy rentes sold by the Netherlands government, even when the interest was guaranteed by municipalities and paid for out of specific civic and domainal revenues.[108] The Magistrat of Lille sold a number of these bonds, nearly all of them

---

104 See, for example, ADN, Tab. 3851, 14 July and 14 August 1565; AML, Reg. 15,434, fols. 29–9v, 77v–8; Reg. 15,435, fols. 6v–7v, 54v–6, 94–5, 132–2v, 169–9v; and, of course, the various marriage contracts analyzed in Appendix B.

105 For Deliot, see Théodore Leuridan, "Statistique féodale du Département du Nord," *BCHDN* 17 (1886):23–4; 20 (1897):194–5; 24 (1900):26–7, 56–7, 162. For holdings by other merchants, see these three volumes, passim, as well as ibid., vol. 25 (1901); AML, Reg. 15,434–5bis; and the tabellions in the ADN.

106 For a more complete explanation, see Herman Van der Wee, "Monetary, Credit and Banking Systems," in *Cambridge Economic History of Europe*, 5:303–5. The most common rate of interest was 6%.

107 Cf. a rente bought in 1521 that was only terminated in 1544 (AML, Reg. 15,434, fols. 104–4v), and another one bought back on 24 January 1566 even though constituted as recently as 1562 (ADN, Tab. 3851).

108 For brief accounts of governmental sales of annuities, see Van der Wee, "Monetary, Credit and Banking Systems," pp. 366–71, and Van Houtte, *Economic History of the Low Countries*, p. 221.

paying 6.25 percent, yet up through midcentury merchants generally acquired few – usually less than 5 percent of the total. Religious communities, widows, and members of the provincial nobility were more substantial purchasers.[109] Even in 1555 and 1557, when towns and provincial estates issued enormous numbers of annuities to help meet the extremely heavy costs of war and a soaring state debt, Lille's merchants apparently bought only between a sixth and a quarter of them.[110]

Finally, merchants made loans. Some were granted (at times under constraint) to various levels of government, municipal and central alike.[111] But in light of the shakiness of Habsburg finance – culminating in the bankruptcy of 1557, when interest payments were suspended and the principal of every loan made to the central government was forcibly converted into annuities – it is not surprising that Lille's merchants preferred to lend to private individuals, who could presumably provide some guarantee of repayment. Much of the credit was granted to people in Lille or its immediate neighborhood: a city notary, a widow in Wambrechies, a laboureur at Linselles. Yet it was also current practice to advance funds to merchants in or from other cities.[112] The credit advanced in the course of many commercial transactions probably earned interest, too, despite the silence of the sources in this regard.[113]

In the absence of sufficient records, there is no way to discover how much of the income of a "typical" merchant – if any such person existed – came from trade and how much from noncommercial investments.

---

[109] See AML, Reg. 16,265, fols. 46–7 (36,000 liv. sold in 1531); Reg. 16,267, fols. 44–6v (40,000 liv., 1533); Reg. 16,269, fols. 35–6 (9,600 liv., 1535); Reg. 16,270, fols. 30v–3 (48,000 liv., 1536); Reg. 16,271, fols. 58–66 (30,650 liv., 1537); Reg. 16,275, fols. 42v–4 (28,480 liv., 1542); Reg. 16,276, fols. 45–7v (16,464 liv., 1543); Reg. 16,277, fols. 48v–9v (7,302 liv., 1544); Reg. 16,283, fol. 54 (3,900 liv., 1549). With the exception of a few yielding 5% (denier 20) issued in 1533, all paid 6.25% interest (denier 16).

[110] AML, Reg. 16,289, fols. 70v–110 (1555); Reg. 16,291, fols. 65–86 (1557). Due to the evident fiscal problems of the Habsburg government, some annuities sold in 1557 yielded 8.33% (denier 12) and 7.14% (denier 14). But all were soon repurchased and replaced with bonds paying the usual 6.25%; see AML, Reg. 16,291, fols. 87–9v (1557); Reg. 16,294, fols. [69v–70] (1560); Reg. 16,295, fol. 60v (1561).

[111] See Appendix E, and Tracy, "Habsburg Grain Policy and Amsterdam Politics," p. 318 n. 135: The de Fourmestraux had, "in a small way," been "among the merchants regularly extending credit to the government in the 1550s."

[112] See AML, Reg. 15434–5bis, passim; ADN, Tab. 3851.

[113] See, for instance, ADN, Tab. 3851, 28 October 1565 (a fuller had to pay within one-half year for the raw materials he bought from the merchant Loys de le Becque), or AML, Reg. 15,435, fols. 90v–1 (a comber had a year to pay Hugues Dancoisne for wool).

Table 2.4. *The estate of Jean de Bertault, 1574*

Type of asset	Value (liv.)	% of total
Capital and merchandise in merchant company	24,600	33.64
Rural land	18,643	25.50
Houses in Lille	14,275	19.52
Annuities	13,099.5	17.92
Miscellaneous	2,500	3.42

The estate inventories compiled after the death of two men do, however, give some idea of the sources and patterns of merchant wealth. Jean de Bertault, called "de Hollande," traded successfully at Antwerp, and although he never served in the municipal government of Lille, his sons did.[114] At his decease, which occurred before 6 March 1574, he left an estate worth 73,117 livres, 10 sols (Table 2.4).[115]

No further information is available regarding Bertault's merchant company, but his investments were extensive. He owned in excess of twenty hectares of land divided into eighteen parcels ranging in size from one-quarter to three and a half hectares. Most were in Baisieux, east of Lille on the present Belgian border, with a few scattered south and west of the city. Within Lille, at least half a dozen houses, the greater part of them on the bustling rue des Malades and the place Saint-Martin, belonged to Bertault. Not all of the sellers of annuities can be identified. But in terms of value, at least one-half of Bertault's rentes had been purchased from villagers (these lived predominantly west and south of Lille, up to twenty kilometers from the city, rather than in the area of his landholdings in Baisieux), and about one-third from Lillois, including merchants and artisans. Only one annuity, with a principal of 800 livres, had been acquired from a member of the nobility, and just three from governments (a total of 800 livres from the crown, 150

[114] He seems to have been the "Janne de Hollander" listed by Coornaert, *Français à Anvers*, 1:360.
[115] Excluded are the six parcels of land, totaling about 7.5 ha., which had been the dowry of his second wife, Marie Mallatrie, who survived him. For what follows, see ADN, Tab. 4237.

livres from the municipal government). Several of the rentes had been established over half a century before – one as early as 1496 – but they had come into Bertault's possession only in the 1560s and early 1570s. All but three of thirty-seven annuities paid "denier 16" (6.25 percent); the others, among which were the oldest, returned 5 percent.

We know much less about Bauduin Galliot, who died on 16 July 1587. He does not appear on Coornaert's list of merchants trading at or with Antwerp before 1585. Nevertheless, the size of his estate, worth 53,144 livres, indicates that he had prospered in trade. In addition, he was appointed to the municipal government in 1585, albeit in the minor position of justice of the peace.[116] Out of Galliot's estate, 11,311 livres was set aside, the bulk of it for the marriage portions of three sons; unfortunately, nothing was recorded about the composition of this sum. Of the remainder, 11,366 livres, or 27 percent, consisted of the principal of twenty-two annuities on individuals, nearly all yielding 6.25 percent per year. Three annuities, totaling 4,000 livres, had been bought from noblemen of Walloon Flanders; the rest of the debtors included fellow Lillois, artisans in nearby towns, and peasants throughout the castellany up to twenty kilometers from Lille. Galliot also left debts receivable (whether from trade or loans cannot be ascertained), an unknown number of houses in Lille, and some sixteen or seventeen hectares of land. None of these was assigned a value in the inventory. Still, by adopting the conservative figure of 700 livres for each hectare of farmland – somewhat below the average for Bertault's holdings – we can calculate that Galliot's rural property constituted another quarter of his overall wealth.

Evidently, the estates left by Bertault and Galliot differed in some respects – annuities formed a larger proportion of the latter's wealth, for example, and he dealt with more nobles. The similarities are, however, even more striking. Not only did farmland account for about a quarter of both merchants' assets, but each man made the same general types of investments – land in the country, houses in the city, annuities -- and avoided government rentes. Such limited evidence has no statistical significance, of course. These two inventories do, however, underline the fact that in addition to their strictly commercial activities, Lille's merchants aggressively purchased rural and urban real estate, acquired

---

116 Galliot's inventory is in ibid.; see also BML, MS. 597.

annuities on private persons in preference to those issued by political authorities, and granted loans.[117]

A few merchants seem to have placed their assets outside trade in order to enable their descendants to take up the life of an official, rentier, or titled landowner. The de Vendeville men who came to maturity in the 1560s largely eschewed commerce, for example. Jean was a professor of law at Louvain, one of the founders of the university of Douai (where he also taught law), and councillor at the Privy Council in Brussels before taking holy orders and being appointed bishop of Tournai (1587–92). His brother Jacques, also a lawyer, became a canon of St. Pierre, Lille. A third son, Guillaume, initially held an important post in the Gouvernance of Walloon Flanders, then was named *maître des requêtes* in the Great Council at Mechelen in 1584. Only the fourth brother, Antoine, became a merchant.[118] But evidence of substantial movement of this kind dates only from the later sixteenth and the seventeenth centuries, when the economic climate appeared less promising and aristocratic values had become dominant in the southern Low Countries. It was then that a few scions of the de Fourmestraux, Deliot, de Thieffries, and other outstanding merchant families purchased patents of nobility, while others became lawyers, government officials, and owners of substantial fiefs.[119]

During much of the sixteenth century, on the contrary, the purchase of land and annuities did not often signify a move into the rentier class. Merchants acquired noncommercial property – and the prestige that accompanied it – but also remained active in trade.[120] Jean de Bertault

---

[117] For several reasons, few merchants farmed municipal taxes. Collection of some levies was reserved to specific groups, usually practitioners of the craft being taxed. The imposts that brought the most to the town coffers – those on wine – were not, moreover, farmed but collected directly by municipal employees. Probably most important of all in discouraging tax farming by merchants was the prohibition against tax farmers concurrently holding office in the city government. This rule was the result of reforms carried out in the mid-fifteenth century at the behest of the dukes of Burgundy in response to the corrupt and anarchic state of municipal finances, for which see Sivéry, "Histoire économique et sociale," pp. 205–7, 229–31.

[118] ADN, Tab. 3852, 4 June 1574; Denis du Péage, *Recueil de généalogies lilloises*, 2:626–7. Cf. ibid., 4:1425–6, 1435–8, for the sons of Etienne Denis, none of whom engaged in commerce.

[119] Idem, "Mélanges généalogiques," *BSEPC* 17 (1912):233–4; idem, *Recueil de généalogies lilloises*, 4:247–58, 265–7 (de Fourmestraux); 2:456–61 (du Beron); 1:104, 108 (Delannoy); 3:1012–13 (le Pippre); 2:772–4 (Miroul); Le Roux, *Recueil de la Noblesse*, pp. 234, 243; BML, MS. Godefroy 112, fols. 81v-2. A similar phenomenon existed in Antwerp; see Hugo Soly, "The 'Betrayal' of the Sixteenth-Century Bourgeoisie: A Myth?" *Acta Historiae Neerlandicae* 8 (1975):31, 39–40, 49.

[120] Cf. Soly, "'Betrayal' of the Bourgeoisie?" pp. 35–6.

and his heirs did precisely this.[121] So did Paul Castellain, who died in 1541. Long after becoming seigneur of Ascq he continued his profitable textile trading. Paul's nephew Guillaume evidently followed in his uncle's footsteps, for he was both a wealthy merchant and seigneur of Wattignies. Near the end of his life, Gilles Castellain, Guillaume's cousin, may have retired to the land, but at least two of his sons were merchants in the early seventeenth century. François Castellain (floruit around 1650), continued the now well-established family tradition of practicing trade even while preferring the title of seigneur.[122] Similarly, members of the Desbuisson, du Forest, du Hot, Desbarbieux, Delobel, Bave, Fasse, du Bosquiel, and Dancoisne families, among others, continued to be vigorously involved in commerce during the seventeenth century despite simultaneously owning feudal land purchased by their ancestors beginning back in the fifteenth century.[123] The Lille data, in short, give but very partial support to the argument put forth by Coornaert and Wittman that merchants bought land in order to gain entry into the feudal class.

Financial rather than social motives appear to have determined merchants' large-scale acquisitions of real estate and annuities during the sixteenth century.[124] Admittedly, a high rate of return may not have been the chief consideration. Whereas annuities usually paid 5 or 6.25 percent and real property about the same, commerce may have earned as much as 7 to 13 percent.[125] But buying property and rentes did make

---

[121] At least during the two generations following Jean's death, members of the family remained merchants; see BML, MS. 597, year 1591; AASL, Reg. J 644, "Testaments."

[122] See Denis du Péage, *Recueil de généalogies lilloises*, 3:921–7, and Appendix E.

[123] See, respectively, Denis du Péage, *Recueil de généalogies lilloises*, 1:44; 2:517–21, 537, 703–5; 1:16, 53–4; 3:1158–9; ibid., 4:1560–7; idem, "Mélanges généalogiques," *BSEPC* 16 (1911):139–41; Leuridan, "Statistique féodale," *BCHDN* 20 (1897):165, 23, 86; ibid., 24 (1900):220; ibid., 20 (1897):59.

[124] Soly, "'Betrayal' of the Bourgeoisie?" pp. 36–9, reaches similar conclusions for Antwerp.

[125] For rates of return on annuities, see the evidence from the estates of Bertault and Galliot, cited previously. There is virtually none of the information needed to calculate real estate profits in Lille. For what it is worth, our one piece of direct data shows that a house with 0.75 ha. of land, located in a suburb, returned 4% in 1574; ADN, Tab. 3852, 4 June 1574 (property valued at 3,600 liv. yields 144 liv. per year). Rents on houses owned by one of Lille's hospices, though increasing over the first two-thirds of the sixteenth century, lagged behind many other prices; see Table 4.1. Thus it seems most unlikely that returns in Lille would have exceeded those found in booming Antwerp, which were no more than 5% for dwellings and 6% for industrial and commercial property; see Soly, "'Betrayal' of the Bourgeoisie?" p. 36. For purposes of the Hundredth Penny tax of 1569, houses were taken to yield 6.25%, all other capital 4.5%. No data exist for trade, but the rates quoted in the text, which were realized in late sixteenth-century Antwerp, offer some guidance; see Ball, *Merchants and Merchandise*, p. 118.

very good sense in terms of security, regularity, and utility in obtaining credit and transferability. A merchant's stock could be lost in a moment, but land and buildings were more durable. Annuities, too, were often paid from income from real property.[126]

Such investments were additionally advantageous because they could provide a regular income while requiring little of the owner's time or attention. That they purchased many small and dispersed holdings – Jacques de Thieffries, for instance, had eight widely scattered parcels of land, of 0.26, 0.44 (two), 0.53, 0.96, 1.9, 4.2 and 8.4 hectares in size[127] – suggests once again that merchant families buying land did so for financial rather than entrepreneurial reasons. Significantly, none of the leases makes any mention of investment or of the encouragement of new techniques. Even the concentrated holdings in a particular village that are occasionally encountered – it will be remembered that most of Bertault's property, for example, was in Baisieux – appear to have been accumulated with an eye toward easing the collection of rents, not with any intent to get involved in agricultural production.

Property could also serve as collateral for credit. Thus Jacques Gerard obtained some much-needed cash by mortgaging land he owned on the road to Douai just outside Lille.[128] Similarly, the transfer of land or rentes was a handy way to raise cash or to settle commercial accounts. Jean Bridoul, for instance, quickly realized 100 florins by disposing of rentes on residents of Comines, while in 1565 Adrien Rotewe paid off a trade debt to his fellow merchant Adrien Henniart by surrendering 400 livres worth of annuities.[129]

Finally, real estate and annuities seem on occasion to have been purchased with an eye to marriage portions. Unfortunately, it is impossible to derive any valid statistics, because only a dozen usable contracts involving sixteen sons and daughters of Lille merchants have survived

---

126 Cf. the very large amount of merchandise lost by the de Fourmestraux in 1557–8; Soly, "'Betrayal' of the Bourgeoisie?" p. 36; and Jan de Vries, *The Economy of Europe in an Age of Crisis, 1600–1750* (Cambridge, 1976), p. 219.

127 AML, Reg. 15,435, 11 April 1550. Cf. François Muette's seigneuries, which were in Verlinghem, Wavrin, and Wazemmes, respectively 5 km. northwest, 8 km. southwest, and just south of Lille, and were 3, 0.2 and 20 ha. in size; Leuridan, "Statistique féodale," *BCHDN* 24 (1900):228.

128 AML, Reg. 15,435, fols. 54v–6, 30 April 1550.

129 ADN, Tab. 3851, 26 September and 5 November 1565; Tab. 3857; cf. Tab. 1146, fol. 25v, no. 64. Once again, practice among Lille's merchants conforms to that among their fellows in Antwerp, for which see Soly, "'Betrayal' of the Bourgeoisie?" pp. 36–7.

for the period before the outbreak of the revolt, and several fail to list the value of the components of the dowry. Still, it is worth noting that at least six of the children received real estate worth between 1,115 and 2,820 livres (representing 46 to 89 percent of their entire marriage portions), and at least four were granted annuities with principals of 100 to 300 livres (3 to 13 percent of their total dowries).[130]

IV

That Lille's merchants were enterprising, competitive, and adaptable is evident not only from the success with which they guided their city to a position of commercial eminence during Antwerp's golden age. It is also manifest in the skill with which they weathered – even profited from – the Brabant port's decline under the impact of growing rivalry from London, Hamburg, and Amsterdam, severe financial difficulties of the Spanish crown, and especially the disruption wrought by the revolt.[131] In the later sixteenth century, the direct links that Lillois had forged with a large number of European cities simultaneously with their close asso- ciation with Antwerp were exploited more intensely. Merchants from Lille also began to appear regularly in cities like Venice that previously they had rarely visited.[132] In addition, large amounts of Flemish cloth, formerly exported through Antwerp, were now assembled at Lille for direct shipment to France, Germany, and Italy via overland routes or English Channel ports.[133] The establishment of a staple for alum like- wise stimulated trade with Italy, while Spanish wool was shipped by road from Rouen, where it was unloaded to avoid the depredations of Dutch privateers in the English Channel.[134] In addition, Lille merchants' long

---

[130] See AML, Reg. 15,434–5bis; ADN, Tab. 3851, 3852. See also Appendix E.

[131] For Antwerp's troubles, see Van der Wee, *Growth of the Antwerp Market*, 2:113–267.

[132] See Dietz, *Frankfurter Handelsgeschichte*, 1:64, 247; Jean-François Bergier, *Genève et l'économie européenne de la Renaissance* (Paris, 1963), p. 201; Coornaert, *Français à Anvers*, 1:157, 282; Wilfrid Brulez, *Marchands flamands à Venise. I. (1568–1605)* (Brussels and Rome, 1965), doc. 664, p. 221, doc. 722, p. 243.

[133] Deyon, *Amiens*, pp. 94–6; Coornaert, *Français à Anvers*, 1:163–4, 166, 179–80, 213, 220, 224, 243, 346, 2:87.

[134] For the alum staple, one of seven in the southern Netherlands, which was acquired by Lille sometime before 1588, see Jules Finot, *Etude historique sur les relations commerciales entre la Flandre et la république de Gênes au Moyen Age* (Paris, 1906), p. 267. Between 1587 and 1589, the Spanish wool staple was transferred to Lille from Saint-Omer, where it had been shifted in 1580 when Bruges was under a radical regime. Even after Bruges regained the staple in 1589, moreover, Lille retained the right of receiving wool directly from Rouen. The revocation of the

82

familiarity with bills of exchange helped turn their native city into one of the chief centers for financial transactions in the Habsburg Low Countries.[135]

Evidence from Lille can lend support, then, to a Pirennean view that the merchants of the sixteenth-century Netherlands were socially and geographically mobile new men characterized by a spirit of initiative. Some traders were Protestants, moreover, which in Pirenne's eyes testified to their estrangement from the established order. At the same time, however, they revealed themselves to be only partially committed to institutional change, they retained familiar investment strategies, and they persisted in seeking local monopolies. This behavior indicates that there is also a good deal of truth in accounts that emphasize the slow pace of innovation and the continued predominance of old attitudes and practices in trade and finance.[136]

Archival records suggest, too, that far from being aggressive entrepreneurs who decisively reorganized production, Lille's merchants preferred to remain primarily traders and financiers.[137] They engaged little of their capital in industrial ventures and played no role in operating the breweries, brickworks, or sandpits that they did acquire, instead treating these properties as sources of steady if unspectacular rental income. Perhaps most surprising of all, the booming light-woolens crafts attracted little merchant intervention.

To understand their behavior in this regard, we must place it in the context of developments in Lille's cloth industry. Had production be-

privilege in 1602 in favor of Bruges's monopoly led simply to widespread evasion, again to the advantage of Lille. See J. A. Van Houtte, "Bruges as a Trading Centre in the Early Modern Period" in *Enterprise and History. Essays in Honour of Charles Wilson*, ed. D. C. Coleman and Peter Mathias (Cambridge, 1984), p. 83. Lille also became the seat of the consulate of the Navarrese nation when this left Bruges in 1586; ibid., p. 82. According to Saint-Omer (ADN, Reg. B 603, fol. 4), by the late 1580s almost all wool went straight to Lille, making that city the main distribution point for Spanish wool destined for the southern Netherlands. Cf. AML, Reg. 15,888, fols. 178–9, 11 July 1592.

135 For Lille's position as a financial center, see Coornaert, *Français à Anvers*, 1:158; Buzelin, *Gallo-Flandria sacra et profana*, p. 14; Wilfrid Brulez, *De Firma Della Faille en de internationale handel van Vlaamse firma's in de 16e eeuw* (Brussels, 1959), pp. 312–13; Henri Lapeyre, *Une famille de marchands – les Ruiz* (Paris, 1955), pp. 293, 303; Dietz, *Frankfurter Handelsgeschichte*, 3:202, 230–1; ADN, Tab. 1146, no. 10, fols. 129v–30; Tab. 3848, 3 June 1593.

136 See esp. Emile Coornaert, "La genèse du système capitaliste: grand capitalisme et économie traditionnelle à Anvers au XVIe siècle," *Annales d'histoire économique et sociale* 8 (1936):127–39, and idem, *Français à Anvers*.

137 On the basis of material in Antwerp, Coornaert, "Commerce de Lille par Anvers," p. 247, comes to the same conclusion.

come "capitalist on the top, proletarian on the bottom," or did "a narrowly corporative spirit" thwart the appearance of new relations of production?[138]

---

[138] The quotations come respectively from Pirenne, *Histoire de Belgique,* 3:245, and Emile Coornaert, "Draperies rurales, draperies urbaines. L'évolution de l'industrie flamande au moyen-âge et au XVIe siècle," *RBPH* 28 (1950):85.

3

"Cloth of every type and price"

I

In the sixteenth as in earlier centuries, only production of woolen textiles for export matched commerce in importance to Lille's economy.[1] A small part of output was accounted for by tapestries, which had acquired a reputation for superior quality soon after being introduced at the end of the fourteenth century, probably by immigrants from Arras. One particularly skilled practitioner of the art wove a set of the "Triumphs of Petrarch" for Giovanni di Cosimo Medici in the mid-fifteenth century, and other Lillois of the time received substantial commissions from England and the Burgundian dukes.[2] Though less celebrated in the sixteenth century, the craft did maintain some activity, for thirty-six masters were counted in 1538, and six years later Charles V issued new regulations.[3]

Not tapestries, however, but the more mundane fabrics used mainly in clothing always constituted by far the predominant sector of Lille's

[1] Linens had also been produced in Lille at least as early as the thirteenth century; see Doehaerd, *Relations commerciales entre Gênes, la Belgique et l'Outremont aux XIIe et XIIIe siècles,* 1:198, and Léone Liagre de Sturler, *Les relations commerciales entre Gênes, la Belgique et l'Outremont d'après les archives notariales génoises, 1320–1400,* 2 vols. (Brussels and Rome, 1969), 1:cxxxvi. The craft appears to have been in poor shape during much of the fifteenth century; Sivéry, "Histoire économique et sociale," pp. 253–4. From all indications it was only after numerous weavers fleeing the war-ravaged villages of Flanders arrived in Lille in the 1580s that linens began to take on some importance in the urban economy; see Jules Flammermont, *Histoire de l'industrie à Lille* (Lille, 1897), pp. 22–4; AML, Aff. gén., C. 1161, d. 23, 28 June 1583 (arrival of refugee linen weavers); and Reg. 16,003, fols. 74v–9, 19 March 1594 (new statutes of the linen guild).
[2] Raymond De Roover, *The Rise and Decline of the Medici Bank 1397–1494* (New York, 1966), p. 144; Jean Lestocquoy, *Deux siècles de l'histoire de la tapisserie (1300–1500)* (Arras, 1978), pp. 90–5; Sivéry, "Histoire économique et sociale," pp. 252–3.
[3] Jules Houdoy, *Les tapisseries de haute-lisse. Histoire de la fabrication lilloise du XIVe au XVIIIe siècle* (Lille and Paris, 1871), pp. 49–60.

woolens industry. The city had long ranked among the major Flemish producers of *draperie* (which historians often refer to as "old drapery"), broadcloth woven mainly from English wool. During the twelfth and thirteenth centuries, when the Flemish industry was at its height, Lille drapery was sent to nearly every corner of Europe: Italy, England, France, the Iberian peninsula, central and eastern Europe, even the Crusader stronghold of Acre in Palestine.[4] Yet despite a strong market position built up over many generations, Lille shared fully in the sharp contraction that affected most urban textile crafts in Flanders from shortly before 1300. Competition from weavers in nearby villages, Brabant, and abroad intensified, and the city's textiles also suffered from the adverse economic and political forces that, as we have seen, were harming trade. As a result, in the course of the fourteenth century Lille's broadcloths became hard to find even in places where they had once been plentiful.[5]

But Lille's craft did survive, as weavers there, like their counterparts in many other towns, adapted to the harsher economic climate by supplementing their customary offerings with what are usually referred to as "new drapery." These cloths imitated fine drapery but were less expensive, largely because they used cheaper wool, some of it English, Scottish, or local, but from the fifteenth century mostly Spanish.[6] Perhaps by dint of these efforts, or simply because of more favorable economic conditions, at various times during the fifteenth century new drapery from Lille could be found in such widely separated places as Bruges, Geneva, Toulouse, and Genoa.[7] The drapery industry had not recovered its former prosperity, however; by the end of the Middle Ages, in fact, everything indicates that it was in a parlous state. In 1516, there are said to have been as few as five active drap weavers in Lille.[8] Though

---

[4] There is no monograph on Lille's textiles in the Middle Ages, but see Sivéry, "Histoire économique et sociale," pp. 163–71, 209; *Histoire d'une métropole*, chaps. 3–4; and Georges Espinas, *La draperie dans la Flandre française au Moyen Age*, 2 vols. (Paris, 1923), esp. 2:487–9, 870–5.

[5] See Derville, "De 1300 à 1500," pp. 161–2; Coornaert, "Draperies rurales, draperies urbaines," pp. 69–70; and Chapter 2, section I.

[6] Coornaert, "Draperies rurales, draperies urbaines," pp. 71–2; Herman Van der Wee, "Structural Changes and Specialization in the Industry of the Southern Netherlands, 1100–1600," *Economic History Review* 2nd ser. 28 (1975):203–18; and John Munro, "The 'New Draperies': The Death and Resurrection of an Old Flemish Industry, 13th to 16th Centuries," in *The New Draperies* (Oxford, forthcoming). I would like to thank Professor Munro for allowing me to consult his essay before publication.

[7] Sivéry, "Histoire économique et sociale," pp. 210–12, 250–2.

[8] Flammermont, *Histoire de l'industrie à Lille*, pp. 44–5.

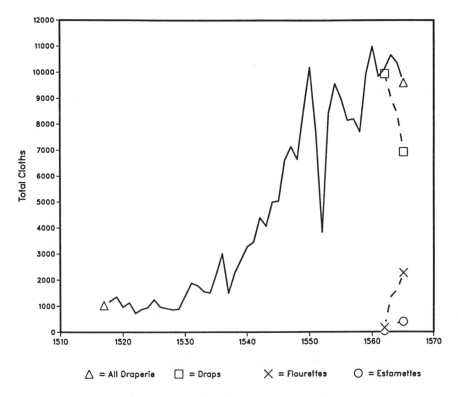

Figure 3.1. Draperie sealed in Lille, 1517–65.

this startlingly low figure may have resulted from short-term factors, municipal tax records from the same period reveal that it was rare for even a thousand pieces of drapery to be "stamped and marked" at the municipal cloth hall or Perche aux draps.[9]

Remarkably enough, in light of the foregoing, the industry managed temporarily to buck the decline common to most long-established drapery cities and stage a final comeback in the sixteenth century (Figure 3.1).[10] Starting in the early 1530s, the number of draps checked at the Perche rose dramatically and steadily, increasing tenfold over the next two decades to reach a total of 10,191 in 1550. A European-wide textile

[9] The quotation comes from the language used in the municipal tax registers. For quantities, see Figure 3.1.
[10] Figure 3.1 is based on data from AML, Reg. 16,253–99, 895.

glut precipitated a steep decline in 1551–2, but recovery was rapid: By 1554 the previous record level had nearly been regained.[11] Once again, production fell off sharply, but after four years rebounded even more quickly. The secular peak of 10,989 pieces was attained in 1560, after which point stagnation – though marked by oscillations from year to year – set in through 1565.

Producers in the countryside, to whom raw materials were put out,[12] accounted for some of the growing output registered at the cloth hall. But Lille's own drapery craft also revived, in large part because its weavers took up less expensive types of fabric often copied from villagers.[13] So by 1572, drapery was described as the second most important trade in the city,[14] albeit far behind Lille's premier industry, the making of light woolens. To be sure, drap making never regained the position it had occupied in its medieval heyday, but it did contribute to quickening the urban economy in the middle decades of the sixteenth century.

The renewal of Lille's drapery was, however, overshadowed by the rise of a light- or dry-woolens industry.[15] Paralleling the city's improving commercial fortunes, its light drapery emerged from insignificance at the end of the fifteenth century to become one of the largest in the Low Countries – in the sixteenth century it was probably second only to the more famous craft at Hondschoote – and indeed in Europe. In consequence of its light-textile crafts, Coornaert declared, Lille became "an industrial center of the very first order."[16]

Contemporary documents, too, underline the importance of the light-woolens trades known as sayetterie and bourgetterie. As early as 1506, sayetterie alone employed "a large part of the people" of Lille, and by

---

11 For the glut, see Peter Ramsey, *Tudor Economic Problems* (London, 1963), pp. 67–8.

12 Cf. a 1544 contract in AML, Reg. 15,434, fols. 116–17.

13 For royal authorization for the weaving in Lille of new kinds of drapery called *pieches* and *crombelistes*, currently being made in the countryside, see Vanhaeck, *Sayetterie à Lille*, 2:48–9, doc. 14, 17 August 1534. For permission to fabricate other types of draps, see AML, Reg. 381, fols. 171v–2, 186v–8v.

14 AML, Reg. 145, fols. 172–2v.

15 In distinguishing traditional (old), new, and light drapery, I am following the usage common among scholars of the Low Countries, as most accessibly expressed in Van der Wee, "Structural Changes and Specialization," and Munro, "The 'New Draperies.'" English historians, on the contrary, recognize just old draperies and new, with light drapery placed in the latter category. See D. C. Coleman, "An Innovation and Its Diffusion: The 'New Draperies,'" *Economic History Review* 2nd ser. 22 (1969):417–29.

16 Coornaert, "Draperies rurales, draperies urbaines," p. 81.

1534 it was characterized as the "principal" craft in the city.[17] Around midcentury, more than two thousand masters worked in sayetterie, described as the industry in which "the greatest number of people [in Lille] earns a living," and at least three hundred masters wove bourgetterie fabrics.[18] At that point, up to half of Lille's population may have been dependent on light drapery. Besides four spinners (typically village women), each loom required the full-time services of a weaver, a comber, two thread doublers, and a spooler, not to mention the contributions of fullers, curriers and dyers.[19] Fragmentary port records from mid-sixteenth-century Antwerp report that Lille's light woolens were sent to Portugal, the Canary Islands, Italy (and thence the Levant), and Spain, from which many went on to Spanish America. Other documents establish that France and Germany should be added to this list.[20]

It has frequently been asserted that this industry began in Lille with the arrival of artisans expelled from Arras in 1479 after its conquest by the French under Louis XI during the wars for the Burgundian inheritance.[21] The claim is incorrect, as *saie* (English "say"), the best known light fabric, had been woven in Lille for export since at least the twelfth century. Thus Lille's early modern light-woolens industry should be understood as the revival of an old craft rather than the sudden implantation of a new one.[22] But the traditional story does specify the period when light cloth began to be important to the city's economy and identifies the catalyst for this development.

In 1480, the Magistrat of Lille petitioned Maximilian and Mary, duke and duchess of Burgundy and counts of Flanders, for permission to

---

[17] Vanhaeck, *Sayetterie à Lille*, 2:23, doc. 7, 2:45, doc. 12.
[18] See the document from 1553 quoted in Michel Baelde, "Un conflit économique entre Lille et Roubaix," *RN* 66 (1984):1072. Another document, dating from about 1575 (AML, Aff. gén., C. 1171, d. 9, fols. 1–1v), mentions about the same number of master sayetteurs.
[19] Pierre Deyon and Alain Lottin, "Evolution de la production textile à Lille aux XVIe et XVIIe siècles," *RN* 49 (1967):23, give the figures regarding the labor force.
[20] J. A. Goris, *Etude sur les colonies marchandes méridionales à Anvers de 1488 à 1567* (Louvain, 1925), pp. 297–8, 308–16; Brulez, "Exportation des Pays-Bas vers l'Italie," p. 483; Alain Lottin, *Vie et mentalité d'un Lillois sous Louis XIV* (Lille, 1968), p. 46. By demonstrating a close correlation between long- and short-term cycles in both the output of light cloth at Lille and Seville's exports to the New World, Deyon and Lottin, "Production textile à Lille," pp. 26–7, have established the importance of this market to the city's light-cloth crafts.
[21] See, for example, Flammermont, *Histoire de l'industrie à Lille*, pp. 48, 209, or, more recently, Lottin, *Vie et mentalité d'un Lillois*, p. 39. Vanhaeck, *Sayetterie à Lille*, 1:12–14, gives the details of the story while criticizing its inaccuracy.
[22] Munro, "The 'New Draperies,'" supersedes all previous accounts of the origins of light drapery throughout Flanders and nearby areas.

issue regulations to encourage further growth in the say making that a "great number of people" was starting to practice in and around Lille. The sovereigns granted the request, directing the aldermen to model rules, inspections, fees, and fines on those found in nearby towns, but cautioned that the authorization would be revoked whenever Arras was freed from foreign occupation.[23] Two years later, after hearing that the many refugee weavers from Arras who wished to remain in Lille no matter what the eventual fate of their native city, as well as the many Lillois who had recently learned the craft, dared not risk investments if their concession might be withdrawn at any moment, Maximilian and Mary made it permanent.[24] The sayetteurs' guild, founded about 1486, formally received its statutes from the municipal government in 1500, four years after bourgetteurs (who also made light textiles) obtained their initial charter upon separating from linen weavers.[25]

By the mid-sixteenth century, light-cloth weavers had developed or – most commonly – imitated fabrics "of," in Guicciardini's words, "every type and price." The most popular were says, *ostades*, woolen satins, velveteens (*tripes de velours*), *changéants*, and other *camelots* (camlets).[26] Like pure worsteds, says and ostades used combed wool for both warp and woof, but like traditional drapery they were fulled (albeit in a rudimentary fashion) and then calendered to obtain a fairly smooth texture. Velveteens, which combined linen or hemp and wool, were woven so as to raise the warp above the woof (a method known as *hautelisse*), giving them an elaborate patterned surface and an air of elegance. The camlet might be made of pure wool or a blend of wool and cotton or even wool and goat hair; in contrast to the say, it was not twilled.[27] A version of the camlet, the changéant or *grosgrain* (known in England as the "grosgram") consisted entirely of wool. It was dyed two or three colors – unlike other fabrics, which were monochromatic – and thus may have been oriented to a fashion-conscious clientele. Although resembling thick cotton cloth of the present day, changéants were so much thinner

---

[23] Vanhaeck, *Sayetterie à Lille*, 2:1–3, doc. 1, 21 December 1480.

[24] Ibid., 2:3–5, doc. 2, 25 March 1482. Thus the return of Artois to Habsburg control in 1493 did not disturb Lille's renascent industry.

[25] Ibid., 1:13–14, 18, 171–2; 2:6–18, doc. 3, 27 February 1500; *Lettres et statuts du corps des bourgeteurs* (Lille, n.d.), p. 2, 28 May 1496.

[26] Guicciardini, *Description de tout le Païs-Bas*, p. 333. For further details about types of light cloth, see the excerpts from Savary des Bruslons, *Dictionnaire universel du commerce* (Paris, 1741), published in Lottin, *Vie et mentalité d'un Lillois*, pp. 382–4.

[27] See Vanhaeck, *Sayetterie à Lille*, 1:240.

and more loosely woven than any other textile then on the market that they were produced much more rapidly.[28] Monopolies granted by the municipal government reserved says and ostades to sayetteurs, velveteens to bourgetteurs; both, however, could weave changéants and all similar very thin textiles.[29]

Notwithstanding the differences among them, all light fabrics were alike in several important respects that were designed to reduce costs in order to undersell competitors.[30] None was more than a millimeter thick (and changéants were only about half that); traditional broadcloth, in contrast, was one and a half or even two millimeters thick. All had a looser weave than broadcloth, which approximated present-day rough felt, and all were noted for having a short nap that, unlike broadcloth, required neither teaseling nor shearing. In addition, the light-cloth industry eschewed the English and Spanish wool used in old and new drapery for less expensive local wools, as well as wool from other provinces of the Netherlands (notably Holland and Friesland), northern France, and central Europe, particularly the Baltic coast area.[31]

Less labor was required to make a light fabric than a piece of old or even new drapery, not only because of the looser weave but also because recourse largely to combed wool enabled several processes to be simplified (e.g., fulling) or even eliminated (e.g., teaseling and shearing).[32]

[28] According to Lottin, *Vie et mentalité d'un Lillois*, pp. 41–2, a wide changéant took three or four days to weave, as against fifteen for a say. A changéant was 19 ells in length, a say 42.75 (Vanhaeck, *Sayetterie à Lille*, 2:55, doc. 18 and p. 28, doc. 9, art. 9), so a weaver's output could be about doubled simply by a switch from the latter to the former. The gain would have been greater with narrow changéants, the only kind made before the later 1570s.

[29] Sayetteurs did manage to win the exclusive privilege of weaving single-color changéants, so long as they were white or blue. Vanhaeck, *Sayetterie à Lille*, 2:57–9, doc. 20, 14 October 1544; the decade of litigation that resulted in this compromise is chronicled in ibid., 1:240–1.

[30] Cf. Pierre Deyon, "La concurrence internationale des manufactures lainières aux XVIe et XVIIe siècles," *AESC* 27 (1972):20–32.

[31] For sources of wool, see Vanhaeck, *Sayetterie à Lille*, 2:48, doc. 14, 17 August 1534; Coornaert, "Draperies rurales, draperies urbaines," p. 83; Adrien Verhulst, "La laine indigène dans les anciens Pays-Bas entre le XIIe et le XVIIe siècle," *Revue historique* 248 (1972):295–6; AML, Aff. gén., C. 1222, d. 10. An aldermanic decree of 25 May 1527 reminded combers that it was illegal to use Spanish wool in says; Vanhaeck, *Sayetterie à Lille*, 2:42, doc. 10. According to sources cited by Deyon, "Concurrence internationale des manufactures lainières," pp. 21–2, wool accounted for 33% to 50% of the total manufacturing costs of good quality woolens but only 21% to 33% of total light-textile costs. As he likewise notes, the admixture of raw materials like linen and hemp was also due to the search for ways to lower costs.

[32] Sayetteurs were permitted to full and bleach their own cloth; Vanhaeck, *Sayetterie à Lille*, 2:15, art. xlvii (1500 statutes); 2:40, art. 67 (1524 statutes). Simplifying finishing was a time-honored way by which Flemish cloth makers cut costs; see Coornaert, "Draperies rurales, draperies urbaines," p. 73.

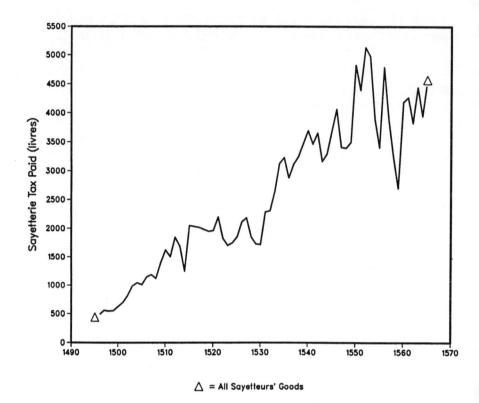

△ = All Sayetteurs' Goods

Figure 3.2. Output of Lille's sayetteurs, 1495–1565.

Owing to cheaper raw materials and fewer labor inputs, light cloth was, of course, of lower quality than traditional woolens. More important, it sold for significantly less: Most types cost no more than half as much as old drapery, changéants only a third.[33] In short, the sayetterie and bourgetterie crafts combined constant innovation in product line, designed to broaden the market, with the adoption of less expensive wools and manufacturing procedures, which by reducing costs would deepen it. A review of the cloth tax receipts listed in the town financial records enables us to gauge just how successful this formula was (Figure 3.2).

During the first two-thirds of the sixteenth century, output of fabrics woven by sayetteurs more than quadrupled, but this long growth span

---

[33] For prices, see Brulez, *Firma Della Faille*, p. 520.

was interrupted by one period of prolonged stagnation interspersed with actual decline and was terminated by another.[34] Thanks to the development of Antwerp and, more generally, the recovery then taking place throughout Europe, an initial phase of rapid expansion occurred between the late fifteenth century and 1512. It was succeeded, however, by nearly two decades of fluctuating production during which no further increase was posted. At the beginning, this downturn – which, as already noted, struck drapery, too – reflected a malaise that was affecting all sectors of the Low Countries' economy, deepened by poor harvests and steep inflation in 1521–2. But it was unwittingly prolonged by a currency revaluation carried out in 1527, because the measure compromised the competitive position of Netherlands cloth in the foreign markets for which a large proportion was destined.[35]

From 1531, growth resumed, stimulated initially by vigorous commercial and industrial recovery throughout the Netherlands, and later by a currency devaluation ordered by Charles V in 1539.[36] Of at least equal importance was the introduction of additional types of light fabrics, notably satins, ostades, changéants, and velveteens, which considerably diversified the product line.[37] A 1534 edict by the central government forbidding say weaving anywhere in the castellany save Lille may also have helped the urban craft.[38] Output of sayetteurs' goods rose smartly for about fifteen years, showing a total increase of 78 percent, with only a few, short-lived, and minor interruptions. In the two decades from the mid-1540s to the mid-1560s, however, it became considerably more erratic.

34 Figure 3.2 is based on data from Vanhaeck, *Sayetterie à Lille,* 1:353–4, and Deyon and Lottin, "Production textile à Lille," pp. 30–1. Light textiles woven outside Lille were not taxed there because they could not receive the seal of the city's crafts, so Figure 3.2 accurately represents urban output.

35 Van der Wee, *Growth of the Antwerp Market,* 2:144–61; Verlinden, Craeybeckx and Scholliers, "Price and Wage Movements in Belgium in the Sixteenth Century," pp. 61, 75 and fig. 8; Ralph Davis, *The Rise of the Atlantic Economies* (Ithaca, N.Y., 1973), p. 106.

36 Van der Wee, *Growth of the Antwerp Market,* 2:166–207.

37 Changéants, ostades, and satins were first mentioned in the definitive sayetterie guild statutes of 1524 (printed in Vanhaeck, *Sayetterie à Lille,* 2:29, doc. 9, art, 16); in 1531, that guild won exclusive rights to weave ostades and satins in Lille (ibid., 2:44–5, doc. 11).

38 Ibid., 2:45–6, doc. 12, 15 May 1534. For a study of the crown's attempts throughout the Netherlands to win urban support and increased tax monies by restricting rural crafts during these years, see E. C. G. Brunner, *"De Order op de Buitennering" van 1531* (Utrecht, 1918). The decision was affirmed in 1547 (Vanhaeck, *Sayetterie à Lille,* 1:271), and again in 1566 (AML, Reg. 16,299, fol. 200v). Corporate rules already forbade fulling, dyeing or trimming says not woven in Lille (Vanhaeck, *Sayetterie à Lille,* 2:12, doc. 3, art. xxxiii, 27 February 1500; 2:34, doc. 9, art. 46, 22 December 1524).

The trend originally continued upward despite marked fluctuations. Production reached its high point for the prerevolt period in 1552, when it was 26 percent above the 1546 level. Subsequently, however, overexpansion among textile makers all over Europe, not to mention a contemporary slump in the Americas trade, provoked a deep decline in sayetterie similar to that affecting drapery. Although broken briefly in 1556, this depression only touched bottom in 1559, when output was barely half of what it had been just seven years earlier.[39] To be sure, sharp recovery was recorded during the next twelve months (an increase of 55 percent), perhaps due to an embargo on English cloth imposed in retaliation for attempts by the Merchant Adventurers to restrict the activities of Netherlands traders.[40] But each year during the early 1560s saw output move in a different direction. Growth nearly stopped. It was just 9 percent over the five years 1560–5, at which point production was still 11 percent below the 1552 peak, and a slight downturn occurred in 1566.

Starting in 1541, data pertaining to changéants and velveteens woven by bourgetteurs become available, making it possible to draw a more complete picture of the evolution of light-cloth output (Figure 3.3).[41] Across the next quarter century, aggregate production of these fabrics rose substantially, although the composition of that output varied across time, very likely as weavers switched in response to changing demand.[42] Changéant production oscillated in both the 1540s and the 1550s. Yet whereas the trend was upward during most of the first decade, it was just the opposite during the second.[43] This depression resembled but was much more pronounced than the downturn experienced by sayetteurs; perhaps the very cheap changéants were especially dependent on New World consumption, itself in crisis. From 1560, however, changéant output shot up, and in 1565 it was three and a half times that of a quarter century earlier.

[39] For the post-1552 "recession" in Spanish exports to the New World, see Deyon and Lottin, "Production textile à Lille," p. 27.

[40] Van Houtte, *Economic History of the Low Countries*, p. 187.

[41] The data for Figure 3.3 come from AML, Reg. 16,274–99.

[42] It is probable that sayetteurs likewise altered their product mix in similar ways. In testimony about 1575, the Vingtaine stated that with the introduction of satins and ostades around 1530, and again of changéants somewhat later, few weavers wanted to go on making says; AML, Aff. gén., C. 1171, d. 9, fols. 2–3v. There is, however, no way of disaggregating the sayetterie data.

[43] Cf. AML, Aff. gén., C. 1160, d. 5: on 7 November 1555 the number of bourgetterie inspectors was raised from seven to ten, "in order to provide against the decline and apparent ruin" of the craft.

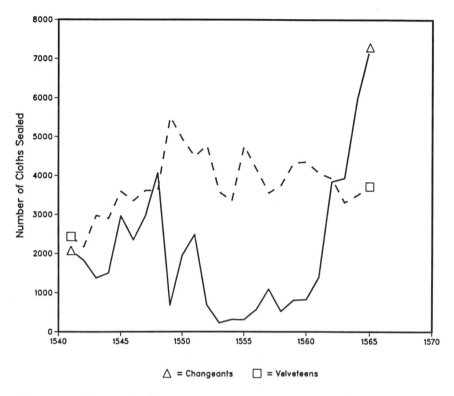

Figure 3.3. Output of changéants and velveteens by Lille's bourgetteurs, 1541–65.

Output of velveteens was also characterized by fluctuations – albeit of much less magnitude than changéants – throughout the entire twenty-five years. During most of the 1540s, production of both fabrics increased. But thereafter their production trends diverged. When changéant output dropped precipitously in 1549, velveteens continued their upward progression. In 1549, in fact, more than twice as many velveteens were sealed as in 1541, despite increasing rural competition.[44] But that proved to be the zenith. Admittedly, across the 1550s

[44] In 1535, owing to the influence wielded by its seigneur, Philippe de Lannoy, *grand maître d'hôtel* of the regent Mary of Hungary, the village of Tourcoing, north of Lille, won the emperor's permission to have twenty-five velveteen and ostade looms. A dozen years later this quota was doubled and weaving of these types of light cloth was sanctioned in the neighboring villages of Roubaix, Leers, and Toufflers. See Vanhaeck, *Sayetterie à Lille,* 1:272–3; and Alexandre de Saint-Léger, "La rivalité industrielle entre la ville de Lille et le plat pays," *Annales de l'Est et du Nord* 2 (1906):375. That these three villages were already engaged in weaving these fabrics

velveteens managed to hold their own much better than other light fabrics, suggesting a lower degree of reliance on markets in Spanish America and less volatile demand within Europe. But yearly oscillations in output were superimposed on a declining trend that by the mid-1560s brought production back to its 1548 level. Perhaps competition from the countryside finally began to bite. Yet because velveteens were one of the most luxurious of the light fabrics, it is tempting to attribute some of their decline – and the recovery of inexpensive changéants – to the effects of spiraling inflation on the eve of the revolt.[45]

Even with the reverses suffered in the 1550s (prolonged into the next decade in the case of velveteens), the overall trend of Lille's woolen-cloth production from the late fifteenth century through the mid-1560s was strongly positive. The repeated adoption of new kinds of cheaper cloth allowed drapers, sayetteurs, and bourgetteurs to benefit from the widening and deepening of domestic and international markets to which the merchants of their city were contributing. At the same time, however, output exhibited a markedly cyclical pattern, as periods of rapid growth alternated with steep downturns. The fact that production cycles varied by craft and by type of cloth may have served to mitigate their impact upon urban society as a whole during much of the period. Yet the increasingly abrupt fluctuations after midcentury eroded much of this advantage and heightened the instability that characterized the industry. What needs to be examined now is whether this period of pronounced but uneven expansion effected any structural changes in the textile industry.

II

Lille's sixteenth-century economy retained the corporate structure that had evolved in the course of the Middle Ages.[46] The rise of the light-

before gaining permission from the Privy Council is clear from the decision (AML, Aff. gén., C. 1161, d. 4, 9 March 1547), which includes a census of looms. It is thus very likely that other illegal looms were also at work.

45 For Lille's price history, see Chapter 4. For rural competition, see the 1560 complaint by a number of cities, printed in *Cartulaire de la commune d'Arras* (Arras, 1863), pp. 402–5. The towns' bid for suppression of rural production was rejected, although the limits cited in the previous note were affirmed; Vanhaeck, *Sayetterie à Lille*, 2:63–6, doc. 27, 14 December 1563.

46 For somewhat different interpretations of the origins and medieval development of Lille's corporations, see Georges Espinas, *Les origines de l'association. I. Les origines du droit d'association dans les villes de l'Artois et de la Flandre française jusqu'au début du XVIe siècle*, 2 vols. (Paris, 1941–2), 2:738–42; and Sivéry, "Institutions lilloises," pp. 298–303.

cloth industry led, in fact, to the formation of new craft associations, from bourgetterie (1496) and sayetterie four years later, to say fulling and dyeing in 1565.[47] But were these guilds vital institutions? Admittedly, through their confraternities they quickly assumed religious and social functions, and their regulations were constantly updated. Yet it has often been argued that market competition and the consequent search for lower costs made the textile trades uniquely vulnerable to efforts at change, especially in a capitalist direction, that corporations might mask but could not prevent. Was this the case in sixteenth-century Lille?

The crafts connected with new drapery seem to have been long familiar with one component of a new economic order, the employment of various kinds of workers paid by the day or, more commonly, by the piece by master artisans and merchants.[48] Some workers, the "free," earned the guild franchise by completing an apprenticeship yet were unable to amass sufficient capital to open their own shops, a prerequisite to receiving mastership.[49] Others never sought the freedom of the craft and the chance, however unlikely in reality, of becoming a master, but chose instead to pay a reduced fee and undergo a briefer training period.[50] Yet others were immigrants who could work in Lille once they paid modest weekly and yearly fees.[51] In every case, workers were subject to detailed corporate regulations governing their pay, hours, and conditions of employment,[52] for next to technical matters, drapery corporations devoted most attention to organizing the labor market.

Still, the information at our disposal indicates that despite the presence of a handful of larger units, petty production remained the norm in the drapery industry. In 1593, date of the only sixteenth-century new drapery census, one of the ninety-two weavers then working had 26 pieces of cloth on his premises. No one else, however, had more than 5. Similarly, the two biggest of fifteen fulling shops were processing 102

[47] Lille's corporate statutes can be found most conveniently in AML, Reg. 16,002–3, "Registres aux Lettres et Ordonnances des stils," and in *Lettres et statuts imprimés des Corps de métiers de la ville de Lille*, 3 vols. (n.p., n.d.), in the BML.

[48] For the earlier period, see Marquant, *Vie économique à Lille sous Philippe le Bon*, pp. 167–70.

[49] In the 1550 redaction of their charter, for example, the shearers specified that a master who could not afford a shop had to enter another's; AML, Reg. 16,002, fols. 122–7.

[50] See ibid., fols. 16v, art. iii (drap weavers), and 125v, arts. 24, 27 (shearers).

[51] The drap weaver's statutes explicitly provided for the employment of outside *varlets;* ibid., fols. 16v–17, arts. ii, vi.

[52] In addition to the statutes already cited, see ibid., fols. 6v–9, 56v–60v (fullers).

and 70 pieces, but the rest from just 1 to 26. Seventeen dyeworks handled between 3 and 73 cloths each, yet the median (25 pieces) and the average (27.4) show a predominance of small producers.[53] In addition, drapery guilds continued to block attempts to amalgamate stages of production, as merchant drapers, for instance, found out in 1554 when they petitioned unsuccessfully for permission to establish fulleries to treat their own cloth.[54] So if wage labor existed in new drapery, the industry seems to have experienced little of the concentration and consolidation that were also fundamental to capitalist development.

Yet however suggestive the evidence from the drapery crafts, the case for a capitalist "economic revolution," in Pirenne's characterization, has rested predominantly on light woolens, at once the most dynamic industrial sector and the one most firmly dependent on export markets. It was here, historians have claimed, that the disjunction with prior forms of production was most complete, here that a new system matured.[55] Thus it is the sayetterie and bourgetterie trades that deserve our closest attention.

Some rules that might be taken as heralding new relations of production were to be found in the corporate statutes of these crafts. For one thing, preference was given to children of masters. They owed only half fees for entry to apprenticeship and for attaining the status of master, and they had no determinate period of training to fulfill, whereas two years were required of other candidates.[56] Corporate regulations, moreover, initially sanctioned the employment of wage labor, both in masters' shops and in putting-out arrangements, and limited workers' mobility and thus their bargaining power.[57] Furthermore, as a 1539 appeal from "numerous" free bourgetterie workers shows, at least some weavers were frustrated when they attempted to attain the status of master. After earning the guild franchise, the petitioners asserted, they borrowed money to open their own shops, the final prerequisite for mastership. Yet

[53] My calculations from data in Henri De Sagher, "Un enquête sur la situation de l'industrie drapière en Flandre à la fin du XVIe siècle," in *Etudes d'histoire dédiées à la mémoire de Henri Pirenne par ses anciens élèves* (Brussels, 1937), p. 479.

[54] AML, Reg. 16,002, fols. 23v, 26v.

[55] Pirenne, *Histoire de Belgique*, 3:257 (quotation); Van der Wee, "Structural Changes and Specialization," p. 217.

[56] Vanhaeck, *Sayetterie à Lille*, 2:9, arts. xvii–xviii (1500 statutes), 2:31–2, arts. 25–6 (1524 statutes); *Lettres et statuts des bourgeteurs*, p. 16.

[57] Vanhaeck, *Sayetterie à Lille*, 2:10, doc. 3, art. xxii; 2:33, doc. 9, art. 30; 2:58–9, doc. 20; *Lettres et statuts des bourgeteurs*, pp. 14–15, arts. xxiv–xxv.

for unspecified reasons they soon lacked "the power to continue" and consequently "entirely lost everything that they had invested" in their businesses.[58]

The innovations registered by the guild rules were, however, limited in extent. The exclusionary provisions were quite mild. The fee differential between masters' children and others' was a matter of only a few livres. Entry to mastership was open to women as well as men and was significantly eased for several specific groups. Orphans in municipal institutions were excused from all fees, while up until 1564 any weaver who had been trained in a town with a chartered light-cloth craft was automatically granted the franchise in Lille.[59]

What is more, from all indications small, autonomous masters dominated light-cloth production. According to a memorandum written around 1575 by the Vingtaine – the six men who administered the sayetterie guild – that craft, "the chief of those practiced in this city and from which the largest number of people gains its living," presently counted about 2,250 weavers. At one extreme stood some 40 or 50 prosperous masters "making use of the craft not only for the necessary support of their families but also for covetousness": Their goal was to become rich. At the other extreme, 200 or so "master [free] workers" were employed by the "more powerful" in return for wages and rent money. But the great majority consisted of 2,000 or more "upright people of slender resources," who were "entirely dependent on the daily practice of the craft" in their own shops.[60] Sixteenth-century loom censuses do not exist. But in enumerations taken in 1638 and 1659, when the corporate structure remained essentially the same, three-quarters of all master sayetteurs possessed three looms or fewer (so that all weaving could be carried out by family members) and none had more than six.[61]

Tax lists and marriage contracts confirm the paucity of wealthy light-cloth producers, especially in comparison with the number of weavers in Lille. Only a handful of sayetteurs and bourgetteurs were among the

58 *Lettres et statuts des bourgeteurs*, pp. 27–8.
59 Vanhaeck, *Sayetterie à Lille*, 2:3, art. v; 2:28, art. 8; 2:51–4, doc. 16; 2:62, doc. 24; *Lettres et statuts des bourgeteurs*, pp. 12–13, arts. xii–xiii; AML, Reg. 380, fols. 147–9v. For a list of the approximately two dozen towns whose crafts were recognized by Lille, see Vanhaeck, *Sayetterie à Lille*, 2:77 n. 1.
60 AML, Aff. gén., C. 1171, d. 9, fols. 1–iv.
61 The censuses (AML, Aff. gén., C. 1170, d. 7) are partially cited in Vanhaeck, *Sayetterie à Lille*, 1:352–3.

250 townspeople who subscribed to a fund for rebuilding the city walls in 1537 or the 297 who bought annuities in 1557 to pay a special aide for the war with France.[62] Again, of the approximately 300 wealthy Lillois who in 1562 each lent the municipal government 20 to 50 florins to buy grain for the poor, just 3 or 4 were light-cloth masters.[63] Finally, very few of the surviving textile craftsmen's assessments for the Hundredth Penny tax in 1569 were much above the minimum payment of 1 livre.[64]

Even the wealthiest cloth maker was far from rich. The average of all contributions in 1537 was 99 livres, yet the sayetteur Jean de Lattre (120 livres) was the only textile artisan who gave more than 50 livres. The few annuities worth 100 or 200 livres bought by cloth makers in 1557 were valued at much less than the mean of 637 livres. And as Appendix C shows, even the highest tax levied on textile producers in 1569 was well below both the median and the mean of merchants.

Appendix B provides another indication of the modest level of assets amassed by light-drapery artisans. The marriage portions that they settled on their children were on the average considerably lower than those given by officials, professionals, nobles, and merchants. The largest light-cloth artisan marriage portion (of the handful in the surviving contracts) was given to Marie Descamps by her father Bauduin, a sayetteur. Composed of 200 florins invested in an annuity yielding 6.25 percent, and 13 florins in cash, it had a total value of 426 livres.[65] More typical were the portions involved when Jean le Gay, a sayetteur, wed Evonne, daughter of the late sayetteur Cornille Zegre. Jean brought to the marriage a loaded loom valued at 10 florins as well as cloth for a wedding robe worth 6 florins. Evonne's dowry, which totaled just under 100 florins, consisted of a loom, clothing, a share in an annuity, and a small amount of cash.[66]

The predominance of small producers was grounded in part in economic conditions. For one thing, light-cloth weaving utilized the labor of nearly all members of a household, including men and women, the young and the old. Men wove; women spun, wove, or, more commonly,

[62] AML, Reg. 902, fols. 86v–92v; Reg. 16,291, fols. 65–86.
[63] Lottin, "Liste des riches lillois," pp. 68–72.
[64] AML, Reg. 966, and Appendix C.
[65] AML, Reg. 15,434, 27 December 1544.
[66] Ibid., 3 March 1544. For other contracts adding up to 100 to 200 liv. and similarly including tools, clothing, rentes, and a little equipment, see ibid., 27 December 1544, and Reg. 15,435, 12 March and 18 May 1550.

doubled thread, twisting two or three skeins together to make tougher strands; children spooled thread or, once they reached age nine or ten, operated looms; the aged assisted in doubling.[67] Of equal importance was the modest amount of capital needed to establish a weaving shop and carry on business, as well as the wide availability of resources to do so. A house with space for a workplace could be rented for as little as 5 livres per year, while looms plus auxiliary tools sold for 15 to 25 livres.[68] Even in 1584, after decades of inflation, the sum of 48 livres was considered sufficient for a sayetteur to open a fully equipped shop stocked with the necessary raw materials.[69] Supplies could readily be obtained through "trade credit," whereby payment was stretched out over several months or more,[70] while as we have seen marriage portions frequently provided both cash and productive equipment. And "many times," as the Vingtaine pointed out and the notarial archives confirm, artisans borrowed from friends and relatives in order to acquire tools and supplies, as well as to overcome temporary liquidity problems.[71]

Necessary as they were, however, in themselves these factors were not sufficient to assure the ascendancy of small producers. After all, the availability of credit did not, as we have seen, prevent some aspiring bourgetterie masters from failing. Surely, too, the periodic light-textile slumps must have made numerous weavers familiar with the plight of men like Jean Vincent. In 1564, Vincent was forced to give up most of his possessions – including a loom, thread, finished cloth, furniture, and clothing – to repay the 106 livres he had borrowed from the merchant Guillaume Rogier.[72] At the same time that capital was widely accessible, moreover, contemporary economic processes enabled some Lillois, mer-

---

67 AML, Aff. gén., C. 1171, d. 9, fol. 5v; Vanhaeck, *Sayetterie à Lille*, 2:84, doc. 38.
68 For rents, see AH Bonnes Filles, Reg. E3-7 (1508–56). For equipment, see AML, Reg. 15,434, 3 May 1544; Reg. 15,435, 12 March 1550; ADN, Tab. 3851, 26 July 1564; Tab. 3858. A few indications of raw material costs can also be gleaned from the notarial archives. In 1564 (ADN, Tab. 3851, 26 July 1564), say thread cost 3.09 liv. a kg., so 10.5 to 13 liv. would have been needed to supply the 3.4 to 4.2 kg. of thread needed for various types of light cloth. The thread requirements have been calculated from figures dating from 1763 printed in Vanhaeck, *Sayetterie à Lille*, 1:355, reduced by one-third because sixteenth-century cloths were two-thirds the length of those woven in the eighteenth.
69 This was the amount granted each year beginning in 1584 by the "Fondation Deliot" to eighteen "honorable" master sayetteurs who through no fault of their own lacked sufficient capital to set up shops; Vanhaeck, *Sayetterie à Lille*, 2:88, doc. 41.
70 For an example, see AML, Reg. 15,435, fols. 90v–1.
71 For the comment, see AML, Aff. gén., C. 1171, d. 9, fol. 3v. Instances of such loans are to be found throughout the notarial registers.
72 ADN, Tab. 3851, 26 July 1564.

chants and artisans alike, to accumulate larger amounts than their fellows, which they then might seek to invest in textile production.

Many historians have insisted that merchants' knowledge of and access to far-flung markets, as well as their financial resources, enabled them to gain control of export-oriented industries, usually by means of the *Verlag* or putting-out system.[73] Long-distance merchants formed, as we know, a wealthy and influential group in Lille, and they had forged strong and intimate commercial links with the great emporium of Antwerp. Furthermore, they were crucial in providing the ready sales that masters needed in order to maintain their liquidity.[74] Contrary to what might be anticipated, however, there is no evidence that Lille's merchants were able to exploit their strategic position and substantial assets to take charge of light cloth. How can we explain this situation?

It is conceivable that a careful assessment of how to maximize returns dictated the behavior of Lille's commercial class in this regard. Precisely because they were the inescapable intermediaries between markets and cloth, merchants enjoyed a strong bargaining position, which was reinforced by guild statutes mandating fines for weavers whose work did not satisfy the traders who bought it.[75] Cognizant of this, merchants may have judged that investment in weaving, subject as it was to abrupt changes in demand, was too risky, particularly when more secure investments such as land and annuities were available to supplement earnings from trade. The costs of supervising putting-out systems, and the myriad possibilities for indiscipline and fraud inherent in them, could have been further disincentives to engaging in this form of activity.

Still, it is clear that not all merchants were reticent about investing in cloth production. Putting out of drapery, as already noted, did occur, and city authorities charged that merchants who placed "concern for their own profit" above "the common good" were employing rural weavers to produce cheap fabrics to the detriment of urban industry.[76] Good reasons can be adduced to explain merchant entrepreneurs' attention to

---

[73] For two classic accounts of the process of alleged merchant takeover of production, see F. Furger, *Zum Verlagssystem als Organisationsform des Frühkapitalismus im Textilgewerbe* (Stuttgart, 1927), and George Unwin, *Industrial Organization in the Sixteenth and Seventeenth Centuries* (Oxford, 1904).

[74] Such rapid turnover was intrinsic to the pattern of petty production, as the Vingtaine attested; see AML, Aff. gén., C. 1171, d. 9, fol. 2; Vanhaeck, *Sayetterie à Lille*, 2:100, doc. 47.

[75] Vanhaeck, *Sayetterie à Lille*, 2:30–1, art. 20 (1524 statutes).

[76] *Cartulaire de la commune d'Arras*, pp. 402–5.

textile making. A contemporary Dutch document mentioned textile profit margins of 13 percent, and a return of 6 to 11 percent can be computed on the basis of Lille data from the mid-eighteenth century, when the industry was in a less flourishing state. If the profits realized in sixteenth-century Lille were anything like these figures, they would have compared favorably with returns from trade and risen above the yield of real estate and annuities.[77] Despite fluctuations, moreover, demand for the cheap textiles in which Lille specialized was incontestably growing. Then, too, the brief time required to make light cloth resulted in a rapid turnover of capital, maintaining an attractive cash flow under normal circumstances and permitting merchants to reduce their exposure quickly when conditions changed. So whereas some members of Lille's commercial class might rationally have construed their best economic interests as recommending avoidance of investment in light-cloth production, others – on equally sensible grounds – could well have wished to attempt this form of enterprise.

Merchants were not, moreover, the only townspeople who might have gained control of light drapery at the expense of small autonomous masters. The growth of the industry distributed affluence unequally among artisans. As early as 1506, a guild document spoke of "rich and powerful" sayetteurs. Seventy years later the Vingtaine claimed that during the long period of light-textile expansion several individuals who had begun with nothing more than petty borrowed capital had ended up with great wealth.[78]

Like merchants, and doubtless for many of the same reasons, prosperous artisans acquired rentes and bought real estate.[79] But they also sought to deploy their capital within the light-textile crafts in ways that would have transformed the existing production system. Wealthy sayetteurs were denounced in 1506 for hiring combers to work in weaving shops for a wage, putting out wool to spinners, and endeavoring to corner the thread market, thereby menacing the great majority of less substantial artisans.[80] Around midcentury, too, the Vingtaine alleged,

---

[77] Charles Wilson, *England's Apprenticeship 1603–1763* (London, 1965), p. 71 (Dutch document); for Lille data, see the material cited from a 1763 memorandum by Vanhaeck, *Sayetterie à Lille*, 1:355–6; for profits on other investments, see Chapter 2, section III.

[78] Vanhaeck, *Sayetterie à Lille*, 2:23, doc. 7; AML, Aff. gén., C. 1171, d. 9, fol. 3v.

[79] See, for example, AML, Reg. 15,434, 27 December 1544, or Reg. 15,435, fol. 18v, 29 March 1550.

[80] Vanhaeck, *Sayetterie à Lille*, 2:23–4, doc. 7.

weavers with "considerable sums" of money had begun to employ many of their fellows as wage laborers.[81]

In short, economic conditions were ripe for the emergence of significant merchant or artisan entrepreneurs in light textiles in Lille, and thus ripe for the further changes in the direction of capitalism that Pirenne and others considered characteristic of new drapery throughout the Low Countries. What ultimately prevented such an outcome was a corpus of regulations that evolved across the sixteenth century, culminating in several critical enactments during the mid-1560s. This regulatory structure did not represent, it must be emphasized, the survival of an older system: No light-cloth rules exist from before the very end of the fifteenth century. Nor was it a copy of the very sketchy code governing new drapery. In addition, the protracted process of constructing the light-textile production system did not proceed smoothly and uninterruptedly, and it was not free of inconsistencies. Neither was it the product of an explicitly articulated theory. Instead, it developed in response to practices regarded as violating deeply held if tacit social relationships and norms of behavior. As we shall observe, however, once the structure of rules was nearly completed, guild leaders gave retrospective expression to the principles lying behind it.

Perhaps because of experience in other crafts and in earlier times, from the very beginning corporate statutes sought to forestall direct merchant involvement in light drapery. Only masters or mistresses were authorized to open sayetterie and bourgetterie shops, employ assistants, and train apprentices. Along with their spouses, moreover, they alone could make the first sales of their cloth.[82] Restrictions on the deployment of artisan capital matured more slowly, but in the first two-thirds of the century, two major problem areas were defined and addressed. One was the monopolization of raw material supplies, the other the employment of low-cost labor, whether in large shops, putting-out arrangements, or other settings.

Each loom consumed the output of four spinning wheels, so thread accounted for a substantial proportion of weaver's total costs.[83] Hence

---

[81] AML, Aff. gén., C. 1171, d. 9, fol. 2.

[82] Vanhaeck, *Sayetterie à Lille*, 2:7, 28, 35 (doc. 3, art. v, and doc. 9, arts. 8, 42); *Lettres et statuts des bourgeteurs*, pp. 13, 14–15 (arts. xv and xxiv).

[83] For the number of spinners required to supply each loom, see AML, Aff. gén., C. 1179, d. 2. Calculations on the basis of figures given in Deyon, "Concurrence internationale des manufac-

Lille's sayetteurs and bourgetteurs sought a plentiful, cheap, and reliable supply, which increasingly could be found only by drawing on the hinterland. Already in 1534, say thread was described as coming "chiefly" from villages in the castellany. By 1572, the urban crafts had reached deeper into the countryside, employing spinners living as far as sixteen leagues away in Hainaut and Artois.[84] Protecting this regional division of labor understandably became a preoccupation of Lille's authorities, lending urgency to their efforts to block village industrialization. As a result, municipal appeals to the central government argued that rural weaving – also under fire for low wages and fraudulent practices – would divert thread from the city, thereby driving up prices and undermining the competitiveness of its cloth.[85]

As we have seen, Lille was but partially successful in its campaign against textile production in the countryside. It did obtain regional monopolies for say and changéant weaving, but several villages in northern Walloon Flanders won the right to make velveteens and ostades. An imperial decree issued in 1547 allowed Roubaix and Tourcoing each to have 50 looms, Leers 25, and Toufflers 12. Over the next few years, complaints by Lille and other towns were rejected and the loom quotas reaffirmed. It is likely, moreover, that these limits were soon flouted, since the next enumeration, taken in 1608, found 720 light-cloth looms in nineteen villages. Thus the issue of thread shortages attributable to rural weaving remained a sore point, ready to flare up whenever the town returned to the offensive.[86]

In terms of possible structural change within urban crafts, however, the major problem regarding thread was internal to the city: assuring equitable distribution among weavers. Attempting to address this issue, the very first guild statutes mandated – and every subsequent redaction reaffirmed – the establishment of a biweekly public market, held every Wednesday and Saturday. All thread used in Lille's light-cloth industry had to be displayed and sold there, and weavers enjoyed the sole right of

---

tures lainières," p. 22, show that raw wool, combing, and spinning equaled close to three-quarters of weavers' total costs.

[84] See respectively Vanhaeck, *Sayetterie à Lille*, 2:45, doc. 12, and AML, Reg. 145, fols. 176–6v, 178–9v. A document from 1506 (Vanhaeck, *Sayetterie à Lille*, 2:23–4, doc. 7) mentions spinners in the city as well as the country, but the later ones cite only those living outside the town.

[85] Cf. Vanhaeck, *Sayetterie à Lille*, 2:45, doc. 12. Villagers viewed the situation differently, emphasizing its exploitative features. See, for example, Roubaix's 1553 statement, printed in Baelde, "Conflit économique," p. 1072.

[86] See nn. 38, 44–5, above; AML. Aff. gén., C. 1164; *Histoire d'une métropole*, p. 198.

purchase during the first hour.[87] This simple institutional structure was explicitly designed, the municipal government avowed, to prevent "rich and powerful" masters from monopolizing raw material stocks and thus to ensure that small producers could obtain all the thread they required.[88]

Unfortunately, the market quickly proved vulnerable not only to those who exploited loopholes in the regulations but also to those who simply ignored them. As early as 1506, "some sayetteurs" were putting out wool to spinners in town and country, then bringing the thread directly to their homes for combing and weaving. In the process, they entirely bypassed the market. Such severe shortages had resulted, it was alleged, that "the greatest part" of the weavers could scrape together barely a quarter of what they needed. Outraged, a "great number" of masters petitioned for better enforcement and heavier penalties: Violators reputedly found the current fine of 40 sols trivial. In response, the Magistrat reiterated the existing rules, strictly forbade all prebuying or even prior consultation between weavers and spinners, enjoined weavers from putting out or otherwise engaging in combing and spinning, and added a new punishment, a fifteen-day suspension from work upon conviction for any offense.[89]

References to thread supply problems dwindled for several decades, but at midcentury – when light-textile output began to fluctuate more frequently and strongly, and rural competition intensified – they became a major concern once again. In 1550, sayetteurs and bourgetteurs who purchased thread in the market for resale were accused of raising prices to the "great prejudice" of their fellows. To counteract this trend, the Magistrat prohibited weavers from buying thread in excess of the amounts that they themselves could work up.[90] The following year, combers were singled out for dealing in thread and putting it out to spinners; they too were told to cease their activities.[91] Enactments then ceased for a decade and a half. But a provision in a 1565 ordinance suggests that attempts at engrossment continued. It threatened banishment "or other severe punishment" to sayetteurs or bourgetteurs who

---

[87] Vanhaeck, *Sayetterie à Lille*, 2:11, 34–5 (doc. 3, arts. xxvii–xxviii, and doc. 9, arts. 37, 41); *Lettres et statuts des bourgeteurs*, p. 16, art. xxix.
[88] See Vanhaeck, *Sayetterie à Lille*, 2:23, doc. 7.
[89] Ibid., 2:23–5, doc. 7.
[90] Ibid., 2:59–60, doc. 21.
[91] Ibid., 2:60, doc. 22.

entered into financial or other relationships with spinners or who obtained thread anywhere but in the public market.[92]

Many of those who engaged in questionable or even illegal practices in regard to the thread supply may have been intending only to turn a tidy profit upon resale, or to cut costs to their individual advantage. But the repeatedly denounced attempts to coordinate spinning, combing, and weaving indicate that some artisans had more far-reaching plans in mind. Certainly in retrospect, at least, corporate officials emphasized that schemes to corner the thread supply had serious implications for the organization of production. Armed with "considerable sums of money," guild officials observed about 1575, "the small number of the most powerful" weavers could "easily find the means of buying all or most thread on market days as well as at other times." By "secretly" arranging with spinners, who preferred assured sales to the risks of the open market, they could virtually monopolize stocks. Consequently, "lesser" masters, unable to find thread at a reasonable price, would have little choice but to abandon their shops and go to work for the wealthy few. It was to forestall this scenario from being played out in Lille, the Vingtaine announced, that the thread market had initially been organized and additional restrictions promulgated across the sixteenth century.[93]

By this point, guild leaders had come to regard the thread supply regulations as crucial elements in a comprehensive strategy. Their goal was to prevent the minority of weavers with sizable accumulations of capital from "drawing to itself all the activity of the craft and finally turning into dependents and wage earners the great number" of small producers who had heretofore predominated.[94] There is little evidence, however, that the authorities had originally imagined that an interventionist approach would be necessary to preserve what they took to be the desirable structure of the light-cloth industry. Nowhere is this clearer than in regard to the employment of labor. Early regulations on this subject had been directed against merchant or other nonartisan capitalists who might seek to open shops in Lille or have cloth, woven more cheaply in the countryside, finished in the city.[95] During the first three

---

[92] Ibid., 2:67, doc. 29. This was not the last decree on thread; see ibid., 2:79, doc. 36, art. iii (1575); 2:86–7, doc. 40 (1580).
[93] AML, Aff. gén., C. 1171, d. 9, fols. 1v–2.
[94] Ibid., fol. 1v.
[95] Vanhaeck, *Sayetterie à Lille*, 2:7, 12 (doc. 3, arts. v, xxxiii), and 2:28, 35, 36 (doc. 9, arts. 8, 42, 46); *Lettres et statuts des bourgeteurs*, pp. 13, 14–15, arts. xv, xxiv, xxv.

decades of the sixteenth century no restrictions on masters' involvement in urban putting out, or on the size of the shops that they could operate, were specified.

Thus it was not foresight but experience, the Vingtaine later declared, that had taught them that only "well-ordered *police*" could ensure that "everyone can have the means of earning a living without the least being crushed and oppressed by the advance of the most powerful." Experience had shown that larger entrepreneurs could offer buyers a combination of quantity, choice of style and color, convenient selection, "more pleasing price," and terms of payment that no modest master could hope to emulate. Experience had also demonstrated that more quickly woven and increasingly popular fabrics like satins, ostades, and eventually changéants generated substantial cash flows that "more powerful" producers could use to buy out their fellows. Had nothing been done, the Vingtaine concluded, eventually this process would have sharply concentrated control of the say industry.[96]

Like most retrospective accounts, this one probably attributes a greater degree of consistency and consciousness than was present when the actions were taken. But it is accurate to the extent that enactments about artisanal employment of labor correlate closely in time with changes in Lille's product mix in the direction of lighter cloth. The critical ordinances dated from the 1530s, the early 1540s, and the early to mid-1560s. These were periods, the Vingtaine later asserted, when the weaving of says was on the verge of abandonment, and when it was feared that the craft would "turn into *satinerie* or *changéanterie* and an infinite number of masters subjugated to the power of just ten or twelve of the most powerful."[97]

The first decrees pertained to the number of looms that each master might own. In 1531, the Magistrat formally granted sayetteurs permission to weave ostades and inverted satins, but also limited each weaver to just one loom for these newer types of cloth.[98] The privilege of making narrow satins in the style of Saint-Pol (conferred in 1537 mainly as a consequence of immigration from that war-ravaged area in Artois) likewise carried with it a quota of one loom per workplace. But this time a proviso – significant in light of the Vingtaine's subsequent testimony –

---

[96] AML, Aff. gén., C. 1171, d. 9, fols. IV–3.
[97] Ibid., fol. 3.
[98] Vanhaeck, *Sayetterie à Lille*, 2:44, doc. 11.

was attached: Only sayetteurs who kept at least one say loom operating in their shops could weave narrow satins.[99] The next year weavers were authorized to have two satin looms (without apparent restriction as to type); just one, however, was permitted if they were unwilling or unable to maintain a say loom.[100]

Other labor practices that compromised the integrity of light drapery had also emerged in these years. In some cases, youths obtained the guild franchise under false pretenses and then were set up in de facto putting-out arrangements rather than opening the independent work-places required for full mastership. Employers thereby circumvented loom limits while profiting from cheap labor. Retaining apprentices after their statutory terms had been completed was another ploy that reduced masters' labor costs.

To combat these "great abuses," the aldermen and council, in con-sultation with corporate leaders and the Chamber of Accounts, in-stituted a compulsory masterpiece: preparing a loom in the proper man-ner and satisfactorily weaving at least half an ell of say or satin in the presence of two guild officials. Further, they specified that the minimum age for reception to mastership would be sixteen years for girls, eighteen for boys. They also declared that new masters and mistresses had to be "duly emancipated and free from paternal authority" (*duement émancipés et mis hors de pain et puissance de père*) and reminded masters that the statutory training period was two years and no longer. At the same time, apprentices were instructed to work only on says in their first year, and on wide satins during their second, thereby eliminating them as a cut-rate labor pool for popular light fabrics.[101]

Finally, after a hiatus of nearly twenty years – during which time the thread supply problems already examined had come to the fore – the Magistrat imposed an important series of regulations during the early 1560s. In 1562, masters in the sayetterie craft were ordered not to put out work to anyone who had not earned the mastership of the trade.[102] Three years later, light-cloth fullers, curriers, and dyers were removed from the sayetterie guild and grouped together into an independent

---

[99] Ibid., 2:51–4, doc. 16.
[100] Ibid., 1:91 n. 2.
[101] Ibid., 2:54–5, doc. 17, 25 February 1540, and 2:56–7, doc. 19, 26 September 1543; AML, Aff. gén., C. 1171, d. 9, fol. 3. The latter document dates a first ordinance to 1538, but I have not located it.
[102] Vanhaeck, *Sayetterie à Lille*, 2:63, doc. 26.

corporation of finishers. This change brought to an end the possibility of integrating weaving and fulling work, one that had existed ever since the original sayetterie statutes had been promulgated in 1500.[103] Just a few months afterward, in what came to be regarded as the keystone of the regulatory corpus, an omnibus ordinance barred any form of putting out whatsoever in changéant weaving and forbade individual master sayetteurs and bourgetteurs to have more than six changéant looms.[104] Because virtually every new kind of cloth invented or adopted after this point was classified as a changéant, the limitation effectively became an industrywide maximum. Fittingly, this decree also reiterated earlier prohibitions on purchases of thread outside the biweekly market. As the Vingtaine subsequently pointed out, if masters could own just six looms, they would have no need to circumvent the market to buy up large amounts of thread.[105]

III

By the eve of the Dutch Revolt, much of Lille's light-cloth industry had been endowed with a structure intended to block the rise of artisan as well as merchant entrepreneurs. Not all forms of change were rejected: In fact, the competitive position of light drapery depended on constant development or copying of new types of fabrics. But the Magistrat had acted to prevent innovation that would benefit individual producers at the expense of the majority. It fostered wide accessibility to raw material supplies, and it also curbed masters' efforts to reduce labor costs by employing apprentices and the unenfranchised, or by establishing large shops promising economies of scale. The regulations that had been put in place by the end of 1565 were designed, in sum, to thwart both the accumulation and the unfettered deployment of significant amounts of capital.

The new system was not constructed without resistance. As we have seen, each restriction on thread commerce led to renewed attempts to circumvent or to monopolize the market. But it was limits on loom

---

103 For the sections of the sayetterie statutes dealing with finishing, see ibid., 2:12, 14–15, arts. xxxii–xxxiii, xxxix–xlix (1500); 2:29, 30, 31, 35–40, arts. 15, 20, 22, 45–6, 52–70 (1524). The charter of the new guild is in AML, Reg. 16,002, fols. 159–61.

104 Violators were threatened with fines of 30 liv., far above the usual 40s. Vanhaeck, *Sayetterie à Lille*, 2:67, doc. 29.

105 AML, Aff. gén., C. 1171, d. 9, fol. 2.

ownership and on putting out – on, that is, ways by which those with sufficient capital could directly dominate production – that gave birth to the most protracted struggle. The quota promulgated in 1565 provoked the most vehement reactions. Some weavers repeatedly violated the law. Louis de Bus, for example, was prosecuted on at least three occasions for having in excess of six changéant looms and for hiring artisans to produce the fabric in their own shops.[106] Simultaneously, a number of masters – du Bus among them – pursued a judicial challenge all the way to the Privy Council in Brussels. Contending that Lille's restrictions were "contrary to the common good and . . . against the liberty allowed all hard-working and industrious folk to employ as many people as they want," the plaintiffs demanded that the entire law be voided and that they be authorized "to set to work as many workers and looms as they think best." But the royal councillors rejected the suit. They agreed with the municipal government (defendant in its capacity as de jure legislator in corporate affairs) that the common good was best served by maintaining the regulations as promulgated.[107]

To convince the Privy Council of the necessity of the disputed rules, the Vingtaine drew up a ten-page memorandum. Dating from a time when the regulative structure was all but complete, it not only justified the stipulations of the 1565 ordinance but specifically defended such earlier enactments as thread-market rules, quotas on satin and ostade looms, and the exclusion of everyone save certified masters from employing weavers. Thus it seems reasonable to take this document, from which I have already quoted several times, as indicative of the ideology underlying the system put together over the prior half century.[108]

The Vingtaine argued that petty production had numerous advantages for the overwhelming majority of Lille's light-cloth weavers, for the prosperity of their craft, and for the city as a whole, and warned that to dismantle the regulations would have dire consequences for each. As it stood, seven-eighths of all sayetteurs were petty artisans working in their own shops. Assured a steady supply of thread, the "daily practice" of weaving, and quick sales, they could support their families. Because, moreover, they earned "more profit than they needed for living ex-

[106] AML, Reg. 15,924, fols. 5v–6. See also Chapters 6 and 7.
[107] AML, Reg. 15,885, fols. 165–5v.
[108] The memorandum, AML, Aff. gén., C. 1171, d. 9, is the source of all remaining quotations in this section unless otherwise noted.

penses," they could even "put away some savings for help in case of illness or bad times." At the same time, the Vingtaine insisted, upward mobility remained a real possibility. With "a little help from relatives or friends," many poor sayetteurs had borrowed money, bought a loom, and eventually acquired several additional ones. Ironically, this had been the path followed by some of the most outspoken opponents of restrictive laws, notably Louis de Bus and the widow à Haighes.

Even those sayetteurs who were wage-earning master workers benefited from the present arrangements, the Vingtaine asserted. Because most masters were self-employed and the hiring of unfree labor was forbidden, the labor pool was small. Yet because some masters sought to exploit the opportunities offered by the expanding market, demand for workers was great. Indeed, with wages high and workers knowing that they would be kept on even when business slowed down, some were becoming "very haughty toward their masters," who were "compelled to put up with a great deal."[109] Jobs, whether in the family workshop or thread doubling and the like, were also widely available for women, children, and the aged.

According to the Vingtaine, small shops made "the opportunity for fraud minute" and thus guarded the "integrity" of the light-cloth crafts. Because a master either did most of the work himself or closely supervised a handful of workers, standards were maintained, "for which he [the master] is honored and the city gets a good reputation." Yet quality was not attained at the price of insufficient output, for merchants had always been able to get as much cloth as they requested. If anything, petty production tended nicely to balance supply and demand, avoiding harmful gluts.

Unfettering production would destroy this desirable order, the Vingtaine cautioned. Should controls be removed, that "small number of more powerful" masters with substantial capital would take control of weaving, reducing all their fellows to the status of mere "dependents and laborers." Willing to accept a lower profit per item in exchange for a larger sales volume, the big producers would undersell the small. Because existing demand was already being adequately filled, moreover, any increase in output on the part of large weavers could only come at

---

[109] Testimony from master bourgetteurs, dating from 1572, that they were reluctant to lay off workers during a slump for fear that few would return once an upturn began corroborates the Vingtaine's claim about workers' favorable position; see AML, Reg. 145, fols. 178–8v.

the expense of the petty. Unable to compete, many masters would be forced to give up their shops and "honorable way of life" and seek employment under the powerful, happy to earn a bare minimum. With the labor pool thus enlarged and jobs controlled by just a few men, workers would no longer enjoy security and wages would soon be pushed down to subsistence level. Should they become sick or get laid off, workers would have accumulated no reserves to fall back on and, like those never lucky enough to get hired, would "find themselves in extreme want." Eventually they would end up on the municipal welfare rolls, "at the expense of the whole community." Under these conditions, opportunities for upward mobility within the craft would sharply contract. The possibility of rising with the aid of borrowed money and hard work "would entirely cease" as the lines of status and income hardened.

Quality would likewise suffer from the reduced control possible in putting-out arrangements. Long hours, night work, and other methods of cutting corners would be unavoidable if workers were to earn enough to survive in the harsh new environment. In the end, predicted the guild leaders, a handful of weavers would "set to work fifty, sixty, 80 or 100 looms" as the entire industry fell under the domination of just ten or twelve men with virtual life-and-death power over their fellows. Such an outcome would result in "very great disadvantages as much for sayet-teurs on their own account as for the whole body of the community [*republicque*]." Should this prophecy be thought baseless speculation, the Vingtaine reported that before 1565 "some people were suspected of having undertaken and begun" just such concentrated control of large numbers of looms.

Thus, the Vingtaine submitted, pragmatic considerations justified sustaining petty production. Admittedly, regulation "hindered freedom," but it also preserved the livelihood of "an infinite number of masters." Although inequality obtained among weavers, upward mobility was a common phenomenon; just as important, polarization between a handful of wealthy, overweening entrepreneurs and a mass of impoverished workers was avoided. And with "strangers and unfree workers" barred from light-cloth weaving, all sorts of "frauds and sinister practices" were more easily repressed.

Defense of the structure that had evolved did not rest, however, solely on calculations of social and economic costs and benefits in comparison with a laissez-faire alternative, but on moral grounds as well. On the one side, the new social relations characteristic of a reorganized light-cloth industry would represent degradation for most weavers. In place of personal and professional autonomy, they would experience subjection, "oppression," and "ruin." Any hope of advancement would be taken away from masters, who could henceforth look forward to nothing but a continual struggle merely "to live from one day to the next." To prevent this from happening – to ensure that "everyone can have the means of earning a living without the lesser being trampled and oppressed by the progress of the most powerful" – had been, the Vingtaine declared, a principal reason for establishing restrictions.

On the other side, the Vingtaine deemed the motivations of the proponents of economic liberty unacceptable, because they consisted of nothing but greed – *avarice* and *convoitise*. It was *convoitise* that drove these well-to-do masters to earn a more than adequate income yet, possessed by the "intention of enriching themselves," to covet still more. It was "because of their *avarice*" that the "most powerful" masters "bear very impatiently that any bridle be put on their *convoitise*." And it was only with "the *avarice* of the rich curbed" that other weavers continued to have a chance of working their way up within the craft. The aspirations of would-be entrepreneurs were, in sum, the product of one of the seven deadly sins and therefore were not to be stimulated or even submitted to but vigorously fought.

Restrictionism was imperative, the Vingtaine implied, because by combatting greed it also expressed even-handed charity to all masters. Discontinuing curbs, on the contrary, would not solely condone transforming the relations of production; it would also sanction sinful conduct. Harmonious social, economic, and personal development would best be served by frustrating individual wishes rather than by liberating them. The drive to accumulate capital without restraint was viewed not as an economic boon but as a profound ethical failing.

IV

The presence of wage labor, the evidence of capital accumulation among some artisans, the indispensable role of merchants in this export-oriented industry, the existence of men proclaiming the virtues of individual initiative and liberty – these features that according to Pirenne signaled the birth of a new mode of production can certainly be found in sixteenth-century Lille's light drapery. It is noteworthy, however, that the

Magistrat increasingly took upon itself the task of forestalling the capitalist reorganization of these, the city's central crafts. Municipally controlled corporate bodies supervised the quality and quantity of output, terms of employment, and training practices. Markets were not freed, for numerous rules governed the acquisition of raw materials, the hiring of labor, and the investment of capital. Little increase was to occur in the scale of productive units: Output was instead to grow by the multiplication of small shops. In short, a body of regulation evolved that was consciously intended to protect autonomous petty masters against potential entrepreneurs, whether merchants or artisans. As far as the authorities were concerned, their actions were crowned with success: "The small and middling" weavers "have been very well off," the aldermen claimed when defending restrictive decrees in 1576, and the light-woolens trade prosperous.[110]

As the Vingtaine noted, there were both rich and poor artisans among Lille's light-cloth weavers,[111] but there are no signs that a proletariat was forming. A requirement that all workers have two years of training[112] – that they achieve, in other words, the same technical qualifications as masters – blurred the distinction between the two groups. This congruence was symbolized by a privilege, codified in the bourgetterie statutes, permitting married workers employed in putting-out arrangements to have an apprentice, and thereby to enjoy one of the defining prerogatives of mastership.[113] The availability of capital and the expansion of the industry also helped make upward as well as downward mobility a common occurrence.

Yet if Lille's sixteenth-century light-cloth trades were not capitalist as Pirenne thought, neither were they, *pace* Coornaert, marked by a "narrowly corporative spirit" or structure. For besides traditional features, sayetterie and bourgetterie incorporated major new elements that combined to form a distinctly urban system of small commodity production.[114] Expansion of output achieved by applying additional labor in-

---

110 The échevins' language was quoted in the Privy Council's 1576 decision, AML, Reg. 15,885, fol. 165v.
111 AML, Aff. gén., C. 1171, d. 9.
112 See Vanhaeck, *Sayetterie à Lille*, 2:10, doc. 3, art. xxii, 2:17, and 2:33, doc. 9, art. 30; *Lettres et statuts des bourgeteurs*, pp. 12–13, 14–15 (arts. xii–xiii, xxiv).
113 *Lettres et statuts des bourgeteurs*, p. 28.
114 For a more general discussion of this form of production, see Robert DuPlessis and Martha Howell, "Reconsidering the Early Modern Urban Economy: The Cases of Leiden and Lille," *PP* 94 (1982):49–84, from which some language in this chapter is taken.

puts and introducing new products, not to mention substantial special-ization and division of labor, effected a specific reconciliation of the pressures created by export-generated economic growth with political aims, social purposes, and moral imperatives. Entrepreneurial activities such as competition and investment were intrinsic to this system. Yet they were to be limited, as well as subordinated to social purposes judged more beneficial to individuals, industry, and society as a whole. Full employment, a moderate standard of living, producer autonomy, and rough equality among artisans were preferred to individual ac-cumulation of wealth and power. Production for the market accom-plished with infusions of capital naturally meant that there was constant impetus for innovation and change. But restrictions on mobilizing cap-ital and turning labor into a commodity frustrated the emergence of a capitalist order.

Lille's light drapery was not set within this regulated but flexible framework by inadvertence. To the contrary, in the course of instituting the urban small commodity system, the authorities knowingly frustrated the wishes of merchants and particularly artisans eager to invest in textile production. They also explicitly rejected an alternative concep-tion of how best to realize individual, craft, and community interests, a view that urged unrestricted latitude for entrepreneurial initiative.[115] Why was it that the ruling class embraced the ideology of small com-modity production rather than this other option?

Calculations of profit and loss, as we have seen, could have led poten-tial capitalists to construe their economic advantage either as compatible with petty production or as antagonistic to it. Although some merchants may have felt that they could better dictate terms to small producers,[116] the Vingtaine itself observed that the efficiencies associated with large units would most likely result in lower prices for traders.[117] Hence strictly economic determinants seem insufficient to account for the sup-port that small commodity production won.

The articulated needs of artisans themselves doubtless carried some

---

115 The most direct rebuff to the entrepreneurial ideal can be found in the aldermen's statement quoted by the Privy Council, AML, Reg. 15,885, fol. 165v, but echoes pervade many of the regulatory documents cited in this chapter.
116 This is, I believe, the position of Alain Derville, "L'héritage des draperies médiévales," *RN* 69 (1987):722–3, although his reference to a merchant oligopoly vis-à-vis producers is confusing both conceptually and empirically.
117 AML, Aff. gén., C. 1171, d. 9, fol. 2.

weight. Certainly, masters were not diffident about asking that their interests be protected. It was they who called for stricter enforcement of thread laws in 1506, and they continued to voice demands all across our period. Yet as we have seen, the distribution of power in Lille was such that merchants allied with professionals and seigneurs controlled the municipal government and, through it, the light-cloth corporations. Weavers could make their wishes known but were in no position to dictate policy to the political leadership. As a result, the small commodity system could not have been implemented had the members of the ruling class not been convinced of its benefits to them.

Assumptions about a proper social and moral order appear to have been important in this regard. Judging by the surviving documents, the city fathers and the Vingtaine subscribed to a paternalistic community ethic. This code obliged them to foster economic arrangements in which "everyone should have the opportunity to earn a living without the humblest being crushed by the advance of the most powerful."[118] It also obliged them to combat sinful behavior. Checking the ambitions of specific people and groups was thus justified in terms of advantages accruing to the city as a whole as well as to individuals.

But what seem to have been decisive in persuading the authorities to implement this ideal in the form and at the time that they did were political considerations: both the wish to solve immediate problems and the hope of perpetuating existing power relations. Surely, it was no accident that enactments on behalf of small masters increased in number and gravity as the established order appeared more seriously threatened after midcentury. The political elite might well have anticipated that favoring petty masters' distinctive status, rights, and obligations would eliminate important sources of disaffection among a large proportion of Lille's population. Assistance of this sort could also help legitimate the current structure of authority. At the same time, it would promote the continued vitality of a substantial middling element largely dependent on the municipal government for protection against would-be capitalist entrepreneurs. The view that a sturdy middle class was of pivotal significance for maintaining political stability was, after all, widely accepted.[119] And as already noted in Chapter 1, an urban economy of

---

[118] Ibid., fol. 1v.
[119] See, for example, Giovanni Botero, *The Reason of State* (1589), trans. P. J. and D. P. Waley (London, 1956), pp. 82–3.

petty producers ruled out the emergence of weighty entrepreneurs, based in the textile trades, who could have challenged merchants' political ascendancy. The system of small commodity production was constituted, in short, because it supported the social, economic, and moral structure of a community that the ruling class valued and of a political order that it intended to continue to dominate.

V

Economic development in sixteenth-century Lille hastened the appearance of new social groups and interests that both resembled and diverged from the picture drawn by Pirenne and his critics. Pirenne was surely correct to emphasize the effects of new men imbued with a spirit of initiative. By seizing opportunities offered by the expanding world market, Lille's merchants, predominantly recent arrivals of modest origins, made the city a leading commercial center. Yet they flourished to a large extent by intensively exploiting old methods, and neither they nor would-be entrepreneurs like Louis de Bus managed to transform the most dynamic sector of Lille's industry in a capitalistic direction. Conversely, the emergence of a system of small commodity production meant that the laboring population in the city's principal crafts consisted neither of proletarians nor of a restricted guild oligarchy, but of autonomous small and middling artisans and skilled workers.

To a large extent, the long-term viability of this sizable group depended on protections afforded by the municipally controlled corporate structure. The Loi's measures in the first two-thirds of the sixteenth century attempted to curb structural change, but they also reveal that endeavors directed at effecting such change persisted. Over the short run, however, the state of the urban economy was a function of the health of markets at home and abroad, over which the municipal authorities had little influence. The economic cycle, in other words, had direct repercussions on the condition of Lillois – and increasingly so as the endemically cyclical woolens crafts experienced sharper oscillations in the decade or so prior to 1566. Because most interpretations point to unsettled material conditions as providing the environment in which Protestantism and political unrest flourished, it seems appropriate at this point to investigate the evolving standard of living in prerevolt Lille.

4

Impoverishment and intervention

In Lille as throughout Europe, vigorous economic growth during the sixteenth century was accompanied by inflation that drove the cost of living to hitherto unimagined heights. Both the long-term trend and the terrible circumstances prevailing in the mid-1560s have led historians to propose that deteriorating material conditions hastened the coming of the Dutch Revolt. But specifying the factors that actually engendered discontent, the manner in which people were affected, and the critical sectors of the populace that were harmed have proved contentious. Was rebellion triggered by widespread absolute deprivation, an interdecennial process of impoverishment that drove the broad masses to acts of desperation?[1] Or was it brought about by the sudden onset of depression in the 1560s, a jolt that threatened to reverse the rising standard of living to which skilled artisans and other middling elements had become accustomed during the previous half century?[2]

I

Thanks to the survival of several series of data, the history of the cost of living in early modern Lille can be charted in some detail. Beginning in 1508, grain prices are provided by the *priserie des bledz et avoines de l'espier et domaine de Lille*, a register of official quotations published yearly to facilitate the conversion into monetary terms of seigneurial

---

[1] This is the position of Pirenne, *Histoire de Belgique*, esp. 3:282–6, 292–5, 450, 466; Erich Kuttner, *Het Hongerjaar 1566* (Amsterdam, 1949); and Verlinden, Craeybeckx, and Scholliers, "Price and Wage Movements."

[2] For this view, see Etienne Scholliers, *De Levensstandaard in de XVe en XVIe eeuw te Antwerpen* (Antwerp, 1960), esp. pp. 133–7, 271–4; and Herman Van der Wee, "The Economy as a Factor in the Start of the Revolt in the Southern Netherlands," *Acta Historiae Neerlandicae* 5 (1971):52–67.

rents originally owed in kind. Archives of hospitals, hospices and asylums contain extensive information on prices of other foodstuffs and household necessities, as well as listings of the rents collected for numerous houses throughout the city that the hospices owned. Finally, the financial accounts of the municipal government provide wage rates for skilled craftsmen and laborers hired to build and maintain civic property, notably fortifications.[3]

Although abundant, these records present numerous difficulties of use and interpretation, which are considered in Appendix F. It is clear from that discussion that ascertaining the standard of living in sixteenth-century Lille entails the use of imperfect information, choice among controversial assumptions, and computations based on both of these. Nonetheless, many of the critical deficiencies in the data can be offset if not corrected. In what follows, the available material is examined from several perspectives. Prices and wages are surveyed to determine the movement of real income; then they are compared with an index of economic activity to pinpoint hard times. Trends are evaluated to deduce the proportions of income needed to meet subsistence requirements. In cases where there is no conclusive reason to prefer one alternative, as in the matter of family size or that of per capita grain consumption, calculations have been carried out according to liberal as well as restrictive criteria. Admittedly, the results obtained are unlikely to recreate the experience of any particular Lillois of the time. But they do help us understand both the relative and the absolute impact of inflation on model families headed by master artisans and laborers, not only over the 1501–65 period as a whole, but also during crises, particularly the one that immediately preceded the initial revolutionary outburst.

Let us begin comparing wages with decennial prices of about a dozen items constituting major family expenditures between 1501 and 1565.[4] Although the rates and schedules of price movements varied among commodities, Table 4.1 shows that all went up in cost. Meat and grains increased the most, beer and salt the least. Most items rose in cost from

---

[3] The grain *priserie* is currently AML, Reg. 797; the hospital archives are in the AH; and the town financial records for the sixteenth century are AML, Reg. 895, 16,237–337.

[4] According to Scholliers, *Levensstandaard*, pp. 34–5, 200–5, 264–5, residents of the Low Countries bought about twice as much cheese as butter, but only butter prices are given in Table 4.1 because of discontinuous cheese price data. Moreover, comparisons indicate that the rate and timing of price movements for butter and cheese coincided, so butter can serve as an accurate indicator of trends in the cost of dairy products. Wax is included because it was the raw material for candles.

Table 4.1. *The evolution of indexes of prices, rents, and wages in Lille, 1501–65*
(100 = mean, 1511–12 through 1520–1)

Period	Prices													Rents	Wages	
	Wheat	Rye	Beef	Pork	Herring	Butter	Red wine	Beer	Coal	Black cloth	Soap	Wax	Salt		Master mason	Laborer
1501–10	86	81	*100*	85	*103*	81	*110*	82	86	95	83	(96)	77	98	100	100
1511–20	100	100	*100*	100	*100*	100	*100*	100	100	100	100	100	100	100	100	100
1521–30	152	138	*136*	141	*136*	107	*143*	107	(150)	111	123	79	*158*	101	100	100
1531–40	167	147	*150*	116	*129*	116	*127*	111	119	105	129	85	120	106	100	106
1541–50	191	155	*184*	119	*151*	145	(110)	106	145	(139)	128	(75)	101	152	100	106
1551–60	253	239	*255*	151	*191*	180	*159*	123	(194)	(178)	(120)	(178)	123	159	117	120
1561–5	296	274	*337*	267	*237*	219	*183*	125	179	209	(225)	216	130	167	143	149

Notes: Numbers in parentheses indicate four or fewer price notations during the decade. Italicized numbers indicate that the index of that commodity equaled or exceeded the wheat index.

Sources: for wheat, AML, Reg. 797 and Françoise Charlet and Claude Lecompte, "Revenus, salaires, profits dans les Flandres sous l'Ancien Régime d'après les revenus de l'Hôpital Comtesse" (Mémoire de maîtrise, Université de Lille III, 1969), p. 70; for rye, *Dokumenten voor de Geschiedenis van Prijzen en Lonen in Vlaanderen en Brabant (XVe–XVIIIe eeun)*, for other commodities and some rents, AH Comtesse, Reg. 4443–532; for additional rents, AH Bonnes Filles, Reg. E3–9; for beer, Louis Dubois, *Le régime de la brasserie à Lille, des origines à la Révolution (1279–1789)* (Lille, 1912), Annexe II; for wages, AML, Reg. 895, 16,237–99.

the very beginning of the century, with the rate of increases quickening during the 1520s. Conversely, prices eased or even declined in the 1530s and 1540s. But then, paced by rents, which after lagging behind jumped steeply in the 1540s, prices of nearly all goods surged ahead once again during the 1550s, continuing upward in the years immediately preceding the outbreak of the revolt. Wages, on the other hand, exhibited remarkable stability. From the 1520s they lagged well behind prices, the gap growing larger as the sixteenth century advanced. Master masons got no raise until 1557, just a few years after laborers received their first significant increase. And although wages rose some more during the early 1560s, they failed utterly to match the simultaneous spurt in prices.

Wheat and rye will be discussed in greater detail later in this chapter but a few peculiarities of the price histories merit brief comment here. The rising cost of beef despite higher grain prices may well provide ammunition for Van der Wee's contention that the middle class was growing in both size and well-being. But it appears also to be symptomatic of supply problems to which a decline in Walloon Flanders cattle herds surely contributed.[5] Conversely, the fact that the great majority of prices lagged behind the cost of grain – often far behind – raises doubts as to the breadth and depth of the supposed wave of prosperity. In a context of sluggish wages, indeed, the slower rates of inflation posted by most commodities strongly suggest that large numbers of Lillois had to use an increasing proportion of their incomes for grain, thereby reducing demand for other goods.

Erratic wine prices can in some degree be attributed to variations in the size and quality of vintages. But like salt prices, which exhibited similar irregularities, they are also testimony to persistent – if only partially successful – speculative and monopolistic efforts.[6] The abrupt acceleration of rental increases during the 1540s indicates that the housing stock was becoming inadequate in the face of heightened immigration called forth by the expansion of the light-cloth industry,[7] and

[5] Comparison of surveys of the castellany taken in 1505 and 1541–9 shows that the number of cattle dropped more than 12%, while population was growing; see ADN, Reg. B 3762–3, and Appendix A.

[6] See the comments of Verlinden, Craeybeckx, and Scholliers, "Price and Wage Movements," esp. pp. 61, 62, 65, 69–71.

[7] For evidence that the number of immigrants may have grown by a third or more between the early sixteenth century and the 1530s, see AML, Reg. 276–7, 955–7.

resulted in unrealized projects for extending the town walls, as cited in Appendix A. When collated with the wage data, the movement of the prices of coal, cloth, and soap – all goods embodying a significant labor component – intimates that in many crafts pay was not raised until well after the beginning of the rise in food prices.

Increasingly inadequate wages and a consequent enforced switch in demand cannot account for the chronically very slow rise in the beer index. Consumption of large quantities of beer – probably about 1.5 liters per day for each adult, judging by information from Louvain and Antwerp[8] – was virtually mandatory if the heavily salted and often excessively mature diet of most early modern Europeans was to be made palatable. The explanation for the price history presented here – and for another peculiarity of the cost of beer, its constant fluctuations within a narrow range – lies rather in the source of the data. What we have are maximum prices, decreed by Lille's aldermen, which varied in relation to the cost of grain according to a formula devised in 1474, not in response to market forces.[9]

Now the posted prices were not necessarily at variance with actual costs to consumers, for the Magistrat employed officials to enforce the regulations and collect the retail beer tax. But they could be. According to one chronicle, a lot (2.12 liters) of beer was selling for 10 deniers in April 1545, when the maximum was 8 deniers, while a year later the market price was 2 deniers below the limit.[10] Such discrepancies become understandable when it is realized that the maximum commonly remained stationary for long period, failing in particular to respond adequately to the rising cost of raw materials. In 1565–6, for example, when the price index of wheat stood at 444, oats at 325, barley at about 300, and hops around 200, beer was supposed to be at 136.[11] Besides outright violations of mandated prices, brewers also circumvented the

---

8 Scholliers, *Levensstandaard*, pp. 61 n. 64, 267.
9 Dubois, *Régime de la brasserie*, pp. 92–101, prints the formula.
10 *Chronique de Mahieu Manteau et de Pierre-Ignace Chavatte*, ed. E. Debrièvre (Lille, 1911), pp. 21–2.
11 For the price data, see AML, Reg. 797, and AH Comtesse, Reg. 4443–500, 4504–32. The Magistrat was quicker to slash the posted beer price as the cost of grain declined, though the reductions – like the increases – were not as great as the change in the grain price. Thus in 1557, when a fine harvest cut wheat prices nearly in half, beer was reduced from 10 to 8 d. a lot, and a further decrease in grain prices the next year led to another lowering of the beer maximum, this time to 7 d.

maximum by diluting their beer. Sometimes they acted illegally,[12] but on crisis occasions at the behest of the Magistrat, which sought to ease the pressure on the grain supply by reserving it for bread.[13] Even more than in regard to other commodities, therefore, it would seem wise not to regard the beer index as precise testimony about the cost of a determinate product. Rather, it should be considered a figure that reflects both the Magistrat's aspirations to influence inflation and the approximate location of the price of a critical yet variable commodity.

Because cereals were central to the diet and thus the cost of living, the price history of grain deserves close scrutiny. Table 4.1 discloses that the cost of wheat and rye rose all across the first two-thirds of the sixteenth century, while Figure 4.1 gives a detailed view of the upward trend, revealing that every decade had a major price peak interspersed with one or more less drastic increases.[14] The graph shows that inflation was concentrated in two longish periods: from the early 1520s to the mid-1530s, and again from the late 1540s to the middle of the 1560s. A century of price stagnation came to an end shortly after 1510,[15] but it was only during the 1520s that inflation noticeably accelerated. The jump in the wheat price from 1523–4 to 1524–5 was, in relative terms, the largest (180 percent) to occur in any single year during the sixteenth century, and substantial increases occurred about every three years from 1521–2 to 1536–7. In the second major period of inflation, the 1550s and early 1560s, increases came even more frequently and reached new heights, the most extreme being recorded in 1565–6. During this phase, too, occurred the worst leap in prices from year to year after the extraor-

[12] In 1512, for instance, Lille's aldermen refused to augment beer prices on the ground that brewers had already increased their profit margins by watering their product; Dubois, *Régime de la brasserie*, pp. 116–17.

[13] In the regular formula, oats comprised 45%, barley 32%, and wheat 23% of the grain component of beer. A temporary recipe employed in 1521 cut the amounts of barley and wheat in half, whereas in 1546 wheat was entirely eliminated; see Dubois, *Régime de la brasserie*, pp. cxxxiii (my calculations are based on information given therein), clxiii, clxv, 151. Verlinden, Craeybeckx, and Scholliers, "Price and Wage Movements," p. 66, note that orders to dilute beer were common during grain shortages.

[14] Figure 4.1 is based on data from AML, Reg. 797, 895, 16,237–99. Comparison with yearly averages derived from accounts of the Hôpital Comtesse suggests that the prices indicated on the figure may be too low for 1521–2, 1564–5, and 1565–6 (they should be raised by as much as a quarter), and too high for 1531–2, 1544–5, 1551–2, and 1558–60 (these figures should be reduced by between a sixth and a half); see Charlet and Lecompte, "Revenus, salaires, profits," p. 70. The only effect that these alterations have on the interpretation outlined below is to emphasize even more the seriousness of the period of high inflation in the mid-1560s.

[15] See Derville, "De 1300 à 1500," p. 160, fig. 16, for fifteenth-century wheat prices.

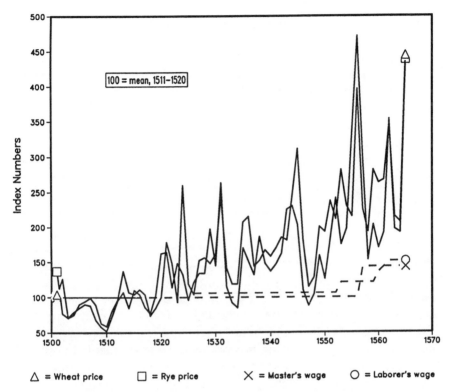

Figure 4.1. Grain prices and wage rates in Lille, 1501–65.

dinary rise of 1524–5. From 1555–6 to 1556–7, the increase for wheat was 84 percent (due to missing data, the comparable figure for rye cannot be calculated), and between 1564–5 and 1565–6 it amounted to 114 percent for wheat, 129 percent for rye. Whereas in earlier crises, moreover, rye prices had generally remained below wheat, in the mid-1550s and early 1560s the price movements of the two grains regularly coincided. During the most difficult years, in fact, rye even attained the highest levels. Thus low-income people who probably often purchased rye were caught in a cruel scissors.

Comparisons with wage rates indicate just how adverse the effects of the price rises must have been. Most likely because continuous immigration fed the labor pool, municipal wage scales did not advance during the entire first half of the sixteenth century, aside from a modest increase

125

in the winter pay of laborers (from 4 sols a day to 5) granted in 1526.[16] It is worth emphasizing that wages stagnated despite both a number of harsh crises when the cost of living shot up and the undramatic but remorseless inflation that characterized the whole period. Only a cluster of bad harvests, sharp rises in the cost of all items, and a visitation of contagious disease – which by killing at least a thousand people must have tightened the urban labor supply – finally forced wages up in the 1550s and early 1560s. As Figure 4.1 reveals, laborers received incremental raises in 1553, 1560, 1561, and 1562 that in the end yielded a daily wage of 8 sols in the summer, 5 in the winter (index 151). For their part, master masons advanced all at once in 1557 from 10 sols (summer) and 8 (winter) to 14 and 12 respectively (index 143).

The augmentation of wages due to exorbitant prices and high mortality was general throughout the Netherlands in the years around 1556–7.[17] Probably because the increases were both substantial and widespread, they generated a controversy that hints at why raises had been granted so tardily and reluctantly, while also disclosing what interested contemporaries thought should be done about inflation. According to one view current among political elites, workers' pay had risen so much that they were "almost holding to ransom and oppressing their masters . . . by refusing to work, preferring to spend almost half their day in idleness, wretchedly spending their huge and unreasonable earnings in taverns and cabarets."[18] Heeding such complaints, in 1561 the government in Brussels considered enforcing a uniform wage reduction everywhere in the Netherlands or at least imposing maximum daily rates of pay. Before any program was implemented, however, provincial officials were asked to express their opinions.

Like most of his colleagues, the lieutenant governor of Walloon Flanders, Denis de le Cambe, advised against the proposal. While describing wages as currently "very excessive," thereby permitting some laborers to give themselves to idleness, and others to purchase clothing and jewelry inappropriate to their station, de le Cambe pointed out that the cost of

---

[16] Hôpital Comtesse records indicate that its employees got no raise at all until 1544.

[17] Cf. Scholliers, *Levensstandaard*, pp. 133–4, 272–3 (the same period of plague and famine likewise resulted in a labor shortage and increased wages in Antwerp); Offermans, *Arbeid en Levensstandaard*, pp. 147–53; Etienne Scholliers, "Le pouvoir d'achat dans les Pays-Bas au XVIe siècle," in *Album Charles Verlinden* (Ghent, 1975), p. 309.

[18] Statement by the Great Council in Mechelen, quoted in Verlinden, Craeybeckx, and Scholliers, "Price and Wage Movements," p. 73.

living had also remained high. Low maxima would thus force many workers and their families to resort to begging. On their side, "honorable" (*honnestes*) people might well seek to attain subsistence by setting their children to work in some craft – which was already current practice among "many villagers," de le Cambe alleged, perhaps alluding to the growing rural textile industry. If this were to occur, laborers and skilled workers alike would be impoverished, presumably because of the increased competition for jobs. Worse, by destroying incentives a standard rate would penalize good workers and pander to bad ones. In any event, it would be all but a dead letter, because a great deal of work was remunerated on a piece-rate rather than a per diem basis.

As for pay cuts, the lieutenant governor judged that they could succeed only if rigorously administered price controls were simultaneously prescribed for food, clothing, and industrial raw materials. Convinced that such measures were not feasible, de le Cambe offered what he considered more realistic advice. Vagabonds should be put to work, forcibly if necessary, and all workers should be bound to their current employers until given permission to leave. Sumptuary laws that had fallen into disuse should be revived, for in their absence many workers and servants purchased expensive but unnecessary clothing, and to support their new tastes they demanded unreasonable salaries.[19]

In the end, the government took no action. Growing religious unrest, as well as demographic recovery and migration,[20] probably had much to do with this outcome. It is striking, nonetheless, how even after decades of inflation the authorities continued to assume that wages should be stable. They thought, too, that raises were undesirable, encouraging the disruption of order and the social hierarchy, and should be exceptional, perhaps even temporary. In common with Lille's Magistrat, these officials were convinced that nonmarket forces, essentially government intervention, could and should regulate labor. Disagreement over whether to rely on mandatory pay scales or to have recourse to limits on mobility and consumption did not shake that fundamental consensus. Little wonder, then, that the price increases of the 1560s, steep though they were, brought such minor wage gains to Lillois.

[19] De le Cambe's letter, dated 22 February 1561, is printed in *Prijzen en Lonenpolitiek in de Nederlanden in 1561 en 1588–1589. Onuitgegeven adviezen, ontwerpen en ordonnanties*, ed. Charles Verlinden and Jan Craeybeckx (Brussels, 1962), pp. 66–9.

[20] Between 1555 and 1565, purchase of citizen status (bourgeoisie) by immigrants to Lille, as calculated from AML, Reg. 956–7, was at its highest level for the entire sixteenth century.

The evidence from Lille confirms that real wages declined almost without interruption across the four decades from the early 1520s to the mid-1550s, and that the end of the period was a time of acute difficulty. But what of the years just preceding the revolt? Did they see a continuing process of impoverishment, or did they form, as Van der Wee and Scholliers maintain, a time of an initially favorable wage–price ratio that abruptly soured?

Comparing grain price and wage indexes helps clarify the situation. The figures in Table 4.2A support the contention that real wages were high during the late 1550s and into the early 1560s: Unbroken impoverishment was not a feature of the prerevolutionary decade.[21] At the same time, Table 4.2B shows that the long-existing gap between prices and income was not wiped out during these years, although examination of Figure 4.1 suggests that the difference had not been so small since the 1520s. But it is equally evident that soaring grain prices and stagnant wages in 1562–3 quickly wiped out the gains of the prior few years and that the hyperinflation of 1565–6 was nothing short of catastrophic. Although the proportional jump in prices from 1564–5 to 1565–6 was less than that registered between 1523–4 and 1524–5, the absolute difference between wheat prices and wages was far above anything previously encountered. Rye prices were also so high that consumers could find little relief by substituting rye for wheat.[22] Table 4.2 also discloses that prices in Lille as elsewhere had already declined noticeably before iconoclasm began in the late summer of 1566 (a time whose price history is captured in the 1566–7 indexes), if not to the levels of two years before. Despite this improvement, it seems reasonable to assume that the shattering experience of the past few years would have created lingering problems and, as Verlinden, Craeybeckx, and Scholliers have contended, widespread resentment.[23]

Besides wage and price levels, the amount of work is of crucial importance to the standard of living. It is impossible, of course, to obtain for sixteenth-century Lille any measurement of the length of the average work week or the unemployment rate, which are the modern criteria.

---

[21] Fragmentary figures available from the Hôpital Comtesse suggest that in 1558–9 and 1559–60 wheat prices were considerably lower than the priserie shows.

[22] Only in 1556–7, when it was the cost of rye that diverged the most from wages, did the gaps approach those of 1565–6.

[23] Verlinden, Craeybeckx, and Scholliers, "Price and Wage Movements," pp. 66–8.

Table 4.2. *Price and wage indexes in Lille,*
1556–7 through 1566–7

Year	Prices		Wages	
	Wheat	Rye	Master mason	Laborer
A. 100 = mean, 1556–7 through 1565–6				
1556–7	139	176	72	89
1557–8	80	113	103	89
1558–9	68	57	103	89
1559–60	99	76	103	89
1560–1	93	64	103	99
1561–2	94	72	103	105
1562–3	123	132	103	110
1563–4	76	74	103	110
1564–5	73	72	103	110
1565–6	156	164	103	110
1566–7	97	86	103	110
B. 100 = mean, 1511–12 through 1520–1				
1556–7	396	471	100	121
1557–8	226	301	143	121
1558–9	193	153	143	121
1559–60	281	203	143	121
1560–1	263	170	143	136
1561–2	267	192	143	143
1562–3	348	353	143	151
1563–4	215	197	143	151
1564–5	207	192	143	151
1565–6	444	438	143	151
1566–7	274	230	143	151

Sources: See Table 4.1.

But the availability of work can be gauged indirectly, if less precisely, by examining the overall level of economic activity. To be sure, no global figures exist, yet we do have very good information, derived from tax receipts, about output of light cloth. This was, as we have seen, by far

Lille's leading industry, and one with linkages to many other sectors of the urban economy.

Deductions for minor administrative expenses, the unavailability of statistics for textiles woven by bourgetteurs before 1541, and the aggregation of different types of fabrics made by sayetteurs complicate the use of these numbers. But these problems do not invalidate the data. The deductions were quite insignificant – less than 1 percent of the reported figures, if that.[24] Bourgetterie output must have been very small before 1541, for in that year revenue from bourgetterie taxes added up to less than 4 percent of the total for all light woolens. Finally, although the numbers cannot tell us how many pieces of cloth were woven, they are a more accurate measurement of total workdays. The different types of fabric were taxed at rates roughly proportional to the length of time it took to make them, so the most rapidly woven stuffs like changéants and ostades paid the least. For the same reason, the tax figures capture the productivity gains realized by the adoption of very light cloth. What with immigration, of course, it would be incorrect to think that light-cloth output data can help us determine the work history of individuals. They do, however, allow us to follow the trend of employment opportunities in the pace-setting sector of the urban economy.[25]

Figure 4.2 compares economic activity, as measured by the taxes levied on light cloth, with the cost of wheat and rye to determine when rising prices coincident with less work might have confronted Lillois with particularly grim material problems. It suggests that once the difficult 1520s were over, the 1530s, 1540s, and much of the 1550s were on the whole times of both high levels of employment and relatively favorable grain prices. With the exception of 1563–4, on the contrary, the years from 1562 through 1566 were grim. Many townspeople must have been squeezed simultaneously by drastic inflation, which wage increases could do little to relieve, and by lower demand for their labor and its products. In terms of the availability of jobs, then, as in the sharp decline in real wages revealed in Table 4.2A, the years immediately preceding the outbreak of the revolt seem to have been characterized by the sudden deterioration in material conditions postulated by the frustrated

[24] Deyon and Lottin, "Production textile à Lille," p. 25 n. 16.
[25] Sources for Figure 4.2: AML, Reg. 797, 895, 16,237–99; Vanhaeck, *Sayetterie à Lille*, 1:353–4; Deyon and Lottin, "Production textile à Lille," pp. 30–1.

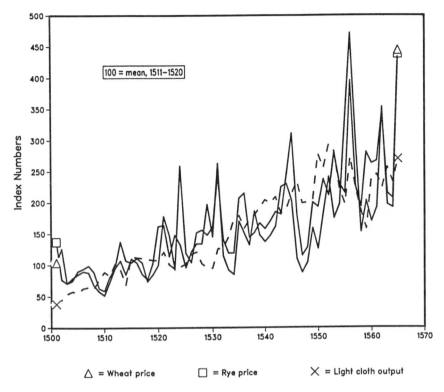

Figure 4.2. Grain prices and economic activity in Lille, 1501–65.

expectations thesis. Further, it seems reasonable to expect that some Lillois might have considered this turn of events a threatening break with a more promising situation – at least in regard to employment – that had characterized much of the reign of Charles V.

Yet a longer view, informed by the data in Tables 4.1 and 4.2B as well as Figure 4.2, lends support to the absolute impoverishment interpretation. From this perspective, too, the harshness of the mid-1560s stands out, but these years can also be understood as constituting one more phase in a protracted erosion of living standards. Conversely, the upturn of 1558–62 looks like simply another of the transitory periods of recovery that once a decade in the past (mid-1520s, early 1530s, late 1540s) had brought a respite in, but no permanent reversal of, the downward trend. All the evidence, in short, converges to underline the calamitous nature of the several years prior to the revolt, though not the final months. But contemporaries could have judged this period of adversity to constitute either a sharp break with more auspicious recent circumstances or the resumption of a relentless process of decay.

Without direct testimony, it is difficult to decide this issue. But we may be able to narrow the possibilities by considering the wage and price data from a different angle: the actual ability of Lillois to obtain sufficient grain for their families. Let us begin by calculating according to assumptions delineated in Appendix F: that the average family size was between four and five, that each person consumed three to four rasières of grain per year, that people worked 250 days a year, that each family had one breadwinner, and that the wage information we have is representative of larger groups of urban dwellers than simply the men employed in the building trades to whom it directly refers. Table 4.3 gives the results of computations made on the basis of these suppositions. The number on the left of each column represents the cost of twelve rasières of grain (three rasières for each of four people), while on the right is the cost of twenty rasières (four for each of five persons). The former can be considered the absolute minimum for a small family, the latter a richer diet or one intended for a larger unit.

Comparison of these figures with the estimates presented in Appendix F makes it clear that an income like that of a fully employed master mason could always provide sufficient wheat to feed even a large family. With the exception of 1556–7, 1562–3, and 1565–6, moreover, a substantial amount would remain for other commodities and perhaps for savings. If some of the grain requirement was filled by rye, a yet larger surplus remained. Unskilled laborers and their families, on the contrary, were consistently much less well off, even if they were fortunate enough to find steady work. Probably as early as the 1520s, as a matter of fact, laborers relying on a single income who wanted to eat wheaten instead of rye bread would have found it difficult to afford the other foodstuffs, clothing, fuel, and housing that composed the rest of their budgets. Ordinarily, masters' families might eat what they wanted. Unskilled workers, in contrast, faced a constant struggle merely to fulfill their households' minimum requirements. Subsistence was a problem for laborers across nearly the entire first two-thirds of the sixteenth century, but it became more acute during the second third.

The greatest loss in purchasing power relative to the cost of grain

Table 4.3. *Percentage of annual income needed to purchase grain for family of four or five persons in sixteenth-century Lille*

Period	Wheat		Rye	
	Master mason	Laborer	Master mason	Laborer
A. Averages				
1501–10	12–20	24–40	10–16	20–32
1511–20	14–23	28–46	12–20	24–40
1521–30	21–35	41–68	17–28	33–55
1531–40	23–38	43–72	18–30	34–57
1541–50	26–44	49–82	19–32	36–60
1551–60	30–50	58–97	25–42	49–82
1561–5	29–48	55–91	24–39	45–75
B. Worst year in each period				
1502–3/1501–2[a]	17–29	35–58	17–28	34–56
1513–4	19–31	38–62	13–22	26–44
1524–5/1529–30[a]	36–60	71–119	24–40	46–76
1531–2	34–56	63–106	32–54	61–101
1545–6/1544–5[a]	43–71	81–134	28–47	53–89
1556–7	38–64	90–150	41–68	95–159
1565–6	43–72	81–135	38–63	71–119
C. Prerevolt period (1556–7 through 1566–7)[b]				
1556–7	38–64	90–150	41–68	95–159
1557–8	22–36	51–86	26–43	61–102
1558–9	19–31 (15–25)	44–73 (35–59)	13–22	31–52
1559–60	27–45 (15–25)	60–100 (33–56)	17–29	39–64
1560–1	25–42	51–86	15–24	30–50
1561–2	26–43	50–83	17–28	32–53
1562–3	34–56	64–106	30–51	57–96
1563–4	21–35	39–65	17–28	32–53
1564–5	20–33 (28–46)	38–63 (52–87)	17–28	31–52
1565–6	43–72 (53–88)	81–135 (99–166)	38–63	71–119
1566–7	27–44 (30–50)	50–83 (56–94)	20–33	37–62

[a]Worst year for wheat/worst year for rye. For other periods, worst year was the same.
[b]Wheat equivalences given in parentheses are derived from material from the Hôpital Comtesse.
Sources: See Table 4.1.

occurred during the 1520s. Yet before midcentury, the nearly total lack of coincidence between peak wheat and rye prices may have cushioned inflationary pressures by allowing the substitution of one cereal for the other. Beginning in 1556–7, however, the worst years tended to synchronize; at the same time, rye prices started to hit heights very close to or even above those of wheat. In these circumstances, wage increases were quickly eroded and savings built up in prior years depleted. Reference back to Figure 4.2, which shows the poor employment situation in 1556–7, 1562–3, and 1564–6, indicates that for many people life in those years must have been even harsher than the data in Table 4.3C suggest.

Other evidence likewise points to a worsening situation in Lille after midcentury. Increasing numbers of children were abandoned and husbands deserted their wives and families.[26] As the crisis struck throughout the Low Countries, beggars and vagabonds swarmed into cities, taxing the grain supply and charity facilities. Starting in late 1554, Lille suffered through an epidemic – considered by many modern authorities to have been influenza, though contemporaries may have been correct when they called it plague – that killed in excess of 1,100 people before it disappeared sometime in 1559.[27] Exasperated by months of high prices, scarcity, and death, in June 1557 disorderly crowds in the grain market showered merchants with such abuse that city officials feared that a riot might be touched off.[28] In the next few months, a good harvest brought some easing of prices, but only a year later they rose precipitously again. From 1559–60 through 1562–3, the cost of wheat remained high, and in the latter year rye actually surpassed it (Table 4.2B; Figures 4.1 and 4.2).

So severe was the dearth that the municipal government sent deputations to search out wheat at the staple markets at Douai and Ghent, at rich abbeys, and from important landowners in the castellany. In 1562,

---

[26] See, for example, AML, Reg. 15,922, fols. 131, 132, 132v, 135, 144v.
[27] For the identification of the contagion as influenza, see Parker, *Dutch Revolt*, p. 39; for the view that it may indeed have been a form of plague, see *The Plague Reconsidered. A New Look at Its Origins and Effects in 16th and 17th Century England* (Matlock, 1977). No fatality figures are available for 1556, though we know the disease persisted. For the other years, see AML, Reg. 16,288, fols. 231v, 238v, 241, 243v, 245v (1554); Reg. 16,289, fols. 303, 305, 306v, 316–16v, 320–2, 330 (1555); Reg. 16,291, fols. 292, 314v–15, 320 (1557); Reg. 16,292, fols. 290, 293 (1558); Reg. 15,922, fols. 154v–8v, 167v.
[28] AML, Reg. 381, fol. 114.

the Magistrat even dispatched several men to Danzig for rye.[29] At the same time, the aldermen inspected warehouses and cellars to discourage hoarding and speculating,[30] while trying to curb provocative conspicuous consumption by enforcing more strictly existing laws that limited attendance at wedding feasts.[31] At least in 1563 the festivities that usually accompanied the municipal procession were suspended because with the prices of foodstuffs rising daily the "small earnings" of many Lillois could not bear the expense.[32] In another sure sign of hard times, the Magistrat repeatedly attempted to restrict entry to Lille, forbid mendicancy, and expel anyone who had not been a resident for at least three years.[33] But in the end, all earthly measures came to naught, so the city fathers ordered taverns shuttered, called townspeople together, and mounted a special procession that wound through the city behind the Host, stopping frequently to pray God for "favorable weather" for crops.[34]

These years of inflation and suffering, although interrupted by a brief respite in 1563–5 – or perhaps, in view of the deteriorating employment situation in 1564, just in 1563–4 – provided the somber background for the "hunger year" of 1565–6. In that dismal time, wheat and rye prices soared in consequence of a poor domestic harvest, temporary cessation of Baltic imports, and speculation. The depth of the crisis can be measured by the many steps the Magistrat took to alleviate shortages. In a flurry of hastily and recurrently enacted ordinances the authorities opened the municipally administered grain market every day (not merely twice a week), demanded that cereals even passing through the city be sold to anyone wishing to buy, revived a requirement that grain exports obtain "passports," then enjoined all such shipments from Lille.[35] Be-

---

29 See AML, Reg. 16,286, fols. 138–8v; Reg. 16,290, fols. 156–6v; Reg. 16,291, fols. 180v–1, 315v, 319; Reg. 277, fol. 153v; Reg. 16,297, fols. 176–6v.
30 AML, Reg. 16,297, fol. 175. In "Price and Wage Movements," Verlinden, Craeybeckx, and Scholliers conclude (p. 60) that in the sixteenth century Netherlands speculators did drive up prices during crises and then maintained them at a higher level than would have resulted from the free play of market forces. "The main effect of external circumstances" like speculation, however, "was to intensify the already existing natural trends towards crisis."
31 AML, Reg. 15,922, fols. 119, 120v.
32 Reg. 381, fol. 193.
33 AML, Reg. 15,922, fols. 162v, 164–4v, 165v; Reg. 381, fols. 102–22.
34 AML, Reg. 382, fols. 2–2v.
35 Ibid., fols. 13v–15, 5 May 1565. For grain passports, first mentioned in January 1552, see AML, Reg. 16,286, fols. 135v, 268–8v, 279, 281v; Reg. 16,288, fols. 231v, 238v, 245v; Reg. 16,299, fols. 217v–19. For the edict prohibiting grain exports, see AML, Reg. 382, fols. 20, 23v–4, 42–2v. First published on 13 August 1565, it was repeated on at least the following occasions: 18

yond trying to increase supplies, the aldermen strove again to curtail consumption by republishing laws banning or restricting banquets and other nonessential gatherings. They also expelled as many poor people as they could lay their hands on.[36] Despite all these efforts, the price spiral proved impossible to master, grain became nearly unobtainable at any cost, and the winter turned out to be one of the coldest on record.

By the eve of the revolt, half a century of rising prices insufficiently matched by wage hikes had impoverished unskilled and casual laborers. In the decade after 1555, moreover, their existence, marginal in the best of times, was regularly menaced by bouts of very high inflation. Although the rate of price increases may have been greater during the 1520s, the gap between earnings and subsistence needs had never been wider than it repeatedly was in 1555–66. Even laborers' families with more than one income must have faced chronic hard times. Concurrently, skilled artisans, who customarily had earned enough to live comfortably, encountered adverse circumstances unknown since the 1520s: repeated wheat and rye price peaks and, if light-cloth output statistics provide any guidance, stagnating employment opportunities or even periodic joblessness.[37]

Thus, despite a recent upturn in light drapery production and a number of emergency policing measures, in late December 1565 the aldermen were forced to admit that Lille had become home to a "great throng of poor people," whose unruly behavior was of great concern.[38] At the same time, however, Lille was endowed with a municipal welfare system that had developed in concert with – and as a result of – the crises of the early sixteenth century. In what ways and to what extent did urban charity address the material problems that we have surveyed?

II

Like most European cities, Lille entered the sixteenth century supplied with diverse foundations and institutions to aid the poor (see Map 1).

September 1565, July 1566, 2 and 28 September 1566, 13 February 1567, 12 June 1574, 17 June 1579.

36 The law on banquets (AML, Reg. 382, fols. 15–17), republished eighteen times between 1565 and 1586, limited wedding feasts to thirty couples, guild and confraternity gatherings to twenty-five individuals, and engagement parties to thirty persons.

37 A 1564 law that imposed mandatory apprenticeship in Lille, even for free workers already trained in approved towns, thereby reducing competition for work, must have been at least in part a response to this situation. See Vanhaeck, *Sayetterie à Lille*, 2:66, doc. 28.

38 AML, Reg. 382, fols. 27–7v, 22 December 1565.

Two hospitals, both opened in the thirteenth century, followed the characteristic medieval practice of providing temporary housing to the homeless as well as ministering to the ill; only in the later sixteenth century did a strict distinction among these functions begin to be made. Four hospices cared for some 120 aged, sick poor. The three founded in the thirteenth century were restricted to impoverished bourgeois of Lille, whereas the fourth, established in 1462, received townspeople without regard to juridical status. The remaining institutions included a home for old women, three orphanages housing about seventy-five children, a foundation that gave a meager supper of bread and soup and a bed to a small number of paupers, an asylum that furnished lodging for a night to twelve or sixteen pilgrims and indigent travelers, and a maternity hospital that also accommodated pilgrims. The municipal government administered the old-age homes and orphanages, even though these establishments, like the others, were staffed by members of religious orders.[39]

Already in 1455 these institutions could care for but a tiny portion of the quarter or more of Lille's population, estimated at between 13,500 and 15,000, thought to have been poor at that date.[40] Nor, despite pronounced urban demographic growth, did the number of residential institutions increase during the next century. To be sure, a hospice for thirteen old women opened its doors in 1541, but just twelve years later the three hospices for ruined citizens were closed and their residual funds converted into modest payments for home relief.[41]

More important in assisting late medieval Lille's poor were the food, clothing, and small sums of money distributed both by the charities (*pauvretés*) that had existed in each parish since at least the thirteenth century, and by the many foundations set up to honor specific individuals. Originally, the parochial establishments were directed by councils of parishioners, whereas the foundations had their own trustees. But as early as 1285 administration of one of the richest foundations was vested in the municipal government. Early in the next century, the al-

---

[39] The best summary account of these institutions is in Platelle, "La vie religieuse à Lille," pp. 338, 342–4, 372–3, 383–6. See also H. Folet, *Hôpitaux lillois disparus* (Lille, 1899).

[40] Derville, "De 1300 à 1500," p. 152, asserts that a fourth of Lille's residents lived constantly at the poverty line during the period he covers, whereas Platelle, "La vie religieuse à Lille," pp. 386–7, concludes that between a quarter and a third of city dwellers were "more or less totally indigent."

[41] Folet, *Hôpitaux lillois disparus*, pp. 17, 23–5.

dermen, who had long supplemented private contributions to the parish bodies, started to impose specific expenditures on them and oblige them to render accounts each year to the city authorities or their designated representatives.[42] Thus even before the sixteenth century the aldermen had some voice in raising aid for and disbursing it to Lille's poor, just as they exercised a measure of control over a number of the city's charitable institutions.

Parish charities continued to assist Lillois in the sixteenth century. Records of the pauvreté of St. Sauveur, for example, detail annual income of between 1,000 and 2,000 livres, derived largely from property rents and bonds, along with about two hundred rasières of wheat and up to forty rasières of oats.[43] Pious townspeople likewise persisted in establishing foundations outside of parish charities. Donors intended simultaneously to benefit their souls and once a year to give several paupers – rarely were more than fifteen helped by any one foundation – bread and a few sols in return for attendance at an anniversary Mass. In St. Etienne parish, for instance, very incomplete documentation reveals that foundations were set up in 1549, 1550, 1554, 1558 (three), and 1559 (two).[44]

Although they commanded substantial resources, however, Lille's parish charities and private foundations had serious inherent problems. As in most late medieval towns, small endowments proliferated,[45] complicating efforts to provide sufficient aid to poor individuals and families. In addition, access to relief was more often a function of residence than of need. Neighborhoods with concentrations of wealthy people enjoyed considerably greater funds than impoverished areas, yet eligibility was strictly determined by parish boundaries.[46] Further, alms were often distributed on dates specified by donors, who might want to honor saints or be remembered on the anniversary of their deaths, although these

---

[42] Platelle, "La vie religieuse à Lille," pp. 346–9.

[43] The accounts, for half a dozen years between the late 1530s and the mid-1560s, are AASL, Reg. F 190–1. No other parish accounts from the period before the revolt seem to have survived. For later decades, see AASL, Reg. D 427 (St. Etienne, 1566–7), Reg. E 301 (Ste. Catherine, 1571–2), Reg. F 192–3 (St. Sauveur, 1573–1625), Reg. G 79 (St. Maurice, 1571–5). AASL, Reg. J 488, is a list of the parish charities' property holdings, made during the 1580s.

[44] AASL, Reg. D 417, "Livre de copies de plusieurs lettres de fondations, pour les pauvres de la paroisse de Saint-Estienne à Lille, tome I," 1336–1567. For other parishes, see AASL, "Inventaire de 1878," unnumbered MS.

[45] See W. P. Blockmans and W. Prevenier, "Poverty in Flanders and Brabant from the Fourteenth to the Mid-Sixteenth Century," *Acta Historiae Neerlandicae* 10 (1978):39.

[46] Platelle, "La vie religieuse à Lille," p. 348.

were not necessarily times when the poor most required assistance. Worst of all, only a fraction of parish charities' expenditures materially benefited the needy. For besides granting cash and grain, the foundations were obliged to pay for religious services in memory of benefactors, acquit seigneurial duties on properties they had been given, and purchase additional income-generating assets. As a result, the subventions received by the poor could be as little as 20 percent of total disbursements, although on occasion they reached 75 percent.[47]

Suggestions for improving the provision of charity in Lille were heard since at least the early sixteenth century. About 1505, the prominent merchant Paul Castellain proposed that the municipal government establish poor commissioners on the model of those recently set up in Antwerp, and three years later his recommendation was carried through. Four central commissioners were delegated the tasks of locating the poor, requesting and receiving alms, and distributing assistance, both in cash and in kind. They also appointed two or three men in each of the five intramural parishes to help with administration and supervision.

Though no records of the "secretaries of poor honorable households" (*ministres des pauvres honnêtes ménages*) have survived, the reform evidently represented a serious attempt to reduce the disorder and inefficiency of the existing charitable arrangements.[48] Unfortunately, by leaving intact the tangled underlying institutional structure, and by continuing to rely entirely on voluntary donations, it failed to resolve the difficulties bedeviling the city's efforts to assist the poor. Still, a first step had been taken toward centralized administration under the control of the municipal government, and the principle of conciliar management accepted. Radical change, however, was not implemented until the effects of worsening material conditions made it impossible to tolerate organizational confusion and insufficient resources any longer.

Throughout Europe, the issue of welfare reform received renewed attention during the harvest failures, epidemics, and ensuing shortages and sharp inflation of the 1520s.[49] In Lille, the stagnant condition of the light-textile industry (Figures 3.2 and 4.2) may have lent additional

---

[47] See the accounts cited in n. 43.

[48] M. Scrive-Bertin, *Les origines de la Bourse commune des pauvres au 16e siècle* (Lille, 1882), pp. 2–3; Paul Bonenfant, "Les origines et le caractère de la réforme de la bienfaisance publique aux Pays-Bas sous le règne de Charles Quint," *RBPH* 6 (1927):209–10.

[49] Cf. Catharina Lis and Hugo Soly, *Poverty and Capitalism in Pre-Industrial Europe* (Atlantic Highlands, N.J., 1979), pp. 84–5.

urgency to the search for a solution. By December 1525, swelling crowds of mendicants had become so importunate that begging was forbidden inside or even near churches, and many paupers were expelled from the city.[50] But in light of the chronically bad economic conditions during these years, measures of this sort were at best temporary palliatives, so the aldermen soon felt compelled to undertake far-reaching changes. To be sure, the new system, like the modifications introduced twenty years before, was neither unique nor original, because it followed reforms adopted at Ypres in 1525, themselves apparently inspired by innovations proposed earlier in Mons and Strasbourg.[51] This time, however, the model chosen entailed a sweeping reorganization of Lille's charity system and an extension of the municipal government's role in furnishing welfare well beyond anything previously undertaken.

The "Order for the poor of Lille" published on 30 April 1527 that embodied the revised charitable regime was concerned as much with the moral and spiritual regeneration of the indigent as with their physical well-being.[52] This objective reflected not only the influence of Ypres and its antecedents but a sentiment winning acceptance in many European communities that welfare ought properly to be employed to foster morality and enhance social discipline.[53]

The repression of begging was commonly regarded as the first step in this campaign, and Lille was no exception. According to a short preamble to the Order, toleration of indiscriminate begging had encouraged "many people" to stop working and live totally from alms. This kind of idleness, "mother of all evils," led quickly to depravity. Men turned to thievery, women to prostitution, and parents taught their children mendicancy rather than a trade. Everyone was "so busy" begging that they

---

50 AML, Reg. 380, fols. 10–10v, 19 December 1525.
51 For the influence of the other cities' efforts on Lille, see J. Nolf, *La réforme de la bienfaisance publique à Ypres au XVIème siècle* (Ghent, 1915), pp. xvii–xxvi, and Bonenfant, "Origins et caractère de la réforme de la bienfaisance publique," pp. 219–21, 229.
52 The Order is in AML, Reg. 380, fols. 21–3v (another copy is in Aff. gén., C. 580, d. 7). It is published in M. de la Fons de Mélicocq, "Ordonnances pour les pauvres de Lille (1527–1556)," *Bulletin du Comité de la langue, de l'histoire et des arts de la France* 3 (1855–6):700–4; Xavier Renouard, *L'assistance publique à Lille de 1527 à l'An VIII* (Lille, 1912), pp. 139–44, and in Nolf, *Réforme de la bienfaisance publique*, pp. 246–50. All quotations in the following five paragraphs are my translations from this document.
53 For model case studies that emphasize this theme, see Gutton, *La société et les pauvres*, and Brian Pullan, *Rich and Poor in Renaissance Venice* (Oxford, 1971). More generally, see Lis and Soly, *Poverty and Capitalism*.

neglected religious obligations, placing their salvation in doubt. Not every pauper was considered shiftless and degenerate, for the Order also recognized the existence of some "true poor beggars." Unfortunately, these rightful mendicants were being prevented access to alms by the lazy who, it was insinuated, had freely chosen joblessness and begging and had been able to persevere in their sloth thanks to mistakenly generous attitudes of the urban community and lax municipal policies. Thus the preamble clearly adopted the view gaining currency in many contemporary industrial centers that the problem of poverty had to be dealt with not simply by furnishing larger amounts of aid but by distinguishing the undeserving from the deserving poor and by forcibly ending indolence and its bad effects.[54]

To put their principles into practice, the aldermen promulgated a series of regulations designed to minimize begging, determine who would be entitled to receive permissible forms of assistance, and establish a structure to deliver that aid. Order, equity, and uplift, it was thought, would simultaneously be fostered. Begging was not unconditionally forbidden, but articles i–iii of the 1527 law restricted it to lepers, prisoners, members of mendicant religious orders, wards of the city's orphanages, and pilgrims. The able-bodied, whether adults or children, risked flogging, imprisonment, expulsion, or worse should they seek alms. After the cessation of begging, assistance would be available, but Lille had no intention of becoming a mecca for the poor. Eligibility rules, set out in articles iv and v, announced that only those who had lived in Lille for two or more years would even be considered. All remaining "vagrants, beggars, lazy people, and others living from the alms of good people" were instructed to leave Lille or get jobs, failing which they would be clapped into jail.

In articles xi–xiiii [*sic*] the aldermen outlined a fundamental reorganization of Lille's system of poor relief. To begin with, the municipal government was to appoint five notables, one from each of the parishes located within the city walls (St. Etienne, St. Maurice, St. Sauveur, St. Pierre, and Ste. Catherine). These men would serve as a panel of *ministres généraux des pauvres* or general secretaries of the poor, a central institution that developed Lille's earlier partial reform in the direction taken by Ypres and several other towns. Assisted by a rudimentary bureaucracy consisting of a clerk, a sergeant, and a page, the

---

[54] Cf. Lis and Soly, *Poverty and Capitalism*, p. 92.

ministres généraux (or "deputies," as they were also called) were charged with "the administration of all the poor" of Lille, whose names were to be listed in a register kept by the clerk.[55] In order to hear the grievances of the poor, investigate the specific needs of groups such as aged paupers, and attempt to bring "discipline and order" to the distribution of relief, the deputies would hold office hours every Monday and Thursday evening. They were also authorized to issue statutes and ordinances they deemed necessary, subject only to aldermanic veto, and required to make a semiannual financial accounting to the Magistrat.

Besides the general secretaries, the 1527 act set up four-man commissions in each intramural parish plus La Madeleine and St. André, which lay outside the walls. Like the members of the central body, the parish commissioners were named by the municipal government (which, in contrast to the earlier reform, now wielded direct control over all levels of the welfare bureaucracy), and one was concurrently designated to head the existing parish charity. Everyday management of the poor relief effort was entrusted to these commissioners, who received and distributed funds, enrolled townspeople newly entitled to aid, and removed those who no longer qualified. The five ministres généraux were clearly in command, however, for it was to them that all funds were turned over, it was they who provided resources to each parish for grants to the poor, and it was to them that the parish commissioners reported eligibility and rendered accounts each month.

In its organizational structure, as in so many other respects, Lille's municipal welfare borrowed from Ypres, which itself had adopted from Bruges the system combining central and parish commissioners. At the same time, these innovations in the Low Countries resembled arrangements that were emerging across western Europe. Even in Venice, where corporate bodies like the *Scuole Grandi* continued to provide much charity, after 1529 the government appointed parish commissions to aid those neglected by the existing institutions.[56]

The capstone of the reform was the establishment in article xii of a

---

55 Although the lists have not survived, we know that they were compiled, for the process gave rise to protests on the part of those denied aid, who even threatened the deputies; see, for example, AML, Reg. 380, fol. 40, 4 January 1528, printed in de la Fons de Mélicocq, "Ordonnances pour les pauvres," pp. 704–5.

56 Nolf, *Réforme de la bienfaisance publique*, pp. xvii, xxviii; Gutton, *La société et les pauvres*, pp. 168–75; Wallace MacCaffrey, *Exeter, 1540–1640. The Growth of an English Country Town* (Cambridge, Mass., 1958), pp. 111–12; Pullan, *Rich and Poor in Renaissance Venice*, pp. 253–6.

Bourse commune des pauvres, created initially by sequestering most existing charitable endowments held by hospitals, brotherhoods, and other organizations. Only benefactions ordained by their founders for specific groups such as mendicant orders were not confiscated. Placed under the immediate supervision of the ministres généraux, the "Common Fund for the poor" also involved the participation of the parish commissioners, who were obliged to solicit and collect donations. All individuals who qualified for aid were compelled to wear fleur-de-lis badges on their sleeves in order "to mark them and also so that good people may see to whom their funds and alms are given."[57] Symbolically as well as in practice, then, the decisions of the Bourse commune as to who would be succored distinguished the deserving from the undeserving, the moral from the immoral poor, while simultaneously presenting signs of their beneficence to the rest of the populace.

For all that the welfare system was reorganized and subjected to lay control, it also gave clergy a conspicuous – if not weighty – role and retained important religious qualities from earlier arrangements. The 1527 law assigned clerics tasks such as encouraging contributions, relaying complaints, and notifying officials when aid was abused or eligible people failed to apply due to shame or "simpleness." What is more, not only were the mendicant orders permitted to pursue their traditional practices, but anniversary Masses established under the aegis of parish charities continued to be celebrated. The deputies also accepted bequests involving payments to religious orders or memorial services in honor of the donors.

These provisions did not, however, initially win unanimous approval for the new arrangements. Parish priests grumbled that the Bourse commune was causing donations to dry up, while parish, confraternity, and chapel officers refused to stop publicly soliciting alms for their own charities. Eventually, to silence these and other adversaries, Lille's Magistrat joined with its counterpart in Ypres in an appeal to the Faculty of Theology at the Sorbonne, which in January 1530 ruled that the Common Fund accorded with the teachings of the church. This decision helped halt challenges to welfare reform in Lille, sparing the city the

---

[57] The quotation is from de la Fons de Mélicocq, "Ordonnances pour les pauvres," pp. 704–5. The requirement was reiterated on 14 April 1556 (printed ibid., p. 710) and enforced thereafter. A sayetteur seeking help from the Bourse commune on 15 March 1557, for example, was told that he could have it only when he joined his wife and children in wearing the badge; AML, Reg. 15,922, fol. 145.

bitter disputes that wracked Ypres for another twenty years.[58] Doubt-less, too, the strength of the Magistrat relative to religious bodies, as suggested in Chapter 1, also lay behind the end of clerical opposition in Lille.

Whatever the attitude of some clergy and administrators of existing charities, perusal of even a tiny random sample of the bequests listed in its account books indicates that the Common Fund soon gained wide acceptance as a legitimate social institution. So, for example, in the last of his many contributions a merchant donated nearly 5,000 livres, an-other 2,300 livres came from the will of Jean de Lattre, seigneur of le Vichte, and a canon at St. Pierre donated 1,600. Less well-off towns-people also gave to the Bourse commune. A woman hotelkeeper left 100 livres, a shopkeeper 6 livres, a plumber 11 sols, while 3 sols 7 deniers was received "from the sale of a gorget by the terms of a poor woman's will."[59]

The new administrative and financial structure quickly proved its viability. In fact, both central and parish commissions soon had to be enlarged and additional sources of income developed in order to handle the many tasks that the municipal welfare system assumed. Already by 1537 a sixth ministre général had been appointed, and in the next few decades the number grew constantly before stabilizing at between twelve and fourteen. By 1537, too, the parish commissions began to expand; eventually, all consisted of at least five men, with St. Etienne and La Madeleine often having eight or even more.[60]

According to the 1527 law, the revenues of the Bourse commune were to be derived from gifts, legacies, poor boxes installed in each parish church, most foundations and property holdings of existing charities, and collections taken in churches. Yet already by the time of the first surviving account book (1 November 1535–30 April 1536), other kinds of income were being tapped, including special door-to-door appeals ordered by the aldermen and a yearly licensing fee levied on every tavern

---

[58] In Ypres, the Dominicans stubbornly maintained that any restriction of begging harmed the practice of Christian charity and that lay control of relief usurped legitimate rights of the religious orders. Lottin, *Lille, citadelle de la Contre-Réforme?* pp. 284–5, introduces new evidence to correct the impression given by Nolf, who published many of the relevant documents in *Réforme de la bienfaisance publique*, pp. l–lx, that only Ypres faced such hostility and that it alone brought the appeal to the Sorbonne.

[59] See, respectively, AASL, Reg. J 566, 568, 573, 581, 566, 563, 570.

[60] See AASL, Reg. J 559, 560, 562, 568, 584; AML, Reg. 16,288, fols. 144–5v. St. Etienne's parish commissioners also served as La Madeleine's.

serving wine. Beginning sometime between 1537 and 1542, the town's share of fines collected for violations of textile guild rules was also turned over to the Common Fund, and from 1539 on some of the income received by Lille's heavily endowed but underused leprosarium was diverted to it. No later than 1546, a lucrative tax of 3 sols for the benefit of the poor was imposed on each box of woad entering Lille. The profits from selling grain that had been donated by the city or by private individuals were also drawn upon from time to time.[61]

In all, six major categories of income can be distinguished: various forms of donations, revenue-producing annuities and property, taxes, grain sales, fines, and loans and grants. From year to year, of course, the amounts registered in any given category could vary considerably, as when the Common Fund received a particularly generous bequest or a large amount of grain was sold.[62] Still, an impression of the size of each source of revenue and of the changes they underwent over time can be obtained by examining averages (Table 4.4).

Although the data are spotty before 1560, several conclusions can safely be drawn. Traditional resources (various forms of contributions and investments) regularly provided the largest share of revenue. Yet these sources of funds quickly proved insufficient to meet the demands placed on the welfare system. To be sure, supplementary donations could be solicited to meet sudden increases in need. In 1546, for instance, householders in the five intramural parishes were visited every week from 25 May to 27 July. Starting in 1565 such appeals, heretofore occasional, were made permanent and participation perhaps compulsory, so perhaps these collections should be considered poor rates, analogous to those instituted or at least attempted in some European cities at about the same time.[63] Thanks to a steady flow of property bequests and

---

61 For the above, see AASL, Reg. J 558–80, and Victor Derode, "Leproseries ou maladreries," *BCHDN* 2 (1844): 261–2, 272. An ordinance of 1531, printed in de la Fons de Mélicocq, "Ordonnances pour les pauvres," p. 707, directed the parish commissioners to solicit alms for the poor at each house every March and September. These biannual collections were not the same as the special ones introduced at about the same time.

62 See, e.g., AASL, Reg. J 566, when in consequence of a donation of 4,700 liv. by the merchant Hubert Deliot the category of contributions represented over four-fifths of all funds received during the six months 1 November 1553–30 April 1554, or Reg. J 575, when about one-fourth of total receipts for the semester 1 November 1562–30 April 1563 came from grain sales. In both cases, the category totals far exceeded the mean reported in Table 4.4.

63 See AASL, Reg. J 561. Although I have found no record of any sort of obligatory poor rate, the stability over long periods of the amounts registered for each parish (see ibid., Reg. J 579ff.) suggests that some element of compulsion may have been employed, as in other cities. For these

Table 4.4. *Major sources of revenue of Lille's Common Fund, 1536–65*
(expressed as % of total)

Period	Contributions[a]	Property and annuities[b]	Taxes	Sales of grain	Fines	Loans and grants
1536–49 (5 accounts)	68.80	19.33	5.10	6.31	0.46	0
1551–60 (7 accounts)	56.96	16.71	15.09	3.95	3.82	3.47
1561–5 (10 accounts)	36.05	32.44	15.43	9.44	6.64	0

[a]Includes gifts, bequests, poor boxes, and special appeals.
[b]Includes income from annuities and property owned both by parish charities and by the Bourse commune.
Sources: AASL, Reg. J 558–80.

some purchases by the ministres généraux, income from investments rose nicely. But unlike the Venetian Scuole, for example, the financial health of Lille's Bourse commune never became heavily dependent on revenues from property.[64] Instead, the viability of the Common Fund came more and more to depend on previously minor types of revenue, including grain sales, proceeds from fines, loans such as the 2,200 livres furnished by the municipal wine cellars in 1552, and especially the woad tax, created for and assigned to the Common Fund. Intensive exploitation of all these measures enabled the semiannual income of the Bourse commune to be raised from an average of about 5,775 livres in 1536–7 to about 8,870 livres in 1561–5.

Over and above the services dispensed by institutions such as hospices and orphanages, charity had historically taken the form of

poor rates, see M. Fosseyeux, "Les premiers budgets municipaux d'assistance. La taxe des pauvres au XVIème siècle," *Revue d'Histoire de l'Eglise de France* 20 (1934):407–32; Gutton, *La société et les pauvres*, pp. 276–7; and John Pound, *Poverty and Vagrancy in Tudor England* (London, 1971), pp. 59–63.

[64] Between 1590 and 1615, for instance, the proportion of income received by the Scuola San Rocco from urban and rural real estate increased from 30% to 84% of the total; Pullan, *Rich and Poor in Renaissance Venice*, pp. 170–5.

Table 4.5. *Leading expenditures of Lille's Common Fund, 1536–65*
(expressed as % of total)[a]

Period	Cash[b]	Food and clothing	Children at wet nurses	Medical assistance	Purchase of annuities
1536–49	81.72	11.55	1.97	2.78	0
(5 accounts)					
1551–60	63.95	10.97	16.24	2.67	1.04
(7 accounts)					
1561–5	52.55	13.13	18.07	2.07	10.14
(10 accounts)					

[a]Percentages do not total 100, as some minor expenses have been omitted.
[b]For absolute amounts of cash outlays, see Appendix E.
Sources: AASL, Reg. J 558–80.

periodic distributions of money, food, clothing, and sometimes fuel. As Table 4.5 shows, the new welfare system continued to emphasize these kinds of aid. Yet the Bourse commune did take on some important additional tasks, notably medical assistance and the support of young children placed with wet nurses. The provision of medical care, which for the most part took the form of paying physicians' bills, had been mandated by a clause in article x of the 1527 law. But the practice of maintaining children – not all of whom were parentless – outside orphanages seems to have developed in the mid-1540s, expanding enormously in the wake of the epidemic that struck Lille a decade later.[65] The other important category of expenditures – the purchase of annuities – did not directly assist the needy but must have been intended to assure the long-term solvency of the Common Fund by broadening its financial base. The municipal welfare system also gave away bread free of charge to the poor (Table 4.6).[66]

---

65 The number of children supported in this way (71 in early 1554) had reached 381 by the time of the next surviving account (May–October 1558). From that level it dropped slowly and erratically to 172 in May–October 1565.

66 It is not clear from the accounts whether no bread was distributed in the May–October semesters of 1546, 1558, and 1559, although the epidemic that so disrupted life in Lille in the late 1550s may be responsible for the absence of data or of distributions in the latter two years. Bread was also handed out during the spring of 1536, but the amounts were not recorded. See AASL, Reg. J 561, 568–9, 558.

Finally, the Bourse commune undertook temporary duties, most prominently providing aid to plague victims in the middle and late 1550s. A special account book dated September 1557, the only one of its kind that appears to have survived, lists 1,218 livres in outlays for guarding infected houses and defraying the living expenses of townspeople who moved into wooden barracks on the Riez de Canteleu, just outside the city walls, for the duration of the outbreak.[67] The regular budget of the Common Fund also absorbed considerable expenses related to the epidemic. Accounts for May–October 1558, for instance, list plague costs of over 1,000 livres, nearly 10 percent of all disbursements during that semester.[68]

The municipal welfare system was capable, then, of delivering an extensive and flexible array of services to Lillois. Compared with the parish charities, moreover, the Bourse commune spent a much larger proportion of its income in ways of direct benefit to the poor. Payments for memorial services and other overhead costs never exceeded 2 percent of total expenditures and were usually much less. As Table 4.7 indicates, by centralizing control of funds the Common Fund also succeeded in overcoming the geographical imbalance between resources and poverty that had characterized previous arrangements.

As the parenthetical figures in Table 4.7 show, important variations in each parish's allotment occurred over the short term. Yet the proportions remained remarkably stable over the three decades for which there are data. St. Sauveur, where textile artisans were concentrated, almost invariably received the greatest part of cash payments. What is more, relief in St. Sauveur, as in Ste. Catherine, St. André, and La Madeleine, was subsidized by the more affluent parishes, St. Pierre and particularly St. Etienne, home to many international merchants. Only St. Maurice, Lille's most diverse parish, got outlays in proportion to both its contributions and its share of the city's population.

Bread allotments reveal a similar transfer of resources. On the one hand, St. Etienne was excluded (for unknown reasons) after 1537, a year in which it received less than 4 percent of the loaves. La Madeleine, on the other hand, was granted nearly twice as much bread as money, perhaps indicating that parishioners were so impoverished that they

---

[67] The account book is AASL, Reg. J 567. For the Riez, see Folet, *Hôpitaux lillois disparus*, pp 47–9.

[68] AASL, Reg. J 568.

Table 4.6. *Loaves of bread distributed by Lille's Common Fund, 1537–66*

Accounting year[a]	November–April[b]	May–October[b]	Year total[b]
1537	37,010	—	—
1542	20,960	—	—
1549	—	16,172	—
1551	—	24,202	—
1552	—	52,487	—
1553	—	29,869	—
1554	48,880	—	—
1560	14,533	—	—
1561	9,346	0	9,346
1562	10,958	0	10,958
1563	16,188	14,563	30,751
1564	20,160	0	20,160
1565	22,400	4,680	27,080
1566	30,509	25,094	55,603

[a]The accounting year coincided with the aldermanic year, beginning in November of the previous calendar year. Thus 1537 extended from November 1536 through October 1537.
[b]Where no number is given, the account book is missing.
Sources: AASL, Reg. J 559–80.

needed free food simply to survive. What is more, variable quotas for grants of bread were established in the mid-1560s. By the terms of these allowances, St. Sauveur took between a third and two-fifths of all loaves, St. Maurice and La Madeleine one-fifth, Ste. Catherine 10 to 13.33 percent, St. Pierre and St. André 5 to 6.67 percent.[69] Apparently, contemporaries recognized a geography of poverty, and the ministres généraux increasingly sought to assign resources as a function of it.

Unlike many private bequests, which were bound to specific distribution schedules and amounts of aid, the Bourse commune could adjust to changes in the cost of living. Thus high grain prices in 1536–7, 1545–6, the early 1550s, 1562–3, and 1565–6 were reflected in large grants of cash and bread, whereas the low cost of grain in 1548–9 brought re-

[69] AASL, Reg. J 577, 579–80.

Table 4.7. *Receipts and disbursements of Lille's Common Fund by parish, 1536–65*

Parish	% of Lille's population, 1566 (est.)	Mean contributions (%)[a]	Mean share of cash outlays (%)[a]	Mean share of bread distributions (%)[a]
St. Etienne	25.60	54.71 (43–75)	7.79 (5–11)	0
St. Maurice	24.70	20.99 (8–39)	24.59 (21–36)	22.19 (14–32)
St. Sauveur	24.00	6.94 (1–16)	34.23 (29–44)	37.31 (31–46)
Ste. Catherine	9.30	3.69 (1–11)	13.06 (9–17)	13.42 (10–19)
St. Pierre	7.00	10.31 (1–20)	5.62 (4–9)	4.97 (0–10)
La Madeleine	4.70	2.03 (0.4–10)	9.43 (7–12)	17.55 (12–23)
St. André	4.70	1.32 (0.4–3)	5.29 (3–9)	4.56 (0–7)

[a]Figures in parentheses give the range of percentages.
Sources: AASL, Reg. J 558–80 (finances); Appendix A (population).

duced levels of assistance.[70] The provision of money and bread was also sensitive to regular short-term cycles of need within each year. Customarily, grants began to increase in September and October, usually hitting their peak during the winter months. In the course of the summer, as dwindling stocks pushed up grain prices before the harvest was brought in, outlays would frequently shoot up again, on occasion attaining their maxima for the year. This pattern suggests that the cost of cereals was the leading factor determining the demand for charity. Yet it is evident that availability of work was also important, for in winter, normally the period of heaviest welfare expenditures, jobs were scarce yet grain prices not necessarily at their height.

70 See Appendix G and Table 4.6. The loss of records makes it impossible to determine what happened in the mid-1550s.

The monthly variations attest, too, that the Common Fund served the two groups of poor that historians have identified in early modern Europe. One consisted of a core of structural paupers, people such as the aged, orphans, and the handicapped who rarely left the welfare rolls and thus received a kind of permanent home relief. The other, less stable in composition and size, comprised the conjuncturally indigent, those who required help – whether unemployment compensation or income maintenance – only at times of crisis.[71] The cyclical pattern of outlays indicates, in other words, that despite the rhetoric of the 1527 Order, Common Fund administrators understood that the able-bodied as well as the infirm could merit assistance and allocated it accordingly. So does a 1541 ordinance declaring eligible for welfare all "poor honorable households" that were unable (due to the presence of children or other "reasonable cause") to support themselves on their earnings (*gaignaiges*).[72]

For all that it represented a significant advance over earlier arrangements, did Lille's reformed welfare system realize the aspirations of its founders for improved morality and behavior among its recipients? Did it provide significant aid to the city's poor? Might it have helped to neutralize the discontent engendered by difficult material conditions?

The Common Fund had one glaring shortcoming. Whether due to the belief that unemployment sprang largely from moral defects, or to a sense that the economy was generally expansive, it was wholly inattentive to policies such as job creation that might have struck at the roots of poverty. In this respect Lille again conformed to the European norm. Lyon was all but unique in seeking to develop the silk industry in the mid-1530s in order to give work to the unemployed poor – and there the popular revolt known as the "Grande Rebeine" (1529) and other episodes of unrest should be credited with stimulating magisterial perspicacity.[73] Lacking that kind of impetus, and perhaps made complacent by decades of textile growth, Lille was content to command the jobless to find work.

Whether morality improved is impossible to gauge. Regardless of the

---

[71] The terms *structural* and *conjunctural* poor were first introduced by Gutton, *La société et les pauvres*, esp. pp. 52–3.

[72] The law, printed in de la Fons de Mélicocq, "Ordonnances pour les pauvres," p. 708, suggests that such households were failing to come to the Bourse because they disliked having to wear the fleur-de-lis badges.

[73] Gutton, *La société et les pauvres*, p. 229.

stress on ethical regeneration in the preamble to the 1527 Order, for a long time little beyond exhortation was attempted in that direction. Article x of the original regulations called upon the commissioners to "compel [poor] children to attend school and learn a trade" so that they could be weaned from their parents' presumed slothful and dissipated ways. Up to the mid-1550s, however, all that was done was to pay a couple of clergymen 30 or 40 livres a year to supply a very rudimentary education to a few children. In 1554 Guillaume Deliot and his son Hubert, members of a leading merchant dynasty and important contributors to the Bourse commune on other occasions, did donate 6,400 florins and property to found a free Sunday school to teach reading, writing, arithmetic, and good morals. Yet although the Deliots' foundation was a forerunner of compulsory Sunday schools for all Lille's youth, before the revolt it could support just eighty poor boys and twenty girls from St. Sauveur and St. Maurice parishes. Thus it is unlikely to have had a major impact.[74]

The suppression of begging, perhaps the major change in the conduct of the poor anticipated from the 1527 reforms, was not accomplished at Lille any more than elsewhere.[75] Failing to qualify for aid, despite having "greatly tormented and molested" the ministres généraux, "many paupers" quickly resumed mendicancy, which to the Magistrat was one more proof of ingrained acedia among the poor.[76] But the frequent republication of prohibitory laws in the decade following the promulgation of the Order, a time marked by high grain prices and slack economic activity, indicates that many of the poor continued to have no choice but to beg. Although the problem eased for a while thereafter, the mid-1550s and early 1560s saw not only a proliferation of repressive ordinances but arrests as well, for the struggle to survive overcame any fear of the law.[77]

---

[74] Jules Houdoy, "L'instruction gratuite et obligatoire depuis le XVIème siècle," *MSSAAL* 3rd ser. 12 (1873):2–3, 9, 22–4.

[75] Claiming that welfare funds in the Low Countries were insufficient, in 1556 Charles V officially permitted begging under certain conditions, thereby reversing three decades of policy; Nolf, *Réforme de la bienfaisance publique*, p. lxvi. In 1514, London decreed a ban on begging, but in later years many of its provisions were relaxed; Pound, *Poverty and Vagrancy*, p. 59. See also Gutton, *La société et les pauvres*, pp. 273, 284; and Pullan, *Rich and Poor in Renaissance Venice*, pp. 238–40, 253, 285, 641.

[76] AML, Reg. 380, fol. 40.

[77] Ibid., fol. 41, 8 April 1528 (republished at least on 5 April 1531, 27 March 1537, 16 April 1538); Reg. 381, fols. 102–22, and Reg. 382, fols. 20, 27, 27v–8, for the 1550s and early 1560s.

The Common Fund's average total expenditures per six-month period grew from 6,780 livres in 1536–42 to 9,045 livres in 1561–5. Did this increase mean that a substantial fraction of poor Lillois received aid? In the absence of poor registers or information about per capita grants, it is impossible to answer this question with certainty. But indirect measurements can provide some useful approximations. Dividing cash disbursements by an estimate of the amount each person received indicates that at least 500 townspeople received aid during months of lowest grants, about 1,550 when outlays were greatest; that is, between 2 and 6 percent of the urban population.[78] By an alternate calculation – dividing the number of loaves of bread handed out each month by four, on the assumption that each week's award consisted of one loaf – as few as 125 or as many as 2,700 people received bread for a month, or between 0.5 and 9.5 percent of the city's residents.

Now, these figures might be taken as testimony that the Common Fund fell short of adequately assisting either the 4 to 6 percent of people in Lille who, according to recent studies of early modern Europe, were permanently impoverished, or the fifth, quarter, or even third of the urban population typically requiring help during crises.[79] Yet it should be emphasized that the estimates of Lillois aided are minima. Not only do they omit anyone helped by surviving parish and other foundations, buy they certainly understate the actual magnitude of Lille's municipal poor relief effort, especially in regard to conjunctural paupers who received a form of income maintenance. For such people, after all, were aided occasionally rather than continually. What is more, it is not likely that everyone received both cash and bread, or that each person was given the maximum allotment. Hence the estimate of the proportion of Lillois succored should certainly be increased, although it would be foolhardy to offer firm numbers.

What was most significant, in any event, was the Common Fund's role during crises. The development of new sources of revenue, the more efficient use of income, and the redeployment of resources made it

The April 1528 ordinance, as well as another dating from 1541, were published by de Fons de Mélicocq, "Ordonnances pour les pauvres," pp. 705–6, 707–9.

[78] I estimate that each person received 1.25 liv. per month, a figure derived from aid given to influenza victims. For a fuller explanation, see DuPlessis, "Charité municipale et autorité publique," pp. 206–9. On the basis of grain prices reported previously such an allowance would have furnished sufficient grain, and left money for other necessities, in every year before 1566.

[79] See Gascon, *Grand commerce et vie urbaine*, 1:403–4; Peter Clark and Paul Slack, *English Towns in Transition 1500–1700* (Oxford, 1976), p. 121.

Table 4.8. *Indexes of Common Fund outlays, grain prices, and employment in Lille, 1561–6 (100 = mean, 1560–1 through 1564–5)*

Year	Cash	Bread	Wheat	Rye	Employment[a]
1560–1	68	48	101	77	100
1561–2	73	56	103	87	91
1562–3	118	156	134	160	105
1563–4	128	103	83	89	95
1564–5	113	138	80[b]	87	110
1565–6	192	283	171[b]	198	109

[a]Employment index calculated from light-cloth output.
[b]Figures derived from Hôpital Comtesse records are slightly higher.
Sources: AASL, Reg. J 559–82 (cash and bread); AML, Reg. 797 (wheat); *Dokumenten voor de Geschiedenis van Prijzen en Lonen*, 4:347 (rye); Deyon and Lottin, "Production textile à Lille," pp. 30–1 (employment).

possible for the ministres généraux to react quickly to changing conditions. The fragmentary records indicate that such responsiveness characterized periods of sharp inflation such as 1546 and the early 1550s. But it also existed during other years, when outlays were doubled from one month to the next in reaction to price oscillations. This practice indicates that the Bourse commune was particularly attuned to the situation of those Lillois – notably the mass of light-cloth artisans – who normally lived above the poverty line but found their prosperity menaced by a rapid inflationary spiral, the more so when it was accompanied by a sluggish employment picture.

From this perspective, it is especially noteworthy that the Common Fund mounted a major effort in the years immediately preceding the outbreak of the revolt (Table 4.8). Information from Table 4.6 and Appendix E corroborates that the flow of both money and food was sharply increased in the critical months from late fall 1565 through the end of 1566.

During the early 1560s, moreover, the municipal government supplemented the Common Fund's efforts with additional relief measures far beyond anything previously attempted. Regular city funds were used to purchase grain for free distribution in September 1561 and October 1562, and (as on a smaller scale in the 1550s) in 1562, 1563, and 1565 the aldermen used annuities to finance the acquisition of cereals.[80] After the disastrous harvest of 1565, for example, the Magistrat sold 100,000 livres of rentes, employing the proceeds for grain that was given away at intervals during the succeeding months.[81] Taking another tack, in November 1562 the aldermen summoned 338 leading residents to city hall and urged them to contribute sums of between 20 and 150 florins apiece. The 13,395 florins eventually raised was spent on wheat and rye that were handed out to the poor throughout the remainder of that winter and on into the following spring and early summer.[82] And when in December 1565 it became clear that numerous people lacked "the means to survive," the city government for once overcame its reluctance and decided to provide jobs on municipal projects for everyone capable of working.[83]

Despite all this aid, we can be certain that the often terrible hardships of these years were keenly felt. Still, it seems likely that relief on such an augmented scale took the edge off both material distress and the discontent attendant upon it, especially among the cloth artisans vulnerable to the scissors of rising foodstuff prices and variable textile output. Whether by design or not, the Bourse commune came to be an integral element in the structure of small commodity production.

III

Reviewing the data at our disposal, there can be little doubt that the evolution of prices and wages followed as gloomy a course at Lille as elsewhere over the first two-thirds of the sixteenth century. Nor can it be gainsaid that the mid-1560s were a particularly harsh period. Even if, as I have maintained in the previous chapter, capitalist development was blunted in Lille, some impoverishment did occur there. Laborers' purchasing power fell the most, over both the long and the short terms, but master artisans had ample cause for worry as they saw the margin between their income and their expenditures consistently decrease. The city's quiescence, in short, did not rest upon any sort of providential

---

80 AML, Reg. 277, fols. 136v, 153v; Reg. 15,923, fol. 22v; Reg. 16,297, fol. 172.
81 AML, Reg. 15,923, fol. 72; Reg. 15,885, fols. 48–9 (24 October 1565), 50v–1 (18 November 1565).
82 Lottin, "Liste des riches lillois," pp. 65–72.
83 AML, Reg. 382, fols. 27–7v, 22 December 1565.

local exemption from the prevalent contemporary pattern of rising living costs and falling real income. Yet if material conditions were unarguably difficult at Lille, the city also had an increasingly elaborate welfare system that was particularly responsive to short-term crises and decisively oriented toward easing the impact of production and price cycles on cloth makers. What is more, the extra resources dispensed by the municipal government notably augmented the total charitable effort during the critical early and mid-1560s.

The Common Fund also included significant regulatory features: frequent reports to the Magistrat by commissioners it appointed, mandatory investigations to determine eligibility for relief, and the compilation of detailed lists of the poor. All these forms of policing – epitomized by the publicly visible badge that recipients of aid from the Common Fund had to wear – could not fail to enhance the municipal authorities' knowledge about, access to, and control over a large segment of the urban population. It seems likely that Lillois' attitudes and behavior were affected by the assistance they received, and the structures through which they received it, as well as by the distress to which it responded. In Tilly's terms, the Bourse commune hampered mobilization prompted by deprivation; that is, it discouraged the poor from rioting in the streets.

In contrast to the emphasis of this chapter, historians have traditionally neglected the role of charitable arrangements in facilitating or retarding the outbreak of the Dutch Revolt. But they have not argued that either destitution or threatened prosperity sufficed by itself to impel people to action. Rather, they contend, it was the appearance of a Calvinist movement that equipped with superb organization and ideology with a broad appeal that proved able to exploit growing but previously inchoate discontent. Verlinden, Craeybeckx, and Scholliers write that "the poverty which periodically afflicted the lower classes drove them to expect an improvement in their situation" from religious change. As a result, "the masses became all the more receptive to Calvinist preaching" in 1565–6 and ultimately were recruited for the iconoclasm that marked the beginning of the revolt.[84] The reformed religion, according to Van der Wee, "fitted in well with the prevailing mood of frustration and protest" of the 1560s.[85]

[84] Verlinden, Craeybeckx, and Scholliers, "Price and Wage Movements," pp. 68, 66.
[85] Van der Wee, "The Economy as a Factor in the Start of the Revolt," p. 66.

Like many industrial and commercial cities in the southern Low Countries, Lille became home to a Reformed movement that might be imagined to have played such a mobilizing role. Did it in fact do so? In light of what we have discovered about the material circumstances affecting townspeople, it now seems appropriate to examine the city's religious situation. We must seek in particular to ascertain the specific relationship between Protestantism and challenges to stability existing in Lille.

〜〜〜〜〜〜〜〜〜〜〜〜〜〜〜〜〜〜〜〜〜〜〜〜〜〜〜〜〜〜〜〜〜

5

Piety and the parameters of reform

I

For more than a century preceding the revolt, the Catholic church experienced considerable institutional growth, physical embellishment, and devotional activity in Lille. Two new religious communities were added to the five already in the city by the early fourteenth century. The Grey Sisters (1453) treated the sick in their own homes, while the Sisters of the Magdalene (1481) received repentant prostitutes who thereafter devoted themselves to the care of ill women.[1] Lille's Dominican monastery, founded in 1224 and the oldest in the Low Countries, also underwent a process of renewal. It helped form the new Congregation of Holland, a step that the monks claimed brought honor to them and salvation to many souls, for conventual discipline improved and the devotion of the rosary was reestablished. Their monastery was entirely rebuilt, too, the new edifice reaching completion in 1486.[2]

Lille's churches, which already disposed of substantial financial and human resources, were further enriched during this period. The collegiate church of St. Pierre was preeminent by virtue of extensive property holdings (including a seigneurie located in the center of Lille), sizable tithe income, and rights of presentation to all seven parishes in the city and twenty-nine others in the castellany. Although it already counted forty canons as well as several chaplains paid by private foundations, at least six new chaplaincies were endowed from 1453 to 1506 and another

---

[1] L. Dancoisne, "Monographie du Couvent des Pauvres claires de Lille (1453–1792)," *MSSAAL* 3rd ser. 5 (1867): 471–81, 491–2; Platelle, "La vie religieuse à Lille," pp. 338–42, 382–4.
[2] Charles-Louis Richard, *Histoire du Couvent des Dominicains de Lille* (Liège, 1781), pp. 25–6.

four between 1537 and 1558.[3] St. Pierre's fabric, on which work had
been suspended for a century, was essentially completed with the addition of several new chapels, a vault over the northern part of the transept
and raised walls in the nave (Plate 4). Then the existing rood screen,
which no longer looked sufficiently monumental, was razed. Its replace-
ment, built in 1532, was adorned with fifty statues that represented
some of the first Renaissance sculpture in Lille. Laying down a fancy
pavement, installing a new organ, and hanging a number of paintings
made the interior yet more impressive. The canons' pride and joy, however, was something that few people ever saw: their new library, built in
1507–8 and ornamented with many statues, pictures, and stained-glass
windows.[4]

Several parish churches also undertook extensive building programs
during the fifteenth and early sixteenth centuries. St. Etienne was almost entirely reconstructed, while at Ste. Catherine, the tower was
rebuilt and the choir greatly enlarged. In St. Maurice, an enormous
choir and apse were constructed and two additional naves begun. These
extensions provided space for the seven horistes, whose positions had
been endowed in 1476.[5] During the first half of the sixteenth century,
wealthy parishioners exhibited their piety in numerous public ways.
Some erected magnificent chapels, such as the one dedicated "to the
honor of God and of the Glorious Virgin Mary and of the Nativity" that
opened in the churchyard of St. Etienne in 1538.[6] Others donated costly

---

3 Platelle, "La vie religieuse à Lille," pp. 325–8, 373; Gonzague Chartier, *Les dîmes du chapitre
Saint-Pierre de Lille* (Lille, 1936); *Documents liturgiques et nécrologiques de l'église collégiale de Saint-
Pierre de Lille*, ed. Edouard Hautcoeur (Lille, 1895), pp. 270–9; Edouard Hautcoeur, *Histoire de
l'église collégiale et du chapitre de Saint-Pierre de Lille*, 3 vols. (Lille, 1896–9), 2:322–3. Hautcoeur
mentions no additional foundations until 1610.
4 Hautcoeur, *Histoire de Saint-Pierre*, 2:130–3, 172.
5 AML, Aff. gén., C. 819, d. 1; Jacques Gardelles, "L'art à Lille," in *Histoire de Lille*, 1:436–43;
Henri Virleux, *L'église St. Maurice à Lille. Etude historique et archéologique* (Lille, 1922), pp. 17–18;
Chronique de Mahieu Manteau, pp. 18–19 (a lottery raised the funds needed to finish the tower of
St. Etienne). Ste. Catherine also got six horistes, endowed in 1558–9 (*Histoire de Lille*, 2:82), as
did, at a minimum, St. Sauveur and St. Etienne, although the dates they were established in these
two parishes are not known.
6 For the chapel, see AET, Fonds Evêché de Tournai, no. 43, 9 October 1538, or AML, Aff. gén., C.
793, d. 2, 3. It was constructed by Jean de Ruffault, treasurer-general of the Netherlands and native
of Lille, where his family had grown rich in trade. Ruffault also paid for the fifty statues decorating
the new rood screen in the church of St. Pierre. For details about the Ruffault family, see Henri
Fremaux, *Histoire généalogique de la famille Ruffault* (Douai, 1887); for Jean, see also Michel Baelde,
De Collaterale Raden onder Karel V en Filips II (1531–1578) (Brussels, 1965), p. 302.

Plate 4. The Collegiate Church of St. Pierre. Nineteenth-century engraving. Lille, Musée de l'Hospice Comtesse.

sculpted copper holy-water basins and baptismal fonts to most of the parish churches.[7]

A revival of beliefs and practices involving substantial numbers of the laity paralleled and at times prompted the material elaboration of the

[7] For the basins and fonts, see *Chronique de Mahieu Manteau*, pp. 13–14, 17, 18, 20, 23, 28. The font placed in St. Sauveur, made in Bruges and adorned with the arms of Charles V, was noted as particularly beautiful.

church. The most weighty and enduring was a recrudescence of Marian devotions. The cult of Notre-Dame de la Treille, founded around the mid-thirteenth century and since then the occasion for Lille's annual procession, had been neglected during long years of plague, war, and economic depression. Between 1430 and 1453, however, the chapel in St. Pierre dedicated to the devotion was thoroughly restored to accommodate a rapidly growing throng of pilgrims: between 500 and 600 per year in the 1460s, 2,000 by the early sixteenth century, a record total of 4,500 in 1520 and some 4,000 in 1546, the last year for which there is information. By 1499 the brotherhood in charge of the shrine was affluent enough to purchase a majestic, costly organ for its chapel, and in 1533 it paid for all copies of the new breviary adopted by the chapter of St. Pierre. Five years later, the sanctuary of Notre-Dame, previously covered with wainscoting, was vaulted in stone.

Notre-Dame de la Treille had long been renowned for curing the possessed, although for many years this had been as disregarded as the rest of the cult. But a revival began in the late fifteenth century, and reports of miracles associated with the devotion soon became a commonplace of popular piety in Lille. An especially abundant series of prodigies – exorcisms, cures for apoplexy, the revival of a stillborn infant – occurred in the chapel between 1519 and 1527, at the dawn of the Reformation. In 1519 alone, twenty-nine miraculous cures were recorded.[8]

Besides the renewed veneration of Notre-Dame de la Treille, several other Marian devotions took hold in this period. The practice of saying the rosary became widespread in Lille as elsewhere by the late fifteenth century. Prayers to Our Lady of the Seven Sorrows, increasingly common since the same time, were endowed in St. Pierre in 1545.[9] The opening of a shrine of Our Lady of Consolation near Lille in 1515, and the fact that the chapel built by Jean de Ruffault quickly became known as Notre-Dame de Laurette to the exclusion of its other patrons,[10] further attest to the popular attachment to the Virgin. Yet another Marian cult made a remarkable debut in 1488 in the sanctuary of the re-

---

[8] Edouard Hautcoeur, *Histoire de Notre-Dame de la Treille* (Lille, 1913), pp. 26–49; [Martin Lhermite], *Histoire des saints de la province de Lille-Douay-Orchies* (Douai, 1638), pp. 502–7.

[9] Platelle, "La vie religieuse à Lille," pp. 404–5. The Dominican order was particularly active in spreading the Marian cult, and it was a Dominican in Lille, Michel Francois, who wrote the first theological study on the compassion of Mary in 1495; see Jacques Toussaert, *Le sentiment religieux en Flandre à la fin du Moyen-Age* (Paris, 1963), p. 284. Lille was also one of the first places where the devotion of the Seven Sorrows arose.

[10] Hautcoeur, *Histoire de Saint-Pierre*, 2:302–4; [Lhermite], *Histoire des saints*, pp. 546–7.

cently opened girls' orphanage, consecrated to the Immaculate Conception. Thanks to prayers to Our Lady in the new chapel, nearly a dozen people – children and adults, women and men, poor and rich – recovered from mysterious illnesses, inflamed legs, debilitating stomach pains, deformed limbs. Their testimony met with immediate credence in many sectors of society, with the result that the sanctuary was nearly overrun with sufferers seeking improved physical and spiritual health.[11]

The many confraternities that arose in these years gave a more organized and collective form to the preoccupation with finding suitable intercessors between God and man, the enthusiasm for devotions and ceremonies, and the keen regard for the tangible benefits that religion was thought to furnish. Brotherhoods were not a recent invention – the first ones in Lille dated back to at least the mid-thirteenth century – but beginning in the fifteenth century their popularity waxed. In the 1430s, for example, at least two confraternities dedicated to venerating St. James and to promoting visits to his tomb in Compostella were founded. Around the same time originated a brotherhood of Jerusalem pilgrims, which over the next century prospered so much that in 1539 it built a new chapel consecrated to the Holy Cross and Sepulcher in the parish church of St. Maurice.[12] The group of rhetoricians known as Notre-Dame du Puy also maintained a confraternity. For their part, the chaplains of St. Pierre controlled a brotherhood of St. John the Evangelist, which by the mid-sixteenth century had gained so many new members and so much wealth that it was able to erect a sumptuous new chapel with altars dedicated to St. John and St. Michael.[13]

The city's four specialized military companies likewise had their own confraternities. The brotherhood of the artillerymen (*canonniers*), for instance, which had a chapel dedicated to Ste. Catherine and Ste. Barbara in the church of St. Etienne, celebrated Masses in honor of its patrons, distributed bread to the poor of Lille on the saints' feast days, and built up a library and furnished its chapel with fine "ecclesiastical ornaments." All of this was said to encourage large numbers of the

---

[11] Théodore Leuridan and H. Leclair, "Faits miraculeux advenus en 1488 et 1489 en la chapelle de la Conception Notre-Dame à Lille," *BSEPC* 7 (1905):9–15.

[12] Platelle, "La vie religieuse à Lille," p. 410; *Chronique de Mahieu Manteau*, p. 21.

[13] M. de la Fons de Mélicocq, "Confrérie de Notre-Dame du Puy, à Lille, aux XIVe, XVe, et XVIe siècles," *Archives historiques et littéraires du Nord de la France* 3rd ser. 4 (1854):466–8; Hautcoeur, *Histoire de Saint-Pierre*, 2:293–6.

faithful to worship there; even more were expected as a result of extensive indulgences granted by Pope Leo X in 1519.[14]

Particularly striking was the proliferation of craft confraternities, which between 1423 and 1484 grew from thirty-three to fifty-seven as a great many occupational groups dedicated themselves to patron saints. Looked at from this angle, masons formed the most pious trade in Lille: They observed all six feast days of the Virgin, together with those of Mary Magdalene and of their principal patron, St. Thomas the Apostle.[15] The rise of light drapery resulted in additional foundations. The first corporate regulations for sayetterie, for example, mention the existence of a fellowship consecrated to St. John, which all guild members were obliged to join. By 1540, their rising numbers and prominence led the members to build their own chapel in the parish church of St. Maurice.[16]

Supported by annual fees assessed on masters and workers alike, brotherhoods were intended to fulfill a number of material, social, and psychic needs. On the most mundane level, they functioned as mutual aid societies, giving money to sick members, burying the dead, and assisting widows and children of deceased fellows. Typically, too, they engaged in various collective observances, such as common prayer, weekly Mass celebrated in the chapels set aside for them in the parish churches, and rites in honor of their patron saints. Most spectacular, confraternities participated in municipal and religious processions, each one proudly displaying its totems – an image of its patron saint, a large candle called a *chandaille*, and a *torse*, a wax torch "mounted on a staff and surrounded by the various attributes of the guild."[17]

Even more than parishes, confraternities made religion an integral part of the daily life of the common people of Lille. Their many activities not only expressed the solidarity of their members but bestowed powerful spiritual meaning upon social relations. The horizontal bonds existing among brothers were to be reinforced and transformed by vertical

---

14 AET, Fonds Evêché de Tournai, no. 40. For confraternities attached to the city's other military companies, see Espinas, *Les origines de l'association. I.*, 2:367–9, 374–5, 439–40; and Victor Derode, *Les milices lilloises* (Lille, 1877), pp. 25–6.
15 See AML, Reg. 16,002, passim, for patron saints.
16 Vanhaeck, *Sayetterie à Lille*, 2:9, doc. 3, arts. xvii, xviii; *Chronique de Mahieu Manteau*, p. 21.
17 Delille [E. Debievre], *Fêtes patronales. Corps de métiers lillois* (Lille, 1896), p. 11, is the source of the quotation. For more information, see Espinas, *Les origines de l'association. I.*, 1:713–904.

links forged between God and man, thereby bringing closer the secular and sacred realms. Embodied in the confraternity, worldly interests and relationships were meant to connect to personal sanctification.

Lille thus provides abundant evidence of the hunger for the divine that, according to many scholars, characterized Europe in the later fifteenth and sixteenth centuries.[18] The profusion of confraternities, the appearance of new cults and devotions, the wave of church building, the eager acceptance of miraculous tales – all these bespeak a deep and passionate involvement in spiritual matters during the period dubbed the "Indian summer of late-medieval piety."[19] Though specific manifestations varied – only the wealthy could endow chapels, for instance – religious fervor appears to have been widely diffused among Lillois, affecting women as well as men, laity in addition to clergy, artisans along with government officials. Significantly, this piety did not set itself against the established church, for after the mid-fifteenth century heresy seems to have died out in Lille as elsewhere.[20]

Much scholarship argues, however, that the religious vitality evident on the eve of the Reformation was accompanied by, indeed often signified, intensifying disorder that ultimately fostered the rise of Protestantism.[21] An ignorant, maldistributed, and mercenary clergy proved incapable of slaking the spiritual thirst of an increasingly literate and critical laity, the more so as the hierarchy, preoccupied with affairs of state, judicial rights, and secular wealth, displayed little pastoral concern. Manifestly anxious about the ills of this life and the hereafter, the faithful were forced to demand or invent new rituals and observances. Although at root not heterodox, this popular piety nonetheless tended to

---

[18] The reference is to a widely cited passage by Lucien Febvre, who wrote of *un immense appétit du divin*. See Febvre, "The Origins of the French Reformation; A Badly-Put Question?" in his *A New Kind of History and Other Essays*, ed. Peter Burke (New York, 1973), p. 65.

[19] A. N. Galpern, *The Religions of the People in Sixteenth-Century Champagne* (Cambridge, Mass., 1976), p. 90.

[20] For evidence of heterodoxy in Lille in the earlier fifteenth century, including the execution of three townspeople in 1418 and, a decade later, the burning of five Lillois suspected of Hussitism, see Fredericq, *Corpus documentorum inquisitionis*, 1:279–80, 281–2, 311, 312–14 (docs. 250, 253, 273, 276); 3:49–51, 55–6 (docs. 42–4, 46–7, 61). In addition, a Franciscan preaching around 1470 was forced to recant publicly after his millenarian doctrines were found suspect: ibid., 1:436–8 (docs. 357–8).

[21] See, e.g., Febvre, "Origins of the French Reformation," esp. pp. 60–74; Toussaert, *Sentiment religieux en Flandre;* Jean Delumeau, *Catholicism between Luther and Voltaire: a New View of the Counter-Reformation* (London and Philadelphia, 1977; trans of French, publ. 1971), esp. pp. 154–61; Steven Ozment, *The Age of Reform 1250–1550* (New Haven, 1980), esp. pp. 205–22.

focus on inessentials and degenerate into empty formalism if not magic, idolatry, and sacrilege. Over time, historians have contended, it could issue in bitter disillusionment or even pave the way for rejection of a church that so inadequately responded to profound religious needs and aspirations.

Some symptoms of spiritual confusion cited in support of this interpretation can be located in Lille. To begin with, the clergy displayed many of its characteristic shortcomings. Absenteeism was rife. Pastors had long since been exempted from residence in most intramural parishes, while in St. Pierre the curé was at the same time lieutenant provost of the chapter and thus, because of the onerous administrative duties involved, was frequently away from Lille. To be sure, deputies were appointed, but they had to pay large sums to the benefice holders.[22] The real income of the priests actually serving in the parishes was therefore lower than the nominal income of the benefice. Combined with the adverse effects of inflation, declining clerical salaries provided a strong incentive to additional benefice hunting and pluralism, the hiring of less qualified substitutes, and neglect of the needs of the faithful.

In St. Etienne, for example, which in the mid-sixteenth century had nineteen clergymen and two clerks – none burdened, it was said, with more than "very light duties" – usually just three or four priests would appear for services, and often only a clerk was present at High Mass. At times, the situation was so bad that Sunday Masses could not be properly celebrated, resulting in "confusion and scandal." Chaplains, cantors, and horistes from the same parish were also accused of competing publicly and heatedly for the privilege of celebrating fee-paying services, arriving for their duties late and in secular clothing, and conversing, laughing, and bickering rather than praying or singing during Mass. Charging that many of the clergymen had "several occupations" and therefore habitually disregarded their obligations to St. Etienne, the Magistrat and the "distinguished parishioners" who brought the complaint agreed that henceforth fees could be received only by those who actually participated in services.[23]

Moral failings of the type that gave rise to anticlericalism elsewhere were also to be found in Lille. Individual horistes, for instance, were dismissed for drunkenness, quarrelsomeness, and misconduct; in 1562

---

[22] Platelle, "La vie religieuse à Lille," p. 394.
[23] AML, Aff. gén., C. 792, d. 8.

every horiste from St. Etienne was reprimanded by the Magistrat, and two discharged, for engaging in "many kinds of disorderliness."[24]

Despite such instances of aldermanic intervention, reform was primarily the responsibility of the church hierarchy. But in Lille as elsewhere knowledgeable and vigilant leadership was lacking, and indeed many abuses profited those who should have been dedicated to eliminating them. The chapter of St. Pierre, to begin with, failed to encourage reform. In fact, faced with the loss of prerogatives and privileges, the canons, like their fellows elsewhere, strenuously resisted publishing the decrees of the Council of Trent.[25]

Even more damaging, the provostship of St. Pierre, the principal ecclesiastical administrative post in the city, was filled by men who took little interest in it because they also held more important offices elsewhere. On the eve of the Reformation, François de Melun, a royal councillor and *maître des requêtes*, was provost between 1508 and 1521. At the same time, he was an apostolic prothonotary, provost in Bruges and St. Omer, and bishop of Arras (1510–12) and of Thérouanne (1512–21).

His successor, Cornille de Berghes (1521–5), concurrently held canonries in Liège, where he was later named bishop. Despite these distinguished appointments, de Berghes's main qualifications for church posts seem to have consisted in noble birth and his father's connections at court, for he never showed any leadership nor even took holy orders. In any event, he soon resigned the provostship at Lille in favor of François de Rosimbos (1525–58), who at the time of his appointment was only nine years old. During his long tenure, Rosimbos's service at court in Brussels kept him so occupied that he rarely if ever came to Lille.

After Rosimbos's death, the provostship remained vacant for several years as episcopal authorities, papacy, and Habsburg government quarreled over whether the position should be given permanently to the bishop of Tournai to compensate him for the loss of substantial parts of his diocese during the episcopal reorganization of the Low Countries after 1559. It was finally attributed, though not by right, to Gilbert

---

24 These cases are all recorded in ibid., d. 4. Cf. ADN, Reg. B 19,456, fol. 176, 7 November 1523, for the case of Gilles aux Chausses, who unsuccessfully sued before the Council of Flanders to get back his post, from which the Magistrat had dismissed him for "scandalous . . . life and conduct," notwithstanding his twenty years of service.

25 Edouard de Moreau, *Histoire de l'église en Belgique*, 6 vols. (Brussels, 1945–52), 5:52.

d'Oignies, who during most of his tenure was in fact also bishop of Tournai.[26]

Similarly detrimental to good clerical order, a general lack of effective episcopal direction afflicted the diocese of Tournai, in which Lille was situated. Either because they were nonresident foreigners or because they were politicians who spent most of their time at the Burgundian and Habsburg courts, the bishops of Tournai had traditionally neglected their charge.[27] Admittedly, Louis Guillard (or Guillart), pupil and follower of the Paris reformer Josse Clichtove, resolved to end fee abuses and make deans more zealous in promoting the spiritual life of the faithful. But his tenure was too short (1518–21) for anything to get accomplished.[28] After him, moreover, the long reign (1525–64) of Charles de Croy, scion of one of the premier noble families of the Netherlands, and a pluralist on a grand scale, marked a return to the familiar pattern. Croy did not take holy orders until 1533, failed to visit his see until 1539, and only celebrated his first Mass at Tournai the following year, after which he was again nearly always absent. Worse, he instituted no changes of any significance whatsoever. Instead, he devoted his energies to building chateaux, providing monetary support for Charles V's wars, and protecting his income when the redrawing of the Netherlands ecclesiastical map carved up his diocese. Upon his death, the bishopric remained vacant for nearly a year before Gilbert d'Oignies was consecrated in October 1565.[29]

If, as historians suggest, disputes over jurisdiction, taxation, and economic competition contributed to anticlericalism, frequent clashes be-

---

[26] See, in general, Hautcoeur, *Histoire de Saint-Pierre*, 2:449–51. For the conflict over the grant of the provostship to the bishop of Tournai, see *Documents inédits sur l'érection des nouveaux diocèses aux Pays-Bas (1521–1570)*, ed. Michel Dierickx, 3 vols. (Brussels, 1960–2), 2:167–9, 324–6, 422–4, 605–6, 3:38–9, 100, 124, 127. For detailed information on Cornille de Berghes, see *Biographie nationale*, 2, cols. 214–18, and *Dictionnaire d'histoire et de géographie ecclésiastique* (Paris, 1912-), 8, col. 457.

[27] Pirenne, *Histoire de Belgique*, 3:336.

[28] *Biographie nationale*, 8, col. 430. Guillard, a Frenchman, was originally named in 1513, but Tournai was seized by the English soon after his elevation. Restored to his throne in 1518, when the English were expelled, Guillard lost it for good when Charles V incorporated the city into his domains.

[29] For Croy, who was concurrently abbot of Afflinghem, Hautmont, and Saint-Ghislain, as well as a canon of Cambrai, see *Nationaal Biografisch Woordenboek*, 10 vols. (Brussels, 1964–83), 2, cols. 148–58. For d'Oignies, see *Biographie nationale*, 16, cols. 112–15. Unfortunately, it is all but impossible to get much of an idea of the functioning of the diocesan administration, or of parish life in sixteenth-century Lille, because the aerial bombing of Tournai in May 1940 destroyed almost all the archives there.

tween the city government and the chapter of St. Pierre created numerous opportunities for the emergence of such attitudes in Lille. The
chapter, for instance, invariably insisted that no resident of its seigneurial enclaves, whether clergy or layman, could be judged by the
municipal courts, even for crimes committed in places subject to the
Magistrat. Just as regularly, the aldermen rejected this claim and summoned offenders to appear before them. Then, too, Lillois were forbidden by town law to buy beer, grain, or anything else in the chapter's
precincts, but the canons continued to abet the tax evasion that such
sales entailed. The Magistrat likewise fought unceasingly to shut down
production of goods on any territory in or near Lille exempt from city
taxes and inspections, and it was St. Pierre's lands that were regularly
cited in this respect.[30]

Relations between city and chapter were further envenomed by a long
dispute over the canons' control of Latin education, increasingly regarded as desirable by a humanist-influenced laity. From at least 1510,
the Magistrat encouraged the opening of private Latin schools independent of St. Pierre's tutelage, only to have them shut down in 1524 by
order of the Gouvernance, which upheld the chapter's traditional monopoly. It took an additional decade of legal wrangling to reach a compromise. By its terms, the municipal authorities were permitted to open
one Latin school in St. Maurice parish and another in St. Sauveur and
choose the teachers. The chapter retained the right to examine and
approve – or, if necessary, reject – instructors, books, and doctrines
taught.[31]

In addition to these shortcomings within the institutional church and
friction between political and ecclesiastical authorities, one can find
troubling signs in some religious practices involving the laity. By the
early sixteenth century, for example, an annual competition among ver-
sifiers writing in the Virgin's honor, sponsored for many years on the
Feast of the Assumption by the rhetorical society of Notre-Dame du
Puy, seems to have degenerated into an occasion for scandalous, even
obscene, ballads attacking women's virtue.[32] The *tableaux vivants* of the

---

[30] The three volumes of Hautcoeur, *Histoire de Saint-Pierre*, contain innumerable examples of
these conflicts, as do AML, Reg. 15,884–6.
[31] See Léon Lefebvre, "Note sur l'enseignement du latin et les jeux en langue latine dans les
écoles de Lille au XVIe siècle," *Annales de l'Est et du Nord* 2 (1906):534–7; AML, Reg. 15,884,
fols. 29v–30v, 30 August 1535.
[32] De la Fons de Mélicocq, "Confrérie de Notre-Dame du Puy," pp. 466–8.

Nativity, Passion, Resurrection, and saints' martyrdoms traditionally staged by the *compagnons* of St. Sauveur, a group of poor men subsidized by the Magistrat, were discontinued after about 1540. Again, on several occasions in the early 1560s the aldermen forbade guilds to display their pious histories, on the ground that the exhibitors were burlesquing spiritual matters.[33] In 1564, to take a final instance, carpenters were ordered to limit expenditures on their confraternal banquet to 10 livres, for a sober religious celebration had turned into a rowdy affair.[34]

Obviously, then, there existed in sixteenth-century Lille phenomena – clerical misbehavior, conflicts between Magistrat and chapter, and a sense of enervating institutional drift – that elsewhere afforded a receptive environment to reforming ideas and movements.[35] Doubtless, too, some religious practice was formal, artificial, and capable of provoking doubt as to its value for helping believers attain salvation. But the evidence also indicates that the traditional faith and the practices that had grown up around it still attracted many Lillois who continued to enrich the church fabric, organize confraternities, or petition the Virgin. Moreover, the city's political leadership strongly supported the orthodox religion, as was ostentatiously demonstrated during the state visit of Emperor Charles V and Prince Philip in 1549. On a stage representing the Triumph of the Faith stood the church personified – dressed in crimson satin and surrounded by figures of a pope, cardinal, archbishop, bishop, St. Gregory, St. Jerome, St. Ambrose, and St. Augustine – trampling wretched heresy underfoot beneath the gaze of Charles. The emperor himself was encircled by Charlemagne, Godefroy de Bouillon, St. Louis, Ferdinand and Isabella, and Philip, and he held in captivity Julian the Apostate, Simon the Magician, Arius, Hus, Luther, Zwingli, and many other heresiarchs.[36]

---

[33] Léon Lefebvre, *La procession de Lille du XVe au XVIIe siècle* (Lille, 1902), pp. 5, 9 n. 1.

[34] AML, Reg. 16,002, fol. 147v.

[35] Though not specifically directing their comments at conditions in Lille, in June 1566 the provincial Estates criticized the ecclesiastical hierarchy of Walloon Flanders for improper behavior and for failing to provide either leadership conducive to public tranquillity or correction of clerical shortcomings, notably greed due to insufficient livings; see the document published by Verheyden, "Chronique de Gaiffier," p. 72 (response to proposed moderation of royal decrees against heretics, 15 June 1566).

[36] See the detailed description of Lille's reception of the Imperial party in Juan Christoval Calvete de Estrella, *Le très-heureux voyage fait par . . . Don Philippe*, trans. Jules Petit, 5 vols. (Brussels, 1873–84; trans. of Spanish, publ. 1552), 2:143–72, esp. p. 166. I owe this reference to Hugo Soly, "Plechtige intochten in de steden van de Zuidelijke Nederlanden tijdens de overgang van Middeleeuwen naar Nieuwe Tijd: communicatie, propaganda, spektakel," *Tijdschrift voor Geschiedenis* 97 (1984):351–2.

Thus, it was amid contradictory signs of the state of the traditional church and faith on the one hand, and displays of Magisterial orthodoxy on the other, that Protestantism developed in Lille.

II

Lille was never, as far as is known, a spot where innovative reforming ideas originated, but several factors facilitated their transmission to and diffusion within the city. Dissent, as is commonly recognized, traveled readily along trade routes, and Lille was a leading commercial center in touch with all parts of Europe.[37] In addition, linguistic and cultural links with France – not to mention geographical propinquity – fostered the spread of Bucerian and Calvinist ideas. Rising literacy among the laity and the advent of printing further enlarged Lillois' range of religious options by allowing heterodox works or simply vernacular Bibles to reach a wide audience. Although no press is known to have operated openly in Lille before 1594, booksellers were present from at least 1509.[38] It is not surprising, therefore, that numerous suspect books had found their way into townspeople's hands by the 1520s, or that they continued to circulate despite official measures ranging from licensing booksellers only after they had sworn to uphold all censorship laws to searches of private homes in search of prohibited literature.[39] Pamphlets, leaflets, and other ephemeral literature also appeared throughout the period. Some of it – to the Magistrat's distress – addressed local issues, suggesting the existence of an underground printing press in or near the city.[40]

Not only members of the educated elite but wool combers, light-cloth weavers, and shopkeepers were prosecuted for reading Protestant writ-

---

37 Cf. Eric Mahieu, "Le Protestantisme à Mons, des origines à 1575," *Annales due Cercle archéologique de Mons* 66 (1965–67):247, where the absence of substantial trade is given much of the credit for the weakness of Protestantism there.

38 In 1594, according to Jules Houdoy, *Les imprimeurs lillois. Bibliographie des impressions lilloises, 1595–1700* (Paris, 1879), p. 39, Antoine Tack was given a bonus by the Magistrat because, in the words of the municipal accounts, "he is the first who has printed in this city." The *Histoire de l'édition française*, ed. Henri-Jean Martin and Roger Chartier, 4 vols. (Paris, 1982–6), 1:218, lists Lille as having a printer in 1509, but the *Bibliotheca bibliographica aureliana. Répertoire bibliographique des livres imprimés en France au XVI siècle*, 30 vols. (Baden-Baden, 1968–80), 9:89–98, shows that while between 1509 and 1594 books were printed in Paris, Antwerp, Bruges, and Douai for Lille booksellers, Tack was the first to print them legally in Lille.

39 AML, Reg. 15,922, fol. 48v, 26 July 1550; Reg. 381, fols. 202v–3; Reg. 382, fol. 6; Reg. 16,290, fol. 160; Reg. 16,295, passim.

40 For mention of such works, see AML, Reg. 381, fols. 191v–2; Frossard, *Eglise sous la Croix*, p. 79; and Jean Crespin, *Histoire des vrays tesmoins de la vérité de l'Evangile* (Geneva, 1570), fol. 665v.

ings and Bibles, a development that inevitably compromised the established church's authority. The master comber Jacques de Lo, for instance, confidently referred to Scripture to explain his repudiation of the Catholic Eucharist service, the doctrine of the real presence, Masses for the dead, fasting, salvation by works, and all sacraments save baptism and Holy Communion.[41] His Reformed coreligionist Robert Oguier similarly defended his beliefs by reference to God's Word. Where, he demanded when interrogated in jail, was the scriptural warrant for the Mass? "One does not," he insisted, "read anywhere in the Holy Bible that the prophets, nor Jesus Christ or his apostles, ever performed the Mass"; it was therefore to be rejected.[42]

Printing did not disseminate the Reformation message in isolation, of course. A 1564 ordinance that forbade bookshops to sell French translations of the psalms of David – a favorite source of the hymns that Protestants sang as propaganda in defiance of the existing church – exemplifies the reciprocal effects of the printed and spoken word.[43] Furthermore, even the literate minority was powerfully influenced by ideas communicated orally, whether in casual conversation or in more structured situations such as the sermons and discussion groups that itinerant evangelists and dedicated townspeople alike repeatedly arranged.[44]

The effects of the new religious teachings thus made available began to be felt early. If Jerome Aleander, papal nuncio in Worms, is correct, heretics denying the doctrine of the real presence were apprehended in Lille just prior to February 1521.[45] Their fate is unknown, nor is it possible to trace the course of heterodoxy during the next few years. Despite the enactment of imperial decrees condemning Lutheran ideas and enjoining the arrest of anyone expressing Lutheran opinions,[46] no

---

[41] Jean Crespin, *Actes des martyrs déduits en sept livres* (Geneva, 1564), pp. 995–8.
[42] Ibid., p. 813; also cited in Willems-Closset, "Protestantisme à Lille," p. 207.
[43] AML, Reg. 382, fol. 6.
[44] Although no public preaching is known to have taken place in the city, the Calvinist minister Paul Chevalier, for example, spoke in houses in Lille (see the document printed in Halkin and Moreau, "Procès de Chevalier," p. 50) while lay leaders hosted gatherings in their own homes. Cf. Robert Scribner, "Oral Culture and the Diffusion of Reformation Ideas," *History of European Ideas* 5 (1984):237–56.
[45] Fredericq, *Corpus documentorum inquisitionis*, 5:394, doc. 749. Aleander, writing to the papal vice-chancellor in Rome, asserted that "many heretics" had been "found and seized" in Artois and Lille, though without being more specific about either total numbers or numbers arrested in each place.
[46] Frossard, *Eglise sous la Croix*, pp. 146–54.

Lillois is known to have been prosecuted again until 1526, when five townspeople were summoned before the bishop's court in Tournai. After a bitter jurisdictional dispute – involving separate trials by episcopal court and aldermanic bench, an interdict, and appeals to Charles V – at least three of the defendants were convicted of holding Lutheran beliefs (a vague and inclusive category) and forced to recant their errors publicly.[47]

The trial demonstrably failed to halt the diffusion of Protestant ideas. In 1528, questionable books were found in the home of a certain Georges Savereulx, and in December 1529 publication of a new imperial law brought a *"grant nombre"* of suspect works into the hands of local officials.[48] Perhaps some sort of Protestant movement emerged in Lille during these years. But a crackdown in 1533, when six or possibly seven townspeople were condemned to death – among them Savereulx[49] – seems to have disrupted whatever developments were underway at that time. The executions may have deprived a nascent heterdox group of leaders before it got established on a firm footing, while frightening away townspeople just beginning to flirt with dissent. Adherents of Luther could particularly have become disillusioned by the recent turn of events. Their movement, after all, placed much of the responsibility for religious reform in the hands of the secular authorities, yet it was now becoming clear that at Lille such officials were not disposed to promote this kind of change. It is equally possible that religious innovation did not yet appeal to many Lillois, caught up in ritual and devotions as they were.

In common with other textile cities, though in sharp contrast to nearby rural cloth areas, none of the sects that composed the so-called Radical Reformation seems to have benefited from the disarray of other reforming currents at Lille during the 1530s or to have taken root there

---

[47] See ibid., pp. 5–6, and Willems-Closset, "Protestantisme à Lille," p. 199 n. 5. On 3 November 1525, the aldermen had won the right to try all transgressions of imperial laws against Lutheranism; see Fredericq, *Corpus documentorum inquisitionis*, 5:38–9, doc. 431. An imperial decision settling the disputes arising out of the 1526 case, dated 4 September 1527, confirmed the right. Although anyone expressing heretical opinions was to be turned over to the inquisition, Jean de Frelin, papal inquisitor for the diocese of Tournai – who had carried out the questioning in the municipal trial – was appointed permanent deputy inquisitor for Lille; see ibid., 5:255–9, doc. 637. Frelin, from the Dominican convent in Lille, had been named papal inquisitor in 1507 (ibid., 3:156, doc. 131); he remained inquisitor at Lille until his death in 1537 (ibid., 5:317–18, doc. 678).

[48] Alexandre de Saint-Léger, *Histoire de Lille, des origines à 1789* (Lille, 1942), p. 160.

[49] Frossard, *Eglise sous la Croix*, pp. 14–17.

later.[50] Granted, Calvin claimed that the Spiritual Libertines – whom he heartily detested and furiously denounced – had been founded by a man named Coppin in his native city of Lille, and several other Libertines are said to have lived and preached in and around Lille about 1540.[51] Yet just one case of all those tried in the city may have involved a member of the sect. In 1545, Jean Laman, a *julier* (Lille dialect for a seller of gold, silver, and other expensive cloth) was prosecuted for having asserted, among other things, that every soul that God created would necessarily be saved, a belief commonly held by Libertines.[52]

Anabaptism also appears to have had scant appeal to city folk. Admittedly, before his execution in 1555, the Reformed leader Baudichon Oguier exhorted his coreligionists to beware dangerous doctrines, in particular those of the Anabaptists.[53] Such exhortations were, however, common practice and need not have had any specific reference to Lille. The one trial of Anabaptists in the city, held in 1563, took place there simply because Lille was the seat of the provincial administration that had jurisdiction over the thirteen accused, all of them villagers from the weaving area along the Lys.[54] If any movement of this type actually existed within Lille, it was very good at evading detection. The sole known Anabaptist from Lille was active elsewhere: a barber deported

50 Cf. George H. Williams, *The Radical Reformation* (Philadelphia, 1962); Johan Decavele, *De Dageraad van de Reformatie in Vlaanderen (1520–1565)* (Brussels, 1975); Willems-Closset, "Protestantisme à Lille," pp. 200, 202 n. 34. Although the maps on pp. xv–xvi of A. L. E. Verheyden, *Anabaptism in Flanders, 1530–1650. A Century of Struggle* (Scottdale, Penn., 1961), cite Lille as the seat of an Anabaptist congregation and as a "known Anabaptist location," the text gives no supporting evidence. It is likely that Verheyden has been misled by Coussemaker's account (see below, no. 54). For the absence of Anabaptists from other cloth towns, see Mahieu, "Protestantisme à Mons," pp. 170–1, and Gérard Moreau, "La corrélation entre milieu social et professionnel et le choix de religion à Tournai," in *Les sources de l'histoire religieuse de la Belgique. Moyen Age et Temps modernes* (Louvain, 1968), pp. 292, 293, 196.

51 To Calvin, Coppin was an "ignorant man" (*vir indoctus*) and his doctrines were "filth" (*faeces*); see excerpt in Fredericq, *Corpus documentorum inquisitionis*, 5:94, doc. 479. Gérard Moreau, *Histoire du protestantisme à Tournai jusqu'à la veille de la Révolution des Pays-Bas* (Paris, 1962), pp. 88, 90, says that Antoine Pocquet successfully disseminated libertine ideas in Lille, Tournai, and Valenciennes in 1540–2. For other libertines, see Phyllis Mack Crew, *Calvinist Preaching and Iconoclasm in the Netherlands, 1544–1569* (Cambridge, 1978), pp. 56–7.

52 Willems-Closset, "Protestantisme à Lille," p. 200. But because Laman was arrested in the aftermath of the Brully affair (see subsequent discussion), he may have been a follower of that preacher.

53 Crespin, *Actes des martyrs*, p. 818.

54 Willems-Closset, "Protestantisme à Lille," p. 215 n. 152. Edmond de Coussemaker, *Troubles religieux du XVIe siècle dans la Flandre maritime, 1560–1570*, 4 vols. (Bruges, 1876), 1:17, 99–101, reported on what appears to have been the same incident. According to him, some of the many Anabaptists who had come to live in Lille in the early 1560s to escape persecution were

from Geneva in 1537 and drowned by order of the magistrates at Metz the year after.[55]

Possibly as early as 1539, a new group of dissenters appeared that was quickly and perhaps from the beginning influenced by Lillois and missionaries with direct links to Bucer and Calvin. It may, in fact, have been the first group with this orientation in the Low Countries. Valerand Poullain, a former priest from Lille who had emigrated to Strasbourg, was particularly important to its development. He sent copies of Calvin's works to his native city and was responsible for the dispatch of Pierre Brully, a minister of the French church in Strasbourg, to preach in and around Lille, Tournai, Valenciennes, Douai, and Arras during the autumn of 1544.

Our first solid information about the group dates from that time, when Brully's capture in Tournai set off a flurry of heresy hunting. Several leading citizens of Lille were implicated, including Jean Fremault, a member of an important political and merchant family who was himself just beginning a career in the Magistrat, and Eustache du Quesnoy, a prominent physician as well as alderman (1540), huithomme (1541), and councillor (1543, 1544). At least half a dozen other Lillois were also prosecuted.

Despite appeals from both the regent Mary of Hungary and Charles V himself, urging that all the accused be treated with the utmost severity, the aldermen's repressive efforts were socially selective. Du Quesnoy was able to flee to Heidelberg, and Fremault and two other men to Antwerp, where in later years they became well-known merchants. Another citizen, though found guilty of having violated imperial placards against heresy, was released because he had always lived a "distinguished and Catholic life" and came from a "virtuous" family. In the end, just two of those apprehended were put to death. The Gouvernance retaliated by confiscating the property of the four who escaped; the Magistrat's appeal to the Great Council at Mechelen failed to get the seizures reversed.[56]

executed by the Gouvernance in 1563 in response to pressure from the ecclesiastical inquisitor. Coussemaker garbled the events he recounted and seems not to have realized that the people executed in Lille had been seized elsewhere. Nor did he understand that had the heretics been townspeople, the Magistrat would have claimed jurisdiction over them. In short, evidence of an Anabaptist community at Lille turns out to have little substance.

55 Willems-Closset, "Protestantisme à Lille," pp. 200–1.

56 Ibid., pp. 201–3 (source of the quotations); BML, MS. 597; Frossard, *Eglise sous la Croix*, p. 26.

As before, the crackdown was soon over, and indeed only one local man was put to death for religious offenses during the next ten years.[57] According to later Calvinist sources, a vigorous Reformed community arose in this milder climate, apparently around a nucleus formed principally of artisan families. The Oguiers were of signal importance. Many conventicles were held in the home of Robert and Jeanne, while their son Baudichon led discussion groups. Guillaume Touart, a mercer, likewise used his house as a meeting place right up to the time he was banished in 1561.[58] The other known lay leader was Jacques de Lo, a master wool comber.[59]

If Crespin is to be believed, all were severe critics of the existing church as well as articulate and knowledgeable exponents of reformed beliefs. "All you want," Jeanne Oguier announced with disgust to the priests examining her for heresy, "is to keep your stomach full, for it's your god, and always to be comfortable."[60] During his interrogation, Jacques de Lo disdained both holy water and the priest's benediction of such sacramentals. Only God can bless things, he declared; furthermore, "everything is pure and spotless to him who is pure." He also refused to listen to Catholic preachers, for they talked of salvation by works, an abomination in his eyes. De Lo maintained too that the true church must be subject to proper ecclesiastical discipline, which he defined in typically Reformed terms.[61] The Mass was a worthless even blasphemous sacrifice, Robert Oguier declared, for by his crucifixion, Christ had once and for all perfected the blessed. Hence to celebrate the act again and again was in effect to deny the Lord. Oguier was confident that he was correct, for he had carefully read his Bible, and it never once referred to the Mass. Christ and the apostles had, Oguier knew, "indeed celebrated the Last Supper, where all the Christian people communed, but," he pointed out, "there was no sacrificing there." For his part,

Du Quesnoy's wife was a de Fourmestraux, and he was related to other distinguished families; see Fremaux, *De Fourmestraux*, p. 202.

57 Willems-Closset, "Protestantisme à Lille," p. 204.
58 Touart went to Antwerp, where he was executed for heresy in 1569. Crespin, *Histoire des vrays tesmoins*, fol. 705v.
59 Willems-Closset, "Protestantisme à Lille," pp. 209, 212–13. She suggests, p. 212 n. 114, that Robert Oguier was also a say-wool comber, but the testimony she cites from Crespin (*Actes des martyrs*, p. 996) says that the two men were of the same *estat*, which could as easily mean social rank as profession. It seems likely, however, that Oguier was also an artisan.
60 Crespin, *Actes des martyrs*, p. 816.
61 Ibid., pp. 1000, p. 998.

Oguier was convinced that the Mass was "invented by men"; as such, he must follow Christ's injunction to avoid all such things.[62]

The community also profited from the return of several Low Countries' refugees trained in England, at that time home to a number of large native and exile Calvinist congregations. First to arrive was the Lillois Symphorien Desbarbieux, but the crucial figure was Guy de Brès (or de Bray), son of a cloth dyer of Mons and himself formerly a glassmaker.[63] Baudichon Oguier mentioned that every Protestant in Lille "knew and approved of" de Brès's teaching, and Jacques de Lo, who directed the group after 1555, declared that he always consulted with de Brès on matters of faith.[64] Jean Crespin's enthusiastic tribute insisted that "there exist few places where the Gospel has been preached and expounded with greater boldness, and received by the people with greater zeal and affection, than in this town." In houses and caves, fields and woods, by night and day, Crespin wrote, the message of salvation had been proclaimed and a large flock of men, women, and children gathered together.[65]

De Brès also sought to set up a proper Reformed hierarchy and a wide range of services. According to Crespin's perhaps idealized description, funds were collected by deacons, who visited the faithful every week, exhorting them to fulfill their duty to the poor. Aid was provided to impoverished, hungry, sick, and imprisoned Protestants and also to *les ignorans*. Youth received proper religious instruction, so that "there was no licentiousness in their lives or in their words."[66]

Between 1552 and 1555, de Brès propagated the faith throughout Walloon Flanders as well as in the nearby cloth cities of Tournai and Valenciennes.[67] Crespin asserted that the "flourishing church" of Lille held large meetings "not only in the city but in villages for four or five leagues around," to which hastened people "as if starving from the wish they had to hear the word of God."[68] A government report on one of

---

62 Ibid., p. 813; also cited in Willems-Closset, "Protestantisme à Lille," pp. 207–8.
63 De Brès, who had left Mons during a crackdown on that city's small Protestant community in 1548, had never been a minister in his hometown; Mahieu, "Protestantisme à Mons," pp. 147–55.
64 See Willems-Closset, "Protestantisme à Lille," pp. 204–5, 212; Crespin, *Actes des martyrs*, p. 998.
65 Crespin, *Actes des martyrs*, p. 812.
66 Ibid; also in Willems-Closset, "Protestantisme à Lille," p. 205.
67 Moreau, *Protestantisme à Tournai*, p. 140 n. 2; Daniel Ollier, *Guy de Brès. Etude historique sur la Réforme au pays wallon (1522–1567)* (Paris, 1883), pp. 33, 52–3.
68 Crespin, *Actes des martyrs*, pp. 812–13.

these *presches*, held at the time of Vespers on Corpus Christi Day 1554 in a wood outside Armentières, fifteen kilometers west of Lille, noted that it was attended by sixty to a hundred people. Singing the Psalms of David opened the meeting, and then an unknown man – circumstantial evidence suggests that it was de Brès – spoke on baptism for more than an hour.[69] A survey carried out the next year for the bishop of Arras testified to the success of evangelizing efforts, particularly in textile villages and towns. The Alleu, a territory with considerable rural industry located on the upper Lys west of Armentières, was of dubious orthodoxy at best. Armentières itself was said to be "infested" with Protestants, while in the entire area few people bothered to fulfill their annual obligation to go to confession.[70]

Early in 1555, however, de Brès's work in Lille was brought to an abrupt end and half a dozen of his followers put to death. Crespin claimed that Lille's Franciscans, learning of Protestant meetings, had undertaken to incite the populace against their fellows and to denounce the Magistrat for failing to uproot heresy.[71] In light of what we have learned about popular attachment to the established religion, it seems plausible that this kind of agitation would have evoked a favorable response among many Lillois, and it might well have put pressure on the authorities. But perhaps just as decisive was the redoubtable Pieter Titelmans, dean of the cathedral at Ronse, inquisitor for all Flanders.

Although named in 1545, Titelmans, his colleague Jean Pollet, canon of St. Pierre in Lille, and several assistants only set about seriously to comb Flanders for dissenters shortly before 1550.[72] Aware that he had to win the cooperation of local authorities if his efforts were to bear fruit, Titelmans approached Lille's aldermen with a proposal designed to allay

[69] Willems-Closset, "Protestantisme à Lille," p. 206.
[70] See Paul Beuzart, "La Réforme dans le diocèse d'Arras en 1555 d'après un document inédit," *BSHPF* 76 (1927):471, 476.
[71] Crespin, *Actes des martyrs*, p. 813.
[72] On Titelmans, see Paul Beuzart, "Pierre Titelmans et l'Inquisition en Flandre (1554–1567)," *BSHPF* 63–4 (1914–15):224–42; Decavele, *Dageraad van de Reformatie*, esp. pp. 11–17; and Johan Van de Wiele, "Itinerarium van inquisiteur Pieter Titelmans en zijn medewerkers (1547–1566)," *BCRHB* 151 (1985):61–144. Titelmans allegedly flirted with Lutheranism before becoming an ardent protagonist of orthodoxy; see Frossard, *Eglise sous la Croix*, p. 58. Pollet, who had begun working for Titelmans at the end of February 1546, continued in this capacity right up to his death on 25 May 1556. From 1557 occasionally, and between March 1563 and at least July 1565 regularly, Joris Immeloot (or Ymmelot), scholaster of St. Pierre, served Titelmans in French Flanders from a home base in Lille; Van de Wiele, "Itinerarium van Titelmans," pp. 66–7; Decavele, *Dageraad van de Reformatie*, p. 17 (who states that Immeloot assisted Titelmans until December 1565).

fears that vigorous pursuit of his mission would damage their power. In return for assistance in apprehending suspects, he promised that all prisoners taken in Lille, and all citizens of the city captured anywhere else, would be handed over to the municipal officials for judgment. His overture succeeded, agreement being reached in early August 1549, just at the time that Charles V and Philip II were being magnificently received in Lille on their tour through the Low Countries. As if to signal that none of the city's privileges had been abridged by this pact, the Magistrat seems not to have proclaimed from the bretesque the emperor's edict of 20 September 1549 ordering the confiscation of condemned heretics' property.[73]

In his quest, Titelmans relied heavily on informers, and indeed Crespin acknowledged that it was a tip from "false brethren" within Lille's heterodox congregation that on 6 March 1555 led the provost and his twelve-man force to the Oguier house, where forbidden books were discovered. Charged with unlawful absence from Sunday Mass and with holding illegal meetings, the four family members in captivity acknowledged their offenses and firmly professed adherence to the new faith. Then they were tortured in an effort to find out the names of other Protestants, convicted, and burned at the stake as obstinate heretics.[74] Two more Lillois were executed at the end of 1555, but de Brès, who presumably was being sought, managed to evade arrest and moved to Ghent.[75] He was not alone in deeming the Lille area no longer safe. Crespin wrote, though perhaps with some overstatement, that the fields and roads of Walloon Flanders were clogged with refugees.[76]

Although investigations proceeded, apparently no one was put to death again for religion during the next five years. When in March 1556, for example, Philippe le Sellier and his wife were prosecuted for conducting conventicles in their house (a capital crime under imperial law),

---

[73] See Jules Houdoy, "Chapitres de l'histoire de Lille. . . . Le privilège de nonconfiscation," *MSSAAL* 3rd ser. 10 (1872):92–6; for the text of the agreement, AML, Reg. 15,922, fol. 37v, 8 August 1549.

[74] Crespin, *Actes des martyrs*, pp. 813–17; idem, *Histoire des vrays tesmoins*, fols. 425–9; Willems-Closset, "Protestantisme à Lille," pp. 206–8.

[75] Frossard, *Eglise sous la Croix*, p. 36; Ollier, *Guy de Brès*, p. 55. De Brès managed to complete his *Le Baston de la Foy* before leaving, but in the preface noted that Lille's Protestants had to wage a daily *guerre et combat* to maintain the true church; E. M. Braekman, *Guy de Brès. I. Sa vie* (Brussels, 1960), pp. 84–5, 87.

[76] Crespin, *Actes des martyrs*, p. 817; cf. Willems-Closset, "Protestantisme à Lille," p. 209. Among those fleeing was Robert Oguier junior, who reached Frankfurt where he later became a wealthy member of the large exile community; Dietz, *Frankfurter Handelsgeschichte*, 2:18.

they were simply forbidden to leave the city for three years and warned not to allow "suspect" people to visit them.[77] But religious dissent had suffered some critical losses. The institutions begun under de Brès seem to have been dismantled – neither Crespin nor any other source makes further mention of them – and formal religious services were not held for some time. Nonetheless, Lille's Protestants did regroup, their survival perhaps aided by an adaptation of the confraternal form.[78] In addition, Jacques de Lo, whom de Brès is said to have designated his representative, was able to convene discussion groups in his home, and apparently similar gatherings took place elsewhere in the city. In 1559, moreover, de Brès went to live in Tournai, which was fast becoming a Calvinist stronghold; from there, he was able to visit Lille and its region.[79]

Starting early in 1560, however, the pace of prosecution stepped up in Lille as elsewhere in Flanders.[80] De Lo and his wife were seized on 30 January, along with a stack of forbidden books and incriminating papers. Two weeks later he was burned at the stake, and she was confined to Lille for a year, compelled to attend Mass every week, and warned not to neglect her Easter duty.[81] On 22 March, failure to attend church for many years and speaking openly against Catholicism earned a tailor banishment from town for six years. In November, a sayetteur was immolated for continuing to speak in a heretical manner despite previous warnings to desist.[82] The next year witnessed an even crueler bout of repression. Between late April and late July, religious offenses resulted in the execution of seven men, including three light-cloth

---

77 AML, Reg. 15,922, fol. 129, 27 March 1556.

78 In May 1556, officials in Brussels advised Jean de Montmorency, governor of Walloon Flanders, of the existence of a secret brotherhood called the comrades (or journeymen) of the doublet (*compaignons du pourpoint*). Its members, "who often go from town to town to see their comrades," included "some who are ill-disposed and some who are suspected of being badly inclined toward the [Catholic] faith." See *Analectes historiques*, ed. L. P. Gachard, vol. 1 (Brussels, 1856), p. 85. Unfortunately, though the governor was directed to make a full investigation, and though the confraternity continued to exist (see a brief passage in an ordinance issued in Douai in 1563, which forbade the brothers of the pourpoint to enter taverns or inns; Archives municipales de Douai, Reg. CC 281, fol. 181), nothing else of substance has come to light.

79 Crespin, *Actes des martyrs*, p. 996.

80 See the information summarized in Decavele, *Dageraad van de Reformatie*, appendixes I and II, presented in graphic form in Parker, *Dutch Revolt*, p. 63, fig. 4.

81 Crespin, *Actes des martyrs*, pp. 995–1003; Crespin, *Histoire des vrays tesmoins*, fols. 563–8; Moreau, *Protestantisme à Tournai*, pp. 180–1 n. 3. Cf. Willems-Closset, "Protestantisme à Lille," pp. 209, 212–13.

82 AML, Reg. 10,813, unfoliated; cf. Willems-Closset, "Protestantisme à Lille," p. 211.

weavers; two *crassiers* or dealers in oil, candles, butter, and similar wares; a trimming maker; and a grain and wood trader.[83] Eight other Lillois suffered less severe punishment ranging from public apology to exile.[84] Little wonder, given this heated atmosphere, that the Gouvernance fiscal officer and government spy Gilles Jovenel deemed suspect the theme – *vray corps de Christ caché soubz pain visible* – set by Lille's chamber of rhetoric for its annual competition in 1561, nor that the governor called off the tournament.[85]

No one was put to death for religion in 1562, although one man was sent to the galleys and four other townspeople were fined.[86] The executioner's grim toll recommenced the next year, when two men were killed and several others punished more mildly.[87] The drive against heresy scored a notable success in 1564, when two of the principal itinerant ministers serving the reformed community were apprehended and executed. On 20 May, Paul Chevalier, formerly a Franciscan friar in Douai and Tournai, was taken by the governor's men in the home of Mathias Remy, current leader of Lille's Protestants, where he was spending the night after preaching in a wood north of Lille. Convicted once by the bishop's court in Tournai, and then again (after the bitter jurisdictional battle narrated in Chapter 1 was settled) by both the Gouvernance and

---

[83] AML, Reg. 10,813, unfoliated; Willems-Closset, "Protestantisme à Lille," pp. 211, 215 n. 149.

[84] AML, Reg. 10,813, unfoliated; Frossard, *Eglise sous la Croix,* p. 54.

[85] The theme had already been approved by local clergymen and scholars when Jovenel got wind of it and judged it heterodox. Failing to convince either the organizers of the contest or local priests to prohibit its use, he rode to Arras to consult Antoine Havet, Dominican, doctor of theology, former confessor to the regent Mary of Hungary, and soon to be bishop of Namur. Havet agreed that the refrain was unorthodox and signed letters to that effect; armed with them, Jovenel got Governor Montmorency to forbid the tournament and direct chambers of other towns to stay home. See "Lettre de Gilles Jovenel . . . 2 août 1561," ed. L. P. Gachard, in *Compte rendu des séances de la Commission royale d'histoire* 3rd ser. 4 (1862);393–4; also printed in *Analectes historiques,* ed. Gachard, vol. 3 (Brussels, 1863), pp. 466–8. Unlike its counterparts in Tournai and other cities, Lille's chamber never, to my knowledge, performed Protestant pieces, so the fears may well have been baseless. Still, it is possible that Lille's Reformed community borrowed its code name, "the Rose," from the chamber, a practice that elsewhere often indicated a link between the two. But the name may have come from an inn, as de Brès is said to have been friendly with the keepers of an establishment called the White Rose; see L. A. van Langeraad, *Guido de Bray* (Zierekzee, 1884), p. 47. Whatever the situation in Lille, royal circles correctly considered many chambers seedbeds of heresy. See Philip II to the law courts of the Netherlands, 30 September 1556, in *Analectes historiques,* ed. Gachard, vol. 2 (Brussels, 1859), pp. 221–2; more generally, see Parker, *Dutch Revolt,* pp. 59–60; Crew, *Calvinist Preaching and Iconoclasm,* pp. 52–3, 63–4; Decavele, *Dageraad van de Reformatie,* pp. 193–220; Henri Liebrecht, *Les chambres de rhétorique* (Brussels, 1948).

[86] Frossard, *Eglise sous la Croix,* pp. 56–7.

[87] Ibid., pp. 60–1; Willems-Closset, "Protestantisme à Lille," pp. 211, 215 n. 151.

the Magistrat in Lille, Chevalier was burned at the stake in mid-December. Jean Castiel (Catel), although caught subsequently to Chevalier, had already been put to death on 14 November.[88]

During 1565, at least eight Lillois were detained for holding conventicles, insulting the Host, attendance at Protestant sermons, and possessing illegal writings. None, however, appears to have suffered capital punishment. The rate of arrest accelerated in the first three months of 1566, when five say-wool combers were apprehended. One, who had gone to preaching but declared that he did not want to change his religion, escaped with some time in the stocks, a public apology, and a promise to attend Mass and receive the sacraments regularly. The rest, who, Crespin reported, had the misfortune to have their forbidden books get into the hands of a Jesuit, paid for their error with their lives.[89]

III

Despite the aldermen's ringing symbolic endorsement of imperial heresy hunting in 1549, before about 1560 they had in fact prosecuted dissenters intermittently and for brief periods. Hence, the sustained campaign mounted during the half decade preceding the revolt, which made Lille a byword for orthodoxy and rigor,[90] represented a break with the Magistrat's previous practice.

In part, the prolonged campaign is testimony to the tireless activity of Titelmans and his assistants, who sharply increased prosecutions throughout Flanders.[91] But novel circumstances help explain the échevins' persistent willingness to continue cooperating with the inquisitor at the same time that they fought royal officials over issues of jurisdiction and confiscation. For one thing, Protestants in the region were gaining

---

[88] Halkin and Moreau, "Procès de Chevalier," pp. 1–74.

[89] AML, Reg. 15,886, fols. 86v–7; Reg. 16,980, fols. 102v–4; Frossard, *Eglise sous la croix*, pp. 70–9; Crespin, *Histoire des vrays tesmoins*, fols. 664v–5v. For the renewed conflict precipitated by the Gouvernance's arrest and prosecution of four of the individuals in 1565, see Chapter 1, section II.

[90] Early in April 1566, a rumor circulated in Brussels that several hundred of the signatories of the Compromise of the Nobility (see Chapter 6) intended to swoop down on the city "because there the sectaries are being prosecuted so severely"; Morillon to Granvelle, 7 April 1566, *CG*, 1:201.

[91] For the upsurge in prosecutions, particularly in 1561–2, see Parker, *Dutch Revolt*, pp. 62–3, based on Decavele, *Dageraad van de Reformatie*, esp. pp. 434, 639. Titelmans himself was rarely in Lille before March 1563, although he was frequently present between that date and February 1565, and again during the summer of 1565; see the chronology compiled by Van de Wiele, "Itinerarium van Titelmans," pp. 78–144.

in numbers and boldness. By 1561, presches attracted up to one thousand people, rather than the several score observed in the mid-1550s, and the crowds, accompanied and protected by armed guards and boldly meeting during the day as well as at night, subsequently grew even larger. Titelmans's campaign seemed, moreover, to result in few permanent gains. Three hundred or more people fled Armentières during the winter of 1560–1 to escape the inquisitor, but most soon returned. Titelmans glumly concluded that he had only aggravated the situation.[92] According to government reports, the gangs of beggars overrunning the countryside of Walloon Flanders in the winter of 1561–2 included many Protestants who preached, sang psalms, and tried, with some success, to convert others.[93] By August 1563, as much as a third of the population of the textile villages of Mouvaux, Wambrechies, Bondues, and Tourcoing was said to be Protestant. Local officials there and elsewhere were often sympathetic to, when not participants in, heretical activities.[94] In these years, too, there were mass Protestant processions in the streets of Valenciennes and Tournai, riots at executions, and attacks on jails to free prisoners.[95]

In view of the links between Lille and the surrounding cloth centers, these developments could only have been profoundly troubling to the Magistrat. Equally ominous was the exodus northward of French Protestants seeking sanctuary from intensified persecution during the Guise regency (1559–60) and once more after the Massacre of Valmy in 1562. Artisans also began to arrive from textile centers like Amiens where Protestantism had become firmly rooted. As the aldermen admitted, they feared that among "the many kinds and types of people" taking refuge in town there might well be adherents of "condemned sects." It was probably these misgivings that made them demand certificates of

---

[92] Letter to Philip II, Bruges, 5 September 1561, *CFMP*, 3:417.

[93] ADN, Reg. B 19,265, no. 46,788, 26 January 1562.

[94] A report on village heresy sent that month to the central government is cited in Willems-Closset, "Protestantisme à Lille," p. 214. According to this document, there were three to four thousand heretics in the four localities; I have calculated the proportion of population represented with the aid of data in ADN, Reg. B 3763. For only a few examples of official connivance with heresy, see Frossard, *Eglise sous la Croix*, pp. 60–1; André Schoonheere, *Histoire du vieux Comines* (Lille, 1961), p. 154; AGR, RB, MS. 65, fols. 33–5, 38v–9v, 43v–5; Beuzart, "La Réforme dans les environs de Lille."

[95] See Geoffrey Clark, "An Urban Study during the Revolt of the Netherlands: Valenciennes 1540–1570" (Ph.D. diss., Columbia University, 1972), pp. 255–333; Adlophe Hocquet, *Tournai et le Tournaisis au XVIe siècle au point de vue politique et social* (Brussels, 1906), pp. 93–106.

orthodoxy from all would-be immigrants from Amiens.[96] The authorities may also have been apprised of and perturbed by the closer contact that was developing among the Reformed churches of the Netherlands. These bonds were fostered by a common confession of faith written by Guy de Brès, which appeared in French in 1561, and by the synods attended by representatives of congregations in Flanders, Artois, Hainaut, and Brabant that were held semiannually between 1563 and 1566.[97]

The material problems encountered by Lillois in those years (outlined in Chapter 4) must also have made the Magistrat apprehensive that the new faith might, as in the surrounding area, serve as a vehicle for mobilizing and focusing discontent. This was a worrisome prospect indeed when townspeople were gathering in Lille's streets and squares in late autumn 1561, a time of acute distress, or reading the books and pamphlets "smacking of sedition and rebellion" that appeared a year later.[98]

The authorities' anxiety could only have become the more lively as prosecutions revealed that heterodoxy in Lille, already heavily artisanal in composition, was taking on a more pronounced class character. Although there are no extant surveys, tax lists, or similar records for any Protestant group in Lille, persecution and emigration have left us occupational information on seventy-five Protestant townspeople between 1544 and April 1566.[99] All but seven of the cases date from 1555–66, and all but one involve people who apparently held Bucerian or Calvinist doctrines (Table 5.1).[100]

---

96 AML, Reg. 381, fols. 159–60 (quotation); David Rosenberg, "Social Experience and Religious Choice: A Case Study, the Protestant Weavers and Woolcombers of Amiens in the Sixteenth Century" (Ph.D. diss., Yale University, 1978), pp. 78–9.

97 Paul Beuzart, *Les hérésies pendant le Moyen Age et la Réforme jusqu'à la mort de Phillippe II, 1598, dans la région de Douai, d'Arras et au Pays de l'Alleu* (Le Puy, 1912), p. 410.

98 AML, Reg. 277, fols. 139–9v; Reg. 381, fols. 191v–2. The Magistrat was so alarmed by the writings that it offered a hefty reward of 50 fl. (100 liv.) to anyone who turned in the authors or publishers.

99 The possible biases of martyrologies, lists of refugees, and registers of emigrés, like those I employ, are perceptively discussed by Benedict, *Rouen during the Wars of Religion*, pp. 72–7. But as he notes, taken together "they can provide a rough picture of the occupational structure of the Protestant community."

100 Sources: AML, Reg. 10,813, passim; AML, Reg. 15,922, fol. 129; ADN, Reg. B 1772, B 7239; Crespin, *Actes des martyrs;* idem, *Histoire des vrays tesmoins;* Willems-Closset, "Protestantisme à Lille"; Frossard, *Eglise sous la Croix,* pp. 40–79; A. L. E. Verheyden. *Le martyrologe protestant des Pays-Bas du Sud au XVIe siècle* (Brussels, 1960), pp. 180, 218–19, 251, 253; *Livre des habitants de Genève. I. 1549–1560,* ed. Paul-F. Geisendorf (Geneva, 1957), pp. 196–201; William J. C.

Table 5.1. *Occupations of Lillois*
who were prosecuted or emigrated
due to their religious beliefs, 1544–66

Clergy		1	(1.3%)
Priest	1		
Professionals		2	(2.7%)
Physician	1		
Teacher	1		
Merchants and shopkeepers		13	(17.3%)
Merchants	9		
Crassiers	2		
Mercer	1		
Julier[a]	1		
Textile artisans		45	(60.0%)
Light-cloth weavers	16		
Say-wool combers	14		
Trimming makers	7		
Drap weavers	5		
Dyer	1		
Fuller	1		
Currier	1		
Miscellaneous artisans		10	(13.3%)
Tailors	2		
Shoemaker	1		
Bookseller	1		
Roofer	1		
Ironsmith	1		
Weaponsmith	1		
Tavern keeper	1		
Unspecified artisans	2		
Others		4	(5.3%)
Sergeants	2		
Steward	1		
Stevedore	1		

[a]Only person known to have been prosecuted for beliefs apparently incompatible with the teachings of Bucer and Calvin.

By sending books and the preacher Brully, the ex-priest Valerand Poullain helped transmit new ideas. The chaplain of the Hôpital Comtesse, Lille's main hospital and asylum, arrested early in 1545 for translating into French a catechism deemed heterodox after publication, may also have been a sympathizer – though his quick release suggests that he had fallen victim to official overreaction in the aftermath of Brully's capture.[101] No suspect clergy appear after that date, indicating that the situation in Lille was much like that found elsewhere: Individual members of the clergy helped implant Protestantism but thereafter heresy made few inroads among them.[102] Perhaps adopting the Reformation was too materially and psychologically costly for clergy, either because of the financial rewards of pluralism, nonresidence, and the like, or because of the honored place that continued to be accorded the priesthood in many religious practices.[103] Or it may be that the Reformed community, once organized, purposely excluded priests of the abhorred old church.[104]

Professionals, government officials, and seigneurs likewise seem to have been little attracted to the new faith. To be sure, such men may have turned Protestant, but as powerful, well-to-do members of the urban community perhaps they succeeded in avoiding prosecution.[105] It is equally likely that caution and a firm sense of what they stood to lose should the existing order be altered governed the behavior of these members of the dominant classes in Lille as in many other cities. At the other extreme of society, unskilled laborers and the very poor are also

Moens, *The Walloon Church of Norwich: Its Registers and History,* 2 vols. (Lymington, 1887–8), 1:153–6; Moreau, *Protestantisme à Tournai,* pp. 319 n. 7, 351; de Schickler, *Eglises du réfuge en Angleterre,* 3:55–6; Decavele, *Dageraad van de Reformatie,* p. 333 n. 54.

[101] The chaplain (not counted in Table 5.1) was freed on the grounds that he had acted in good faith and bore no blame for the contents of the booklet, written by Cornelis van der Heyden, canon of Mechelen, and published in Ghent, possibly under a false license. See Frossard, *Eglise sous la croix,* p. 27; Willems-Closset, "Protestantisme à Lille," p. 203.

[102] Cf. Mahieu, "Protestantisme à Mons," pp. 143, 246; Decavele, *Dageraad van de Reformatie,* esp. table on p. 549; Moreau, "Corrélation entre milieu social et choix de religion à Tournai," pp. 292, 299.

[103] That the many supplementary posts continued to be a good source of income for Lille's clergy is suggested by the financial accounts of, e.g., the horistes of St. Etienne (AML, Reg. 14,718) or Ruffault's chapel (AML, Reg. 15,026), neither of which note any disruption during the sixteenth century.

[104] A suggestion that Protestants spurned potential recruits from among Catholic clergy was made in the discussion following Moreau's paper, "Corrélation entre milieu et choix de religion à Tournai," p. 300.

[105] Alain Lottin, in *Histoire de Lille,* 2:95, hypothesizes that the Magistrat was unwilling to prosecute prosperous members of the community for fear that their property would be confiscated.

nearly completely absent from the list, again a common phenomenon throughout Europe.

A pronounced gender imbalance – all the records together list fewer than a dozen female Protestants – also deserves comment. Perhaps there were numerous heretic women in Lille but prevalent notions of female weakness, dependency, and irresponsibility largely exempted them from the close attention of the authorities.[106] Conversely, women may have been less susceptible to Protestant messages than men. Some historians have contended that lower levels of female literacy hindered the diffusion of the new doctrines, allegedly dependent on written forms of propaganda.[107] The wide use of oral means of communication by Lille's Protestants, however, raises questions about the validity of such an explanation. Perhaps adherence to practices condemned by reformers was stronger among women: In the one instance of suspected iconoclasm in Lille it was women who raised the alarm.[108] Or perhaps the many rituals associated with the Virgin provided a satisfactory way of integrating female spirituality into the established church.

Confirming what scholars have found in many other cities, Table 5.1 reveals that the bulk of Lille's Bucerians and Calvinists consisted of merchants (17.3 percent) and artisans (73.3 percent). Long since, of course, Pirenne noted the marked appeal of Protestantism to merchants. In his account, a "capitalist spirit" and experience of upward social mobility predisposed industrious, self-made businessmen to reject tradition in favor of the individualism and radicalism that distinguished the Reformed religion.[109] Certainly a number of successful parvenu merchants benefited from Lille's sixteenth-century economic growth, and some of them seem to have found the new faith more congenial than the old. But if the evidence presented in Chapter 2 is any guide, their interest in religious novelty was not the concomitant of a capitalist mentality rooted in structural change.

Merchants' occupational experience seems more likely to have influenced their religious choice. In particular, the repeated travel and resi-

---

[106] It is worth noting that Jeanne Oguier is the only Lilloise known to have been executed. Jacques de Lo's wife, though arrested with her husband, received a considerably milder sentence than he did.

[107] See, e.g., Natalie Davis, "City Women and Religious Change," in her *Society and Culture in Early Modern France* (Stanford, 1975), pp. 65–95.

[108] For this incident, see Chapter 6.

[109] Pirenne, *Histoire de Belgique*, 3:434–5.

dence abroad traced in Chapter 2 both detached merchants from still-vital institutions like confraternities that promoted integration into the established church, and put them in contact with new currents of belief. In this context, it is surely significant that many merchants of Lille typically spent much time in – or at the very least maintained constant close communication with – ports in which Protestantism had become strongly rooted, Antwerp being the outstanding but by no means sole example.[110] It is telling that, as Table 2.4 demonstrates, Lille's principal merchant families had substantially greater contact with Antwerp than their less distinguished counterparts, for the former figure much more prominently among those denounced as heretics.[111]

Yet if among the great long-distance merchants of Lille Protestants or sympathizers, they were all but invisible in their hometown. Jean Fremault, in 1544, was the only prominent merchant subject to judicial pursuit in his own city. Perhaps like other elite Lillois they too benefited from an aldermanic blind eye. But several examples suggest that some of those who were inclined to religious dissent migrated to or remained in Antwerp, a strategy adopted by numerous dissenters from all over the Netherlands. Besides the merchants from Lille accused of heresy by a government spy in Antwerp in 1566, there were the members of the de Fourmestraux clan settled in Antwerp who subscribed 100,000 florins to an abortive project to purchase religious freedom from Philip II, as well as Gerard Delobel, a Lille merchant indicted for adherence to the Reformed religion and banned from Antwerp in 1568.[112] Those of their fellows who remained in Lille were prudently quiescent, whether by choice or by constraint. As far as can be ascertained, none of the merchants who routinely constituted a majority on Lille's Magistrat played a

[110] For relations with Antwerp, see Chapter 2; for contact between Lille and Rouen, another major Calvinist center, see Benedict, *Rouen during the Wars of Religion*, p. 79.

[111] Only three of the individuals or families cited in 1566 (Chapter 1, section I) are not found among the two dozen chief commercial families mentioned in Chapter 2. In addition, in the aftermath of the events of 1566–7, both Marie Deliot, widow of Guillaume Castellain, and Jean Dupont had property confiscated as a result of alleged heretical and seditious activities; ADN, Reg. B 7239.

[112] For the denunciations, see the previous note. (Those named are not included in Table 5.1.) For the project to purchase toleration, for which 3 million fl. were raised, see Chapter 2, section III, and Crew, *Calvinist Preaching and Iconoclasm*, p. 17. For Delobel, see Van der Essen, "Progrès du luthéranisme et du calvinisme dans le monde commercial d'Anvers," p. 211, no. 19. William of Orange's physician, the botanist Mathieu Delobel, came from the same Lille family; de Schickler, *Eglises du Refuge*, 1:248 n. 1. Cf. Decavele, *Dageraad van de Reformatie*, esp. pp. 572–3, 585–6, who argues that movement to Antwerp for refuge was as significant as emigration abroad.

leadership role among heretics during the critical years from de Brès's ministry to the outbreak of the revolt.[113] On the contrary, the artisans who composed the great majority of the Reformed movement also came to direct it. Members of Lille's upper class may have helped introduce this form of religious dissent, but craftsmen developed it.

Not all types of artisans were equally tempted by the new doctrines. Brewers, bakers, fishmongers, grocers, and their fellows in the provisioning trades generally remained Catholic in Lille as elsewhere. In contrast to some cities, moreover, the artisanal elite of goldsmiths, apothecaries, dyers, and the like were but little represented among Lille's Protestants.[114] The evidence from Lille, then, gives little support to interpretations postulating that relatively high levels of wealth, status, skill, and education endowed some craftsmen with a degree of self-assurance and independence of mind that prompted them to reject the authority of church and curé in favor of Protestant notions of the priesthood of all believers and the promise of an unmediated relationship with God.[115]

As in the city's population as a whole, practitioners of cloth crafts – none of whom enjoyed the elevated levels of training, income, or prestige – predominated in the ranks of the Reformed. Table 5.1 suggests that Protestantism found most adepts in four occupations: say and bourgetterie weaving, say-wool combing, trimming making (*parementerie* or *passementerie*), and drap weaving. In Chapter 3 we have seen that drap weaving employed many wage earners, and although there is little information regarding the situation of trimming makers before the late six-

---

113 The only mention of merchant involvement in heresy at Lille that I have encountered during the period 1555–66 concerns the unnamed merchant's house where, Chevalier testified, he had preached at some point during the months before his arrest; see the document printed in Halkin and Moreau, "Procès de Chevalier," p. 50.
114 Cf. Mahieu, "Protestantisme à Mons," p. 243; Moreau, "Corrélation entre milieu et choix de religion à Tournai"; Clark, "Valenciennes," pp. 176, 418–19; Van Roey, "Correlatie tussen sociale-beroepsmilieu en godsdienstkeuze," pp. 252–3.
115 For versions of this hypothesis, see esp. Natalie Davis, "Strikes and Salvation in Lyon," in her *Society and Culture in Early Modern France*, pp. 1–18; idem, "The Sacred and the Body Social in Lyon," *PP* 90 (1981):40–70; Benedict, *Rouen during the Wars of Religion*, pp. 71–94; John Martin, "Salvation and Society in Sixteenth-Century Venice," *Journal of Modern History*, 60 (1988):221–6. For a similar argument, cast as the spiritual emancipation of the prospering middle classes, see Herman Van der Wee, "La Réforme protestante dans l'optique de la conjoncture économique et sociale des Pays-Bas méridionaux au XVIe siècle," in *Sources de l'histoire religieuse de la Belgique*, pp. 303–15.

teenth century, at that time workers appear to have been common in that craft as well.[116] Perhaps their receptivity to Reformed religion is to be accounted for by a Pirennean explanation. Perhaps, that is, proletarianization and impoverishment engendered a workers' Protestantism of resentment and revolt. The material problems traced in Chapter 4 may lend support to such a hypothesis, especially in light of the Reformed response under de Brès's leadership. For if Crespin is to be believed, the "works of mercy" offered the poor, the sick, and the imprisoned during de Brès's tenure in Lille had brought "many" of "the uninstructed" (*les ignorans*) "to a knowledge of Jesus Christ."[117]

It would be a mistake, however, to consider Protestantism simply a refuge for wretched cloth makers. For one thing, although after de Brès's enforced departure the welfare and other services attributed to his inspiration apparently disappeared, Reformed textile artisans did not. More important, explanations of this type do not help us much with respect to the largest groups of textile Protestants, light-cloth weavers and wool combers. They, as we have found in Chapter 3, were mainly not impoverished wage earners but autonomous petty masters and master workers.

As in the case of merchants, then, it was probably the specific occupational experiences of light-cloth artisans that were the main social determinants of their religious allegiance. Unlike merchants, however, it seems that textile producers were touched less by the effects of recurrent uprooting from Lille than by what happened to them within the city. Admittedly, the aldermen worried lest the light-drapery industry lure immigrants who would introduce the suspect ideas pullulating in many cloth towns. Witness the requirement that say weavers and combers

---

[116] Parementiers, among whom were included seamstresses (*cousturiers*) and embroiderers (*broudeurs*), only received corporate statues in 1559, and these were sketchy; AML, Reg. 16002, fols 129–31. To judge from numerous regulations, women were very common in this craft as both mistresses and workers. It was, however, male parementiers who were arrested for heresy. Revised statutes dating from 1588 suggest that wage labor, putting out, and excessive hours were common features of trimming makers' work experience; AML, Reg. 16003, fols. 79v–82v.

[117] Crespin, *Actes des martyrs*, p. 812. Cf. Robert Oguier's last remarks to his coreligionists: "Don't forget the poor who are among you: be diligent in helping them in their poverty, and mainly the faithful"; reported in ibid., p. 818. De Brès also used alms to help spread heresy in Tournai; Moreau, *Protestantisme à Tournai*, p. 138. At about the same time, Mons's magistrates feared that Protestants there might make inroads among the poor; Mahieu, "Protestantisme à Mons," p. 163.

from Amiens seeking to settle in Lille in the early 1560s produce documents attesting to their Catholicism.[118]

Yet the contribution of immigration to artisan Protestantism ought not be exaggerated. Although some of those prosecuted for heresy were natives of Cambrai, La Bassée, Artois, and elsewhere, apparently the majority was Lillois by origin.[119] In addition, craft and other confraternal organizations remained vigorous in Lille. In contrast to the results of merchant mobility, then, immigration was structurally less likely to release artisans from accustomed religious obligations and associations.

But if light-drapery Protestants were neither proletarians nor rootless outsiders, during much of the decade or so prior to the outbreak of the revolt they were people facing entrepreneurial efforts that threatened to change profoundly the structure of the textile trades. In particular, producers' highly prized autonomy was menaced by attempts to establish larger shops and putting-out arrangements, employ unfree labor, and reorganize thread supplies. The danger was especially acute because such efforts were inaugurated or intensified against a backdrop of more pronounced oscillations in cloth output and greater material hardship. Although, in the absence of corporate records, it is impossible to be certain, the series of ordinances and rulings issued in the early 1560s designed to defend producer independence against entrepreneurial innovation strongly suggests that the Magistrat was responding to pressure from small and middling masters.[120]

This desire to protect their way of life against proposed changes may have influenced cloth producers' religious allegiance because it found an echo in important Reformed themes, notably the need to preserve the

---

[118] For immigration, see the registers of citizenship, AML, Reg. 276–80, 955–7 and Chapter 6, section IV. Cf. Decavele, *Dageraad van de Reformatie*, pp. 564, 570, for links between immigration and heresy in other cities. Ibid., p. 256, cites the case of one Wouter Bassee, originally of Bruges, who learned Lutheranism during a stay in Nuremberg in the late 1520s, then moved to Lille, which exiled him in 1533 for attacking priestly authority, church law, and images of saints. For the ruling about Amiénois, see Rosenberg, "Social Experience and Religious Choice," pp. 78–9, 96–7, and Appendix VI. The Magistrat's revocation in 1564 of the automatic grant of mastership to weavers trained in other corporately regulated towns (Vanhaeck, *Sayetterie à Lille*, 2:62, doc. 24) may also reflect apprehension about the importation of heresy, because Tournai, Valenciennes, and other say centers had become Protestant strongholds by that date.

[119] For places of origin, see Frossard, *Eglise sous la Croix*, and Willems-Closset, "Protestantisme à Lille." Of the seventeen relevant individuals on the "Liste des personnes executées à Lille" (ibid., pp. 210–11, nos. 11–27), thirteen were Lillois.

[120] For the enactments, see Chapter 3, section II.

true faith against harmful human innovations and the emphasis on the autonomous believer who was answerable for his or her salvation.[121] After all, men like Oguier and de Lo focused their denunciations on the Mass, fasting, salvation by works, and a host of other doctrines and practices that they condemned as human inventions. Furthermore, in their bearing as well as in their statements they proudly – even defiantly – accepted full responsibility for their fate before God. It is possible, in short, that some light-textile artisans embraced Reformed religion because it resonated with and thus validated ideas born of their own experience.

Yet if occupational experience could decisively predispose some light-textile artisans to alternative forms of belief, it also ultimately limited the attraction of the new faith. For as we have seen in Chapters 3 and 4, precisely during the early 1560s – and very probably in the knowledge that the Reformation had established a foothold among cloth makers – the Magistrat resolutely and repeatedly addressed basic sources of disgruntlement and distress. In so acting, the authorities helped safeguard artisans' imperiled autonomy. Some sayetteurs, bourgetteurs, and combers, like their fellows in other trades, changed religious allegiance, of course. But the consolidation of the system of small commodity production and the Common Fund's relief campaigns functioned as brakes on widespread Protestant recruitment. In Amiens, the municipal government condoned, even encouraged, change in the textile industry. Such connivance prompted a critique of secular authority that, it has been postulated, coincided with Protestant critiques of religious authority, prompting that city's say weavers and combers to favor Reform.[122] Similar criticism may have emerged in Lille, but its development was effectively limited by the actions taken by the city fathers to curb innovation.

The menace or even onset of structural change in a context of material insecurity could, in short, generate an audience for dissent. Yet insofar as effective steps were taken to address these problems, the size of that audience was circumscribed. Against such a restricted group, the Magistrat's repressive efforts were effective, assuring that never again would Lille boast a strong dissenting community. Nor would the city

---

121 I am grateful to Pierre Deyon for comments that helped clarify my thinking about possible relations between autonomy and responsibility.
122 Rosenberg, "Social Experience and Religious Change," esp. chap. III.

continue to serve as heresy's regional center of gravity, which now shifted to Tournai and the villages of the textile belt. It seems symbolic that after de Lo's execution in 1560 the new leader of the city's Protestants, Mathieu Remy, though apparently a resident of Lille, was employed as a *receveur* by rural nobles rather than having an urban occupation.[123]

IV

The Magistrat was understandably preoccupied with Protestantism during the 1560s. If the argument of this chapter is correct, however, even during this period the danger from dissent in Lille was more apparent than real. Persecution crippled organized Protestantism in the city; more important, the kinds of social conditions encouraging attachment to religious reform were being eliminated.

Further, the Reformed represented themselves as concerned only with the achievement of religious toleration and otherwise humbly obedient to the powers that be. This stance had been enunciated under de Brès. Every conventicle, Baudichon Oguier explained to his interrogators, prayed not only that the "Word of God be openly declared and purely preached" but also that God bless the civil powers. "We offer prayers," he stated,

for our lord [*sire*] the Emperor and for all his council, that the common weal [*chose publique*] be governed in peace for the glory of God: And also you are not forgotten, Gentlemen [of the Magistrat], for we greatly recommend you as our lords [*seigneurs*] and superiors, beseeching God for you and for all the city that He support you in all good things.[124]

It remained the stated position of Lille's Reformed in August 1566, when they sent the Loi a written request for permission to live "according to the reformation of the Gospel" as revealed by God's Word, for they insisted that religious freedom implied no rejection of the existing political order.[125]

These denials that dissent constituted a movement of social protest and political change may, of course, have been nothing but a smoke

---

[123] For Remy, who worked for (among others) Philippe, seigneur of Bailleul, one of the first signatories of the Compromise of the Nobility in 1566, see Willems-Closset, "Protestantisme à Lille," p. 213; Halkin and Moreau, "Procès de Chevalier," p. 15; and Decavele, *Dageraad van de Reformatie*, p. 334.

[124] Crespin, *Actes des martyrs*, pp. 813–14.

[125] Printed in Verheyden, "Chronique de Gaiffier," pp. 74–6.

screen. Certainly the Magistrat would have been troubled by Oguier's insistence elsewhere that he had to act in keeping with his interpretation of Scripture. The aldermen would similarly have taken umbrage at other declarations in the 1566 letter that emphasized the primacy of the individual conscience – "which no one may dominate" – or intimating a conditional loyalty wherein "fidelity" was owed "first to God, then to His Majesty." They might even have noted that this statement echoed an earlier and equally contingent avowal by Jacques de Lo that he obeyed worldly authority "in everything that is not against God."[126] Taken together, however, the pronouncements suggest an ambivalence among the Reformed about the legitimacy of demands going beyond the strictly religious, an ambivalence that must have hobbled them in the face of a Magistrat that harbored no such doubts about its actions. If nothing else, Lille's Protestants seem far from Pirenne's picture of committed radicals consciously determined to foment far-reaching revolt.[127]

Despite the established church's evident problems, moreover, attachment to the orthodox religion remained strong in Lille. The Magistrat had a hand in this matter, and not only by means of persecution. It also revived the custom of subsidizing preachers to deliver sermons at Advent and Lent in at least the major parishes of St. Etienne, St. Maurice, St. Sauveur, and Ste. Catherine.[128] In 1564, for example, the aldermen paid the prior of the Dominican monastery near Arras 20 livres to "admonish the people" of St. Etienne, while an Augustinian friar from Tournai and a Franciscan from Douai each received 16 livres for preaching in St. Sauveur and St. Maurice respectively.[129] Although none of the homilies has been preserved, the municipal accounts for

---

126 For Oguier and the 1566 letter, see the two previous notes. For de Lo, see Crespin, *Actes des martyrs*, p. 998.

127 Cf. Crew, *Calvinist Preaching and Iconoclasm*, who argues that initially the heretical movement was socially and politically conservative, its proponents interested only in religious reform. In her view, radicalization was the effect rather than the cause of mass mobilization and official repression.

128 The practice, begun about 1463, had lapsed for about half a century after 1480, but was reestablished by 1541 if not earlier. Some of the preaching in Ste. Catherine was in Flemish, probably for immigrants. Edmond Leclair, "Gratifications accordées par la ville de Lille à des prédicateurs aux XVe, XVIe et XVIIe siècles," in *Etudes historiques dédiées à la mémoire de M. Roger Rodière* (Arras, 1947), pp. 157–8. The four parishes where we know preaching to have occurred housed some five-sixths of Lille's population. One wonders whether friction with the chapter, documented in section I, explains the omission of St. Pierre, the only intramural parish not supplied with a preacher.

129 AML, Reg. 16,298, fol. 191v.

1556 record that the parishoners of St. Sauveur heard an exposition of some Gospels and were exhorted to "live well."[130]

Whatever the efficacy of these measures, it is clear that allegiance to the traditional faith continued to run deep among many Lillois. This adherence can be seen in the unceasing popularity of devotions and practices that lent orthodox worship a more dynamic appeal without entailing the renunciation of long-accepted beliefs. It is equally obvious from the constant endowment of chaplaincies, horistes, and anniversary Masses for the repose of the donors' souls.[131] This loyalty is revealed as well by the large crowds that attended the sermons of the celebrated Dominican Alexandre Fremault or the popular Jesuit Father Bernard Olivier, who in June 1556 filled the church of St. Etienne to overflowing several times.[132]

Dedication to the established religion is even more conspicuously manifested in the passionate denunciations of heretics that Crespin has preserved. When Baudichon Oguier was being bound to the stake, for example, several spectators fulminated against him, demanding that he be grilled slowly like St. Lawrence or declaring, "if you were my brother, I'd sell everything I own to buy faggots to burn you."[133] It comes through, too, in the relieved comment by an observer at Chevalier's execution in December 1564. The crowd's conduct, he wrote, demonstrated that "most of the people of Lille are still sound" in matters of religion.[134]

In Lille in the early 1560s, the conjunction of material hardship with the beginnings of change that threatened to alter the economic order cut some townspeople adrift from traditional religious institutions, creating something of a public for the Protestant message. But the appeal of Reformed religion proved socially and temporally limited, and the Roman church retained or regained its doctrinal and experiential relevance to Lillois, who remained small producers firmly ensconced within the corporative and confraternal framework. At Lille, the purported Calvinist moment turned out to be a Catholic moment instead.

[130] AML., Reg. 16,290, fol. 235v.

[131] AASL., Reg. D 417; Hautcoeur, *Histoire de Saint-Pierre*, 2:323; *Histoire de Lille*, 2:82.

[132] Hautcoeur, *Histoire de Saint-Pierre*, 2:428; Paul Debuchy, *Un apôtre du pays wallon. Le Père Bernard Olivier de la Compagnie de Jésus (1523–1556)* (Antoing, 1911), pp. 162–4. The aldermen pressed Olivier to return soon, but he died before he could do so.

[133] Crespin, *Actes des martyrs*, p. 815; also in Willems-Closset, "Protestantisme à Lille," p. 208.

[134] "Le général du peuple de Lille est encores bon"; *Papiers d'Etat du Cardinal Granvelle*, ed. Ch. Weiss, 9 vols. (Paris, 1841–52), 8:583.

Epilogue

~~~~~~

Stress and stability

Every year since at least 1301, when the *Deposuit potentes* was chanted during Vespers on the eve of Epiphany, the young clerks, chaplains, and cantors of the collegiate church of St. Pierre at Lille had elected one of their number "Bishop of Fools." The youth chosen was charged with supervising several days of literary competitions, plays based on biblical themes and saints' lives, and, as time went on, general merrymaking involving laity and clergy alike. This celebration of the world upside down had long offended ecclesiastical officials, and in the course of the fifteenth century repeated condemnations by chapter and councils had succeeded in driving the proceedings out of the church choir into the street. Municipal authorities had traditionally been more tolerant: Successive Magistrats subsidized the Feast of Fools with greater or lesser regularity until at least the end of the fifteenth century. By no later than 1519, however, the aldermen had come to share the canons' objections, so they forbade the revels, now considered scandalous and disrespectful. Their decree evidently encountered resistance, for bishops were again named at least in 1525 and 1526, and townspeople joined in the customary activities. But in the early 1530s concerted common efforts by chapter and magistracy finally brought the festivities to an end.[1]

A number of the convivial and didactic aspects of the Feast of Fools were duplicated (and perhaps absorbed) by the Feast of the Holy Innocents, observed a week earlier on St. John's Day and its eve (27–28 December) as another element of the twelve-day Christmas cycle. Like the Feast of Fools, the Innocents dated from the early fourteenth cen-

---

[1] Léon Lefebvre, *L'évêque des fous et la fête des Innocents à Lille du XIVe au XVIe siècle* (Lille, 1902), pp. 3–10; Hautcoeur, *Histoire de Saint-Pierre*, 2:217–22.

tury if not before, and it too had originally taken place in St. Pierre, later moving out of the church and attracting lay participation. The Feast of the Innocents likewise comprised the election of a bishop, in this case by the choirboys of St. Pierre from among their fellows. The tasks assigned to the bishop of the Innocents were, however, more solemn than those of his foolish counterpart. He presided over a dinner and then, carrying an episcopal cross, led a procession through town during which he distributed engraved medals depicting pious stories and moral lessons: the prodigal son, a youth debauched by vice, sensual temptation, the triumph of chastity. Simultaneous with this edifying display, all manner of farces were presented and masked young men paraded through Lille on foot and on horseback, dispensing sweets, engraved medallions, and even little coin-filled boxes to unmarried girls. The feast had evolved, in short, into a combined rite of fertility, passage, and inversion, marking the entrance of Lille's youth into sexual maturity, reminding them of the morality they were expected to assume, and permitting a final time of indulgence.

Initially in the 1520s – at the same time, that is, as the campaign against the Feast of Fools – and more tenaciously after midcentury, the aldermen turned their fire on the Innocents. The intrusion of adults playing all manner of games, throwing flour, cinders, and even excrement, chanting "dissolute" songs, brandishing weapons, and beating passers-by had turned the Innocents into a riotous occasion, the Magistrat alleged in 1552. So in that year, and again annually between 1556 and 1560, the city fathers decreed that youngsters alone could parade through city streets. Any participant or spectator engaging in *insolences* and *deshonettetés* risked severe punishment. For the next few years, the feast apparently enjoyed a respite from official attention, but in 1565 and 1566 the entire celebration was flatly prohibited on the grounds that it promoted "useless expense" and disorder.[2]

During the early 1560s, too, the civic procession dedicated to the Virgin, held every year on the Sunday after the Feast of Trinity, became a cause for magisterial concern. Central event in the communal ritual calendar since at least 1270, when it had been chartered by the legendary beneficent Countess Jeanne of Flanders, the long stately parade

---

2 Lefebvre, *Evêque des fous et fête des Innocents*, pp. 10–11; idem, *Histoire du théâtre de Lille de ses origines à nos jours*, vol. 1 (Lille, 1907), pp. 14–15; Hautcoeur, *Histoire de Saint-Pierre*, 2:226–7; AML, Reg. 381, fols. 35–5v; Reg. 382, fols. 27v, 52v–3.

wound for hours through the city and out the gates to circle the ramparts. Led by the four sworn military companies, the procession included the corporate brotherhoods carrying images, torses, chandailles, and depictions of biblical scenes; the pilgrimage and devotional confraternities; the magistrates in their official robes; and at the end – denoting highest status – the clergy carrying every reliquary in the city. Beginning in 1560, it was felt wise to augment the number of guards along the route of march to prevent "impudent acts" by participants and onlookers alike, and in 1565 the aldermen resolved to end the display of tableaux vivants on the ground that guild members often put on burlesques rather than pious scenes.[3] In the same years, restrictions were also placed on other aspects of urban public amusements. Plays given by wandering troupes, a favorite form of urban entertainment, were subjected to prior aldermanic censorship. The three-day feast of the Prince of Love, celebrated with the assistance of delegations from neighboring towns, held its Mass, tableaux, morality plays, procession, burlesques, and banquets for the last time. The magistrates mounted their severest and most prolonged assault on street games and masquerades, 1566 in particular witnessing a continual stream of edicts banning all such activities.[4]

In a broad perspective, the steps taken in Lille can be understood as aspects of the elite offensive to regulate and reform popular culture across early modern Europe that scholars have recently identified.[5] More immediately, the Magistrat's closer policing of Lille's ludic and festive life betrays a growing anxiety lest ceremony, performance, or play metamorphose into unmanageable disruption. The municipal *registres aux ordonnances* had never been devoid of enactments on these subjects. But in the years just prior to the outbreak of the revolt the municipal authorities evidently concluded that youth festivities, games, even the communal procession, might augment rather than release tension, im-

---

3 Lefebvre, *Procession de Lille*, pp. 1–9; AML, Reg. 16,294–9, "Procession"; Reg. 382, fols. 19v–20.

4 AML, Reg. 381, fols. 190v–1v; Lefebvre, *Théâtre de Lille*, 1:65–73; Isabelle Paresys, "L'ordre en jeu: les autorités face aux passions ludiques des lillois (1400–1668)," *RN* 69 (1987):535–51, esp. fig. 1.

5 See, e.g., Peter Burke, *Popular Culture in Early Modern Europe* (London, 1978); Robert Muchembled, *Popular Culture and Elite Culture in France, 1400–1750* (Baton Rouge, La, 1985; trans. of French, publ. 1978); Hugo Soly, "Openbare feesten in Brabantse en Vlaamse steden, 16de–18de eeuw," in *L'initiative publique des communes en Belgique. Fondements historiques (Ancien Régime)* (Brussels, 1984), pp. 605–31.

pair rather than promote civic solidarity, question rather than legitimate religious and secular norms.

Such fears are comprehensible in light of the unsettling forces, traced in Chapters 1–5, impinging on sixteenth-century Lille. Renascent long-distance trade had given birth to an essentially parvenu merchant class, some of whose members adopted novel techniques, values, and religious commitments. Increasingly integrated into a nascent world market, an expanding woolens industry simultaneously experienced recurrent slumps that periodically threatened cloth makers' security and attracted would-be entrepreneurs committed to effecting structural change. Chronic inflation, exacerbated by recurrent drastic material crises, eroded living standards, striking especially hard at unskilled wage earners. Consolidation of power at the municipal level was accompanied by conflict between Magistrat and central government bred principally by infringements of important local privileges. Beset by clerical shortcomings and inadequate leadership, the established church confronted determined Protestant agitation, rooted locally in urban socioeconomic groups affected by occupational mobility, economic uncertainty, and the onset or portents of socioeconomic change. The origins of many of these issues can be traced back to the time of Charles V if not earlier, but they worsened in the early years of Philip II's reign. Even skilled artisans faced intensified material distress, conditions in the textile industry became more unsettled, manifestations of heresy and hostility to the established order took more overt and menacing forms, and political tensions between Brussels and Lille sharpened.

Yet if many of the preconditions emphasized in accounts of the Dutch Revolt existed in the city by the mid-1560s, arrangements that could foster stability had also evolved over the preceding decades. Small commodity production had emerged in the light-drapery crafts. Hence the premier sector of the urban economy was characterized neither by a capitalist mode of production breeding disruptive social polarization and alienation, nor by an inflexible, stagnant corporate order benefiting a narrow elite at the cost of mass impoverishment. Instead, there prevailed a system that managed market forces, product innovation, and inputs of capital and labor to maintain a mass of autonomous masters. At the same time, a well-funded municipal welfare system flexibly and visibly assisted needy townspeople with a variety of programs, while also attempting to reform or at least regulate their behavior. Many townspeople remained wedded to orthodox beliefs and devotional practices and favored the established church with unbroken material support, in large part because confraternities integral to a still vital corporate structure promoted spiritual and worldly community. Municipal government, finally, was not in the hands of a closed patriciate increasingly isolated from the city's dynamic social and economic sectors, riven by debilitating factionalism, and dependent upon the central regime. To the contrary, Lille's political life was directed by a cohesive yet open ruling stratum, dominated by leading merchants, that intervened decisively in every strategic area of urban activity.

The coexistence of these contradictory elements led contemporaries to divergent perceptions of Lille's prospects on the eve of the iconoclasm that swept over the Netherlands in late summer 1566. Should an occasion present itself, Governor Rassenghien believed, Protestants and the poor might start a sanguinary riot.[6] But when public preaching, psalm chanting, and other heretical acts erupted inside Tournai, the bishop and many other clergy abandoned that city for Lille, "where it's safer."[7] To understand why the governor's fears proved misplaced, and Bishop d'Oignies's confidence correct, we need to examine the interplay of forces at work in Lille during a decade and a half of unrest and rebellion.

---

[6] Rassenghien to Margaret of Parma, 29 June 1566, AGR, EA, Reg. 282, fols. 200–1 (incomplete summary in *CFMP*, 2:250).
[7] Morillon to Granvelle, 21 July 1566, *CG*, 1:278–9.

PART TWO

Revolution and stability

6

A city's "fine duty": Lille in the iconoclastic fury, 1566–1567

Ushered in by extreme cold, a poor harvest, the interruption of grain imports, and extensive unemployment, the terrible "hunger year" of 1566 soon metamorphosed into the celebrated "wonder year" of religious and political revolt. Despite intensifying agitation on the part of both the Reformed and the political elite, Philip II had stubbornly refused to ease the placards against the heresy. On 5 April, however, some three hundred nobles submitted a "Compromise" to Margaret of Parma, urging that religious repression be tempered, and this step brought to a head a crisis that had been brewing for nearly a decade.

Lacking sufficient military and political resources to overawe opponents, the regent attempted conciliation. On 9 April, she directed judges and magistrates to treat heretics less harshly; simultaneously, she asked the Estates of every province to comment on a plan to ease tensions by suspending prosecutions for private belief. Margaret intended that the Moderation, as her proposal was known, not be promulgated until Philip II's assent had been received, but its terms soon leaked out. Warmly greeted by many people, the Moderation nonetheless failed to have the effects on which its backers had counted. In particular, its continuation of the long-standing ban on public Protestant meetings was widely disregarded. Open-air presches and other gatherings proliferated throughout the Low Countries, exploiting the leniency or even active support of numerous seigneurs and local officials, the zeal of exiles who streamed home now that persecution had ceased, and the government's conspicuous shortage of troops.

As the crowds at presches swelled in size and audacity during the early summer, government agents became more and more apprehensive of some sort of outburst. It turned out that their fears were amply justified. On 10 August, after a sermon near Steenvoorde in Flanders (some forty-five kilometers west of Lille), the audience set upon a nearby convent and destroyed every image. Three days later a monastery outside Bailleul, fifteen kilometers closer to Lille, was sacked. From there, the iconoclastic movement spread both spontaneously and by organized bands across much of Flanders, Hainaut, Brabant, Zeeland, Holland, and the northeastern provinces during the rest of August, September, and on into October. Only small groups actually carried out the work of destruction. Yet the movement evidently tapped widespread sentiments of anger and revenge, for in many places multitudes watched approvingly and militia companies stood idly by.

Struggling to stem the tide, Margaret continued to be hobbled by inadequate supplies of soldiers and money, and by divisions among political leaders. On 23 August, therefore, she allowed Protestants to deliver sermons and to worship openly wherever they had done so up to that time, though not to perform baptisms, offer communion, or raise money. But events once again overtook her measures. Far from being content with a concession unattainable only a few weeks earlier, Protestants refused to halt iconoclasm, continued to organize worship in new places, administered sacraments, and began to solicit funds. Several governors accepted local settlements that permitted services within towns, thereby exceeding anything Brussels had envisaged. By late summer 1566, central authority was being swept aside, while on the provincial and local levels new arrangements were emerging. It seemed to many people that a revolution had begun.

I

Protestant activity burgeoned throughout the textile districts of Walloon Flanders during the late winter and spring of 1566. Even before Margaret of Parma resigned herself to the Compromise, unauthorized meetings pullulated in homes and fields, flouting royal law and the futile mandates of the harried lieutenant governor Baude Cuvillon.[1] Once the

---

[1] See his order forbidding such gatherings in the interest of keeping "the people in tranquillity and security"; AML, Reg. 16,980, fol. 104v, 3 April 1566.

regent capitulated, moreover, presches attracting large audiences occurred with ever-increasing frequency: By the end of June, daytime
meetings of three to four thousand had become commonplace.[2]

Many open-air sermons were delivered west of Lille, notably in the
vicinity of Armentières and in the Alleu region of the upper Lys valley.
In the latter area, according to one informant, Protestants boasted that
"the law would not be strong enough to prevent them" from holding a
public communion service. Early in June, a striking series of presches
took place in the neighborhood of Estaires, one of the principal towns in
the Alleu: two on 5 June, the second of which drew some two to three
thousand people; one each on 6, 7, and 8 June; two more on the 9 June;
and another the following day.[3] Protestant assemblies were also held east
of Lille, particularly once Cornille de le Zenne (De Lesenne), one of the
first evangelists around Armentières and in the weaving villages of the
Lys valley, extended his ministry to the region between Tournai and
Lille.[4]

But for sheer size and audacity, the presches held in the neighborhood
of Bondues, 10 kilometers north of Lille, held pride of place. Already at
the end of May, a mammoth gathering at the seigneurie of Vertbois near
Bondues attracted some four or five thousand auditors, many of them
armed. From ten o'clock in the evening until nearly three the next
morning they sang, heard a sermon that, among other things, rejected
the veneration of the Virgin and saints, prayed for the conversion of the
king, and took up a collection for the poor.[5] Then, on 2 July, as many as
eight thousand people gathered at three in the afternoon outside the

---

[2] Rassenghien to Margaret, 29 June 1566, *CFMP*, 2:250. An inquiry conducted in September 1567
for the Council of Troubles by Cuvillon and Zegre de Hove, counsellor at the Gouvernance,
argued (incorrectly, as it happens) that presches and night meetings held in Walloon Flanders
prior to the Moderation had uniformly been met with firmness by all officials. "But immediately
the said request [Compromise] had been presented, at the urging of their preachers the sectaries
rose and armed themselves to resist the officers of the law and, what is worse, shortly afterward
began (as elsewhere) to hold presches and public assemblies with a very large number of armed
people"; AGR, RB, MS. 65, fol. 31.

[3] Undated memorandum, *CFMP*, 2:231.

[4] Rassenghien to Margaret, 30 June 1566, ibid., 2:251–2; Magistrat of Tournai to Margaret, 8 July
1566, in Hocquet, *Tournai et le Tournaisis*, pp. 312–19; AGR, RB, MS. 65, fol. 33v.

[5] This description has been assembled from information published in *CFMP*, 2:223–4 (letter from
Rassenghien to Margaret, 7 June 1566); 2:226–8 (information gathered by Cuvillon and by the
aldermen of Lille, 28–9 May and 1 June 1566); 2:231–2 (undated anonymous memorandum and
information gathered by the bishop of Tournai and the dean of the Lille District of the diocese,
29 May and 2 June 1566). Estimates of attendance at the presche ranged from two to five
thousand; the figure used in the text was provided by Rassenghien.

parish church of the village for a service described as "the biggest held so far." In the course of this *presche*, baptisms and marriages were performed in accordance with Reformed precepts, something which, it was noted, had "never before taken place here [in Walloon Flanders] in public."[6]

Clergy throughout the area reported that parishioners had forsaken Mass for presches, for taverns, or – "to show off their wicked souls more amply," in the words of the pastor of Bondues – for bowls, which they played right next to the church, "jeering and making fun" of him when he objected to their irreverence. Priests from villages along the Lys related threats to beat them or throw them into the river, as well as remarks that "soon there'll be no more Mass or confession." Pointing to the dangers they faced and their dwindling congregations – at Frelinghien only two hundred of the seven to eight hundred parishioners bothered to show up on Sundays once presches had begun in late May – a dozen curés asked to be relieved of their duties.[7]

Critical to this upsurge was tireless propagandizing by a handful of hedge preachers. None of them, Governor Rassenghien lamented, could be captured, for they knew many tricks and constantly changed the sites of their meetings as well as their garb.[8] Chief among them was de le Zenne, a farrier's son and former lace maker from Roubaix known to contemporaries as "Maître Cornille."[9] Among his fellows was an unnamed say-wool comber noted at Tourcoing.[10] Comines, a cloth town straddling both the Lys and the linguistic border, was perhaps best served, for there sermons were delivered in two languages. Four preachers, two of them apostate monks from Ypres, spoke in Flemish and two others (one the ubiquitous de le Zenne) in French. In addition, one of the renegade monks regularly sold Protestant books to people who went to the home of a sympathizer.[11]

---

[6] Rassenghien to Margaret, 2 July 1566, *CFMP*, 2:252; Margaret to Philip, 7 July 1566, ibid., 2:246. The estimate of the size of the crowd comes from the 1567 probe; AGR, RB, MS. 65, fol. 43v.

[7] Information gathered by the dean of the district, 29 May 1566, *CFMP*, 2:232–3.

[8] Letter to Margaret, 7 June 1566, *CFMP*, 2:225–6. For an excellent and extensive discussion of these preachers, see Crew, *Calvinist Preaching and Iconoclasm*.

[9] "Mémoires de Bauduin de Croix," fol. 10. The identification of de le Zenne's background comes from a letter from Rassenghien to Margaret, 30 June 1566, *CFMP*, 2:251. In AGR, RB, MS. 65, fol. 33v, however, de le Zenne is mentioned as a native of Camphin, a village 12 km. southeast of Roubaix.

[10] See AGR, RB, MS. 65, fols. 38, 39, 43–4.

[11] Ibid., fols. 44–4v.

During these months, too, Protestants in Walloon Flanders, like their counterparts elsewhere in the Netherlands, struggled to channel the growing enthusiasm for their cause into more durable structures. Armentières was one of the first places to establish a consistory complete with elders and deacons, who soon entered into close relations with a similar body at Laventie in the Alleu. In the course of the summer, consistories were organized in several villages in the northern part of the province, including Tourcoing, Quesnoy-sur-Deûle, Wambrechies, and Bondues. Important allies helped found or protect the nascent congregations. Later testimony implicated, among others, four aldermen and the town treasurer of Armentières (not to mention merchants and other substantial property owners); the bailiff, clerk and an alderman at Bondues; the bailiff's lieutenant at Tourcoing; and the bailiff, clerk, and two aldermen at Quesnoy. All were cited for attending presches or otherwise showing favor to the new religion.[12]

Maximilian Vilain, baron of Rassenghien – subsequently described by Bauduin de Croix as "entirely devoted to God, the king and the *patrie*"[13] – thus faced a herculean task upon assuming the governorship of Walloon Flanders on 1 June. Already in mid-June he reported that "the audacity and number of sectaries is [*sic*] growing by the day," while expressing fear that more and more of them were arming themselves and that Protestant ministers were in touch with coreligionists in France.[14] By the end of the month, Rassenghien was relaying tidings of incipient revolt. Crowds at presches, he wrote, were barely being restrained from committing violence, and after the harvest, due in two or three weeks, rural Protestants planned to withhold grain from the towns in order to provoke famine and "by means of poverty attract a greater throng." Fugitives were flooding back, and he had heard that four thousand French nobles were prepared to cross the border to assist any rising that should break out.[15]

The situation did not improve in July. In just a single week, a new

---

[12] Ibid., esp. fols. 33v–5, 38–9, 43–4v. No consistory was mentioned in Comines, but some of the prominent Reformed of the village were reported to have taken up collections for the poor after each presche; ibid., fol. 44v.

[13] "Mémoires de Bauduin de Croix," fol. 9. Parker, *Dutch Revolt*, p. 33 and n. 8, pp. 281–2, discusses the ambiguous meaning of *patrie* in the sixteenth century: The word could refer to one's home province as well as to the entire Netherlands.

[14] Letter to Egmont, 14 June 1566, *CFMP*, 2:230–1.

[15] Letter to Margaret, 30 June 1566, ibid., 2:251–2.

French-speaking evangelist began to preach on Wednesdays and Saturdays outside Lille; armed peasants passed muster at Sailly-sur-Lys, not far from Armentières, vowing retaliation if any Protestant were molested; and following a sermon close to Poperinghe some of the five or six thousand listeners stormed the jail in Armentières and freed a Calvinist and an Anabaptist.[16] Although earlier convinced that a timely edict from Margaret could bring "the corrupt people" back to their senses,[17] Rassenghien was now persuaded that compulsion alone could restore order. He had few troops at his disposal, however, and he knew that the provincial nobility was reluctant to crack down on presches and other forms of religious unrest. So on 26 July the governor informed Margaret that because he lacked "sufficient force," he could not "assure public calm and maintain the authority of the king."[18]

As early as 2 June the bishop of Tournai, whose diocese encompassed much of the troubled area around Lille – along with the Tournésis, another Protestant hotbed – had surmised that the public meetings, absence from church services, and rampant anticlericalism presaged "pillage" of ecclesiastical buildings and assaults on the persons and goods of priests.[19] Two weeks later, Rassenghien himself worried that country folk might take up arms and be incited to "go beyond the bounds of reason."[20] For the moment, the governor informed Margaret on 30 June, the hedge preachers were dissuading their restless flocks from taking action. But he found the implications of their messages unsettling. Cornille de le Zenne, for example, warned his listeners not to start trouble or engage in seditious acts, but he simultaneously assured them of rescue should they be arrested for Protestant beliefs or for attending outdoor gatherings. After inveighing against "idolatrous papists," he nonetheless cautioned, "our time hasn't yet arrived." Another evangelist likewise had to restrain members of his audience who wanted

---

[16] Margaret to Philip, 19 July 1566, ibid., 2:261.
[17] For the governor's pleas for a decree that would suspend laws concerning private belief and end the Inquisition while ordering Protestants to cease meeting, see ibid., 2:225, 231, 250–1, 251–2. Although Philip's response to the original Compromise had not yet arrived, on 9 July Margaret finally issued such an edict – in effect promulgating the Moderation – but it did not check the Protestant mobilization.
[18] AGR, EA, MS. 282, fol. 275. For the reticence of the "leading gentlemen" of Walloon Flanders to try to repress religious dissent, see Rassenghien to Margaret, 7 June 1566, *CFMP*, 2:224–5.
[19] Letter to Margaret, *CFMP*, 2:231–2.
[20] Letter to Egmont, 14 June 1566, ibid., 2:230.

to attack a house near Tournai, telling them "it's not yet time." Yet the preacher added that he would announce at once when the hour for action had struck, voicing his fervent hope that it would not be long delayed.[21]

Given this impatient mood, not to mention the government's demonstrated impotence, it is hardly surprising that the iconoclastic movement spread rapidly after the initial outbreaks in West Flanders on 10 and 13 August.[22] On 18 August alone, Margaret learned, ten to twelve churches had been plundered in the vicinity of Lille. A week later, on the basis of information that was already outdated, Granvelle was told that two hundred churches and monasteries around Lille and in nearby lower Flanders had been despoiled.[23]

Some religious houses in the vicinity of Lille sustained massive destruction: At the monastery at Marquette, just north of the city, for instance, the damage was estimated at 22,000 livres. At times, too, assault accompanied demolition. After ruining statues and books and defecating in grain sacks, the crowd that descended upon the abbey of Loos, also in view of Lille's walls, mistreated several servants. Besides roasting the bottoms of one man's feet, the throng beat another, then threatened to hang him by the genitals or even shoot him, and finally dumped him head first into a privy – all in the vain pursuit of weapons. But generally fury was focused on images. Although the iconoclasts at Marquette entered the premises during Mass, Bauduin de Croix recounted with some amazement, "they committed no other impudence against the monks and the priest; all their rage was turned against the paintings, statues and other objects." After smashing them, the band drank wine and beer and ate food from the monastery's cellars before departing "very joyful and singing psalms."[24]

Outsiders often played an important role in iconoclastic activity. Many of those who attacked Loos had traveled the twenty or thirty kilometers from the Alleu, stopping off on the way to vandalize the parish churches

---

21 Rassenghien to Margaret, 30 June 1566, ibid., 2:251.

22 Of the numerous works on the iconoclastic movement, the best is J. Scheerder, *De beeldenstorm* (Bussum, 1974). See also Deyon and Lottin, *Les casseurs de l'été 1566.*

23 Margaret to Philip, relaying a report from Rassenghien, 19 August 1566, *CFMP*, 1:153; Morillon to Granvelle, 25 August 1566, *CG*, 1:428.

24 This account has been assembled from "Mémoires de Bauduin de Croix," fols. 17–19, 21, and AGR, RB, MS. 65, fols. 37–7v.

at Capinghem and Lomme.[25] Some of the indefatigable hedge preachers were also involved. After allegedly assisting in the two bouts of iconoclasm that struck Wambrechies, Cornille de le Zenne spoke in one of the scarred churches. Leading his audience of eight hundred in cheers of "Long live the Beggars!" and "The time has come, long live the Beggars!" he then ordered images cast down wherever they remained.[26]

In most cases, however, participation by local people was crucial to the onset and success of iconoclasm. The "breaking, smashing, and pillaging" of churches and religious houses in Armentières, for example, was said to have been instigated by Reformed ministers and elders and carried out by merchants, artisans, and others living in the town.[27] Sometimes villagers and strangers made common cause: The band on its way to Loos, estimated at eight hundred people when it passed through Lomme, had swelled to twelve hundred by the time it reached the next village.[28] Conversely, the inhabitants of an area could quickly halt if not entirely prevent destruction. The day after three hundred image smashers marched south from Loos to plunder the collegiate church at Seclin, the "very Catholic" villagers of the area routed them in a pitched battle. At the end of the fighting, at least fifty iconoclasts lay dead in the fields or were cut down while trying to scramble across the Deûle at Bac-à-Wavrin. The defeat brought an abrupt end to all such activity in the area.[29] The despoilers of the abbey of Marchiennes were likewise driven off with heavy losses (allegedly including some 150 dead) in two battles with the peasants of the vicinity led by local officials.[30] Even before reaching the monastery, moreover, the band had suffered a humiliating setback at Orchies. Halting before the town walls, the crowd demanded entry, claiming to have an order from the king authorizing iconoclasm there. But when no document could be produced, the mag-

---

[25] AGR, RB, MS. 65, fols. 37v, 42–2v. Similarly, a group from Tournai said to number between six hundred and eight hundred people was responsible for much of the extensive damage to the monastery at Marchiennes, east of Douai, as well as defacing village churches in Aix and Nomain near Orchies; ibid., fols. 32, 40, 41v.

[26] Ibid., fols. 42v–3. The epithet "Beggars," which a royal minister had disparagingly bestowed upon the mainly young minor nobles who submitted the Compromise in April, had quickly been adopted by the Confederates themselves as a badge of honor.

[27] Ibid., fol. 34v.

[28] Ibid., fols. 42v, 32. In like manner, four hundred to five hundred individuals from the neighborhood lent a hand to the Tournaisiens sacking Marchiennes; ibid., fol. 40.

[29] "Chronique de Gaiffier," p. 24 (source of the quotation); AGR, RB, MS. 65, fols. 31v–2.

[30] AGR, RB, MS. 65, fol. 40v, and "Chronique de Gaiffier," p. 24.

istrates and townspeople refused to open the gates and the sectaries were forced to move on.[31]

By September the iconoclastic fury had swept on past Walloon Flanders, but the situation remained tense. On the seventh of the month, Rassenghien informed the Regent that he was still unable "to calm down the riotous people in the countryside [or] quell their furious rage." In some respects, things actually seemed to be getting worse, because large number of people were arming and organizing in anticipation of attempts to punish them for the image breaking.[32] Within towns and villages, Protestants stayed on the offensive, openly disregarding even the more lenient terms of Margaret's concessions granted on 23 August. The Reformed in Armentières forcibly appropriated the recently sacked parish church, occupying it night and day with up to three hundred riflemen and refusing to permit the celebration of Mass. They agreed to leave only when Egmont, seigneur of the town, authorized construction of a temple just outside the walls. Door-to-door solicitations in every neighborhood quickly raised nearly 1700 livres, which a duly constituted works committee spent on a brick edifice thirty meters on each side and five meters tall.[33] People in Wambrechies also canvassed the idea of building a temple there; nothing, however, seems to have come of the plan. And although the Calvinists of Comines failed to oust the bailiff, clerk, and an alderman in favor of men from the ranks of the Reformed, they did manage to erect their own house of worship, despite opposition by Catholics so vehement that it nearly ended in bloodshed.[34]

II

Had the Moderation not been issued, Lille's aldermen claimed, they would have continued meting out "exemplary punishment" to religious

---

[31] AGR, RB, MS. 65, fol. 41. An appeal to the authority of the Protestant preacher accompanying the group had no more effect.

[32] *CFMP*, 2:392–3. Even at the end of the month, Lille's hinterland allegedly remained "very infected" with heresy; Margaret to Philip, 27 September 1566, ibid., 1:172.

[33] AGR, RB, MS. 65, fols. 34v–5v; Philippe Fremault to Wallerand Hangouart, dean of St. Pierre, Lille, 1 September 1566, ADN, Reg. B 18,061: Intervention by two nobles, the seigneur of Escaubecque (reputedly a Protestant sympathizer) and Adrien de Noyelles, one of the bailiffs of Walloon Flanders, had succeeded that day in having a Mass said in Armentières.

[34] AGR, RB, MS. 65, fols. 43v, 44v–5. The nominee for alderman in Comines had reputedly directed iconoclasm in the village. For Protestant building of the temple *à main armée*, see BN, Fonds français MS. 9009, fol. 178 [146].

dissenters as they had right up to the presentation of the Compromise. But Margaret's concessions, along with her instructions that heresy laws henceforth be applied with "all modesty, discretion, and prudence," led Lille like the rest of the country to abandon a policy of "rigor."[35] Lille thus stood in sharp contrast to the surrounding textile areas, not to mention many other parts of the Netherlands. For its Magistrat stopped persecuting heretics not as the outgrowth of nor the prelude to local religious or political insurrection but because of a policy shift in Brussels. Conditions elsewhere dictated the change in Lille, not those prevailing inside the city itself. No hymn-chanting processions took place within Lille's walls, much less presches or open Protestant worship. Armed heretics never mustered in the city, nor did crowds storm its jail. Its churches sustained no iconoclastic onslaught and were not turned into Reformed temples. More striking still, the hopes expressed when the Estates of Walloon Flanders, like their counterparts in most other provinces, endorsed the Moderation as "appropriate and useful in the present circumstances to preserve the Catholic faith and ancient religion"[36] were far better realized in Lille than in numerous other cities. What explains this achievement?

It cannot be attributed to a more favorable price and employment situation than elsewhere. Just as both the general inflationary trend of the sixteenth century and particularly harsh conjunctures had struck Lille in common with the other seventeen provinces, so in 1565–6 a material crisis developed there as throughout the Low Countries. Grain prices, which had begun rising in autumn of 1565, continued to move dramatically upward across the winter and on into the next spring. The cost of wheat eventually reached index 444 – up from 207 the previous year and by far the highest attained up to that point – while rye climbed from index 192 to 438 (Figure 4.2).[37] Despite the inflationary spiral, neither masters nor laborers received wage hikes. The former's pay rate

---

35 AGR, EA, Reg. 282, fol. 173, Magistrat of Lille to Margaret, 30 May 1566; "Grands devoirs," fols. 572–4.

36 The document, signed by the four bailiffs of the province and by Jean de le Forterie, municipal attorney of Lille, and dated 15 June 1566, is printed in "Chronique de Gaiffier," pp. 68–72; the quotation is at p. 69. In a brief memorandum, dated 16 June (ibid., p. 73), the clergy also approved Margaret's step in the expectation that it "would redound to the honor of God and at the present time would result in calm and tranquillity for the public good."

37 Rye prices had been marginally higher in 1556–7. The price and wage indexes cited here and below use averages between 1511 and 1520 as base 100. For sources and further discussion, see Tables 4.1 and 4.2.

remained stuck at index 143 from 1557 through 1569, while the latter (index 151) saw no improvement between 1562 and 1573. As a result, 1565–6 was the most difficult year of the decade in terms of the proportion of putative income required to buy sufficient grain to feed a family, and it was little short of catastrophic for unskilled wage earners.[38]

Sayetteurs' stagnant output (taxes of 4,575 livres were paid in 1565, 4,520 in 1566) suggests that extra work to help fill the earnings gap was hard to come by. Bourgetteurs seem to have been little better off, since a 25 percent gain in changéant production (7,292 cloths in 1565, 9,700 the next year) was offset by a drop in the number of the more labor-intensive velveteens from 3,721 to 3,396 pieces. For its part, the drapery craft was in the midst of a sharp slump, which hit its nadir in 1566 (8,332 pieces as opposed to the previous year's 9,597, and 10,349 in 1564).[39] Trade with Antwerp, as measured by Coornaert, was at its lowest point since the late 1540s.[40] As summer approached, finally, grain shortages began to crop up. So on 20 May the Magistrat banned all grain sales save those negotiated in the town market on specified days, and in late July shipments of grain from Lille, as well as sales outside posted hours, were made punishable by a very heavy fine of 60 livres.[41]

Nor can the city's stability during the wonder year be traced to religious indifference. Townspeople frequented the nocturnal open-air preaching that took place in villages like Marcq, Bondues, Linselles, and Marquette, just a few kilometers north of the city. According to Bauduin de Croix, that "seducer of the people" Cornille de le Zenne played a pivotal role. Lillois "went openly to find him in one of the neighboring villages, either to learn about the new religion or to strengthen themselves in it."[42] Participants confirmed de Croix's account, if not his evaluation of the preacher. Between two hundred and one thousand city residents were estimated to have heard de le Zenne speak at the large gathering held in the Vertbois in late May. One informant deduced that the largest groups had come from Lille and Tournai because at the end,

---

38 Wheat would have consumed between 43% and 72% of a master's earnings and a staggering 81% to 135% of a laborer's, whereas rye would have taken respectively 38% to 63% and 71% to 119%.

39 For 1566 output, see AML, Reg. 16,300; for comparisons, see Figures 3.1, 3.2, and 3.3.

40 Coornaert, *Français à Anvers*, fig. "Nombre de marchands" at end of vol. 2.

41 AML, Reg. 382, fols. 38v–9, 42–2v. Informers were offered one-third of the fines. The fine of 60 liv. was the equivalent of two-thirds of a laborer's yearly wages.

42 "Mémoires de Bauduin de Croix," fol. 11.

when groups were being assembled for the journey home, "people called out Lille and Tournay [*sic*] more than other places."[43] By early July, Rassenghien was confiding to Margaret that "more than half of this town [Lille] would have gone" to the giant presche at Bondues where Reformed baptisms and marriages were celebrated, had the city gates not been closely watched; even so, over two thousand inhabitants managed to attend.[44] A few Lillois even traveled to presches in places like la Gorgue, thirty kilometers west of the city in the upper Lys textile belt.[45]

As the summer wore on, Lille's Protestants became emboldened, as evidenced first of all by their requesting the new Reformed Academy at Orléans to assign trained ministers to their town.[46] More dramatically, in early July "the citizens, manans, and habitans of the city of Lille who want to live according to the reformation of the Gospel" called on the Magistrat to assure liberty of conscience and permit the free exercise of their faith.[47] Assuring the authorities of their "entire obedience" as witnessed by the persecution they had "patiently suffered and borne," the petitioners also pledged "their goods, their bodies and their lives" to the service of the king, "their head and natural prince" established by God, and offered to prove their fidelity by swearing an oath as guarantee. In return, they asked "to have their conscience free and unconstrained [*franche et libre*] in the service of God, without your [the Magistrat's] authority putting any obstacle in the way." They sought, in short, toleration based on the primacy of conscience as instructed by the Word of God.

On their side, the authorities feared that material hardship might trigger disorder. Should the Antwerp trade be interrupted, Rassenghien

---

[43] Information gathered by lieutenant governor Cuvillon and by the Magistrat of Lille, 28–9 May and 1 June 1566, *CFMP*, 2:226–8.

[44] Letter of 2 July 1566, ibid., 2:252.

[45] Undated report, from early or mid-June 1566, printed ibid., 2:231; see also another report from the same period, ibid., pp. 236–7.

[46] Des Gellars to Beza, Orléans, 12 August 1566, *Correspondance de Théodore de Bèze*, ed. H. Meylan et al., 10 vols. (Geneva, 1960–80), 7:195, no. 488. Because so many had already been sent elsewhere, only one person was found, "who may help the Lillois for some time." Whether the unidentified person ever went to Lille is not known, but a Protestant minister seems to have been in Lille by the fall of 1566; see section IV.

[47] The document, from which the quotations in this paragraph come, is found in AGR, EA, Reg. 282, fols. 248–9, and AEN, MS. 399, fols. 29v–30v. It is printed from the latter in "Chronique de Gaiffier," pp. 74–6. The appeal is undated but on the basis of internal evidence, as well as its placement in AEN, MS. 399, it seems to have been a response to letters in the king's name, issued at Brussels on 3 July and published in Lille three days later (AEN, MS. 399, fols. 28–9), which once again condemned and forbade all conventicles and presches.

confided to the regent, a "popular uproar due to poverty" could well break out.[48] Magistrat and governor alike found religious agitation even more troubling. Presches were considered especially pernicious, for they promoted "conspiracies and sinister practices" against public order and undermined the obedience owed the king.[49] What is more, these assemblies knit more closely the existing links between urban and rural Protestants, perhaps paving the way for common action. In late June, Margaret informed Rassenghien of reports that

> those from the vicinity of Lille who are badly inclined toward the Catholic religion and faith would set a market day to enter the said city in disguise and, hiding themselves in the houses of their collaborators there, take up arms together and make themselves masters of the city.[50]

Thanks to the "great collusion" between them, the governor replied, "it would be very easy" for sectaries inside and outside Lille to cooperate and attempt a coup.[51] According to later testimony by the Magistrat, rumors current during the summer of 1566 had it that Protestants from Flanders and elsewhere intended to attack Lille if the open practice of their religion were not permitted there. The aldermen averred that they took this news very seriously, because "the great number of sectaries united on every side against the city" would have made resistance "very difficult."[52]

Within Lille, too, emotions were running high. Already in early June the shouting of "names and words that could inflame quarreling, discord or dissension" had reached troubling dimensions. Soon thereafter, even children were uttering taunts and threats.[53] Despite aldermanic orders that such behavior cease, epithets like "Papist!" "Beggar!" and "Huguenot!" were shouted all summer long.[54] More alarming, the populace was said to be stocking pistols and other weapons in their homes; the *menus gens*, Rassenghien fretted, were better armed than the rich.[55]

---

[48] Letter to Margaret, AGR, EA, Reg. 282, fol. 258v, 20 July 1566.
[49] *CFMP*, 2:229, June 1566.
[50] Margaret to Rassenghien, 30 June 1566, ibid., 2:252.
[51] Rassenghien to Margaret, 2 July 1566, ibid.
[52] "Grands devoirs," fols. 574–5.
[53] *CFMP*, 2:229; AML, Reg. 382, fol. 41v, 25 June 1566.
[54] AML, Reg. 382, fol. 44, 5 August 1566.
[55] Rassenghien to Margaret, 29 June 1566, AGR, EA, Reg. 282, fols. 200–1; incomplete summary in *CFMP*, 2:250. For a letter from the governor of Avesnes to Margaret on 21 July, reporting that merchants from Lille, Tournai, and Valenciennes were said to have bought arms at Antwerp on 17 July, see ibid., 2:303.

Ominously, too, in the governor's eyes, the city's Protestants began to measure their support by asking people which side they were on, lest they be abandoned "in a pinch" (*au besoing*).[56]

Rassenghien was all the more dismayed because he judged the force available to defend Lille woefully inadequate. Granted, a round-the-clock watch overseen by two aldermen and backed up by cannons on the ramparts and harquebusiers at the gates had been mounted at the end of March. At the same time, the city gates were fitted with new locks to which only members of the Loi had keys, thereby enabling, the Magistrat later boasted, closer surveillance of the gates "in order to prevent any secret machinations that might have been mounted against the city."[57] The authorities also ordered innkeepers to report the names and hometowns of all new guests by nine o'clock each evening, while visitors lodged in private homes had to be registered every Saturday. Bauduin de Croix claimed that houses were searched for prohibited books and for Protestants who might have entered town secretly;[58] such measures have, however, left no traces in official records. At the beginning of April, a comprehensive ordinance designed to prevent an "enemy" take-over forbade unauthorized meetings as well as "unlawful talk smacking of disturbance or brawling," and instructed all males between the ages of twenty and sixty to arm themselves with staffs and pass muster. Should trouble break out, those assigned to the *centaines* organized in each parish had to appear at once at the scene of disorder, while the rest were to assemble on the central market square.[59]

In the governor's opinion, however, these precautions fell far short of what was needed. He dismissed the citizen watch as practically useless – perhaps an accurate appraisal, given that (to judge from recent municipal edicts) men failed to show up or left before their tours of guard duty were completed, and lent or even sold their weapons. He also pronounced the sworn companies not entirely dependable.[60] But no matter

56 Letter to Margaret, 14 July 1566, AGR, EA, Reg. 282, fol. 245.
57 "Grands devoirs," fols. 576–7.
58 AML, Reg. 382, fols. 32–2v, 30 March 1566 (republished 9 and 17 September 1566, 25 May 1572, and 13 February 1573); "Mémoires de Bauduin de Croix," fol. 12.
59 AML, Reg. 382, fols 35–5v, 2 April 1566. A survey of the houses of the men in the *centaines* to make certain that they had weapons is mentioned in AML, Reg. 16,300, section "Salaires," unfoliated, and Reg. 277, fols. 203v–4.
60 For Rassenghien's judgments, see his letters to Margaret, AGR, EA, Reg. 282, fols. 180, 200–200v, 1 and 29 June 1566; for the ordinances, see AML, Reg. 382, fols. 39v–40, 28 May 1566; Reg. 277, fols. 203v–4, 10 May 1566.

what the state of the bourgeois guard, Rassenghien's unease arose most of all from his firm conviction that only professional soldiers, who would both strengthen the citizen forces and expand the tiny garrison at his command, could adequately protect Lille.

Unfortunately for the governor, the regime's lingering financial crisis meant that little assistance was forthcoming from Brussels. On his first day in Lille, Rassenghien requested the dispatch of a company of harquebusiers. Six cavalry and twelve foot soldiers were sent in late June, but Rassenghien still had to make do with fewer than forty men.[61] Given his responsibility for countryside as well as cities, these troops were, as he repeatedly complained, utterly insufficient. Worse, their pay was far in arrears.[62] Although Margaret authorized the levy of at least sixty additional men, she refused the governor's plea to offer higher wages than normal, despite his declaration that at present rates few enlistments had been secured.[63]

Even during the iconoclastic crisis Brussels was unable to send troops, despite Rassenghien's gloomy predictions of imminent disaster should help not be forthcoming immediately. On 16 August, for example, he wrote Margaret that insurgents were fast approaching Lille and boasting that they would soon enter the city to do their work there. Lacking enough soldiers, the governor lamented, he dared not make a sally against the image breakers' vanguard, even though they were just "disorderly peasants" who could easily be routed.[64]

The next day Rassenghien stepped up his rhetoric to lend greater weight to his request. He could not leave Lille to try to defend rural churches against the onslaught of thousands of "sectaries" spreading "devastation" across "the greater part" of the castellany, lest in his absence townspeople sympathetic to the iconoclasts "revolt." Because he was not sure who these seditious Lillois were, he feared them even more than outsiders. Urging haste, he declared, "the rage of the people, once roused, doesn't understand reason, and it's to be feared that from

[61] Rassenghien to Margaret, 1 June 1566, AGR, EA, Reg. 282, fol. 180; Margaret to Rassenghien, 5 July 1566, *CFMP*, 2:253.
[62] Rassenghien to Margaret, 29 June and 10 July 1566, *CFMP*, 2:251, 265; and 20 July 1566, AGR, EA, Reg. 282, fol. 259.
[63] See correspondence between Margaret and Rassenghien, stretching across July 1566: *CFMP*, 2:253, and AGR, EA, Reg. 282, fols. 259, 273v–4.
[64] *CFMP*, 2:339–40. The Magistrat added its plea for soldiers to withstand external assault and "evil people" within Lille; ibid., p. 340.

churches they'll proceed to pillage and, at an extreme, to arson."[65] Margaret could only respond by authorizing the governor to raise up to two hundred troops on his own and promising to send Montigny's cavalry band as soon as possible (it did not arrive, however, until early September, when the danger was over).[66]

The period between 16 August and 23 August, when iconoclasts were ravaging the castellany as well as neighboring parts of Flanders, Artois, and Hainaut, was a time of great anxiety in Lille. In response to reports that rural image breakers intended to join up with their fellows from Tournai and smash idols in the city, the Magistrat reinforced guard patrols on 18 August. The next day, the city fathers put the bourgeois companies on alert and told everyone else to return home quietly. Those ordered to arm themselves were instructed, under penalty of the gallows, "not to do nor attempt anything" or to leave their posts, unless commanded by their captains.[67]

Tension reached a climax on 20 August, its fever pitched manifested by the canons of St. Pierre, who received permission to cut their hair, dress like laymen, and bear arms for protection in case of attack.[68] That same day, the eve of the feast of St. Sauveur, an unknown man was observed in the parish of that name, home to Lille's greatest concentration of light-cloth artisans. Immediately the rumor flew around that he was an iconoclast who, having already sown destruction in Tournai and around Lille, would now continue his wicked task with the aid of accomplices who had secretly entered the city. Hearing this, a crowd of women pursued the man to the church, where he was seized by armed parishioners. Then the *petit peuple* dragged him off to the Château de Courtrai and begged Rassenghien to execute justice. But after examining the man, named Gervais Delplace (or de le Place), Rassenghien decided either that the accusation was unfounded or, according to Carette, that the *diversité du tems* made it impossible to act. So the governor released Gervais through a hidden back doorway giving directly onto the country, then told the throng milling around at the castle gate that the miscreant had been corporally punished.[69]

Carette concluded that the mobilization to capture Gervais disproved

65 AGR, EA, Reg. 282, fol. 310.
66 Margaret to Rassenghien, 18 August 1566, *CFMP*, 2:341. The promise of Montigny's company of one hundred horsemen was repeated in a letter of 21 August; AEN, MS. 399, fol. 48.
67 AGR, EA, Reg. 282, fol. 310; AML, Reg. 382, fols. 43v–4.
68 Carette, "Recueil," fol. [80v]; Hautcoeur, *Histoire de Saint-Pierre*, 2:409 n. 2.

any fear that iconoclasts might have had *cousins* in St. Sauveur.[70] Yet although the iconoclastic scare turned out to be a false alarm,[71] the authorities evidently continued to be apprehensive lest townspeople mount an attack in concert with outsiders. On 21 August, for example, the Magistrat forbade all male Lillois to leave the city under any circumstances. Whereas women and children could depart, they could not take any jewelry or other valuables with them, only the clothes on their backs. Anyone wearing a shirt of mail had to turn it over to the watch before entering Lille. In order that trade not be interrupted, the aldermen allowed merchants to come and go freely, but their goods had to be inspected and approved before passing through the city gates.[72] Two days later, the magistrates reiterated the prohibition on removing valuables and barred entry to armed outsiders.[73]

On 23 August, too, came a final alarm. As Tournai's churches were being plundered, Rassenghien was alerted (by whom, we unfortunately do not know) that Protestants from that town, the Alleu, Armentières, and Flanders were planning an imminent raid on Lille, aided by confederates within the walls who would put the city to the torch. Although

---

69 The story can be found in both the "Mémoires de Bauduin de Croix," fols. 21–3, and Carette, "Recueil," fols. [80–80v]. The account in Hautcoeur, *Histoire de Saint-Pierre*, 2:408, is based on the latter. Despite his escape on this occasion, in July 1567 Delplace was condemned by the Gouvernance for taking part in rebellious acts and banished for twelve years; AML, Reg. 12,121 (also reported in Frossard, *Eglise sous la Croix*, p. 85).

70 " . . . on doutoit qu'ils [iconoclasts] eussent des cousins en cette dite paroisse, combien que fut trouvé le contraire, car ils [the parishioners] garderent leur eglise et prirent" Delplace; Carette, "Recueil," fol. [80v]. Carette may not have meant relatives, for the word *cousins* could also indicate "friends" "cronies," or "dupes."

71 A mid-seventeenth-century chronicler reported that in 1567 [*sic*], "lors que les geux et briseurs d'images l'ont assailly [Lille] y voulans introduire l'heresie lutherienne et calvinienne, briser les Images et profaner tout les eglises, avec toutes les lieux saincts et sacrees," Rassenghien stood in front of the church of St. Etienne, "l'espee nue en main," and "menacait severement ceulx qui auroint l'asseurance de commetre quelque desordre contre lhonneur de Dieu et de son Eglise, de les tuer, exhortant aussi la bourgeoisie de ne riens permettre de semblable"; BML, MS. 319–20, Jean de le Barre, "L'héraclée flamand et catholique," 1618–58, fols. 124–4v (1024–4v). The passage comes amid news from the year 1655. Though de le Barre, a Lillois by birth and fervent Catholic, says that his information "m'at este fidelement raporte par les tesmoins oculaires," no contemporary document that I am aware of mentions the incident. It is in neither Carette nor de Croix – both of whom were contemporaries who had a great deal to say about the events of 1566 – nor even in Rassenghien's letters, which are typically not reticent about narrating his exploits. I owe the reference to the manuscript to Lottin, *Lille, citadelle de la Contre-Réforme?* p. 143, who credits Rassenghien with stopping an impending attack. To me, however, the passage – not to mention the verb *auroint* – suggests that the governor's act, if it occurred, was not necessarily related to any actual threat.

72 AML, Reg. 382, fols. 44v–5.

73 Ibid., fols. 45v–6, 23 August 1566.

apprehensive lest the citizen companies prove unreliable, the governor at once put them and his few available soldiers on armed watch, but in the event nothing materialized.[74]

Soon thereafter, it became obvious to everyone that Lille was going to be spared iconoclasm. Margaret wrote Rassenghien on 27 August to praise the "guardianship, care and protection of the city of Lille" that he and the aldermen had accomplished so well.[75] Then on 1 September, the prominent citizen Philippe Fremault reported that "things are going better and better" in Lille and that most of those who had fled out of fear of attack had already returned.[76] A week later, while still expressing anxiety that outside sectaries retained evil designs on Lille, Rassenghien was willing to admit that the city had remained "intact" despite them.[77]

III

Writing from Spain in early October, Philip II congratulated Lille's officials on having "done such fine duty" that their city had been spared the "turmoil and other evils" convulsing the Netherlands.[78] The aldermen gladly took much of the credit for the failure of iconoclasm in their city. Quoting Philip's praise, the exculpatory *Grands devoirs* placed great stress on military preparations and close watch of churches, which allowed them to remain "whole" and in their "former condition," even though Lille had been "very threatened." The city fathers also emphasized their measures to assure "union and tranquillity, without uproar, sedition or public scandal" among residents.

Admittedly, townspeople had not been kept away from presches. Closing the gates on the side of the city from which arteries led to Protestant meeting places had not worked. Nor had forcing everyone wanting to leave Lille to obtain tokens at city hall, where officials allegedly took care to distribute them only to people "known to be Catholics." For Lillois had slipped away "very secretly," using gates on the

---

74 This account is based on "Grands devoirs," fol. 578, and on a letter from Rassenghien to Margaret, 25 August 1566, AGR, EA, Reg. 282, fol. 325, also printed as an appendix to Pasquier de le Barre's *Mémoires*, in *Mémoires de Pasquier de le Barre et de Nicolas Soldoyer pour servir à l'histoire de Tournai, 1565–1570*, ed. Alexandre Pinchart, 2 vols. (Brussels, 1859–65), 1:342–3.
75 AGR, EA, Reg. 282, fol. 338.
76 ADN, Reg. B 18,061.
77 Letter to Margaret, 7 September 1566, *CFMP*, 2:393.
78 Letter of 3 October 1566, AEN, MS. 399, fol. 66v.

opposite side of town from their destinations and, once outside, striking out overland, avoiding roads. Still, the Magistrat claimed, it had prevented arms from being taken to presches, had broken up possibly dangerous groups of returning Protestants by obliging them to enter singly through a small and well-guarded door in the city wall, and had banished anyone who had actively participated in a service, such as by having a child baptized there.

All those steps, the aldermen concluded, had deterred any presche or "other exercise of the new religion" from taking place in the city. The measures had also led many clergy and laymen to take refuge in Lille, where Mass continued to be celebrated without interruption.[79] A contemporary diarist agreed that these measures had been vital: "As for the city of Lille," wrote Pierre Gaiffier, "it was protected from such a disaster and failing [as iconoclasm] by the good order, watch and guard and policing that the Magistrat established."[80]

Its internal unity contributed importantly to the Magistrat's effectiveness in promoting public order. The Loi governing Lille from November 1565 through October 1566 shared many of the attributes of its predecessors during the quarter century 1541–65, and the differences that did exist enhanced the magistracy's coherence. It included men from all the occupational groups usually represented, but merchant dominance was more pronounced both within the municipal government as a whole and on the policy-making councils of aldermen, jurés, and huit-hommes.[81] Of the thirty-three positions in the Conclave, moreover, sixteen were held by men who were, or would soon become, members of the inner circle, as against just eight or nine in an average year between 1541 and 1565. Finally, entry of new men into the Magistrat and the number of officials serving for the first time in a given

---

79 "Grands devoirs," fols. 573–6, 579–80. They might have pointed out, too, as the agents of the Council of Troubles did (AGR, RB, MS. 65, fol. 32), that Lille had been the place where Catholic villagers had hid "the best vessels and ornaments of their churches" during the troubles.

80 Printed in Verheyden, "Chronique de Gaiffier," p. 24.

81 The entire Loi consisted of twenty-eight merchants (the 1541–65 mean was twenty-three), four seigneurs (as against five or six), three physicians and three lawyers (typically two or three and three, respectively), one rentier and one administrator (also the norm), one artisan (a well-to-do apothecary who belonged to the inner circle) in place of two, and two men whose profession is unknown (down from the usual four or five). On the three councils, where they usually formed a majority or very close to a majority, merchants held nine of eleven aldermanic seats, eight of twelve of the voir-juré and juré positions, and were five of the huit-hommes. For 1541–65 figures, see Chapter 1, section I.

position were below the norm.[82] This was, in short, a more homogeneous and experienced ruling body than usual. Whereas the typical Lillois selected for the Loi served 7.58 terms over his entire political career, these men had on the average already sat 8.88 times and would go on to be named a mean of 15.06.

Understandably, perhaps, the aldermen's account was reticent about Rassenghien's contributions. He had urged, for instance, that Lille copy "well-policed larger towns" and divide the "distinguished bourgeois and merchants" into quarter organizations captained by "the most capable and adequate gentlemen of the city." The *Grands devoirs* does not mention this suggestion, even though in late June the Magistrat set up six companies, armed them, and appointed as officers six seigneurs including the provost and rewart but no current alderman or councillor.[83] The governor also had convinced the Magistrat (again without later receiving credit) to recast guard detachments in the proportion of four reliable men to one who was "doubtful" as a way of minimizing threats to the city's security by Protestants and their sympathizers serving on the watch. And as the wording of the oath suggests (as well as the fact that it is not mentioned in aldermanic records), it was at Rassenghien's behest that in mid-July citizens were obliged to pledge publicly "to devote themselves loyally to the guard and defense of the city against all disturbances and disorders and to maintain their duty to the king under the authority of the Governor and Magistrat."[84]

Equally comprehensible was the Magistrat's failure to note their long resistance to Rassenghien's attempts to bring in mercenaries, their outright refusal to countenance any of his requests thought likely to infringe municipal privileges, and their irresolution when seeming to accede to

---

[82] Two aldermen were new to municipal government (the 1541–65 mean was 2.4) and three were first-time échevins (4.6); among councillors (voir-jurés and jurés), the figures were zero (0.64) and three (3.08); and among huit-hommes one (2.28) and three (3.76).

[83] Rassenghien to Margaret, 29 June 1566, *CMPF*, 2:250. The composition of the captaincy may also reflect Rassenghien's influence, for he expressed his displeasure that the current Loi contained no nobleman who had proper military experience; see letter to Margaret, 2 July 1566, ibid., 2:252. Of those selected as captains (listed in "Mémoires de Bauduin de Croix," fols. 14–15) Philippe de la Riviere, seigneur of Warnes, a member of the inner circle who served twenty-one terms between 1560 and 1601 and had been rewart the previous year (he was not currently in office), was to play a critical role in the late 1570s; see Chapter 8.

[84] Rassenghien to Margaret, 20 July 1566, AGR, EA, Reg. 282, fol. 258v. Nearly everyone swore, Rassenghien reported, with the exception of "some malevolent people" who feigned not to understand what was meant by the term "loyalty" (*fidelité*). If they did not conform (and the governor was hopeful that all would "come to their senses") they were to be expelled from Lille "as useless members of the body politic." What actually happened is not known.

his importunities. Thus, although the city fathers apparently agreed on
10 July to contract with either a cavalry troop or 50 armed foot soldiers
to serve under Rassenghien, ten days later the understanding fell apart.
Instead, the aldermen engaged (and placed under their own sole direction) 100 harquebusiers to serve 20 at a time with the 160 citizens who
patrolled each night.[85] At the same time, the Magistrat rejected the
governor's proposal that the excellent municipal ordnance and powder
stores ("Lille is," he wrote, "rather better stocked with heavy artillery
and munitions than any other city of its type in this country") be moved
to the Château de Courtrai for safekeeping. Claiming that any such
transfer required the express consent of the citizenry, the échevins declined to seek such approval on grounds that it was unlikely to be
given.[86]

The presches, which "everyday come closer to the city," along with
fear of sedition and pillage by "the multitude of poor people" in Lille,
finally persuaded the Magistrat to heed Rassenghien's admonitions and
ask again for a company of cavalry – so long as it was well behaved and
therefore would not disrupt trade. Unfortunately, by late July Margaret
had nothing to send but a promise that horsemen would come "as soon
as possible."[87] So on its own the Magistrat raised several hundred more
infantrymen and harquebusiers, who joined the bourgeois guard around
the city's churches. Like those already hired, these forces were placed
under the aldermen's control.[88]

Although the city fathers likewise neglected to mention them, a
number of welfare measures they undertook must also have helped deter
religious violence in Lille. To increase supplies, the magistrates emptied
private warehouses and cellars of their stocks and used city funds to

---

85 Rassenghien to Margaret, 10 July 1566, *CFMP*, 2:265; 20 July 1566, AGR, EA, Reg. 282, fol.
258v.
86 AGR, EA, Reg. 282, fol. 259.
87 Rassenghien to Margaret, 26 July 1566, ibid., fols. 275–5v. Magistrat to Margaret, 27 July 1566,
ibid., fol. 278; Margaret to Magistrat, 31 July 1566, ibid., fol. 288v.
88 "Grands devoirs," fol. 577. To help pay for the troops, a special tax was instituted on wine, with
no exemptions permitted; AML, Reg. 15,885, fols. 96v, 98v–9v, 106–7v. The levy remained in
place through the end of 1567, by which time it had brought in 62,858 liv.; "Grands devoirs,"
fol. 577. It was, however, insufficient by itself to cover all expenses, so St. Pierre's share of a
"free gift" granted the crown by fourteen religious institutions in Walloon Flanders was diverted
to the city to help pay the infantry (AML, Reg. 137, fol. 1; ADN, Reg. B 18,064) and a special
tax on sales in Lille's biweekly horse market was added; AML, Reg. 277, fol. 207. The canons of
St. Pierre guarded their own church with the aid of one hundred paid soldiers; Carette,
"Recueil," fol. [80v]; Hautcoeur, *Histoire de Saint-Pierre*, 2:409.

Table 6.1. *Indexes of cash and bread distributions by Lille's Common Fund, January–December 1565 and 1566 compared (100 = mean, 1561–5)*

Month	1565		1566	
	Cash	Bread	Cash	Bread
January	103	113	172	235
February	142	124	187	191
March	166	142	225	163
April	89	292	221	565
May	110	0	166	2083
June	124	0	148	1310
July	100	0	158	608
August	125	0	244	0
September	77	266	160	299
October	112	199	182	506
November	173	*a*	152	*a*
December	163	50	116	114

*a*Bread was never distributed in November between 1561 and 1566.
Sources: AASL, Reg. J571–83.

purchase grain on staple markets, directly from producers, or wherever they could find it on their frequent buying expeditions.[89] Doing their part, the ministres généraux set Common Fund grants of money and bread at levels substantially above those recorded in 1565 and far superior to average outlays across the first half of the decade (Table 6.1).[90]

Disbursements continued at high levels throughout the late summer and into the fall, despite an abundant harvest that had brought grain prices tumbling down (wheat to index 274 from 444, rye all the way from 438 to 230). Only in November and December did outlays decline below those of the previous year, and even then they remained substantial. These massive increases testify eloquently to the authorities' ability to augment quickly and considerably the flow of monies into the Bourse

[89] AML, Reg. 16,300, sections "Salaires" and "Voyages," unfoliated.
[90] Cf. Tables 4.6 and 4.8 and Appendix G.

commune.[91] But they indicate even more vividly the way in which the welfare institutions elaborated over the preceding decades had come to play a critical role in promoting stability in Lille. In particular, the large amount of cash handed out in August 1566, nearly twice as much as in August 1565, when the harvest had just failed and prices were soaring, makes it clear that welfare had purposes beyond alleviating material distress. The steps were successful, moreover: Lille avoided the fate of Ghent, for instance, where a bread riot was the prelude to iconoclasm.[92]

The Bourse commune shows most dramatically the stabilizing effects of arrangements previously developed. Yet the weakness and isolation of challenges during the wonder year suggest that the small commodity production system also contributed to creating an environment in which more immediate measures could work effectively. There was a cluster of critical enactments tending to stabilize petty masters' position – those imposing limits on loom ownership and prohibiting putting out and the employment of cheap labor – in the early and mid-1560s. It was, however, not simply these steps but the long structuring of the light-textile industry, a process that had gone on during nearly the entire first two-thirds of the sixteenth century, that allowed the shocks of 1566 to be absorbed and Lille's stability preserved. It was the structuring of small commodity production, more specifically, that accounts for Carette's previously cited observation that the residents of St. Sauveur, the cloth workers' parish, were not accomplices to iconoclasm.

The consequence of all these factors, in the words of investigators for the Council of Troubles, was that the orthodoxy and loyalty of the city's residents, who "so displayed and supported . . . the service of God and of His Majesty," helped calm the Protestant storm. The priory of Fives, the Franciscan church and convent, and the parish churches of La Madeleine and St. André were untouched by iconoclasts,[93] even though they lay outside the city walls and were in sight of such places as Marquette and Lomme that were ravaged.

As a matter of fact, it was not Protestants but Catholics who were most decisively mobilized in 1566 Lille, for popular vigilantism was directed not only against presumptive image breakers like Delplace but

---

91 A total of 4,961 liv. was gathered by special solicitations in 1565; in 1566, the sum was 8,721 liv.; AASL, Reg. J 580–3.
92 Parker, *Dutch Revolt*. pp. 76, 78.
93 AGR, RB, MS. 65, fol. 32.

also against those who went to presches or were just imagined to be partial to the new doctrines. On 19 August, for example, Lille's Reformed, meeting in the relative safety of the Tournésis, protested the "outrages" and "violence" being perpetrated against them. The next day their coreligionists from Tournai repeated that even those suspected of "some little spark" of interest in the reformed religion faced "intolerable trouble and molestation." Verbal insult and actual physical assault, even rape, awaited such unlucky Lillois, and they might well have their houses ransacked and arms seized.[94] Conceding the truth of the allegations, the aldermen emphasized that "the common people" (*la commune*) were "very stirred up" against those who would deprive them of the free exercise of their religion.[95] If the argument of this book is correct, such a popular religious temper – which rendered military steps almost gratuitous – was another, albeit indirect and probably unintended, result of sixteenth-century Lille's social and economic development.

IV

Passions did not abate as soon as the iconoclastic scare was over. In Lille, popular Catholic sentiment continued to issue in vigilante action. At least once a crowd seized Protestant children from their parents and forcibly rebaptized them. On other occasions, Lillois took justice into their own hands – stoning the houses of reputed heretics or even arresting them instead of calling the proper authorities.[96] Significantly, the Magistrat felt it prudent to warn several times about the dangerous *division* and *esmotion* that insults and other forms of expression, including children's songs, might arouse.[97]

Outside Lille, however, the Reformed typically kept the upper hand. Protestants in the castellany constituted a union with coreligionists in Tournai and Valenciennes and formed groups armed with weapons sent from Germany to Ghent and thence up the Lys.[98] Some Lillois, more-

---

94 The letters are printed in Verheyden, "Chronique de Gaiffier," pp. 77–80.
95 Letter of 21 August 1566, printed ibid., pp. 80–3. Cf. "Grands devoirs," fol. 574: Some townspeople returning from presches had been roughed up by "others holding the ancient and catholic religion."
96 Alexandre de Saint-Léger, *Lille sous les dominations autrichienne et espagnole (première partie)* (Lille, 1910), p. 71; AML, Reg. 382, fols. 46v, 49–50, 28 August and 16 October 1566.
97 AML, Reg. 382, fol. 50, 5 November 1566 (republished 18 January 1567).
98 Wilfrid Brulez, "De Opstand van het industriegebied in 1566," *Standen en Landen* 4 (1952):83.

over, continued to go to the large presches and meetings that went on in the surrounding countryside all autumn.[99] And in early October Margaret learned that a Protestant minister from Lille had met secretly in Ghent with some fifteen or sixteen colleagues from Antwerp, Valenciennes, Tournai, Armentières, and elsewhere, to what effect was not known though the worst was feared.[100]

Other disturbing news came in November or December. Nobles in many parts of the Low Countries had taken fright at the iconoclastic movement, disowning their erstwhile allies or even joining in the work of repression. But consistories held in the Alleu and the Lys valley during October had been attended by numerous seigneurs, including Noyelles and Escaubecque, signatories of the Compromise and already noted by Rassenghien as disaffected and lethargic at best in controlling popular unrest,[101] and by Huguenot leaders from France, including Coligny. It was rumored that weapons had been purchased and distributed, so that twenty to thirty thousand armed Protestants could now be quickly assembled in the Lys area. Nearly the entire textile region north and west of Lille had become a Protestant fortress, it was alleged, and (yet again!) the "Beggars" were said to be announcing that whenever they wished they could raise fifty thousand men "to hurl at Lille." The government agent who reported this alarming news argued that the city could be saved only by swiftly putting an end to all Protestant preaching and meetings in the countryside and disarming the peasants. Longer-term stability depended, in his eyes, on garrisoning the entire Lys valley.[102]

In the face of reports like this, Lille's authorities could take heart from news that a proposal that Escaubecque try to capture the city for the Protestants had been shelved as unfeasible due to "the paucity of faithful living in the said city."[103] What is more, central authority was

---

[99] Margaret to Philip, 18 November 1566, *CFMP*, 1:215; BN, Fonds français, MS. 9009, fol. 175v (143v).

[100] Margaret to Philip, 10 October 1566, *CFMP*, 1:190.

[101] See Rassenghien's letter to Margaret, 7 September 1566, ibid., 2:393. But cf. the report by Philippe Fremault a week earlier that these two men had intervened to persuade Protestants in Armentières to allow Mass to be celebrated there; ADN, Reg. B 18,061 (see n. 33).

[102] Report by Gilles Jovenel, BN, Fonds français, MS. 9009, fols. 174–80 (142–8). This report is also discussed in Brulez, "Opstand van het industriegebied," p. 87. Jovenel seems to have been something of a scaremonger, but he was a heresy hunter of long date: It was he who had gotten the 1561 rhetorical competition canceled; see Chapter 5, section III.

[103] Apparently, the Antwerp consistory had raised decisive objections after talking to "Cornille" (most likely de le Zenne) and others; report of November or December 1566, printed in *CFMP*, 3:324, and cited by Brulez, "Opstand van het industriegebied," p. 85.

beginning to revive. Once the first shock of iconoclasm had worn off, Margaret of Parma had begun to hire soldiers, demand strict adherence to the Moderation and subsequent concessions, enjoin the reestablishment of Catholic worship in places where it had been suspended, and threaten military action if compliance were not forthcoming. As the autumn wore on, Margaret adopted an increasingly hard line. First, she forbade as a capital crime performance of or attendance at Reformed baptism, communion, or marriage – indeed anything save sermons and worship. Then she decided to garrison Tournai and Valenciennes, which had turned into heretical bastions, declared them traitors and rebels when they closed their gates on the troops she sent, and finally ordered them besieged.

The steps taken by the regent were in part a response to Confederate and Reformed attempts to raise money to purchase toleration or, failing that, to hire troops of their own.[104] Conversely, nobles and Protestants answered Margaret by redoubling their efforts. In early December, the textile area rose in revolt.[105] It is not clear whether this event was a dramatic riposte to the government's moves against Tournai and Valenciennes, or the culmination of several weeks of agitation by preachers exhorting their listeners to seize some town and turn it into a Reformed stronghold – the same campaign that had concocted the plan for Escaubecque to fall upon Lille. But whatever the reason, four different Protestant forces, each numbering up to 1,000 men, assembled in various towns and villages and marched north of Lille toward Tournai. Initially outflanked, Rassenghien managed to engage the second and third bands, but he had too few troops and in the end was glad to withdraw "without considerable losses." He was better able to handle the final group, some 200 men from the sayetterie center of Hondschoote and its environs in West Flanders. Learning of its arrival in Wattrelos, about fifteen kilometers northeast of Lille, he dispatched 50 light cavalry and 150 infantry who surprised the rebels on 27 December, forcing them into the parish church which was then set afire, burning many people to death.

Upon hearing of the slaughter, men already gathered in Tournai set

---

104 Cf. the unsuccessful project to purchase religious freedom from Philip for 3 million fl., to which the Protestant wing of Lille's wealthy de Fourmestraux commercial clan, resident at Antwerp, subscribed 100,000 liv. in October, cited in Chapter 2, section III.

105 The following account draws chiefly on Brulez, "Opstand in het industriegebied." For a summary and a different interpretation, see Parker, *Dutch Revolt*, pp. 94–6.

off. According to some rumors, they were headed toward Lille: One man from Erquinghem-sur-Lys, for example, was reported to have said "before long the *rôtisseurs* of Lille will be roasted in their turn."[106] But near Wattrelos, on the morning of 29 December, they met Rassenghien, who had hurriedly raised more forces and now commanded a total of 1,000 cavalry, 300 harquebusiers, and 2,000 armed peasants. An inconclusive skirmish ended when the rebels retreated toward the nearby walled bourg of Lannoy, while Rassenghien, fearing that his peasant soldiers were becoming disorderly, and hearing that Protestant reinforcements were on the way from Tournai, withdrew to Lille. In the early afternoon, however, while the insurgents milled around outside Lannoy, the baron of Noircarmes drew near with 650 cavalry and 950 infantry diverted from the siege of Valenciennes. Once 500 additional horsemen appeared, Noircarmes attacked. Although the 3,000 or so rebels fought well, with but 30 cavalry they were doomed to failure. Leaving at least 600 dead on the field, the rest of their force melted away. A few days later 100 to 150 men gathered close to Bailleul, on the edge of West Flanders, but they quickly dispersed on their own, without taking any action.

The defeat before Lannoy marked the end of armed resistance in the areas around Lille. It also marked the beginning of the end of the first revolt. Tournai admitted a royal garrison on 2 January 1567; Valenciennes, after continuing for several months to resist in the hope of aid from the Confederates, from France, from anywhere, submitted to Noircarmes on 24 March. To be sure, Protestants at Armentières tried to remain on the offensive, demanding that the Magistrat select some men from a list of prominent Reformed residents so that they could "deal with political affairs" together. But the aldermen flatly rejected this attempt to win recognition for a parallel authority, and by February the Protestant preacher Gilles du Mont had fled to Antwerp.[107]

Emboldened by the recent military successes, Rassenghien summarily punished numerous disorderly people in the countryside and disarmed peasants in all places where trouble had occurred or seemed likely. He also outlawed bearing weapons, or even mere possession. Pursuant to

---

106 AGR, RB, MS. 65, fol. 37; also printed in Beuzart, "La Réforme dans les environs de Lille," p. 57.

107 AGR, RB, MS. 65, fols. 36v, 33v. See also Beuzart, "La Réforme dans les environs de Lille," pp. 48, 56.

Margaret's second agreement with the Confederates in late August 1566, no one was to be prosecuted for Protestant belief, yet parish priests reported that over four hundred people had reconverted to Catholicism in the first week of January alone.[108] On 11 January, Margaret confirmed that presches were still allowed, though nothing else (whether baptisms, marriages, communion, consistory meetings, or collection of funds).[109] But royal investigators later found that even preaching had stopped in January. Thereafter, the inhabitants had "showed obedience," and though "some sectaries fled, others returned to the church and some of the most seditious suffered capital punishment."[110] In the wake of Valenciennes' surrender, other Reformed strongholds quickly capitulated. At Comines, where Protestantism had been noted as still strong in January, cowed residents complied with Aerschot's command to demolish the temple, and the execution of several men for rebellion proceeded without disturbance. On their side, "the good Catholics" of Armentières demolished the Protestant temple "of their own accord."[111]

During the autumn, the Magistrat took steps to prevent rural disorder from spilling over – or being deliberately imported – into Lille. Because four-fifths or more of those who purchased citizen status came from the castellany or adjacent districts of Flanders, limiting access to the bourgeoisie was an indirect but durable way to keep out potential troublemakers. Because, further, citizenship involved participation in the bourgeois militia, which now entailed significant security duties, the city fathers must have considered it especially urgent to monitor closely entry into the bourgeoisie.[112] Acquisition of citizenship had already been sharply if informally curtailed during the summer of 1566: Only four men were received in July, one in August, and none in September,

[108] Rassenghien to Margaret, 8 January 1567, *CFMP*, 3:165–7.
[109] See Frossard, *Eglise sous la Croix*, pp. 83–4.
[110] AGR, RB, MS. 65, fol. 33.
[111] Schoonheere, *Histoire de vieux Comines*, p. 156; AGR, RB, MS. 65, fol. 35v.
[112] Access had already been restricted in December 1561: Each applicant was henceforth required to find a citizen in good standing to serve as his sponsor and guarantor; AML, Reg. 277, fol. 189v, 5 December 1561. This measure did diminish the rapid increase in admissions registered since the mid-1550s plague, but the numbers of new citizens remained well above the level of the second quarter of the sixteenth century. Samples taken every five years in AML, Reg. 277 suggest an average of about 64 purchases of bourgeoisie each year between 1525 and 1550, jumping to 119 in 1555 and 153 in 1560, before declining to 109 in 1565. For the geographical origins of new bourgeois, see Croquez, *Histoire de Lille*, 2:66, and Dal, "Bourgeoisie à Lille," pp. 245–6.

as against a monthly average of more than ten over the previous decade. It was permanently curbed after 4 October, when the price of citizenship jumped from 3 to 25.5 livres.

A proposal that only residents of Lille be permitted to attain citizen status was dropped. But the new fee schedule, probably in tandem with the informal mechanisms that had been put in operation during the months prior to its introduction, moved de facto far in that direction. No additional purchases of citizenship occurred until December 1566, and for several years thereafter the monthly average was less than two. Many months recorded no admissions at all.[113] The minimal charges owed by descendants of current bourgeois were not raised, however, so during the subsequent two decades an average of about seventy natives continued to become citizens *par relief* each year, along with thirty or forty *par achat.*[114] Thus, although ingress to bourgeoisie was restricted, the supply of (presumably trustworthy) new citizens required for guard duty and governmental service was maintained.

The need for a reliable citizen militia seemed to become more pressing as winter approached and rural heretics armed themselves. The Magistrat instituted round-the-clock watch in the tower of St. Etienne from 2 November 1566 through 8 February of the following year,[115] and in mid-November put the six bourgeois companies on armed alert and ordered everyone else home until further notice.[116] As in the summer, scouts were sent out to gather information, notably in the textile districts of the Lys valley and the West Quarter of Flanders. The aldermen summoned the company of Ste. Barbe for guard duty from 10 December until January, and on 13 December again called out the militia, which stayed in readiness into the following April.[117]

Between 20 and 22 December, the bands passing just north of the city renewed iconoclastic attacks on cloisters and churches. In response, the Magistrat posted particularly close guard at every gate and gave permission to leave town only to individuals who had obtained passports (in the

---

[113] The monthly listings are in AML, Reg. 277; the decision to raise the fee is on fol. 206. Dal, "Bourgeoisie à Lille," p. 70, explains the various components of the new fee.

[114] Just seventeen new citizens *par achat* were registered in 1567, thirty in 1570, forty in 1575, thirty-one in 1580. Never again across the sixteenth century did purchases reach 1525–50 levels, much less those of 1555–65: the mean between 1570 and 1600 was forty-seven. These figures are calculated from listings in AML, Reg. 277–80, 955–7.

[115] AML, Reg. 16,301, section "Despence commune," unfoliated.

[116] AML, Reg. 382, fol. 50v, 16 November 1566.

[117] AML, Reg. 16,301, section "Despence commune," unfoliated; Reg. 382, fol. 51.

form of green wax stamps stuck on the back of the right hand) and who were known as "upright" and "beyond suspicion" of heretical sympathies.[118] Celebration of the Feast of the Innocents, openly acknowledged to create the possibility for disorder, was forbidden once again.[119] To ensure that no fugitives from rebel bands took refuge in Lille, in early January the Magistrat summarily expelled all outsiders without exception.[120]

After that, however, repressive decrees tapered off, as the string of defeats inflicted on sectaries removed any threat to Lille. On 5 April, the aldermen called a celebratory procession to thank God "for the victory won at Valenciennes without bloodshed," and about this time the clergy of St. Pierre was informed that it was safe to resume wearing clerical garb.[121] As seat of the Gouvernance, Lille saw judgment meted out to iconoclasts and rebels from the castellany.[122] But few people in the city were prosecuted, and the Magistrat assured the government that the small number of Lillois suspected of image breaking anywhere in the area had been banished.[123]

Persistent rural disorder did prompt a few measures designed to insulate Lille as much as possible from sources of contagion. In mid-April, the aldermen told all Lillois, even citizens, who had fled the city that they could not come home, nor could immigrants settle there, without having first obtained official permission. At the end of June, outsiders were again summarily expelled.[124] Yet the dismissal of all remaining mercenaries on 7 June 1567 indicates that the authorities thought that any danger had passed.[125] As far as the Magistrat was concerned, an acceptable level of stability had been restored to the city. It was now time, as a general procession held in July proclaimed, for the king finally to make good on his promises and come in person to the Low Countries to resolve its problems.[126]

---

[118] AML, Reg. 382, fols. 50v–1, 52. It was due to these precautions, the magistrates subsequently claimed, that no Lillois were among the armed Protestant sectaries at Wattrelos or Lannoy; "Grands devoirs," fols. 580–1.

[119] AML, Reg. 382, fols. 52v–3, 23 December 1566.

[120] Ibid., fols. 53–3v.

[121] Ibid., fols. 57–7v; Hautcoeur, *Histoire de Saint-Pierre*, 2:410.

[122] See Frossard, *Eglise sous la Croix*, pp. 84–5.

[123] "Grands devoirs," fol. 581. The merchant Jacques de Hellin was among the exiles (Frossard, *Eglise sous la Croix*, p. 82); no other names are known.

[124] AML, Reg. 382, fols. 58v–59, 15 April 1567; fol. 65v, 28 June 1567.

[125] AML, Reg. 277, fols. 207v–8.

[126] AML, Reg. 382, fols. 66–6v, 21 July 1567.

7

"Trampling and oppression": Lille under Alba and Requesens, 1567–1576

Even before the duke of Alba reached the Low Countries, the first revolt was effectively over. Margaret of Parma, in fact, had presciently, if futilely, dispatched a special emissary to dissuade Philip from sending troops who might only stir up trouble again. But the king refused to countermand his orders, and on 22 August 1567 Alba arrived in Brussels at the head of an occupying army. Meting out punishment to those deemed responsible for the recent disorders was central to the duke's mission. So between 1567 and 1573, the Council of Troubles, a special tribunal established to judge iconoclasts and other rebels, tried more than twelve thousand people. Three-quarters of them were convicted and nearly eleven hundred executed. Yet the ambitions of Philip and his advisors reached far beyond chastisement. They dreamed of extirpating heresy and instituting changes that would foreclose any chance of renewed rebellion.

In pursuit of these objectives, Alba, who upon Margaret's departure at the end of December 1567 became regent as well as supreme military commander, sometimes carried through plans inaugurated previously. With the appointment of bishops to the new dioceses, for example, the redrawing of the episcopal map was finally accomplished in 1570, more than a decade after it had been decreed. But other policies were novel, particularly a project for new forms of taxation, unveiled in 1569. This scheme was designed to pay for the thousands of troops who were to garrison the Low Countries permanently, as well as to cover the costs of an expanded central state administration.

Despite – or because of – Alba's policies and ready recourse to force

to implement them, Protestantism was not uprooted nor the Netherlands entirely pacified. Yet regardless of wide and bitter hostility to the
proposed taxes, before 1572 continued Spanish rule faced no serious
threat. To be sure, William of Orange had attempted both to defeat the
Spanish militarily and to unite the opposition to the crown on a broad
platform of religious toleration, the restoration of traditional privileges,
and an appeal to national feeling against foreign overlordship. But even
though William had become the acknowledged leader of opposition
once the principal signatories of the Compromise had died or been
killed, all his efforts had miscarried.

In the spring of 1572, however, a conjunction of events finally favored
the renewal of revolt. After a winter marked (as in 1565–6) by harsh
weather and grain shortages, as well as the reappearance of plague,
Alba, having failed to win the provincial Estates' assent for his new taxes,
ordered collection to begin without it. Merchants throughout the Low
Countries responded by going on strike. This step, in combination with
adverse cyclical movements and a French embargo on cloth from the
Netherlands, sharply reduced commerce and industrial production,
triggering widespread unemployment and exacerbating already mounting distress and discontent. Rapprochement between the Huguenots
and the French king, trade conflict between England and Spain, and
Spanish entanglement in the Ridolfi plot designed to put Mary Queen of
Scots on the English throne in place of Elizabeth coincidentally created
a propitious international context.

On 1 April, the Orangist Sea Beggar privateers, who for several years
had preyed on shipping in the English Channel and North Sea, seized
the strategic port of Brill in Zeeland in a surprise attack. In the following
days, they took additional towns across that province and Holland virtually without a fight. During the next few months, a new political order
was consolidated in the northern provinces, as supporters of the Spanish
government were purged from city councils and replaced by men
pledged to Orange. William himself was installed as governor of Holland, Zeeland, and Utrecht, mandated to fight with them to restore
traditional liberties. Protestants won the free exercise of their religion,
whereas Catholics, though guaranteed equal treatment, began to face
discrimination.

Large areas of the southern and eastern Netherlands had also fallen easily to Orangist forces, often assisted by local sympathizers. In the course of the autumn, however, Alba recaptured much of the territory he had lost, in the process gruesomely sacking several cities to sow terror. By the end of 1572, however, his reconquest had ground to a halt, blocked equally by the heroic determination displayed by residents of cities in the northern provinces and by growing Spanish money problems that left his soldiers without pay and unwilling to fight. A year later, lacking new initiatives to supersede his discredited coercive policies, Alba was replaced by Don Luis de Requesens, grand commander of Castile.

The change failed, however, to restore the Spanish position. Losses mounted under Requesens, as royal troops mutinied over wage arrears. When interest payments on the enormous Castilian state debt were suspended on 1 September 1575, the flow of funds to forces in the Low Countries was reduced to a trickle. By the time of Requesens's death in early March 1576, even the areas under the control of the royal government were rife with disaffection. The long tax battle had alienated significant sectors of the ruling strata, peace negotiations with Holland and Zeeland had broken off with no prospect of resumption, and predatory bands of unpaid troops and Beggar guerrillas prowled the countryside and threatened cities. Unhappily, although Requesens had been ineffectual, his decease presaged worse, for he had left no successor, so authority devolved upon an aged and divided Council of State.

I

Alba's punitive campaign struck Lille and its immediate neighborhood much less harshly than other parts of the Low Countries. Between 1567 and 1573, 68 convictions can be credited to the four men sitting at Lille who, relying on investigations and denunciations, transmitted names to the Council of Troubles in Brussels.[1] Compared with the 1,063 people condemned at Tournai, the 525 at Antwerp, or the 425 at Valenciennes – to cite some of the most impressive figures – or even the 106 punished at Armentières, this was a small number indeed. What is more, the

---

[1] For a description of the workings of the system, see William S. Maltby, *Alba* (Berkeley, 1983), p. 154.

urban population was little affected. Of those found guilty by the council, only 4 at most came from the city, the rest from villages in the castellany.[2]

Some Lillois doubtless escaped prosecution by going into exile, despite a placard signed by Philip II forbidding emigration on pain of automatically being considered a suspect in the past disorders.[3] Several merchants who had long traded with Germany moved to Cologne for a while in the worst years of repression,[4] while a handful of artisans was recorded in Geneva.[5] Other townspeople surely went to France before the St. Bartholomew's Day Massacre in 1572. But the majority of refugees apparently fled the shorter distance to England. Many went to the textile center of Norwich, where in May 1568 twenty-three of the eighty-three members of the Walloon church with known birthplaces were credited with having come from Lille, though this designation apparently encompassed the castellany as well as the city.[6]

At least temporarily, expatriation reduced the number of dissenters, unwittingly aiding the government's attempts to crush heresy. Yet the faithful who remained – and the many others who soon began to filter back – managed to revive Protestant communities in a number of villages before the end of the decade. The fragility of government control over the countryside was reflected, too, in the anticlerical activity and brigandage that became endemic during these years. Much of it was carried out by bands composed of men condemned by the Council of Troubles and perhaps protected by nobles.[7] Reacting to reports from Ypres, the Alleu, and places around Lille, in January 1568 Alba an-

---

[2] A. L. E. Verheyden, *Le Conseil des Troubles. Liste des condamnés (1567–1573)* (Brussels, 1961); Frossard, *Eglise sous la Croix*, pp. 86–107. A roofer from Lille who was punished at Ghent for iconoclasm should also be noted; see Verheyden, *Martyrologe protestant des Pays-Bas du Sud*, p. 253, no. 127.

[3] Placard of 15 September 1567, in BML, MS. 245, fols. 270–3v.

[4] Coornaert, *Français à Anvers*, 1:168 n. 3, names André, Guillaume, Gaspard, and Toussaint de Fourmestraux; Pierre Coene; Alart and Pierre Delannoy; and Dominique Poulle.

[5] *Livre des habitants de Genève. II. 1572–74 et 1585–87*, ed. Paul–F. Geisendorf (Geneva, 1963), pp. 15, 102, 105. As the published records relevant here cover only 1572–4, they omit people who would have arrived in the previous few years, because earlier records stop at 1560.

[6] Only the province of Flanders, with twenty-seven, had sent more. Moens, *Walloon Church of Norwich*, 1:153–6; Beauzart, *Les Hérésies dans la région de Douai, d'Arras et au pays de l'Alleu*, p. 442 n. 1. Some of the spouses and children of these twenty-three people were also probably natives of Lille or the region. All but four of the exiles had arrived in 1566 or later, most in 1567. A few Lillois were also noted in the Southampton church registers during the early 1570s; *Registre de l'Eglise Wallonne de Southampton*, ed. Humphrey M. Godfray (Lymington, 1890), pp. 6–7.

[7] Cf. a deposition by the curé at Auberch (or Aubers); AGR, RB, MS. 65, fols. 67–8v.

nounced that villagers would be held collectively responsible for protecting pastors against the assaults, even murders, being perpetrated "daily." These assaults, the duke alleged, were carried out by people acting "under the pretext of the new religion" to drive the clergy from the parishes.[8] Despite a flurry of similar edicts, however, the situation continued to deteriorate across the late 1560s. Churches and curés' houses were burned down and priests held to ransom, while Beggars were able to break into jails and free Protestants.[9]

To some observers, the government's failure to achieve mastery over the castellany menaced the security of Lille, so often the object of Protestant fulminations but never yet conquered. Gilles Jovenel expressed his disquiet in a long, rambling memorandum drawn up in the late summer of 1569, when Huguenot strength was rapidly growing in nearby France. The presence of abbesses, priors, monks, and nuns of French nationality at Marquette, Fives, Loos, and other nearby religious houses was extremely dangerous, he wrote, for their guests included heretic noblemen who plotted to seize Lille to make good the Protestant failure to do so in 1566.[10]

From all indications, however, such an attack would have been even more ill-advised in the late 1560s than during 1566 – and, if actually mooted about, just as wisely rejected – for conditions in Lille did not at all resemble those prevailing in the countryside. Admittedly, there were signs of political and religious disaffection. As Alba's grip tightened, popular antipathy became more visible and vociferous: To the magistrates' chagrin, for example, songs "tending to dishonor" the crown and its officials could be heard openly in the streets.[11] On occasion, sacred objects and church property were vandalized. Some townspeople threw rocks at church windows, a crucifix in a chapel on the market square dedicated to the Virgin was defaced, and cemeteries were profaned by people who played bowls, practiced archery, and used them as garbage dumps.[12] Indifference to traditional religious duties seems also to have existed – for example, among those sayetteurs who allegedly no longer observed the feast of their patron St. John the Baptist as a holiday, but

8 Printed in Verheyden, "Chronique de Gaiffier," pp. 66–7.
9 AGR, RB. MS. 65, fols. 67, 68; Schoonheere, *Histoire de vieux Comines*, p. 157.
10 AGR, RB, MS. 65, fols. 54–60.
11 AML, Reg. 382, fol. 84v.
12 Ibid., fols. 103, 85, 95v–6.

seated at their looms treated it " like other days."[13] Finally, investigators sent around his diocese by the bishop of Tournai at Alba's behest in late 1568 or early 1569 questioned the orthodoxy of four instructors in the parish elementary schools and found condemned works in two book-sellers' shops.[14]

But this is the only piece of evidence of its kind, and – because all four masters had been admitted to their posts by the Magistrat – a very inconclusive one at that. It is hardly, in any event, suggestive of the existence of vigorous, numerous, organized, or dangerous heresy. What is more, no material crisis fueled discontent, because economic conditions in late 1560s Lille were more uniformly favorable than they had been for a decade. As the top five lines of Table 7.1 show, the city's textiles recovered smartly from their mid-1560s slump. Led by the say craft, light-cloth output grew fastest in 1567–9, but – with the exception of changéants – expansion continued into 1571. As for drap production, it increased by a fourth between 1566–7 and 1568–9 and stayed at a high level through 1571–2.[15]

Lille's merchants once again frequented Antwerp in large numbers – their presence reaching its secular peak in 1570 – while also resuming their travels across the length and breadth of Europe.[16] Table 7.2 indicates that grain prices were essentially stable from 1566–7 through 1569–70 and only showed a slight increase the following year, whereas wages remained in a generally good relationship to prices. Although below the levels attained in the middle of the decade, substantial outlays of both cash and bread were maintained by the Bourse commune through 1569–70, using funds generated by special door-to-door solic-

---

13 Ordinance of 20 August 1569, commanding renewed observance of the feast, printed in Van-haeck, *Sayetterie à Lille*, 2:74, no. 33.

14 One master taught in St. Sauveur, another at St. Maurice, the remaining two in St. Etienne. In only a single instance were reasons given for the doubts: One master was said to have fallen under suspicion during the iconoclastic period, although he now produced an attestation from his parish priest documenting that he fulfilled his duties as a Catholic. See Ernest Matthieu, "Statistique scolaire du diocèse de Tournai au XVIe siècle," *Analectes pour servir à l'histoire ecclésiastique de la Belgique* 38 (1912):385–6; René Hoven, "Ecoles primaires et Ecoles latines dans le Diocèse de Tournai en 1569," in *Horae Tornacenses* (Tournai, 1971), pp. 178–80; A. Delmasure "L'enseignement primaire au XVIe siècle dans la 'partie française' du diocèse de Tournai," *RN* 55 (1973):93–8.

15 The contrary movements of changéant and velveteen output indicate that bourgetteurs were essentially switching from one fabric to the other, presumably in response to changes in demand. Hence it was sayetterie that fueled growth at this time.

16 Coornaert, *Français à Anvers*, fig. "Nombre de marchands" at end of vol. 2; ibid., 1:168, n. 17 for one example of extensive travel.

Table 7.1. *Indexes of textile output in Lille, 1566–76*
(100 = mean, 1561–2 through 1570–1)

Year	Sayetterie	Changéants	Velveteens	Draps
1566–7	98	127	96	85
1567–8	101	122	81	87
1568–9	108	177	78	108
1569–70	118	157	100	100
1570–1	119	123	125	100
1571–2	81	164	125	104
1572–3	106	184	96	82
1573–4	119	212	99	81
1574–5	123	287	94	82
1575–6	169	314	121	89

Sources: Deyon and Lottin, "Production textile à Lille," p. 31 (sayetterie); AML, Reg. 16,300–9 (all other types of cloth).

itations, a practice instituted earlier in the decade. Thus an additional cushion was provided against material problems or the dissatisfaction to which they might have given birth.

For their part, the aldermen displayed a firm commitment to Catholicism and political conformity. Magistrat, citizens, guilds, and clergy participated in numerous processions, along with governor, crown officials, and titled gentlemen. They extolled papal grants of indulgences, thanked God for Alba's triumph over the "rebels and sectaries" in Friesland, praised "the maintenance of the ancient Catholic religion," toasted Philip's health, and celebrated the French king's victory over the Huguenots at St. Valéry.[17] The city fathers also duly published royal placards commanding that books be inspected and all forbidden works turned in, or calling for close supervision of bookstores, schoolmasters, and midwives.[18] Teachers were summoned before the aldermen to check that they could produce proper permits.[19] Finally, the Magistrat

[17] For general processions held just in 1567–9, see AML, Reg. 382, fols. 71, 71bis–1bisv, 75v–6, 84–4v, 92v, 93v–4, 106v, 111v; BML, MS. 725, fol. [25v].
[18] AML, Reg. 382, fols. 120v–1, 13 May 1570; Reg. 16,980, fols. 165–8, 19 May 1570.
[19] AML, Reg. 382, fol. 115, 30 January 1570. The fact that a year had passed since suspicions had been voiced regarding four teachers suggests that as always the Magistrat resented interference by outside authorities, whether clerical or lay, in the city's affairs.

Table 7.2. *Index of Common Fund outlays, grain prices, wages, and employment in Lille, 1566–76 (100 = mean, 1561–2 through 1570–1)*

	Common Fund Outlays		Prices		Wages		
					Master		
Year	Cash	Bread	Wheat	Rye	mason	Laborer	Employment[a]
1566–7	121	102	96	91	102	101	99
1567–8	104	102	94	89	102	101	101
1568–9	115	98	91	87	102	101	110
1569–70	108	102	96	87	102	101	119
1570–1	85	79	100	104	86	101	120
1571–2	89	144	123	145	102	101	86
1572–3	99	112	112	130	86	101	109
1573–4	91	71	176	165	97	101	122
1574–5	130	61	177	130	107	105	129
1575–6	128	93	136	95	117	105	173

[a]Employment index calculated from light-cloth output.
Sources: AASL, Reg. J 583–602 (Common Fund outlays); AML, Reg. 797 (wheat prices); *Dokumenten voor de Geschiedenis van Prijzen en Lonen*, 4:347 (rye prices); AML, Reg. 16,300–9 (wages); Deyon and Lottin, "Production textile à Lille," p. 31 (employment).

once again banned boisterous games at which crowds might gather, prohibited unauthorized meetings, and suspended the celebration of the Feast of the Innocents for several years in a row.[20]

Such measures, like those enacted before and during the iconoclastic crisis, make it clear that Lille's ruling class had little quarrel with Alba's goals of restoring order and reestablishing the hegemony of the traditional faith. Nor, at least initially, did the Magistrat object to the duke's tactics. In his memoirs, Bauduin de Croix eulogized Alba's administration, in particular applauding his determination to provide sufficient permanent troops to forestall future unrest.[21] The three (of a total of four) local representatives of the Council of Troubles who were current or former members of the Loi constituted a more immediately tangible

[20] Ibid., fols. 30–30v, 52v–3, 85v–6. Cf. Paresys, "Ordre en jeu," fig. 1.
[21] "Mémoires de Bauduin de Croix," fols. 38–40.

endorsement of Alba's actions.[22] In addition, under the city's guidance the provincial Estates willingly voted 40,000 livres in early 1568 to help defray the costs of Tournai's garrison of twelve hundred cavalry. This force was intended both to control that former Calvinist citadel and to help put down marauding bands in the rural Tournésis and Walloon Flanders.[23]

As Alba's regime proceeded, however, increasingly sharp points of friction arose. Later in 1568 the aldermen engaged in an acrimonious wrangle over the duke's resolve to confiscate the goods of exiles,[24] an echo of earlier battles. But the greatest conflict by far erupted after the government's project for tax reform was presented in March 1569.

II

On 13 April, the Estates of Walloon Flanders – the usual delegates from Lille's Magistrat and the four bailiffs representing the countryside were joined on this important occasion by two officials each from Douai and Orchies – met in the aldermanic hall at Lille to consider Alba's demand for what were known as the Tenth, Twentieth, and Hundredth Pennies.[25] The latter was a one-time levy of 1 percent of the annual income of real property, including annuities but exempting all movable property worth less than 100 florins. Both the Twentieth Penny (a tax of 5 percent of the sale price of all real property, to be paid by the seller at each transaction) and the Tenth (10 percent of the sale price of everything else, including exports) were, in contrast, meant to be permanent. Breaking with past practice, moreover, special officials responsible solely to the central government would gather the Tenth and Twentieth Pennies.

---

22 The four were Phillippe Hangouart, royal councillor and provincial collector of aides, who had served on the Loi for three years during the late 1540s (other men from his family were appointed to the Loi all across the sixteenth century); Sebastien le Prevost, also a collector of aides, named to the Magistrat nine times between 1559 and 1577, including five terms as alderman and two as councillor; Jean de Warenghien, an official at the Chamber of Accounts, selected for the municipal government in 1565, 1566, and 1567; and Jean de Quemble, the only one with no known connection with Lille's Magistrat. It is, of course, significant that the three who can be identified worked for the central government: These jobs were probably the primary reason for their appointment to the council. For names, see Verheyden, *Conseil des Troubles*, pp. 3, 4, 8; for terms in city office, BML, MS. 597.

23 AML, Reg. 15,885, fols. 116–17v, 31 March 1568.

24 AML, Reg. 16,302, fol. [170]. The outcome of the dispute is unknown.

25 Unless otherwise indicated, the following account is based on the register of the deliberations of the provincial Estates, AML, Reg. 145. Houdoy, *L'impôt sur le revenu*, though helpful, is not always reliable.

The governor-general's plan was a manifest onslaught on the Estates' main raison d'être and mode of political leverage – namely, the right to vote taxes, determine how they were to be raised, and collect and administer them. The assembly's response, however, emphasized the nefarious economic consequences of the proposed fiscal innovations: higher food prices, but most of all severe damage to trade and manufacture. What with goods passing through many hands between producer and purchaser, the 10 percent tax would be levied five or six times. Textiles, which involved numerous stages and raw materials, would no longer remain competitive with foreign cloth. Urging the plan's withdrawal, the Estates offered 160,000 florins in its place.

Although offers and counterproposals were the accustomed way by which the sovereign's tax requests were handled in the Netherlands, Alba would have none of it. He ordered the Estates to gather again, this time in the presence of Rassenghien, an egregious violation of their liberties that can only have damaged the governor's ability to gain consent for the project. At this new meeting, Rassenghien relayed several messages from Alba that indicate the duke's conviction (probably well founded, given the content of the Estates' statement and later developments) that Lille was spearheading the opposition. The city was menaced with garrisoning or even sacking, while the mayor, two aldermen, and the city attorney were cited as holdouts who would regret their recalcitrance. Should the delegates persist in their refusal, Rassenghien concluded, they would be summoned individually to Brussels to justify their position at the court. This was a warning that no one would take lightly after Egmont and Hornes, prominent signatories of the Compromise of the Nobility, had been seized and executed in the capital on 5 June 1568. The intimidation did not entirely succeed. But after Lille's Magistrat met with notables of the city, agreement was reached to accept the Hundredth Penny and sweeten the substitute for the other two taxes by offering 200,000 florins over six years.

This proposal turned out to settle the matter of the 1 percent levy, which began to be collected in Walloon Flanders as throughout the Low Countries late in 1569. Alba spurned the rest of the compromise, however, and decided to try to smash his adversaries once and for all. So both to indicate his displeasure and to win compliance for the original plan in its entirety, he carried through an earlier threat, announcing in late summer 1569 that troops would be billeted in cities across the Low

Countries until the Tenth and Twentieth Pennies were voted. On 4 October, ten companies of Spanish soldiers entered Lille; they were destined to remain until 2 July 1570.[26]

In December 1568, just a brief stay by light cavalry fresh from victories over Orange's forces nearly led to brawls between troops and townspeople.[27] Since that time, the tax proposals had so focused and spurred popular protest that "seditious remarks" on the subject were widely heard around the city.[28] Hence, the échevins could only regard the arrival of the soldiers with deep foreboding. Hoping to forestall problems, they warned townspeople not to "vilify, mistreat or otherwise molest" the troops.[29] But residents remained hostile, many refusing to admit the soldiers into their homes, where they were to be lodged.[30]

Sure enough, relations worsened as the months dragged on. According to a flood of complaints by Lillois, soldiers incurred large debts and then refused to pay them, reducing some citizens to indigence. There must have been a measure of truth to these allegations, for to reimburse townspeople the Magistrat imposed special consumption taxes.[31] Within a few weeks of their arrival, soldiers were involved in a serious clash with the citizenry, leading the commanding officer to summon reinforcements – through alderman Sebastien le Prevost rushed to Brussels and managed to dissuade the court from sending any more men. A riot during the annual procession in June 1570 was narrowly averted when the provost's force intervened.[32] In the words of a contemporary, the troops "committed several murders and thousands of outrages," and the normally reticent municipal financial accounts also commented on the "trampling and oppression" of Lillois.[33]

Over Rassenghien's objections, envoys from the Magistrat went to Brussels to plead for the removal of the troops almost as soon as they got

---

26 Carette, "Recueil," fol. [85v]; AML, Reg. 15,885, fols. 148v–9v, 7 April 1571; Reg. 382, fols. 107v, 109. In contrast to these documents, the *Histoire de Lille*, 2:122, places the troops' arrival on 13 March 1569.
27 AML, Reg. 382, fol. 93; Reg. 16,303, fol. 230v.
28 AML, Reg. 382, fol. 98v, 23 May 1569.
29 Ibid., fols. 107v, 109v–11, 27 September and 14 October 1569.
30 Ibid., fol. 109, 5 October 1569.
31 Ibid., fols. 114, 115v; Reg. 15,885, fols. 129–30, 148v–9v. The taxes were not revoked until 1574.
32 AML, Reg. 16,305, fols. 124v, 202v. Le Prevost probably enjoyed some credit at the court, for he concurrently sat on the Council of Troubles.
33 Carette, "Recueil," fol. [85v]; AML, Reg. 16,304, fols. 128–8v.

to Lille. Another fruitless delegation visited the court early in 1570.[34] In the end, the garrison departed not because of these entreaties but because Alba, unable to overcome resistance anywhere in the Netherlands and in desperate need of money, agreed to negotiate. In early summer 1570, the Estates of Walloon Flanders subscribed to the arrangement worked out with other provinces, whereby an aide of 2 million florins annually was granted retroactively for the two years from August 1569 to August 1571. At the same time, the Hundredth Penny (already being collected) was ratified: Of the 3.63 million florins it yielded in the Netherlands as a whole, Walloon Flanders paid 232,057 florins, or about 6.4 percent. Lille's contribution placed it fourth among Netherlands cities, behind Antwerp (which paid four times as much as the next town), Brussels, and Bruges, but ahead of Ghent, Tournai, and Valenciennes.[35] Its share of the aide cost the province 81,250 florins per year, 4.06 percent of the total, or just below the 4.2 percent agreed to in 1558 but still above the proportions the province had paid before midcentury. Lille owed 18,055.5 florins.[36]

Alba was not at all satisfied with these sums, which fell far short of what he had counted on from the Tenth and Twentieth Pennies. A crucial misunderstanding, moreover, made another battle inevitable. Netherlanders interpreted Alba's acceptance of the aide as indicating that he would be amenable to bargaining and compromise when taxes were discussed once again. The duke, however, was resolved to secure a permanent financial base for the central government, preferably by sales taxes.[37] At the expiration of the aide, therefore, Walloon Flanders like the rest of the provinces still declined to accept any form of the 5 percent and 10 percent levies. But on 31 July 1571 the duke directed Rassenghien along with the other governors to ignore the Estates, appoint collectors, and set about gathering them.[38]

The struggle was far from over, however. Disregarding the threats and warnings once more passed on by Rassenghien (with whom they engaged in a fierce verbal war in late December 1571), the Estates

---

[34] AML, Reg. 277, fols. 217–18, 13 October 1569; Reg. 16,304, fol. 133.

[35] Maurice-A. Arnould, "L'impôt sur le capital en Belgique au XVIe siècle," *Le Hainaut Economique* 1 (1946):17–45.

[36] AML, Reg. 15,885, fols. 130–1, 140v–1, 144–5v. See also Reg. 145, fols. 84–5. For the earlier figures, see Chapter 1, section III.

[37] See Maltby, *Alba*, p. 218.

[38] AML, Reg. 145, fols. 109, 117–28.

immediately resorted to obstructionism. They repeatedly asked for further explanations and refused to receive the oaths of the few men who did consent to serve as collectors; at the same time, they offered to renew the aide for another two years.[39] But most of all they labored to put flesh on their contention that the taxes would have disastrous effects – that indeed just the attempt to impose the new levies had already sharply curtailed economic activity, in particular by drying up the credit that was the lifeblood of trade and industry.

As part of this campaign, at the end of January and the beginning of February 1572 depositions were taken from guild leaders in Lille and several other towns for submission to Alba. Sayetteurs in Lille testified that output was down by over seven thousand cloths a month and would drop further should the duke's proposal go through. At least six hundred masters operating 634 looms had been or would be idled, throwing out of work some two thousand people, including weavers, dyers, fullers, combers, and spinners, and affecting villagers up to six leagues from the city. Equally dire predictions came from drapers, who slyly added that the collapse of textile production in Lille would end the city's large imports of Spanish wool. Bourgetteurs endorsed the grim prophecies outlined by the other weavers and noted that most textile makers had unwittingly accumulated stocks of unsold cloth. Hosiers agreed that Spanish wool merchants in Bruges would suffer along with Lillois and added that workers had already been reduced to "extreme poverty." Retailers of cloth claimed that sales were down by a half and, what was worse, customers were unable to settle debts for goods bought previously. Finally, mercers and apothecaries, along with drap weavers from Armentières and Comines, reported cutting production and releasing workers.[40] The directors of Lille's Bourse commune and parish charities announced that the number of poor had risen by a third since Alba had ordered the collection of the Tenth and Twentieth Pennies. Unfortunately, gifts had fallen sharply, so that the Common Fund was months behind in annuity payments and would be unable to distribute any new clothes to the needy.[41]

Whether or not it was correct in all particulars, Lille's remonstrance

---

[39] Ibid., fols. 109, 112, 132–58. On at least three occasions (19 September, 20 October, and 13 December 1571), Alba again rejected Walloon Flanders' complaints and ordered collection to begin at once.

[40] Ibid., fols. 176–84v.

[41] Ibid., fols. 66–7.

was supported by other evidence – a description of conditions in Flanders presented to the king in January 1572 confided that the new taxes were causing merchants from Lille, Douai, Arras, Brussels, and Antwerp to emigrate to France[42] – so Alba agreed to modify his proposals. In the final version, the 10 percent levy would fall only on the first and last sale of merchandise rather than on every transaction. Many foodstuffs, industrial raw materials, and goods in transit would be wholly exempt and only the final sales of agricultural products and cattle would be assessed. The export tax was also reduced to the thirtieth penny or 3.33 percent. But Alba insisted that the levies be permanent and that a new corps of tax officials, beholden only to the central government, be established.[43]

Moreover, the duke was stubborn. Ignoring advice that the inhabitants of Lille, Douai, and Orchies would not hear of the Tenth Penny and that the magistrates of these towns feared being "massacred" should they consent to name receivers, in March 1572 he ordered that the taxes be collected on pain of a 12,000 florin fine for Lille and substantial amounts for Douai and Orchies.[44] At the same time, he wrote to the king urging the rejection of all requests for relief.[45] But the decision was no longer in his hands. Having failed to receive a reply to their earlier detailed petition, the Estates had convoked additional meetings to which important citizens and members of the local nobility were summoned. In them, it was decided to follow Hainaut's example and send a three-man delegation to Spain to speak with the king himself. Rassenghien's fulminations were no more effective this time than before.[46]

On 20 April 1572, the deputies from Walloon Flanders appeared before Philip shortly after their counterparts from Hainaut. In the name of the entire delegation, the provost of Douai asserted that the Tenth and Twentieth Pennies would ruin the province economically: Indeed, trade and industry had already diminished by a third and were still falling. He then cautioned that the new taxes would be spiritually deleterious as well, creating such bad feeling and estrangement, and

---

[42] The report, by Francés de Alava, is printed in *CP*, ed. Gachard, 2:215–16, no. 1073.
[43] Craeybeckx, "Aperçu sur l'histoire des impôts," p. 102.
[44] Morillon to Granvelle, 31 March 1572, *CG*, 4:157.
[45] Letter of 19 March 1572, *CP*, ed. Gachard, 2:234–5, no. 1095.
[46] Alba to Philip, 11 March 1572, ibid., p. 230, no. 1091; Morillon to Granvelle, *CG*, 4:123. The delegates included one of the bailiffs from the castellany, along with the pensionary of Lille and the provost of Douai.

prompting such substantial emigration, that "an infinity" of souls would be lost. In an injured – and likely sincere – tone, the envoy pointedly recalled to the king the province's loyalty to him and to the Catholic faith. "Even during the recent troubles," Philip was reminded, Lille had served "as a shelter and refuge" for clergy and sacred objects, and its citizens had "repulsed, at their cost, expense and risk of life, the efforts of seditious and disorderly enemies." The statement went on to accuse Alba of duplicity, rigidity, and overbearing behavior and protested, too, Rassenghien's frequent attempts at intimidation. In sum, it concluded, Walloon Flanders "judged and knew" the Tenth and Twentieth Pennies to be "unquestionably repugnant to the honor of God, [his subjects'] consciences, the service of Your Majesty, and the public weal of your lands and subjects." The province would, however, consent to pay its aide of 81,250 florins for four more years.[47]

After emissaries from Artois, Brabant, and Flanders had presented their cases – all concluded by agreeing to prolong the aide of 2 million florins – there was a two-month wait for Philip's decision. On 26 June 1572, the king finally agreed to suspend the proposed taxes in return for the aide promised by the provinces.[48] Philip's response did not go into the reasons for his decision. Nevertheless, it seems probable that the petitioners succeeded only partly (if at all) on the basis of their arguments.[49] More likely, the king realized that he needed to bring the tax revolt to an end and assure some flow of revenue into the royal coffers in the Netherlands to repel the recent Sea Beggar invasions, which, ironically, met with such initial success precisely because of the discontent engendered by his tax policy.[50]

Like its resistance to the confiscation of heretics' property, the Magistrat's opposition to the new levies should not be taken as denoting

---

[47] The statement, AML, Reg. 145, fols. 189–91v, has been printed as an appendix to *CG*, 4:607–11. See also *CP*, ed. Gachard, 2:243–4, no. 1105, for a summary in a letter from Philip to Alba.

[48] AML, Reg. 145, fols. 191v–5v.

[49] Morillon may, however, have been echoing court opinion when he wrote Granvelle that the representatives from Lille "raised the liveliest and most justified objections to the Tenth and Twentieth" Pennies; *CG*, 4:189.

[50] In a letter dated 20 April 1572, the day on which Lille's envoys appeared before him, Philip informed Alba that he had received them with clear signs of his displeasure, although he stopped short of rejecting the provinces' demands, as the duke had requested; *CP*, ed. Gachard, 2:240, no. 1104. Two days later Philip learned of the fall of Brill and on 8 June of Mons's capture, although before making up his mind he probably had not heard of Alba's decision, taken on 15 June, to abandon the northern provinces to concentrate on the defense of the South; Parker, *Dutch Revolt*, pp. 60–1, 135.

disagreement with central government poilicies as a whole. Rather, the dispute over the Tenth and Twentieth Pennies shows once again that the municipal government would object – and object vociferously – to specific initiatives that threatened traditional civic privileges and arrangements between crown and locality. But the Loi's fundamental loyalty to the status quo remained unshaken. Hence, the aldermen evinced no sympathy for the urban revolts stimulated by the 1572 invasions. To be sure, like several other towns, Lille refused to admit the Spanish and Italian forces that in the wake of the Beggar coups Brussels suggested as reinforcements for existing garrisons.[51] Doubtless the experience of what had happened just two years before remained vivid, and the troops could also be used in any last-ditch bid to enforce the Tenth and Twentieth Pennies. But when Orangists seized Mons on 24 May, the Magistrat immediately took steps to guard against the occurrence of any similar event in Lille. Ordinances dating from 1566 were republished, commanding daily registration of outsiders, expelling beggars, prohibiting unauthorized meetings, ordering boats removed from the moats at night, enjoining all males between twenty and sixty to arm themselves with staffs and put themselves at the ready.[52] In addition, three infantry companies from the area were hired.[53]

The economic situation, which had been deteriorating for nearly a year, must have contributed to the authorities' worries. Lille's business with Antwerp, already diminished in 1571, dwindled even further the next year, slumping to the depressed levels of 1566–7.[54] Sayetteurs' production plummeted (Table 7.1), wages remained frozen, and wheat and especially rye prices soared.[55] Common Fund disbursements of cash, already reduced in the previous year, stayed low in comparison with the recent past (Table 7.2). Masters ought to have been able to feed their families without too much difficulty even in 1571–2.[56] Laborers' families dependent on a single income, however, must have found it all

[51] Morillon to Granvelle, 28 April 1572, CG, 4:203.
[52] AML, Reg. 382, fols. 32–2v, 34–5v (three ordinances from March and April 1566, republished 25 May 1572), 140 (8 August 1572).
[53] "Mémoires de Bauduin de Croix," fol. 47.
[54] Coornaert, *Français à Anvers*, fig. "Nombre de marchands" at end of vol. 2.
[55] Even more spectacularly, the price of salt more than tripled between 1570 and 1572, after the Sea Beggars captured much of Zeeland, a major source for the southern Netherlands. AH Comtesse, Reg. 4536–40; cf. Verlinden, Craeybeckx, and Scholliers, "Price and Wage Movements in Belgium," pp. 69–70.
[56] According to the method of calculation outlined in Appendix F, supplying wheat to the family of a fully employed master would have required 33% to 56% of putative earnings, rye 31% to

but impossible to make ends meet, because buying sufficient wheat would have swallowed from 63 to 106 percent of putative earnings, and even rye from 60 to 99 percent.

Incidents in the light-cloth industry may also have troubled the Magistrat. In the late 1560s, some urban artisans seem to have begun putting out work to rural producers, perhaps to circumvent the six-loom limit imposed in 1565.[57] Others engaged city weavers. By 1571, the master sayetteur Jacques Masurel was giving work to seven weavers, five of them Lillois,[58] leading the Magistrat to republish the 1565 ordinance in its entirety, reaffirming the six-loom limit and the ban on putting out.[59]

The extent of the crisis ought not be exaggerated, however, for it was neither so broad nor so harsh as the one that had occurred in 1565–6. Although sayetteurs were producing less cloth in 1571–2, changéant output was significantly superior to that of either 1569–70 or 1570–1, while velveteens stayed at the same high level (Table 7.1), indicating real growth rather than redistribution of work within the bourgetterie trade. Cause and effect of this same vitality, bourgetteurs began to weave a wide variety of popular new fabrics, winning the aldermen's sanction in October 1571.[60] The drapery industry likewise more than held its own (Table 7.1). The Bourse commune, for its part, managed to hand out many more loaves of bread than in any year since 1565–6 (Table 7.2), thereby easing the plight of the destitute. In 1572–3, moreover, changéant output continued to increase and sayetterie rebounded nicely, so overall employment rose sharply, while a good harvest brought grain prices down and trade with Antwerp picked up. After 1569, finally, the

52%. Even correcting for the downward turn in output and thus in employment, only three-quarters of income at most would have been needed for foodstuffs, even less if we take into account the earnings of other family members.

57 An ordinance of 17 April 1567 (AML, Reg. 382, fols. 60–60v) reiterated the long-standing prohibition on dyeing and finishing in Lille cloth woven elsewhere. The steep increase in fines from 3 liv. to 10 liv. per single cloth and 20 liv. per double piece suggests that violations were occurring with some frequency. That it was urban weavers in particular who engaged in the practice can be deduced from the much heavier penalties threatening convicted sayetteurs (up to ten years' suspension from their craft) as compared with the penalty for finishers (a one-year suspension). A similar law to the same effect issued on 26 May 1568 (printed in Vanhaeck, *Sayetterie à Lille*, 2:69–70, doc. 31) raised all fines to 30 liv. but lowered the terms of weavers' suspension to six months. These provisions were republished on 6 Octoer 1568 (printed ibid., 2:71–4, doc. 32) because, it was expressly noted, violations were continuing. For an analagous ordinance directed at bourgetteurs, see AML, Reg. 382, fol. 105, 13 August 1569.

58 AML, Aff. gèn., C. 1161, d. 18, 9 April–5 May 1571. Among them, the seven operated thirteen looms. Two men had three looms apiece, two others had two, and three just one.

59 Ibid., C. 1160, d. 5, 16 June 1571.

60 Ibid., C. 1160, d. 5.

spate of ordinances reaffirming loom limits and the urban light-cloth monopoly came to an end, suggesting that the situation was once more in hand, at least for the moment.

Similarly, although information wrung from the linen merchant Antoine Douchet, arrested in early July 1572,[61] indicates that there were Orangist sympathizers in Lille, nothing suggests that they constituted a real danger. Douchet himself had provided at least 1,200 florins to hire rebel soldiers for attempts on several cities (not including Lille) and when seized was carrying letters between the occupiers of Mons and Beggars in the Alleu. Under torture, he named five merchants from Lille, along with others from Tournai and one from Antwerp (whose wife was a Lilloise), as rebel accomplices. Douchet testified that he had talked to each man individually, telling them that William of Orange, Louis of Nassau, and some French noblemen planned to conquer the Netherlands, then "plant liberty" so that everyone could recover their possessions (presumably a reference to exiles' property). After this appeal, the Lillois Nicolas Melantois and Antoine Lecat had each promised 100 florins, Helie Desplancques 300, with another 1,500 pledged by Antoine de Flandres.[62] On the basis of "frequent conversations" and correspondence with them, Douchet claimed that all four of the Lille merchants were Protestants and favored Orange.[63] He asserted, too, that François Delobel, a merchant from Lille resident in Rouen, had also promised money.[64]

Yet even though Douchet reported a plan for a coup in Tournai, he mentioned no plot of any sort against Lille. What is more, his allegations had no repercussions in the city, where Antoine de Flandres, for example, continued to live and thrive, marrying off his son Jean in 1574 with

---

[61] The report on Douchet is printed in *CG*, 4:634–46.

[62] A wealthy dyer and trader with connections via Antwerp throughout Europe, de Flandres had been a councillor four times and alderman twice between 1549 and 1555, but thereafter he was never again appointed. For his service in the Loi, see BML, MS. 597; for other evidence regarding his considerable wealth, see Chapter 2, section III. Granvelle's correspondent Morillon reported that Douchet was a "rich man who traded in France" and had never been suspected before; see letter of 27 July 1572, *CG*, 4:329. Of the seventy-eight merchants whose Hundredth Penny tax levies have survived, de Flandres ranked eleventh, paying 24 liv. Desplancques paid 8 liv., Douchet 2.5. No information is available regarding the other two men. The mean tax for merchants was 14.53 liv.; see AML, Reg. 966, summarized in Appendix C.

[63] None of the men named by Douchet appears on the list of suspected Protestant merchants in the Antwerp trade, for which see Chapter 1, section I.

[64] For Helie Desplancques's wine trading partnerships with the Delobels, see Chapter 2, section II.

an enormous portion valued at 14,000 livres.[65] It seems, too, that the Magistrat was not concerned about any Orangist threat once Alba recaptured Mons on 22 September, for the citizen guard was immediately relaxed and the mercenaries released.[66]

III

During the period from late 1572 to early 1576, Holland and Zeeland became the focus of military and political activity in the Netherlands. Yet although Walloon Flanders was now at the periphery of events, its rural districts were far from pacified. Unpaid Spanish and Walloon soldiers, initially brought in to recapture rebel cities but kept on to garrison suspect areas, ravaged the countryside. With few reliable troops at their disposal, government officials could only push the marauders from one area to another. One band, for example, successively expelled from Artois, Hainaut, and the castellany of Lille, then moved into Flanders where it continued its depredations. Another, turned out by the armed inhabitants of Menen, who refused to pay the soldiers' back wages, resorted to plundering and burning nearby villages in revenge.[67] "Forest Beggars" or just plain "Beggars," Protestant partisans who had never been eradicated and indeed had flourished during the tax protest years,[68] continued to attack rural priests and extort money from peasants.[69] At the same time, hostility to Catholicism resurfaced in the villages. At least in the spring of 1573, farces mocking the established church, its clergy, and its doctrines were performed widely. The authorities were dismayed, because they were persuaded that the plays promoted the spread of heresy.[70] In Lille, too, the aldermen saw possibilities for disorder. As a precaution, they canceled the Feast of the Innocents in 1572, 1573, and 1574, and on two occasions in 1573

[65] See Chapter 2, section III. Jean was, however, expelled from Lille in 1579; see Chapter 8, section VII.
[66] "Mémoires de Bauduin de Croix," fol. 47.
[67] For the first band, see Morillon to Granvelle, 16 December 1572, *CG*, 4:530; for the second, BML, MS. 725, fols. [26v–7]. Cf. *CG*, 4:429, 434, 464 n. 1, 5:25; AML, Reg. 15,885, fols. 157v–60, and Reg. 16,980, passim.
[68] Cf. Carette, "Recueil," fol. [93v]; AML, Reg. 15,885, fols. 147v–8, 149v–50v; Reg. 32, fols. 55–7; *CG*, 4:310, 429–30.
[69] See Carette, "Recueil," fol. [102v], for assaults on clergy in 1573 and a report that two Beggars who had wrung money out of villagers by hanging them up and burning their feet had been executed in Lille on 9 February 1575.
[70] AML, Reg. 16,980, fol. 252v.

banned all meetings on the grounds that townspeople gathering to "grumble" (*murmurer*) were voicing sentiments that might trigger a disturbance.[71]

The Magistrat probably acted with an eye more on deteriorating material conditions than on religious or political problems. As Table 7.2 demonstrates, 1572–3 showed some improvement over the preceding year in terms of grain prices, employment, and cash grants from the welfare bureau, although masters' wage situation seems to have regressed and bread was less generously distributed. But these moderately good times were short-lived, as soaring inflation made 1573–4 a very difficult year. The cost of wheat reached its highest level recorded up to that point, and rye was close behind. Wages retained their long-term immobility, so even the fully employed must have struggled simply to provide their families with the bare essentials.[72] Nor could they expect much help from the Bourse commune. Probably in consequence of the steep price rise and the Hundredth Penny, which had sucked a great deal of liquid capital out of townspeople's pockets, donations to special collections diminished by about a fifth, and no supplementary sources of income were developed.[73] By April 1574, some people receiving alms from the municipal fund reportedly had to beg publicly in order to survive.[74] That Lille's merchants' dealings with Antwerp were at their lowest point in a quarter century cannot have helped matters either.[75]

To be sure, the light-cloth trades remained vigorous (Tables 7.1 and 7.2). For the first time in almost ten years, in fact, a magisterial decree of June 1573 permitted immigration of masters trained elsewhere.[76] But to judge from the republication of regulations, the long battle between advocates of entrepreneurial liberty and those of restriction revived. The employment of unfree labor and the operation of shops by anyone save registered masters were again prohibited, and the thread-market mo-

---

[71] AML, Reg. 382, fols. 52v–3 (December 1572, 1573, 1574), 145v (6 March 1573), 154–5 (28 August 1573).

[72] Wheat would have taken 51% to 84% of a master's putative income, rye 38% to 63%. A laborer would have expended between 91% and 152% for wheat, 68% to 113% for rye.

[73] AASL, Reg. J 593–8.

[74] AML, Reg. 382, fols. 162v–3.

[75] Coornaert, *Français à Anvers*, fig. "Nombre de marchands" at end of vol. 2.

[76] Ordinance of 6 June 1573, printed in Vanhaeck, *Sayetterie à Lille*, 2:76, doc. 34. The permission was tacit, part of a provision mandating that every candidate for mastership must have woven a masterpiece in Lille. In effect, then, it repealed a 1564 ruling (ibid., 2:66, doc. 28) that no sayetteur could set up as master in Lille unless he had finished a two-year apprenticeship there.

nopoly – acknowledged to be frequently violated – was reasserted.[77] But infractions continued. In February 1574, for instance, Loys de Bus was convicted for the third time of having more than six looms in his shop and of putting out changéants to be woven.[78]

Some economic indicators recovered in 1574–5 and 1575–6. All cloth production was buoyant (Table 7.1),[79] wages finally began to move upward, rye prices were markedly lower, and Common Fund cash grants reached totals of a decade before (Table 7.2). Commercial activity reinvigorated as substantial numbers of Lillois reappeared in Antwerp and connections were developed with other trading outlets, notably Calais.[80] But conditions did not uniformly turn for the better. The Bourse commune financed higher cash outlays by selling substantial parts of its grain reserves, so bread allotments had to be curtailed.[81] The paucity of free bread must have created particular hardship in 1574–5, when the wheat price hit its secular high for the second year in a row, for even rye would have taken a big bite out of laborers' income.[82]

Complicating the picture yet further was the reappearance of "plague." First noted in the late summer of 1572, it had become serious enough by September 1575 that the Magistrat reopened the quarantine barracks in the Riez de Canteleu, which had last been used in the 1550s. In order to support victims, whether they moved to the Riez or remained in their own homes, the aldermen established a new tax on beer as well as an additional door-to-door collection each month.[83] Finally, some Lillois tried to take advantage of these difficult times by cornering the thread supply or putting out work to desperate weavers.[84]

---

[77] Ibid., 2:75–6.
[78] AML, Reg. 15,924, fols. 5v–6.
[79] Textile workers were so much in demand that they were said to change employers without having repaid advances; Vanhaeck, *Sayetterie à Lille*, 2:80, doc. 36, art. VI, 6 July 1575.
[80] Coornaert, *Français à Anvers*, fig. "Nombre de marchands" at end of vol. 2, and 1:163, 166.
[81] AASL, Reg. J 599–602.
[82] Despite the modest wage increase noted in Table 7.2, wheat would have consumed 88% to 147% of laborers' income, rye 51% to 85%.
[83] The first official reports of plague can be found in AML, Reg. 16,306 (accounts for 1572), fols. 262v, 263v, 269–9v. For later references, see Reg. 16,307–10 (accounts for 1573–6), passim, and Reg. 15,924, passim. Letters patent for the tax are in Reg. 15,885, fols. 161–1v, 31 August 1575; authorization to continue it due to the persistence of sickness is ibid., fols. 165v–6, 11 February 1576. The introduction of a collection just for the benefit of *pestiférés* is in AASL, Reg. J 600, as are the records of payments. Whether the sickness actually was the plague, influenza, or some other disease altogether cannot be determined.
[84] Both of these practices were condemned in July 1575; Vanhaeck, *Sayetterie à Lille*, 2:79–80, doc. 36, arts. III, VIII.

In light of the pressures on townspeople – not to mention the obvious crumbling of Spanish power, which only accelerated after Alba's departure at the end of 1573 – it is understandable that the Magistrat was apprehensive when Requesens presented a tax request reminiscent of Alba's during the summer of 1574. Evidently hoping to ensure the loyalty and orthodoxy of the citizen guard, in September the aldermen required each member to swear to aid the king and his allies without fail and to maintain the Catholic faith. All the militia companies were also obliged to select patron saints (apostles and martyrs were signaled as particularly appropriate) and venerate them by offering Masses. Trying to foresee any eventuality, the Magistrat then forbade blasphemy, contact with fugitives or the king's enemies, meetings not explicitly authorized by the aldermen, and departing from Lille with one's weapons unless a militia captain's permission and a passport had been previously obtained.[85]

No matter how menacing the outlook may have seemed to the ruling class at that time, however, the shades of 1566 were unlikely to descend again. Despite the harsh inflationary spiral of 1573–5, the textile industry unflaggingly maintained its vigor, in late 1574 wages and welfare benefits began to rise, and grain prices finally fell in 1575–6 (Tables 7.1 and 7.2). In addition, the keystone of the regulated urban economy, the 1565 ordinance limiting loom ownership and putting out, was upheld by the Privy Council on 16 January 1576, despite opponents' appeals to entrepreneurial freedom.[86] Finally, Protestantism seems to have gone into decline in the city. Not only were the public voices of religious dissent stilled but no representative from Lille attended the second synod of Netherlands Reformed churches, which took place at Antwerp in February 1576. In contrast, delegates from the two churches of the Olive, comprising Tourcoing, Bondues, Wambrechies, Quesnoy, and other places around Lille, were present at the conference.[87]

This continuing weakness of urban Protestantism, as well as the displacement of active revolt far away from the city, meant that there was no local focus for discontent, the more so as the Magistrat renewed its opposition to any version of the Tenth and Twentieth Pennies. The Loi

[85] AML, Aff. gén., C. 284, d. 1.
[86] AML, Reg. 15,885, fols. 165–5v; another copy is in Aff. gén., Pièce 89/1646. For a fuller discussion, see Chapter 3, section III.
[87] *Livre synodal contenant les articles résolus dans les Synodes des Eglises Wallonnes des Pays-Bas. Tome I, 1563–1685* (The Hague, 1896), pp. 25–6.

(and through it the provincial Estates) cooperated fully with the delaying tactics employed by the assemblies of Flanders and Brabant to thwart Requesens's tax proposals. The maneuvering ceased only in October 1575, when in the wake of his bankruptcy decree Philip found himself in a parlous financial state yet in need of immediate funds to pay his restive troops. Shorn of any other option, the king agreed to discard the idea of the Tenth and Twentieth Pennies once and for all, convert a projected second Hundredth Penny into a lump sum payment, adjourn the Council of Troubles, and confirm the privilege of nonconfiscation enjoyed by Lille along with many other cities.[88]

This accord represented a victory of sorts for the Netherlands, and Requesens was convinced that Philip's suspension of payments on the debt had doomed a promising military campaign against Holland and Zeeland.[89] Yet the country remained at war, with no peaceful resolution in sight once negotiations between Brussels and Orange broke down in July 1575. Lille's Magistrat continued to favor conciliation rather than repression to solve the problems of the Low Countries. So just as on the eve of Alba's arrival, upon hearing of Requesens's death on 5 March 1576 the aldermen mounted a general procession. This time – with an additional decade of bitter experience lending force to their plea – the city fathers implored God to persuade Philip to leash the Spanish soldiers and appoint a native as governor-general of the Low Countries.[90]

---

88 For Requesens's complaints to Philip about the Estates, see *CP*, ed. Gachard, 3:149, 183, 310, 342, nos. 1395, 1417, 1471, 1493, 16 September 1574 to 23 July 1575. The settlement is in AML, Reg. 15,885, fols. 162–5, 12 October 1575.
89 For Requesens's despondent appraisal of his situation, see Parker, *Dutch Revolt*, pp. 169–70.
90 BML, MS. 725, fol. [27].

8

From "common cause" to "special league": Lille between Estates-General and reconciliation, 1576–1582

By March 1576, nearly ten years had elapsed since the first revolt. Yet not only had Netherlanders' initial grievances not been resolved to their satisfaction, but the government's response had given rise to new discontents. In contrast with 1566–7, however, rebels had conquered and held territory, for the new order had become firmly rooted in Holland and Zeeland and steps taken in the direction of legal independence. Equally significant, the disarray of the Brussels regime set the stage for the renewed involvement of the southern provinces, the center of insurgency in the mid-1560s but only intermittently engaged since then. Events there, in fact, determined the scope, intensity, and success of the revolt.

The first result of Requesens's death was paralysis. For want of anything better, authority devolved upon the Council of State, dominated by the Catholic but strongly anti-Spanish duke of Aerschot, who was convinced that peace would return if the unpopular foreign troops were withdrawn and traditional liberties restored. But neither Aerschot nor the council proved able to make constructive use of the opportunities at hand. They did not resume negotiations for a peace treaty with Holland and Zeeland. Worse, they could not put an end to the continued depradations of the unpaid royal mercenaries, although this behavior stoked popular rage while simultaneously preventing the government from consolidating its rare military gains. But what precipitated the councillors' downfall was their refusal to allow the Hainaut and Brabant Estates to meet together and discuss common means of defense. Even though the Pragmatic Sanction of 1549 authorized assistance among provinces in the event of war, the council dared not uphold Netherlands privileges that conflicted with royal policy, and Philip was adamantly opposed to any joint assemblies of the provincial estates.

On his side, the king's attempt to regain control was stymied by his nominee for governor-general, his illegitimate half-brother Don John of Austria. Don John insisted that he consult with Philip in person before taking up his new post, thereby delaying his arrival in the Low Countries until 3 November 1576. By that date, however, the situation had changed fundamentally, and a new stage of revolt had begun. On 4 September, troops from among those hired by the Estates of Brabant to crush the insubordinate Spanish soldiers – an assignment they had signally failed to fulfill – arrested the Council of State. Two days later, deputies from Brabant and Hainaut met in Brussels in defiance of the king's express orders and summoned every province save Holland and Zeeland to gather in the capital and organize means of safeguarding the country.

Defensive in nature, the stated purposes of this Estates-General were much the same as those of the Council of State under Aerschot. Most generally, the assembly wanted to restore peace to the Low Countries; more specifically, it meant to subdue and if possible drive out the hated mercenaries. The urgency of this latter task, already clear from the bloody sack of the Brabantine town of Aalst on 25 July, was tragically underlined by the "Spanish fury" in early November, when mutineers desolated much of Antwerp, massacring up to eight thousand people.

To realize its objectives, the Estates-General soon assumed many of the attributes of government – borrowing money, levying taxes, raising forces of its own, and bargaining with foreign governments for aid. Its most notable early achievement was the Pacification of Ghent, signed on 8 November 1576. This agreement provided for a prompt ceasefire, maintenance of the religious status quo (Catholicism alone could be practiced in all provinces save Holland and Zeeland, where Calvinism was to prevail), and common action to expel the Spanish. Once the foreign soldiers had been driven out, the assembly proposed to settle all outstanding religious and political issues.

For all its increasing independence, the Estates-General was far from repudiating royal authority. But relations did become strained, because Don John refused to take his oath as governor-general until his responsibilities had been clearly delineated and ratified by the deputies in Brussels. Several months of negotiations finally produced an accord and the restoration of royal supremacy, at least on paper. By the terms of this "Perpetual Edict," signed on 12 February 1577, Don John accepted the Pacification of Ghent and pledged to remove the Spanish troops. For its part, the Estates-General undertook to uphold Catholicism, supply back pay for German and Netherlands contingents in the king's army, welcome Don John to office once the Spanish forces had gone, and then dissolve in favor of a new assembly summoned by the governor-general.

I

The dramatic events unfolding in Brussels in early September 1576 initially evoked a cautious, even negative reaction in Walloon Flanders. Upon hearing of the detention of the Council of State, Lille's aldermen alerted the citizen militia companies and positioned artillery pieces at key locations throughout the city.[1] The call for a meeting of the Estates-General was greeted with little enthusiasm by the provincial Estates to which it was addressed. Some members declared that only the king could rightfully convene such a gathering, others felt that "in a matter of such importance you ought not to bind yourself boldly lest you have to repent quickly." The influential abbot of Marchiennes voiced his fear that seditious and heretical sentiments would be aired.[2]

Walloon Flanders' recalcitrance did not last long, however. Soon released from confinement and purged of the king's loyal advisors, the Council of State wrote urging participation so that action could be taken at once against insubordinate royal troops. In response, the provincial Estates reversed course.[3] Meeting again on 1 October, the delegates unanimously resolved to send representatives to the Estates-General on condition that its business be limited to raising forces to defeat the Spanish mutineers – "enemies of the *patrie*" – and that nothing be done to the detriment of Catholicism or royal authority. The next day, the Estates took security measures of their own by engaging four infantry companies and one of mounted harquebusiers, placing them under the captaincy of members of the local nobility and the acting governor of the

[1] AML, Reg. 278, fols. 36–7, 9 September 1576; BML, MS. 725, fols. [26v–7].
[2] AMD, Reg. BB3, fol. 44, 17 September 1576; "Mémoires de Bauduin de Croix," fol. 50.

province, François de Montmorency. Then they selected two deputies to go to Brussels: François de Hennin (or Haynin), seigneur du Breucq and a bailiff of the castellany of Lille, and Antoine Muyssart, pensionary of Lille, whose knowledge of court and capital, dating back to at least 1566, was unsurpassed. They were instructed to vote for levies of troops provided that the forces were pledged to defend church and crown.[4]

On 12 October, the two delegates put in their first appearance at the Brussels assembly, joining representatives from Brabant, Hainaut, Flanders, and Tournai who had preceded them.[5] Whether in anticipation of the administrative burden the Estates-General had to shoulder, or to involve the province more fully in the assembly, Walloon Flanders was asked soon after to increase the size of its contingent. It was also requested to grant all deputies full powers to decide about the "withdrawal or expulsion" of Spanish troops as well as peacemaking, negotiations with Holland and Zeeland having recommenced on 10 October.[6] Both demands were quickly satisfied. Walloon Flanders expanded its delegation to nine men, including another bailiff from the castellany, the first alderman and pensionary of Douai, the first alderman of Orchies, representatives of the clergy and the nobility, and Bauduin de Croix, who was seigneur of Wayembourg, alderman of Lille, and a memoir writer. As before, all were charged to safeguard Catholicism and the king's authority.[7]

If the Spanish soldiers, who became more menacing as the fall wore on, were to be pacified, the Estates-General had to raise its own army. Because, as we have seen, winning approval for aides was normally time-consuming in the extreme, at first the assembly had recourse to loans and the sale of annuities. Lille's commercial and financial activities

---

3 The change of mind may have had something to do with the fact that Rassenghien had agreed to work with the Estates-General and indeed had already departed on a mission to Spain; see Poullet, *Gouverneurs de province*, p. 179.

4 "Mémoires de Bauduin de Croix," fols. 50–5. One of the captains, Jean de Vlieghe, seigneur of la Grurie, had been rewart of Lille in 1558 and mayor in 1562. A letter from the Council of State, dated 4 October 1576, for the second time asking Walloon Flanders and several other provinces to send deputies to Brussels, is in *Actes des Etats Généraux*, 1:429–30; by that time, the decision had already been taken.

5 *RSG*, 1:10–11.

6 "Mémoires de Bauduin de Croix," fol. 57; *Actes des Etats Généraux*, 1:436–7.

7 The deputies' names are given in *RSG*, 1:3, and in " Mémoires de Bauduin de Croix," fol. 58. In 1577, a total of fifteen men from Walloon Flanders attended the Estates-General at one time or another, including seven of the nine who had served the previous year. Among those who returned were François de Hennin and Antoine Muyssart, but not Bauduin de Croix nor any other member of Lille's Magistrat; *RSG*, 1:150.

made it an obvious place to seek funds. On 22 October, therefore, Roland de Vicq, seigneur of Northoven and bailiff of Wavrin, who had recently arrived in Brussels as the second representative of the rural districts of Walloon Flanders, went back to Lille to persuade merchants there to purchase rentes guaranteed by the Estates-General.[8]

What results his mission had are not known, but soon thereafter the Spanish Fury elicited a remarkably speedy agreement to the substantial aides that the Estates-General immediately proposed. In early December the Estates of Lille, Douai, and Orchies offered 400,000 livres in place of a new Hundredth Penny, half to be paid at Christmas, the balance at Easter,[9] and other provinces settled at the same time. Once troops were hired, Walloon Flanders was asked to remit additional sums – 100,000 livres to pay Count Lalaing's band in December, another 20,000 livres for three Walloon regiments the next month.[10] These substantial levies could only make the Perpetual Edict the more welcome, for Don John's promised removal of all Spanish troops would allow sharp cuts in military expenditures. But first the German and Netherlands units had to be indemnified. Walloon Flanders was to contribute 70,000 livres, although the amount seems subsequently to have been reduced to 25,000 florins. This sum was to be collected through loans (voluntary if possible, forced if necessary), annuities at interest rates as high as 16.67 percent for one life or 8.33 percent if inheritable, the donation of plate, or even sequestration of monies held by the towns.[11]

Whether the province actually provided its full quota is unclear. Rassenghien, who had returned and been put in charge of collection, reported at the end of February that the Estates had voted only 18,000 florins although he had hopes for more.[12] But enough was gathered throughout the Low Countries that the Spanish troops could be satisfied; they left from Maastricht on 28 April. Two days before, the Estates-General had decided to send Netherlands soldiers back to the provinces in which they had been hired, and to disband some after

[8] *RSG*, 1:114.

[9] Ibid., p. 123; AML, Reg. 15,885, fols. 173v–5, 177v–9v. The payment schedule for the 400,000 liv. was eventually changed, half being due in February, the other half in March; *RSG*, 1:466.

[10] *RSG*, 1:110, 241. The province apparently satisfied the requests by paying 25,000 liv.; AML, Reg. 15,885, fols. 177–7v.

[11] *RSG*, 1:246, 469–72.

[12] Ibid., p. 474.

Table 8.1. *Indexes of textile output in Lille, 1576–82*
(100 = mean, 1561–2 through 1570–1)

Year	Sayetterie	Changéants	Velveteens	Draps
1575–6	169	314	121	89
1576–7	104	295	135	57
1577–8	131	263	167	68
1578–9	135	391	157	44
1579–80	126	443	96	37
1580–1	170	363	189	53
1581–2	131	278	187	57

Sources: Deyon and Lottin, "Production textile à Lille," p. 31 (sayetterie); AML, Reg. 16,310–15 (all other types of cloth).

paying them off. As a result, the four infantry companies raised the previous October and subsequently put under the command of the Estates-General were sent back to Walloon Flanders, where they were released in early April.[13] The province pledged a final 20,000 livres as its contribution to the common expense, although eventually it seems to have turned over the equivalent of 32,000 livres (26,000 in the form of grants, 6,000 as a loan).[14]

In all, 621,000 livres had been requested from Walloon Flanders and at least 477,000 actually remitted, Lille's portion coming to 138,000 and 106,000 livres respectively.[15] The lion's share of this heavy burden was borne, of course, by ordinary people. In Lille, for example, the necessary sums were raised by imposing special consumption taxes, notably on grain and beer. Adverse economic conditions assured that these additional levies would be keenly felt. Employment had dropped sharply (in 1576–7 output of both light cloth and drapery was off by one-third from 1575–6), wheat prices were up about 13 percent and rye nearly 37 percent, and Common Fund cash outlays had declined while bread distributions had been suspended (Tables 8.1 and 8.2). Little wonder,

[13] AML, Reg. 383, fol. 11v, 11 April 1577.
[14] *RSG*, 1:346, 356, 357–8, 481, 485.
[15] The tax totals are figured from the information given in *RSG*, 1:110, 123, 241, 246, 469–72, 474; and in AML, Reg. 15,885, fols. 173v–5, 177–9v. When Lille's quota has not been specified, it has been calculated according to the traditional formula, for which see Chapter 1, section III.

then, that in the spring the taxes inspired so many and such vociferous "insults, nasty and shameful remarks," even attempted assaults, that the aldermen threatened to banish anyone who verbally abused or tried to stir up trouble against collectors.[16]

The provincial ruling classes, however, had reason to be content with the results of the Estates-General's work, for by early summer 1577 the objectives outlined in the deputies' instructions the previous October seemed to have been realized. The Spanish troops had departed, peace officially reigned, the Catholic religion was still maintained, and, with the swearing-in of Don John as governor-general on 6 May, royal authority continued to be recognized.

II

In reality, the Estates-General's achievement was tenuous, and sharp conflicts quickly arose when it came time to carry out decisions mandated by the Pacification of Ghent and the Perpetual Edict. Holland and Zeeland protested clauses in the agreements that foresaw the restoration of Catholicism throughout the country. Deputies from other provinces, not to mention the populace of Brussels, did not trust Don John or Philip to honor their promises, and Orange and his agents did their best to heighten these doubts as well as to oppose the abolition of Calvinism in Holland and Zeeland.

For his part, Don John was loath to make any substantive concessions on religion to gain the adherence of Orange and the two rebel provinces. He was resentful, too, that although governor-general he had neither an army nor close advisors of his own, and that he was forced to deal with an assembly and a nobility that had grown accustomed to wielding real power during the past year and showed no willingness to relinquish it.[17] Failing to make any headway in negotiations with Orange, and realizing that popular sentiment was running against him, Don John made a desperate bid to turn the tide by seizing the citadel at Namur on 24 July 1577. From there he tried to dictate terms, insisting that he be granted

---

16 AML, Reg. 383, fols. 14–14v, 19 April 1577. The taxes, imposed as of 30 March, were terminated after 1 October; ibid., fols. 12–13, 25–5v.

17 The Estates-General, for example, continued to raise money on its own authority; see *RSG*, 1:489, for a request dated 8 July 1577. For the nobles, see Geyl, *Revolt of the Netherlands*, pp. 151, 153.

Table 8.2. *Index of Common Fund outlays, grain prices, wages, and employment in Lille, 1576–82 (100 = mean, 1561–2 through 1570–1)*

	Common Fund Outlays		Prices		Wages		
Year	Cash	Bread	Wheat	Rye	Master mason	Laborer	Employment[a]
1575–6	128	93	136	95	117	105	173
1576–7	119	—	154	130	117	105	112
1577–8	93	—	130	160	117	105	138
1578–9	57	165	123	139	117	113	145
1579–80	64	140	110	156	117	123	137
1580–1	59	115	115	139	117	123	176
1581–2	96	—	125	156	117	123	138

[a]Employment index calculated from light-cloth output.
Sources: AASL, Reg. J 601–14 (cash and bread); AML, Reg. 797 (wheat); *Dokumenten voor de Geschiedenis van Prijzen en Lonen*, 4:347 (rye); AML, Reg. 16,310–16 (wages); Deyon and Lottin, "Production textile à Lille," p. 31 (employment).

greater authority, that certain supporters of Orange be purged from the Estates-General, and that he be aided in fighting William. But his *coup de main,* coupled with an unsuccessful attempt on Antwerp a week later and – in utter violation of the Perpetual Edict – his urgent request to Philip for the return of Spanish forces, served instead to confirm earlier misgivings and harden public opinion against him.

Don John may have hoped to take advantage of divisions within the Estates-General, winning the support of deputies hostile to Protestantism and capitalizing on particularism and loyalties to crown and church. If Walloon Flanders' current delegation was at all representative of the more conservative provinces, his prospects could have seemed auspicious. The group was dominated by Catholic, royalist nobles. Chief among them was Maximilien de Hennin, count of Bossu, governor of Holland under Alba and currently sitting on the reconstituted Council of State and the Estates-General's Council of War. Two other members of the Hennin clan accompanied Bossu: Jacques, seigneur of Ghislinghien and bailiff of Comines, and (continuing from the previous fall) François, seigneur du Breucq and a bailiff of the castellany of Lille. The deputation also included Claude de Berlaymont, seigneur of Hault-penne, whose relative Charles, councillor of state under Requesens, was ardently pro-Spanish and indeed rallied to Don John after the capture of Namur.[18]

In the weeks before Don John's coup, moreover, the deputies from Walloon Flanders had shown a marked reluctance to surrender traditional provincial prerogatives, even though their position could hobble the Estates-General. Several times they joined with their colleagues from Namur, Artois, and Tournai and the Tournésis to refuse assent to money bills before receiving approval from "their masters." They also balked at voting 25,000 florins a month for an unlimited period, preferring to determine every month whether the money was needed.[19] At home, the provincial ruling elites trumpeted their religious and political orthodoxy. When pledging to carry out the terms of the Pacification of Ghent, for example, the Estates of Lille, Douai, and Orchies drafted a statement in concert with representatives of the clergy and nobility declaring that no religion save Catholicism was to be permitted in the province.[20]

Whatever chance for success Don John may initially have had, however, vanished once he recalled Spanish troops. Much of the Netherlands had had bitter first-hand experience of these soldiers, and memories of the mutinies and massacres of the past few years were still fresh. The abrupt change in sentiment was obvious in Walloon Flanders. When the Estates-General voted on 10 August to raise a total of 2.78 million florins for troops to resist Don John, the province agreed in just a month to supply its quota (226,667 livres) by selling annuities and borrowing money at high interest rates, as well as by retaining or even increasing existing taxes.[21]

Exasperation with Don John and concern lest he attack once reinforcements arrived from Spain was evident in Lille. So, according to

---

18 The list of members is in *RSG*, 1:150; the appointments to councils ibid., pp. 152–3. No Lillois sat on any major council.
19 See ibid., pp. 441, 447, 449.
20 M. Baelde and P. van Peteghem, "De Pacificatie van Gent," in *Opstand en Pacificatie in de Lage Landen* (Ghent, 1976), p. 38.
21 *RSG*, 1:495–8. As before, the province offered yields up to 16.67% on life annuities; interest on loans was expected to be between 8% and 12%; AML, Reg. 15,885, fols. 184–5.

Bauduin de Croix, was wariness in regard to the Protestants beginning to reappear in many southern Netherlands towns. In response, the Magistrat thoroughly reorganized the citizen militia in early September, raising the number of companies from six to sixteen. Each was to contain 200 men officered by a captain, two lieutenants, and two sergeants and accompanied by a standard bearer and a drummer. Beyond its immediate implications, the change was clearly intended to enhance permanently the Magistrat's control over the city. In sharp contrast to the 1566 reorganization, when on Rassenghien's advice the Loi had handed militia leadership over to seigneurs outside the municipal ruling class, this time nearly all captains were selected from current aldermen and councillors, and most were members of the inner circle. For several months at least, 125 men from the companies were posted to guard duty every day and an equal number at night. Under the direction of an Italian engineer, moreover, earthen ramparts were built outside the city walls for additional protection.[22]

Taking a cue from Antwerp, Ghent, Utrecht, Valenciennes, and Béthune, all of which sought to forestall any further surprises by Don John or his allies, Lille concomitantly petitioned the Estates-General for permission to raze the royal citadel located just north of and adjacent to the city walls. In their request, the aldermen told of their fear that the troops garrisoned in the castle might "pillage and sack" the town, "rape and do violence to women and girls, burn houses, hold the inhabitants to ransom, and in addition commit no end of murders, oppression, violence and many other loathsome crimes."[23] The negotiations were concluded rapidly, as Lille promised in return to remain Catholic and loyal to the king, make a grant of 60,000 livres and loan 50,000 livres. Although the Estates-General delayed for a few days to get Rassenghien's opinion, when it was not quickly forthcoming the castle was turned over to municipal authorities for dismantling.[24]

Demolition began at once, first by citizens alone under the watchful eye of the Magistrat, which prudently posted guards to keep onlookers

---

22 "Mémoires de Bauduin de Croix," fols. 64–6 (Croix was one of the captains); AML, Aff. gén., C. 284, d. 1; [Thiroux], *Histoire de Lille et de sa chatellenie* (Lille, 1730), pp. 75–6. For 1566, see Chapter 6, section II.

23 AML, Reg. 15,885, fols. 185–5v. See also "Mémoires de Bauduin de Croix," fol. 66.

24 AML, Reg. 15,885, fols. 185v–6; *RSG*, 1:283, 387, 389–90, 392, 403; *Mémoires anonymes*, 2:56, 58. One factor making for rapid agreement was the Estates-General's urgent need for money to pay restive troops at Maastricht and Breda.

from attacking the soldiers still quartered there.[25] But when the task proved more difficult and time-consuming than foreseen, all *manans* (residents who were not citizens) were also compelled to pitch in or contribute eight sols a day to hire substitutes.[26] Eventually, every Lillois, including officials at the Chambre des Comptes and Gouvernance and even canons of St. Pierre, was obliged to take a turn. The municipal government likewise recognized no exemptions when levying taxes totaling 20,000 livres to repair the small portion of the citadel left standing and integrate some of its walls into the existing urban ramparts, which on this occasion were strengthened where needed.[27]

In the spring, the new indirect taxes imposed to pay the arrears of government troops had been met with some protests, probably because none of the soldiers were in Lille. But there was no hint of resistance to levies when local concerns were at stake, whether to guard against Don John or to raze the castle, though taken together these decisions obligated the city to grant the Estates-General outright over 110,000 livres and loan another 50,000. Nor, apparently, did anyone refuse to help pull down the fortress.

III

When Don John suddenly fled to Namur and declared war on the Estates-General, most of the Catholic nobles who had been his strongest advocates found it prudent to abandon him. But they did not renounce their search – lent urgency in their eyes by the growing popularity of William of Orange – for a means to perpetuate the substantial power they had acquired in the Estates and central councils and to maintain the traditional religion. The young and inexperienced Archduke Matthias of Austria, son of the late emperor Maximilian II and nephew to Philip II, seemed the perfect instrument to Aerschot, the Hennins, and many other leading aristocrats. So despite the fact that Don John's mandate had not been revoked, and despite the fact that it lacked the authority to make such an appointment, the Estates-General

---

[25] AML, Reg. 383, fols. 24v–5, 30 September 1577.

[26] Ibid., fols. 26–6v, 21 October 1577. On 14 January 1578, a longer workday and higher indemnity were imposed to speed up the job; ibid., fols. 29–9v.

[27] AML, Reg. 15,885, fols. 186–7, 194–5; "Mémoires de Bauduin de Croix," fols. 66–7; and *RSG*, 2:142–3. In April 1578, the city bought the land and buildings of the citadel for 33,000 liv., then rented them out; AML, Reg. 15,885, fols. 196–7.

was persuaded to offer the governor-generalship to Matthias. He accepted with alacrity, arriving in the Netherlands on 20 October 1577.

No more than Don John's exploit did this venture accomplish its aims. Orange enjoyed the support of numerous delegates to the Estates-General and significant sectors of the populace. His most strategic backing lay in Brussels, where the eighteen councillors named by the craft guilds had come not only to dominate the municipal government but to wield considerable influence on provincial and national politics. Already in late autumn 1576 they had assembled large crowds to prod the Brabant Estates to adopt the Pacification of Ghent. The next year, they pressured the Estates-General to invite Orange to come to Brussels to give advice. On 23 September 1577, a decade after fleeing Alba, Orange made a triumphal entry into the capital. Shortly afterward, the eighteen convinced both Brabant and the Estates-General to appoint Orange *ruwart* or governor of Brabant, a post created specifically for him, because normally the governor-general presided over the province.

Determined not to be outmaneuvered, Aerschot, in his capacity as stadtholder of Flanders, persuaded the Estates of that province to object to William's appointment. But instead the step sparked a revolt in Ghent. The rising resulted not only in the arrest of Aerschot and his entourage (including Rassenghien, destined to be held captive until June 1579) on 28 October, but also in the revival of Ghent's old communal government in which guildsmen predominated. Soon, too, a committee of eighteen was established on the model of Brussels. It wielded authority with the aid of a reorganized militia drawn from artisans rather than more well-to-do citizens, as was customary.

Although quiescent heretofore, Lille was drawn into the complex power struggles of autumn 1577 – not, however, through insurrection, but through obscure intrigues regarding the selection of the incoming Loi. According to Estates-General records, on 27 October 1577 Antoine Muyssart, Lille's long-time pensionary and a delegate to the Estates-General from the beginning, requested that the term of the current Magistrat be extended past the usual renewal on 1 November until the start of the new year. Evidently convinced that the petition came from the Magistrat, the Estates-General consented, emphasizing that the change was exceptional. A week later, however, two emissaries sent in haste by the municipal government announced that Muyssart had acted without authorization and that the Loi wanted the assembly's action nullified. This demand was granted on 6 November, but by then the normal election date had passed without the proper commissioners having been sent. Only on 18 December were four men – including the seigneur du Breucq, like Muyssart a delegate to the Estates-General from the outset – named in conformity with the usual practice. On 1 January 1578 they selected a new Magistrat, which took office without further ado.[28]

The meaning of this incident is not easy to decipher. On the one hand, the Magistrat's own register of appointments notes only that the Loi was continued in office by the Estates-General "for some reasons" (*pour aucunes raisons*).[29] On the other, circumstantial evidence can be adduced to support both the aldermen's accusation that Muyssart had acted of his own accord and the view that the Magistrat contrived its own continuation. Let us examine each possibility in turn.

It is conceivable that Muyssart tried to use the confused conditions prevailing in the autumn of 1577 to provoke political change in Lille, perhaps in an Orangist direction. During his long service in the Estates-General, after all, Muyssart had often been brought into close contact with William and his supporters. In July 1577, for instance, he had been named to a five-member committee charged with drawing up a response from William to Don John after the breakdown of negotiations between them. At about the same time, he was one of four men assigned the task of dealing with Utrecht, where pro-Orangist sentiment was very strong. Again, in mid-September, he, along with the clerk of Hainaut, was delegated to examine all correspondence between Orange and the duke of Alençon, brother of the French king Henry III, and ascertain the promises made on behalf of the Estates-General to pay Alençon's expenses should he agree to provide help against Don John. As a result of all these experiences, Muyssart – like many other people in the assembly – could have come to favor William's ascendancy.[30] It may, in fact, be indicative of his sympathies that in early November he was one of six pensionaries designated to handle requests to the Estates-General when

28 The story can be traced in *RSG*, 1:561, 565, 576, 578.
29 BML, MS 597, year 1576. This language echoes that of the Estates-General's records, *pour certains respectz; RSG*, 1:578.
30 Cf. the experience of Den Bosc's first alderman Dirck Aertsen, who came to advocate a more radical and Orangist position after he took up nearly full-time residence in Antwerp as a delegate from his city to the Estates-General; see L. P. L. Pirenne, *'s Hertogenbosch tussen Atrecht en Utrecht; staatkundige geschiedenis, 1576–1579* (Tongerlo, 1959).

it was not in session. The other members of the group were his counter-parts from Brussels and Ghent (home to revolutionary committees), the Hague and Middelburg (for the past several years under Orangist administrations), and Valenciennes, which had a long history of rebel-liousness.[31]

If Muyssart had indeed sought to alter the municipal regime, he might have anticipated that postponement of the election would abet his plans. He certainly knew of the situation in Ghent and may even have been aware that an attempt would be made to seize Rassenghien. This circumstance could be counted on to leave the provincial government at least temporarily in disarray and, more specifically, provide an opportunity to name a suitable substitute to head the election committee for Lille.[32] Or Muyssart might have counted on assistance from the Ghent revolutionaries, who in the next few months fomented or patronized risings in Oudenaarde, Courtrai, Bruges, and other towns in the southern provinces, each revolt followed by the appointment of a radical committee to conduct municipal affairs.

Muyssart could have been operating in concert with a faction of the Magistrat, misleading the Estates-General into believing that his backing was broader than it actually was. If such were the case, the conspirators might have calculated that keeping the existing Loi in office would provoke a popular upheaval, which in turn would facilitate overthrowing the current regime and installing a new one with the aid of the militia. Nothing of the sort happened, of course, but the hypothesis should not be dismissed out of hand. To begin with, a number of men with family members who had previously been accused or even convicted of Protestant sympathies currently sat on the Magistrat. They included the aldermen Guillaume Deliot, Robert Delobel, and François Fasse, and the councillors Antoine de Bertault (de Hollande), Jean Castellain, and Jean de Fourmestraux. All might have been imagined to favor Orange. Another councillor was Gilles Delecousture, whose Protestant son and namesake subsequently went into exile in England.[33]

---

[31] For the appointments, see *RSG*, 1:169, 552, 296, 159.

[32] Hugues de Bournel, seigneur of Steenbecque or Estaimbeke, was not installed as acting governor of Walloon Flanders until 6 February 1578; Poullet, *Gouverneurs de province*, p. 180. For the governor's electoral role, see above, Chapter 1, section I.

[33] The roster of the Magistrat appointed on 1 November 1576 is in BML, MS. 597. The voluntary exile of Gilles Delecousture, junior, is noted in AML, Reg. 278, fol. 93, 3 October 1583, a sentence of the Magistrat officially expelling him some time after his departure.

Muyssart might also have been anticipating more forceful assistance from accomplices within the municipal government. Militia companies occupied a pivotal position in Lille as in every Netherlands town, and Deliot captained one. As we shall see, moreover, the companies proved to be threatening centers of discontent against aldermanic policy in 1578. Further, the missed election did not sit well with Lillois: The Magistrat's own envoys reported to the Estates-General that some townspeople had denounced the magistrates for a "vile deed" (*infamie*) when they remained in office past 1 November.[34] The final piece of evidence suggesting Muyssart's culpability is his firing as pensionary in December 1579. His dismissal was later upheld by then governor-general Alexander Farnese on the grounds of Muyssart's "life, qualifications and behavior."[35]

It is worth remarking, nonetheless, that if Muyssart was responsible for the incident, he kept the pensionary's post for two years and his seat in the Estates-General until 1578 – scarcely the treatment one would anticipate for an unmasked plotter. His eventual loss of position thus seems more likely a consequence of the reconciliation with Spain than of any conspiracy two years before. What is more, none of the magistrates with real or alleged Protestant connections suffered politically. If they had composed a faction allied with Muyssart, at the very least one would expect that the defeat of his maneuvering would have resulted in their subsequent exclusion from the Loi. Yet after the delayed election, Jean Castellain moved onto the échevinal bench and Gilles Delecousture remained a councillor. To be sure, none of the three 1576 aldermen from suspected Protestant families was rotated onto the council the next year, but all served elsewhere in the municipal government. Moreover, Guillaume Deliot returned as alderman in 1580, Antoine de Bertault went on to be alderman in 1581, and it was Jean de Fourmestraux's death in early 1578 that removed him from further consideration.[36] In short, the suggestion that Muyssart was an Orangist plotting a coup with the support of a section of the Magistrat seems unlikely.

---

[34] *RSG*, 1:565.
[35] For Muyssart's firing (with no reasons specified), see BML, MS. 597, year 1579. On 15 April 1581, Farnese rejected Muyssart's attempt to sue the Magistrat before the Council of Flanders for his ouster, concluding that the former pensionary was lucky that the aldermen had not used "harsher methods" against him than merely loss of employment; AML, Reg. 15,886, fols. 57–7v.
[36] See BML, MS. 597.

It seems more fruitful, then, to explore the second possibility, that Muyssart was doing the Magistrat's bidding when he asked for the delay. If this is the correct interpretation, the city fathers' later repudiation of his step would mean that he was scapegoated when the plot encountered popular objections – or once the delay had served its purpose. Several good reasons for the Loi's actions are imaginable. For one thing, some officials could have feared that commissioners named by the Estates-General at a time when Orange was enjoying great popularity would themselves favor William and thus appoint magistrates with similar views. This conjecture acquires a retrospective logic from allegations, examined later, that biased electoral commissioners were chosen the next year. If more reliable commissioners and thus an orthodox magistracy was in fact the objective of the maneuvering, it was a goal largely realized. Among the new members of the Loi were the aldermen Sebastien le Prevost, formerly on the provincial Council of Troubles, and Michel Gommer, related by marriage to members of Aerschot's entourage. Our old acquaintance Bauduin de Croix became a councillor.[37]

Alternatively, the magistrates as a whole could have schemed to prolong their terms in order to settle a pressing but unfinished piece of business regarding the light-cloth industry. The struggle between the mass of weavers and would-be entrepreneurs had resumed in recent months, probably stoked by difficulties stemming from the textile downturn and foodstuff inflation of 1576–7, to which the Common Fund for once responded inadequately (Tables 8.1 and 8.2). During the autumn of 1577, "a large number of masters and members" (*supôts*) of the sayetterie craft appealed to the Magistrat to put an end to some nascent "evil practices" (*inconvénients*). These maneuvers, it was alleged, threatened to subvert the crucial 1565 ordinance regulating the industry, jeopardizing "the preservation of the common people" dependent on it.

According to the petitioners, "several" sayetteurs had recently adopted a lucrative, perfectly legal, but indirect means of evading the limit on loom ownership instituted a decade earlier. Specifically, they had begun to weave changéants one aune and five-quarters in width, rather than "the former and customary" size, which was about three-quarters narrower. In consequence, six of the new looms produced as much cloth as ten regular ones. Such an increase of course recom-

---

[37] Ibid. For le Prevost, see also Chapter 7, section II; for Gommer, see n. 46.

mended the innovation to those Lillois who chafed at the loom quota. But widespread adoption of the new looms would, it was said, prove gravely detrimental to the mass of small producers. Masters' children who, beginning as young as age nine or ten, could "easily" weave ordinary changéants would become unemployed, because to operate the wider looms "requires the strength of a highly skilled adult." In addition, shops turning out broader cloth could (presumably due to greater productivity) offer higher wages and thus lure the best workers away from shops that continued to fabricate narrow changéants.[38]

Economic conditions in Lille during these months can only have intensified light-cloth makers' discontent (Tables 8.1 and 8.2). Admittedly, as the 1577–8 figures show, textile production was picking up and the cost of wheat was falling. At the same time, however, the rye price was approaching its secular peak and welfare assistance declining: For the second year in a row no bread was forthcoming. Commerce at Antwerp was again in the doldrums.[39] Finally, the plague that struck so harshly in 1575–6 had, after receding in early 1577, returned with renewed virulence between September and November of that year.[40]

On 9 November – a week after it normally would have left office – the Magistrat finally came up with a workable compromise permitting every master and mistress to use a maximum of two wide looms.[41] Weavers with surplus capital to invest got some advantage from this solution, but not enough to eliminate the family workshops that formed the backbone of the trade. In retrospect, it is worth emphasizing that this controversy was the last overt challenge to the regulatory framework of Lille's light-cloth industry for nearly a century. Following close on the heels of the decision by the Privy Council upholding the six-loom limit, and the Vingtaine's forceful articulation of its ideology,[42] the Magistrat's ordinance marked the completion of Lille's system of small commodity production. At the moment, however, it was doubtless sufficient that the ordinance resolved a potentially explosive dispute.

The various scenarios outlined are not, of course, mutually exclusive, for both Magistrat and Muyssart might have been scheming simul-

---

[38] Vanhaeck, *Sayetterie à Lille,* 2:84–5, doc. 38.
[39] Coornaert, *Français à Anvers,* fig. "Nombre de marchands," at end of vol. 2.
[40] See AASL, Reg. J 601–4.
[41] Vanhaeck, *Sayetterie à Lille,* 2:85.
[42] For these, see Chapter 3, section III.

taneously. But only the former prevailed. Whatever the correct explanation of the affair, the outcome was not a shift in municipal regime. Rather, the political hegemony of the cautious Catholic oligarchy that had long ruled Lille was reaffirmed. Amid a major crisis of the central regime, which opened the way for significant political and religious change in numerous urban centers, any challenge that may have been mounted at Lille was quickly snuffed out. If Muyssart had been conspiring, his abortive attempt to involve the Estates-General testifies eloquently to the weakness of insurgency within the city. More likely, it was the Magistrat that had the initiative all along, finding the means both to assure its reproduction along acceptable lines and to carry through an important policy. From this perspective, the appeal to the Estates-General was a clever expedient to gain time, a success despite the objections raised back home. In any event, no Protestants, Orangists, or any one else capitalized on discontent in Lille. Indeed, it was the ruling class that effectively responded to the one mobilized group that did appear, the sayetterie masters.

IV

At the Estates-General, however, as in many towns, changes were taking place that served William of Orange and the forces allied with him. With many of his backers captive in Ghent, on 8 December Matthias accepted the supremacy of the national assembly, which would appoint a council to advise him and have final say over all his enactments. Two days later, the Estates adopted the "Closer Union," which proclaimed Don John an enemy of the fatherland and its people and promised aid to Holland and Zeeland in case of attack by royal troops.[43] Early in January 1578, once again under the prompting of the Brussels populace, the Estates-General named Orange permanent governor of Brabant as well as Matthias's lieutenant, deputy, and principal advisor. Only then, after William had become in effect chief of state, was Matthias permitted to take office as governor-general.

The ruling class of Walloon Flanders may have been uneasy about the growing prominence of Orange and his supporters. The provincial dep-

---

[43] It may have been at this time that, according to a later report, inhabitants of Lille stopped shipments of Arras's sayetterie for a month in a successful endeavor to force Artois to join the union; see Pedro Arcanti to Philip, Paris, 22 May 1578, *CP*, ed. Lefèvre, 1:285, no. 468.

uties, for example, objected to the appointment of Steenbecque as interim governor of Walloon Flanders during Rassenghien's imprisonment.
Ostensibly, their challenge was based on the principle that governors
should not hold more than one office at a time, and Steenbecque was
already governor of the frontier fortress of Bapaume, temporary governor of Artois, and a member of the Council of State.[44] But the real cause
of their recalcitrance may well have been a conviction that he was one of
William's men.[45] Perhaps, too, it was to balance Orangist influence that
the province nominated Adrien, seigneur of Rebrievettes, a client and
ally of Aerschot, for a place on the Council of State.[46]

But whatever misgivings the provincial elite may have had about the
tendency of Estates-General politics, they did not benefit Don John. Not
even his rout of the Netherlands' forces at Gembloux on 31 January or
his subsequent capture of Louvain and several other cities – which
caused the Estates-General to flee Brussels for the comparative safety of
Antwerp – convinced Walloon Flanders to rally to him. To the contrary,
the province continued to pledge substantial sums to the effort to defeat
the erstwhile governor-general and his foreign troops. It promised
15,000 florins on 10 January; 3,500 (nearly as much as Brabant) plus an
additional 2,000 in emergency funds on 23 February; and another
25,000 later that same month and early the next.[47] Nor did Walloon
Flanders evince any interest in a political rapprochement. The provincial Estates indignantly rejected overtures from the clergy and nobility of
Artois proposing the dissolution of the Estates-General and a peace
treaty with Don John.[48] Similarly, when Maximilien de Longueval, seig-

---

[44] *RSG*, 1:454.

[45] See the letter of Maximilien de Longueval, seigneur of Vaux, to Don John, 15 February 1578,
mentioning that Orangist governors had been named to several provinces, among them
"Estiembecque" for Lille, Douai, and Orchies; *CG*, 7:486.

[46] *RSG*, 1:423. The Estates-General refused to appoint him, however. De Rebreviettes, whom we
shall encounter again, was related (as son?) to Martin de Rebreviettes, seigneur of Thibauville,
at his death in 1569 chief bailiff of the duke of Aerschot in Flanders and the castellany of Lille
and former rewart of Lille; see BML, MS. 597, year 1557. By marriage, Adrien was related to
Michel Gommer, seigneur of Schoonvelde, who served twenty-five terms in Lille's Magistrat
between 1572 and 1605. In the current year – aldermanic 1577 – Gommer was an alderman,
and the next fall he was to be sent as a delegate to the Estates-General and the Council of State;
BML, MS. 597; AGR, EA, Reg. 580, fol. 407.

[47] *RSG*, 2:139, 155, 180, 277, 294. Yet another 12,322 fl. was requested in mid-March (ibid.,
p. 252), but with unknown results.

[48] Leon Van der Essen, *Alexandre Farnèse, prince de Parme, gouverneur général des Pays-Bas (1545–
1592)*, 5 vols. (Brussels, 1933–7), 2:96. The Estates of Tournai joined Walloon Flanders in
turning down these ideas, but those of Hainaut approved of Artois's initiative. For an early
report, see *CS*, p. 25, 2 March 1578.

neur of Vaux, who had just gone over to Don John's camp wrote to Lille's magistrates urging them to change sides, the letters were instead forwarded to the Estates-General.[49]

Don John's offensive also prompted security precautions within Lille. A census of foreigners resident in or moving to the city was taken in March, and updated reports were required every evening at nine o'clock, after the town gates had closed. To forestall any surprises, the elite companies of crossbowmen, archers, and cannoneers joined the militia on guard duty.[50] Judging from political slogans,[51] John had his partisans in town – their sentiments perhaps encouraged, as the national assembly charged, by Catholic clergy.[52] Whatever the truth of that accusation, the Loi took no chances but obliged each member of the militia companies to swear to guard Lille against Don John and his supporters.[53] All clergy, nobles, and bourgeois not enrolled in the citizen guard were likewise required to take the oath and to promise to inform the aldermen should they hear of any conspiracies and intrigues.[54] A deputation also went to the Chamber of Accounts to get its adherence to the pledge, which now included an extra clause, "for the king, the Estates [General] and the fatherland." The officials – many of whom were reported to be "patriots" on the surface but firm Johanists and opponents of the Estates-General underneath[55] – refused to accept the codicil, however, and in the end were permitted to subscribe to the oath in its original form.[56]

By the end of April 1578, shortages of money and manpower had brought Don John's campaign to a standstill. As the threat from him waned, however, fissures closed in the face of common danger began to reopen within the uneasy Estates-General coalition. In the revolutionary cities, complex conflicts developed between artisans and patricians, Catholics and Protestants, partisans of the former magistracies and

---

[49] *RSG*, 2:41.

[50] AML, Reg. 15,924, fol. 75v; S. Monnoier, "Journal," BML, MS. 725, fol. [55].

[51] See ordinance of 15 April 1578, AML, Reg. 383, fol. 32v.

[52] AML, Reg. 32, fols. 119–20, 12 April 1578. A short time after receiving this letter from Brussels, the Magistrat expelled a Franciscan preacher, telling him never to return to Lille; AML, Reg. 15,924, fol. 77, 26 April 1578.

[53] AML, Reg. 278, fol. 44v, 24 March 1578. The names of those who refused were to be noted, but if any did, no records have survived.

[54] Ibid., fols. 44v–5, 2 April 1578. Students and faculty at the tiny seminary established at St. Pierre in 1569 were also obliged to bind themselves.

[55] *Mémoires anonymes*, 3:21–2.

[56] AML, Reg. 278, fol. 45v, 10 April 1578.

champions of the new.[57] Several provinces refused to recognize fully the national assembly's authority and reduced their financial contributions; others opposed negotiations aimed at securing assistance from foreign powers. But it was the troops raised to fight Don John that posed the most immediately pressing issue. By summer they numbered some fifty thousand, costing an estimated 800,000 florins per month. This sum was far beyond the financial capacity of the Estates-General, which quickly lost control of them.[58]

Between mid-April and early July, Walloon Flanders contributed at least 77,600 livres and perhaps as much as 227,600 for soldiers' pay,[59] yet the province still felt under siege from its purported defenders. Already while voting a general subsidy at the end of April, the Estates of Lille, Douai, and Orchies had insisted that the revenues be used to satisfy the unruly troops who "tormented, extorted, and oppressed" the countryside,[60] a baleful echo of complaints voiced earlier against royal forces. Over the summer, the situation only deteriorated. Despite voting a new common subsidy for three additional months (August through October),[61] the Brussels assembly could not amass sufficient funds or restore military discipline.[62] Replying in late August to yet another request for money, Walloon Flanders declared its eagerness to subscribe to the "common cause." But it begged that the troops be withdrawn "immediately" and that provincial authorities be given full powers to repress the disorders "by whatever means they deem suitable."[63]

Religious grievances were an even more potent source of disaffection in Walloon Flanders, particularly among the political elites. The Pacification of Ghent and its guarantee of a Catholic monopoly everywhere

---

[57] See esp. Wittman, *Les gueux dans les "bonnes villes" de Flandre*.

[58] See Parker, *Dutch Revolt*, p. 192.

[59] *RSG*, 2:168, 170, 187, 198, 207, 310–11, 314–15, 319, 325. Cf. ibid., p. 255, for a proposed loan of 40,000 fl.

[60] Ibid., p. 314.

[61] Ibid., p. 352, 28 July 1578. Lille revived a grain tax to help pay its share of this subsidy; AML, Reg. 383, fols. 38v–9, 13 August 1578.

[62] It was probably to get help in dealing with these troubles that the provincial Estates made a special contribution of 3,000 liv. to the central treasury. The sum assured the appointment of Adrien d'Oignies, seigneur of Willerval, as acting governor when Steenbecque left office shortly before his death in late June. The appointment stipulated that Willerval would relinquish his seat on the Council of State and reside in Walloon Flanders. *RSG*, 2:459; "Mémoires de Bauduin de Croix," fols. 68–9. Willerval was, of course, a substitute for Rassenghien, still a captive at Ghent. Officially appointed on 12 June 1578, he served until Rassenghien's return a year later.

[63] *RSG*, 2:359, 21 August 1578 (request); p. 216, 1 September 1578 (reply).

outside Holland and Zeeland notwithstanding, in cities ruled by revolutionary committees public Protestant worship was established and the old church restricted. In these circumstances, the project for a "Religious Peace," which would have compelled local magistrates to grant freedom of worship wherever at least one hundred families requested it, could hardly have failed to ignite a firestorm of protest when a Reformed synod presented it to the Estates-General in April. Responding to a proposal to promulgate the peace, the provincial Estates wrote angrily that under no circumstances would the practice of "the so-called reformed religion" be allowed anywhere in the castellany of Lille, Douai, and Orchies. On the contrary, these areas would remain within the bosom of the "Catholic, apostolic, Roman" church, as promised in the Pacification of Ghent, Union of Brussels, and other agreements.[64]

A recrudescence of Protestant activity within the province proved equally disturbing. In July, for instance, open-air preaching took place in Premesques, less than ten kilometers west of Lille, and the preacher arrested by the provost was freed by the crowd.[65] Lille's Magistrat was also alarmed by townspeople who proclaimed that Protestant services were now permitted in and around the city. So it reaffirmed that all heretical practices, whether preaching, meetings, or worship, remained strictly forbidden.[66]

In this context of military insecurity and religious agitation, even a minor incident was bound to have major reverberations. One soon appeared in Lille. As de Croix recounted it, he was inspecting a guardhouse at one of the city gates on 20 July, in his role as councillor and captain of a militia company. Suddenly, an unnamed but reputedly Protestant Lillois, accompanied by "several other evil rogues," accosted him, shouting, "Do you want to cut our throats?" Becoming more excited, the man tried to rouse citizens against the "notables," but the small uproar that resulted was easily crushed.[67] De Croix was convinced that the suspects had intended to open the gates to men from Ghent, but that their failure, along with the armed watch then on patrol, persuaded the

---

[64] Ibid., pp. 437–8, 16 August 1578. The proposal was withdrawn in the face of uncompromising rejections by Walloon Flanders, Artois, and Hainaut, although each province or town was left free to decide for itself. Only a few, including Antwerp, actually made a settlement of the type suggested.

[65] *Mémoires anonymes*, 2:314.

[66] AML, Reg. 383, fols. 37v–8, 6 August 1578.

[67] "Mémoires de Bauduin de Croix," fols. 74–7.

attackers to avoid Lille and fall instead upon Ypres. That city was, in fact, seized on the same day and soon reorganized on the model of the other towns ruled by revolutionary committees. The Estates of Walloon Flanders, too, formally charged in the Estates-General that Ghent's sponsorship of presches in the castellany betrayed an intent to descend on Lille.[68]

Whether or not these accusations were true, acting governor Willerval exploited the situation to stampede the Magistrat into accepting a garrison for the city. At a dramatic meeting on 21 July, he informed the city fathers of Ypres's capture and quickly won authorization to raise 250 to 300 soldiers at once and place them under the seigneur du Breucq, whom we have met before as bailiff of the castellany of Lille, representative to the Estates-General since it had opened, and commissioner for the delayed selection of the Loi in 1577.[69]

A case could perhaps be made for the wisdom of engaging troops as a defensive measure, in view of the presence nearby of radical municipal regimes; unruly mercenaries; the duke of Alençon (recently elevated to duke of Anjou), who had arrived in Mons on 10 July; and, a little further off in Brabant, Don John. But the aldermen's hasty acquiescence in the entry of mercenaries contrasts markedly with the reluctance that had greeted Rassenghien's similar suggestions during the correspondingly threatening summer of 1566. In light of what the 1578 decision provoked, the caution that had delayed consent twelve years earlier should probably have been in evidence this time as well.

To be sure, the aldermen may have felt that little protest was to be feared, given the local military situation and favorable material circumstances (see Tables 8.1 and 8.2; cf., for 1566, Tables 4.2 and 4.8). Further, the Magistrat tried to forestall objections by sending two influential councillors (one of them the ubiquitous Bauduin de Croix) to assure the Estates-General that the troops were being levied solely for protection.[70] Yet despite these precautions, news of the decision set off a

---

[68] *RSG*, 2:463, 26 July 1578. According to the *Mémoires anonymes*, 3:29, 38, the accusation was dropped once Ghent sent envoys to reassure the Magistrat that no raid would occur.

[69] "Mémoires de Bauduin de Croix," fol. 78 (where the force is given as 300 infantry); AML, Reg. 15,924, fol. 82 (where 200 foot and 50 cavalry are mentioned). In 1566, du Breucq's father Guislain, then seigneur of the same fief, had commanded 300 foot soldiers in the castellany under the bailiffs' authority; "Mémoires de Bauduin de Croix," fol. 15. The present seigneur was de Croix's brother-in-law.

[70] "Mémoires de Bauduin de Croix," fol. 79.

wave of rumors, demands, and meetings that kept the city in a state of turbulence for several months.

As usual, Bauduin de Croix blamed Lille's Protestants, though acknowledging that they were few in number. They, he claimed, spread a story that the soldiers' true mission was to help the city leave the union of all provinces and reconcile with Don John, in consequence of which commerce would be destroyed and the city ruined. But whatever the role of religious dissenters in disseminating rumors, the recent defections of Vaux and de la Motte to the Spanish side, not to mention the visibly shaky loyalty of the mercenary troops led by other Walloon nobles, must have raised doubts about the intent behind Willerval's proposal.[71] Bitter memories of Alba's occupation, too, probably motivated many of the townspeople. As de Croix ruefully acknowledged, they "readily accepted such talk [the allegedly Protestant-inspired rumor] tending to sedition," and "openly opposed" the efforts of governor and Magistrat.[72]

Subordinate officers of the bourgeois militia took the lead in objecting to the garrison. Probably they were angry at the magistrates – ten of whom were currently militia captains – for having agreed to a plan that would take the city's defense largely out of citizen hands. Upon learning of the arrangement, the lieutenants of the companies "gathered tumultuously" (de Croix's words) in a tavern and summoned their captains to meet with them. Before doing so, the worried captains took counsel with Willerval, who – although his ultimate objective, as we shall see, was to bring mercenaries under his control into Lille – evidently decided not to press his luck at this moment. So he advised the captains to convince the lieutenants to petition the Magistrat not to garrison the city, in return for a promise that no troubles would break out at Lille nor any

---

71 As we shall see (section VII), in the aftermath of the reconciliation with Spain numerous townspeople were banished from Lille and several others were executed or imprisoned in connection with a plot to seize the city. Among them were all the subofficers of the militia company captained by Michel Gommer in 1578, the only company so affected. Another company had a lieutenant and its standard bearer exiled, and a third perhaps its standard bearer; the remaining thirteen companies were apparently untouched. Gommer was related by marriage to Adrien de Rebreviettes – client and ally of Aerschot (see n. 46) and subsequently counsellor to the count of Lalaing (see n. 87), one of the Walloon nobles and mercenary captains who were in the process of entering into open rebellion against the Estates-General that would soon lead them to change allegiance to the Spanish side (see section V). In light of all this, one wonders (probably in vain) whether the later expulsions had anything to do with those exiled having taken leading roles in the July 1578 events; and, if so, whether the dissent expressed in Gommer's company had anything to do with their captain's link with the dissident Walloon nobility.

72 "Mémoires de Bauduin de Croix," fols. 79–80.

harm come to Catholicism. Agreement was quickly reached on this basis. The captains, lieutenants, and standard bearers, asserting that Lillois could adequately defend their town, solemnly pledged to tighten up discipline, carry out the orders of aldermen and governor, and uphold the Pacification of Ghent. The Loi then directed du Breucq to cease enrolling troops, and he left for Douai soon thereafter.[73]

As the militia had been critical to the overthrow of municipal governments in Ghent, Arras, and elsewhere, the ruling elite must have found the resistance within the companies ominous. Certainly the governor's and Magistrat's hasty retreat implies recognition of the proposal's explosive potential at a time when, to judge by de Croix's reports and public taunts, popular feeling was running high.[74] The authorities may also have felt that the dispute menaced the unity of the urban ruling class as well as the city's security. At least two of the thirty-two lieutenants currently sat in the Magistrat along with ten captains. The remaining six captains, two other lieutenants, and perhaps two standard bearers had been members of the Loi in the past, and no fewer than nine of the lieutenants and eight of the standard bearers belonged to Magistrat families.[75]

Notwithstanding the accord, Willerval remained determined to bring mercenaries into Lille. Early in the autumn, he tried to introduce a company of cavalry commanded by his son into the city under cover of darkness. The attempt was, however, foiled by a militia lieutenant who called out his company and some nearby townspeople.[76] Aversion to a garrison was so widespread, Sarrazin reported, that Willerval's attempt resulted in "a tremendous uproar."[77] It is not known whether the Magistrat had been apprised of the governor's plan of (in Sarrazin's words) "slipping in" troops – exactly what the authorities had promised not to do back in July. But de Croix's characterization of those who blocked the cavalry's entry as "seditious" suggests that at least one well-connected and influential councillor sympathized with the scheme. Nor did the Loi

---

[73] Ibid., fols. 80–3; AML, Reg. 15,924, fols. 81v–2, for the oath and the names of all the officers.

[74] Cf. AML, Reg. 383, fol. 37v, 4 August 1578, an ordinance prohibiting jeers like "Papist," "Johanist," "Huguenot," "Beggar," "heretic," and many others.

[75] The officers have been identified from the incomplete list of those who pledged to defend the city in AML, Reg. 15,924, fols. 82–2v; for government service, see BML, MS. 597.

[76] "Mémoires de Bauduin de Croix," fol. 84. Unfortunately, de Croix does not name the lieutenant.

[77] *CS*, p. 87, 28 September 1578.

distance itself from the governor. On the contrary, perhaps recognizing that Willerval's duplicity had engendered a good deal of enmity, it assigned him a full-time guard, paid for out of municipal funds.[78]

Willerval's second fiasco did not quiet the unrest in Lille. But the next initiative apparently came from people unfriendly to the existing order, although the acting governor once again played a leading role. According to de Croix, Lille's Protestants continued to stir up trouble in the city.[79] Realizing, however, that most Lillois remained too devoted to Catholicism to revolt in favor of Orange, and that the authorities had taken too firm precautions for a rising to succeed unaided, the heretics turned to the central government for assistance. Calling themselves the "Zealots for the public weal" (*Zélateurs du bien public*), they secretly petitioned Matthias and the Estates-General, contending that Lille was in danger of falling to a surprise attack or some other calamity due to the carelessness of an overworked Magistrat. Because most militia captains simultaneously served in the Loi, they could not pay adequate attention to their security duties. The only solution, the Zealots declared, was to replace either the aldermen or the captains with new men having only one responsibility.

Two commissioners were sent from Antwerp to investigate. One of them, Bussaert van Surbise, was, if de Croix is correct, a Protestant predisposed to if not allied with the Zealots. Upon arrival in Lille, the delegates first visited the acting governor, who, after speaking with them, at once conferred with the Magistrat through the intermediary of the mayor, Philippe de la Riviere, seigneur of Warnes.[80] During his discussion with the Loi, Willerval railed against his inability to repress heresy with the slender means at his disposal, the unwillingness of the town to receive a garrison, and the fact that a majority of Lillois had become "factious" under Protestant influence. He concluded by urging that the city's Catholics publicly manifest their resolve. Following the governor's recommendation, Warnes then consulted with the parish priests, who in turn convoked citizens known to be particularly antagonistic to the Reformed, encouraging them to appear en masse before the commissioners and voice their opinions about the Zealots' charges.

[78] AML, Reg. 15,924, fol. 83v.
[79] For the material in this and the next two paragraphs, see "Mémoires de Bauduin de Croix," fols. 86–92.
[80] As a councillor, de Croix must have been a party to these talks, but he also had access to additional information from Warnes, his half-brother.

So when the inquiry opened, a crowd of three hundred citizens appeared behind Charles de Boisot, a counsellor-assessor at the Gouvernance, demanding that the Zealots appear in public and prove their allegations. For their part, these Catholic bourgeois announced, they were entirely satisfied with both the Magistrat and the captains; what the Zealots desired was simply to stir up trouble so that their faction could take control of the municipal government and militia in order to introduce Protestantism. Intimidated by this show of force, no Zealot dared reveal his identity nor did anyone speak in support of their appeal. With that, the investigation abruptly ended and Surbise hurried away from Lille, having failed, de Croix smugly claimed, to get what he had wanted.

It is not possible to ascertain whether the Zealots were simply citizens – perhaps the lieutenants once again – concerned, as their remonstrance stated, with Lille's security, or, as de Croix and Willerval believed, heretics seeking to provoke an Orangist rising. Yet no matter which was the case, the episode underlines once again the daunting obstacles insurgency faced in Lille. On the one hand, a Magistrat united against Orangism and Protestantism cooperated closely with the provincial leadership. On the other, both the appeal to the Estates-General and the Zealots' inability to find townspeople who would stand up for them in public indicate the lack of any substantial organized social base in support of change. Nor, from all indications, were there adverse social and economic conditions to inflame discontent. Prosecutions for violating light-cloth rules disappear from the registers, while output and thus employment were rising and grain prices falling (Tables 8.1 and 8.2).

What the Zealot affair shows, in sum, is that even at the high tide of urban revolution elsewhere in the Netherlands, it was easier to mobilize Lillois against political and religious innovation than for it. This was even more true because the changes demanded by the Zealots could plausibly be seen – and were so represented by Boisot and his retinue – as favoring factional objectives.

V

The incident also must have further strained relations between provincial elite and Estates-General. Thus it probably contributed to Walloon Flanders's move away from the national assembly toward rapprochement with Spain that became evident as the autumn wore on. This drift, almost certainly urged by Willerval, was encouraged, too, by Don John's successor Alexander Farnese, prince of Parma, son of Margaret, regent at the beginning of the revolt. An able soldier, Parma was an equally skilled diplomat whose preferred strategy was to bring the Walloon provinces back to the Spanish side by means of compromise and then tempt the other provinces until they too settled separately.[81] Just ten days after replacing Don John on 1 October, Farnese wrote to the Estates and major towns of the Walloon provinces, inviting them to reconcile with the king in order to protect Catholicism and their positions and to gain the restoration of all privileges and liberties that had existed under Charles V.[82] With the discredited Don John out of the way, Farnese's efforts quickly began to bear fruit. Hainaut suggested that the French-speaking provinces form an alliance "against the dangers and oppression of Catholics and nobles" from a league that Flanders, Holland, Zeeland, and several other provinces were rumored to be forming.[83] There was even a revival of the idea, first broached by Artois in the spring, of a separate peace with Spain.

Mutiny among the Estates-General's troops likewise fostered divisions between national assembly and provincial ruling classes. Convinced that their pay was being deliberately withheld for religious reasons, the companies captained by French-speaking nobles dubbed themselves "Malcontents" and refused to obey the Estates until they received the wages owed them.[84] At the end of September, a band led by Montigny seized Menen, on the Lys less than twenty kilometers north of Lille, cutting Ghent off from Walloon Protestants and radicals. In response, Ghent and its allies in Ypres and Courtrai called on other cities in the area to join in common military action against the Malcontents, but these pleas were rebuffed. Lille, for instance, replied that Ghent would first have to "reinstate the [Catholic] religion."[85] An appeal to John Casimir, administrator of the Rhine Palatinate, produced better results: On 10 October this ardent Calvinist arrived with twelve thousand troops initially supported by Queen Elizabeth of England. Open

---

81 Van der Essen, *Alexandre Farnese*, 2:50–1.
82 Ibid., p. 99. Farnese's promises here were close to the terms of the reconciliation negotiated the next spring.
83 Besides Lille, Douai, and Orchies, Artois and Tournai and the Tournésis were approached; *RSG*, 2:438, 20 October 1578.
84 *RSG*, 2:224, 20 September 1578.
85 *CS*, p. 89.

warfare soon broke out between the Malcontents and Casimir's soldiers, though both were still nominally under the command of the Estates-General.

Involving a religious as well as a political protest, the Malcontent rebellion focused magisterial discontent in Walloon Flanders and nearby provinces, helping to push them away from the Estates-General. Echoing the troops' complaints, officials like Bauduin de Croix (and, according to him, many of his counterparts in other Walloon towns) charged that the Antwerp assembly deliberately neglected to pay the soldiers as part of a larger plot to weaken Catholicism.[86] If de Croix is to be believed, moreover, at least some members of Lille's Magistrat knew about, and thus presumably approved of, gunpowder sent to the insurgents by Adrien de Rebreviettes, counsellor to the count of Lalaing, Montigny's brother, and the same man whom the Estates of Lille, Douai, and Orchies had tried to place on the Council of State early in 1578.[87] Equally suggestive of changing attitudes among the ruling groups was Willerval's report that it was becoming difficult to raise loans in the name of the Estates-General, even though the receipts were to be employed "in better dislodging" the unruly soldiery in the vicinity.[88]

In short, signs of sympathy for the Malcontents began to emerge among political leaders – many of them linked by family, clientage, or friendship to the mutineers' commanders, whom in addition they had engaged on various occasions from 1566 to the present to help defend their cities. Yet the dominant popular sentiment was animosity, based in large part on months of depredations by the undisciplined troops.[89] De Croix admitted that Lillois' antipathy was so great that supplies sent to the Malcontents by de Rebrievettes had to be hidden in herring barrels.[90] There seems as well to have been a prevailing aversion to anything smacking of reconciliation. Even though "a spark of obedience to the king" flickered among some people, Sarrazin wrote, the general

---

[86] See "Mémoires de Bauduin de Croix," fol. 93. Other diarists were convinced that the captains were lining their own pockets; *Mémoires anonymes*, 3:93.
[87] "Mémoires de Bauduin de Croix," fols. 104–5. De Croix was, once again, probably well informed, for he was both a counsellor and brother-in-law to du Breucq, who had reemerged, now as an active Malcontent conspirator.
[88] *RSG*, 2:260, 2 October 1578.
[89] Cf. the complaints listed in the instructions for Michel Gommer, sent to the Estates-General in early October; AGR, EA, Reg. 580, fol. 407. See also *RSG*, 2:471, 7 October 1578.
[90] "Mémoires de Bauduin de Croix," fol. 105.

"loathing" for the Spanish prevented any Catholic league from being formed.[91]

Very likely it was public opinion of this tenor that accounts for the Magistrat's denial that it had assisted the Malcontents, a charge that had prompted radicals in Ypres to sequester Lillois' "goods and merchandise."[92] The Loi also agreed to receive the pensionary of Bruges, sent by the Estates-General to discourage the formation of "special leagues" or any other disruptive step. Reminding his listeners that the Union was needed to fight "the common enemy of this fatherland" and that religious conflict would be fatal to "so just a cause," the emissary carried letters intended to allay Lille's fears. In them, the Estates-General scorned Hainaut's contention that some provinces were planning a league to extirpate Catholicism and assured Lille, Douai, and Orchies that it was taking energetic measures to repress disorders. Stressing that a civil war would result in the "entire ruin of all these countries," the assembly contended that such hostilities would inevitably end by making Spain once again "masters of us and our posterity, placing us in eternal bondage, to the mockery of the whole world."[93]

But these efforts to hold the provinces together were destined to fail. Whatever the magistrates' real or professed attitude as late as 20 October, renewed intrigue over the upcoming selection of the Loi almost immediately chilled their relations with the Estates-General. At the same time, this new affair presented the political elite with a superb opportunity to manipulate a strategic segment of popular sentiment against purported Protestant and Orangist machinations in order – at last – to bring a garrison into Lille.

Bauduin de Croix, once more a leading participant in the story he narrated, presented the episode as one more in a long series of Protestant attempts to take over Catholic Lille.[94] In his account, the only first-hand one we have, the city's Reformed grew angry upon learning that one of the commissioners for the *renouvellement de la Loi* was to be du

[91] *CS*, p. 93.

[92] AGR, EA, Reg. 580, fols. 407–8v; *Documents historiques inédits concernant les troubles des Pays-Bas (1577–1584)*, ed. Philippe Kervyn de Volkaersbeke and J. L. A. Diegerick, 2 vols. (Ghent, 1849–50), 1:37–8, 41–2, nos. XXII, XXV, 22 and 27 October 1578. At Lille's request, the Estates-General dispatched mediators (*RSG*, 2:471), but Sarrazin reported with undisguised glee that Flemings and Walloons were at each others' throats; *CS*, p. 92.

[93] *RSG*, 2:438–40, 20 and 22 October 1578.

[94] "Mémoires de Bauduin de Croix," fols. 107–20. De Croix may have inflated his importance in the events, but as we shall see he occupied several strategic positions.

Breucq, for it was in his house in the neighboring village of Seclin that Montigny had planned the Malcontents' seizure of Menen. Taking their case to Matthias, and perhaps also to Orange, they got du Breucq replaced by the sieur of Longastre, a recent convert to Calvinism. They also drew up a list of candidates for the Magistrat. "Apart from four or five," de Croix reported with disgust, "there was neither a gentleman nor a rich personage, not one, so to speak, who had well-formed judgment, but several were of suspect faith." The slate was forwarded to Matthias, who in turn sent it on to Willerval (who as acting governor headed the election commission), along with a personal envoy who was instructed to help put in office a new Loi containing the men named on it.

As might be expected, Willerval adamantly opposed such an outcome and set about to frustrate it. He immediately contacted the mayor, who summoned his brother-in-law Bauduin de Croix and the officers of the militia company he captained. Currently responsible for the night watch, their reliability, it will be recalled, had been determined back in July when they had foiled the rising at the town gate. Together, they planned preemptive moves. First, they posted the list of nominees throughout Lille, intending thereby to "unmask" them [95] – and also, it may safely be assumed, intimidate them. Next, they persuaded the Magistrat to send de Croix and Toussaint Muyssart, councillor and captain of another militia company, to remonstrate with Matthias, the Council of State, and the Estates-General about both the list and the revocation of du Breucq's commission.[96]

On 4 November, the two men appeared before the Estates-General, where they demanded that Matthias be informed that the recent actions had seriously infringed the city's privileges.[97] The bailiff of Ypres responded that du Breucq had been removed for his own safety: Reports had it that he was so widely hated by the people that his life was in jeopardy. Although there was probably some truth in this explanation – as we have seen, du Breucq hastily left Lille after the lieutenants' protest in July – de Croix indignantly rejected it, claiming that in Catholic Lille

---

[95] The list has not survived.

[96] Muyssart, whose relation if any to Antoine Muyssart (see section III) I have not been able to discover, later acquired the seigneury of Estevele and became the receiver of the provincial Estates. He was related to the provincial nobility by birth (his mother was Marguerite de Rebreviettes) and marriage (his wife was Catherine de Hennin). See BML, MS. 597.

[97] A brief summary of their statement is in *RSG*, 2:480.

it was Longastre who had cause for fear, not du Breucq. This unsatisfactory session completed, the Lillois, accompanied by the pensionaries of Friesland and Tournai representing the national assembly, had an audience with the Council of State. There a similar exchange took place. This time, de Croix and Muyssart added a new allegation: It was the colonels of Antwerp's militia, with whom Lille's Protestants had conspired, who had applied pressure leading to du Breucq's revocation.

While awaiting the outcome of these discussions, the elections had been postponed, but the authorities' efforts to influence the results had proceeded. On the afternoon of 1 November, when the names of the incoming Loi were traditionally announced, some one thousand citizens assembled before the governor's palace behind their spokesman François de le Fortrie, lawyer and one of the militia officers who had previously participated in planning countermeasures. De le Fortrie announced that the crowd had gathered upon learning of a plot to introduce Protestants, suspected Protestants, or even people "of evil repute, living only from the product of their labor," into the Magistrat. He insisted that the governor block any such nominations to ensure that none save "worthy people" would sit on the Loi.

Taking this cue, Willerval assured the crowd that he shared their concerns but was unable to act decisively because of sentiment in favor of the Protestants and, even worse, against the entry of troops that would strengthen his hand. At this, voices were heard crying out, "*Levez, levez les troupes!*" assuring Willerval that they were prepared to receive any garrison that would be necessary to exclude Protestants from the Magistrat. This favorable news was quickly communicated to de Croix and Muyssart in Antwerp, who at once demanded another hearing before the Council of State. At first, the council temporized, then directed the envoys to speak with Orange, which they refused to do. A few days later Matthias gave in and conferred on Willerval total authority over the election process.

Sarrazin, writing from Arras perhaps on the basis of information supplied him by Charles de Boisot,[98] the official at the Gouvernance who had been spokesman for the earlier staged rally against the Zealots, saw Orange's hand in the events. William "named commissioners of his *secte*" to carry out the annual elections, wrote the prior of St. Vaast. After

---

98 In April 1579, Boisot sent Alexander Farnese a report that closely resembled Sarrazin's earlier letter; *CS*, p. 118, n. 1.

they were "rejected" (by whom, we are not told), it was again William who drew up the list of candidates, which consisted of men that he "meant to be placed in the Magistrat."[99] Cardinal Granvelle, at Rome, concurred, though his briefer reference to the incident had it that Longastre, though ostensibly named commissioner by Matthias, had actually been appointed by Orange to "pack" the Loi.[100] Both Sarrazin and Granvelle agreed with Bauduin de Croix that the goal was to put Reformed (Sarrazin calls them *huguenots*, Granvelle *consistoriaulx*) in the municipal government. Like de Croix, too, both Sarrazin and Granvelle contended that it was (in the latter's words) "the people" who blocked the attempt: two thousand *bons*, in Sarrazin's version, who gathered of their own account to warn Willerval that if even a single Protestant were selected "they would cut his throat."[101]

It is not difficult to imagine that Orange and his followers, local Protestants, and others dissatisfied with the existing regime all might have cooperated in the incident. But whatever their relative contributions, these forces of change were badly outmaneuvered by Willerval and his allies in the Magistrat. These men obviously realized that the election affair, like the Zealots' protest, could be used to strengthen the existing system by mobilizing a body of citizens to overawe insurgents and defeat their demands. What is more, although in form the mobilization resembled the one mounted a few months before, the crowd was considerably larger and more careful preparations had evidently been made to manipulate it. Hence the authorities were able not simply to gain endorsement for the status quo but to create a momentum in favor of measures that previously had failed to win popular approval.

Shortly before the election, the outgoing Loi authorized the levying of a garrison, whereupon Willerval immediately brought in one hundred cavalry under his son, the seigneur of Philomez – the same company that had been refused entry the prior September.[102] Finally, on 15 November, a Magistrat characterized equally by religious orthodoxy and political experience was inducted. All its members were Catholics and just four of forty-three were inexperienced in municipal government, compared with an average of 7.23 across the period between 1541 and

---

[99] Ibid., p. 117.
[100] Granvelle to Farnese, 18 November 1578, *CG*, 7:211.
[101] *CS*, pp. 117–18; cf. *CG*, 7:211.
[102] "Mémoires de Bauduin de Croix," fol. 122.

1580. Only one alderman had never previously served in the Magistrat, and no councillor, as against means of 2.13 and 0.6 respectively. Just two of the twenty-four men (both were aldermen, one the person new to the Loi) on these two central bodies had served fewer than three terms.[103]

VI

By late 1578, the growing disenchantment of the Walloon provinces with the Estates-General regime was common knowledge. From Rome, Granvelle reported to Philip that Artois, Hainaut, and Walloon Flanders were showing "great discontent" with William of Orange because of the anti-Catholic activities occurring with his apparent consent.[104] Another informant claimed that Walloon Flanders and Artois wished to reconcile with the king if moderate terms could be secured; should they be won over, they would draw the other Catholic provinces in their wake.[105] But the actual separation took several months and was marked by false starts and apparent reversals.

The Estates-General, of course, tried hard to maintain the common front.[106] Among other things, a member of the Council of State was sent to Lille, Tournai, and Arras to oppose a separate peace treaty between the Walloons and Spain by assuring that the ancient faith would be respected.[107] The emissary seemed to have been successful: Willerval, for example, had promised to do whatever he could. Even Farnese thought for a moment that the Estates-General had turned the tide back in its favor, frustrating his expectation that Artois, Walloon Flanders, and Tournai would quickly reconcile.[108] Yet the national assembly's initiative had no lasting impact. On 6 January 1579, deputies from Artois, Hainaut, and the city of Douai, meeting at Arras, announced the formation of a league to uphold the Pacification of Ghent, especially its "main point,"

103 Derived from BML, MS. 597. One of the neophyte aldermen was Toussaint Muyssart, doubtless rewarded for meritorous service.
104 *CG*, 7:233.
105 François de Moncheau to Pedro de Arcanti, 15 December 1578, *CP*, ed. Lefèvre, 1:461, no. 797.
106 At times, however, the national assembly acted in heavy-handed ways. In early December, for instance, Walloon Flanders was asked to provide 150,000 of the more than 750,000 liv. needed to keep the Estates' army from dissolving over the winter – an amount equal to that requested from Brabant, Gelderland, Holland, and Zeeland combined and far in excess of its usual share; *RSG*, 2:389 n. 3.
107 Ibid., 2:739–40, report dated 4 January 1579.
108 Farnese to Borja, 29 December 1578, *CP*, ed. Lefèvre, 1:473, no. 811.

the defense of Catholicism; to guarantee obedience to the king; and to maintain the privileges of the country. The representatives also pledged to try to find "reasonable, certain and assured means" of making peace between Philip and his subjects.[109]

Lille initially held back from the Union of Arras, as the new league came to be called. Although the Magistrat had sent delegates to the talks, they were asked to leave because the powers granted them were insufficient. As a result, no Lillois signed the 6 January statement.[110] The banishments that, as we shall see, followed reconciliation when it finally occurred indicate that aversion to such a move within the city, noted in the fall, had not disappeared. But contemporaries emphasized another source of Lille's reticence – the fact that the Magistrat disapproved of any settlement until the king agreed to observe the terms of the Pacification of Ghent.[111]

Nevertheless, the drift of the city's policy, doubtless encouraged by Willerval, continued to be away from the Estates-General and toward common action with the other French-speaking cities and provinces. If de Croix is correct, relations with the Malcontents became warmer and closer under the new Loi. To be sure, when in the late fall the mutineers seized Lannoy, a walled textile town fifteen kilometers northeast of Lille, the magistrates were briefly apprehensive for Lille's security. But they quickly accepted Montigny's reassurances that the step had been taken to keep out Flemings who could otherwise menace Lille. So deep, in fact, was their abhorrence of the Flemish cities' Protestantism, de Croix contended, that a short time later Lille's aldermen decided to "league together openly" with the Malcontents and recalled Denis le Guillebert, their only deputy still remaining at the Estates-General. Additional troops were also brought into Lille, in the form of two infantry companies lodged in what remained of the former citadel. By late January 1579, the Magistrat was secretly in touch with de la Motte, the Catholic nobleman who had been first to switch sides back in April 1578 and was now working for Parma.[112]

Responding to Lille's public avowals of support for the Pacification of

---

[109] See Van der Essen, *Alexandre Farnèse*, 2:124; *Actes des Etats-Généraux*, 2:452–4, for the text of the Union of Arras.

[110] Cf. Farnese to Philip, January 1579, *CP*, ed. Lefèvre, 1:489, no. 829.

[111] See letter of Moulart and Valhoun to Farnese, 22 January 1579, *CP*, ed. Lefèvre, 1:497, no. 846.

[112] "Mémoires de Bauduin de Croix," fols. 129–38.

Ghent, the Estates-General pledged that all provisos of the treaty would be scrupulously respected; in particular, no changes in the practice of Catholicism would be permitted.[113] Such statements were of no avail, however, both because the national assembly could not satisfactorily enforce the compact and because the Walloon provinces emphasized every lapse. At Arras on 23 February, for instance, representatives of Artois, Hainaut, and Douai complained once again that the Estates-General had failed to halt infractions of the Pacification. The reply from Antwerp underscored the cruelty and tyranny of Spanish overlordship, claiming that keeping out the Spanish had to be the main objective. After that was accomplished, every other issue could be settled. But the letter implicitly admitted that the Pacification had been violated by arguing that its goal was not to "set up new inquisitions about the faith and religion" of Netherlanders but to form a union dedicated to liberty and the expulsion of Spain.[114]

Farnese skillfully exploited the Walloon sense of grievance, repeatedly insisting that with peace Catholicism and local privileges would be protected. Moreover, once he had won over Malcontents and their strongholds at Menen, Estaires, and Cassel in mid-December 1578, he disposed of sufficiently numerous loyal Walloon soldiers that he could confidently promise that no Spanish troops would be brought into reconciled towns.[115] So even though delegates from Lille were still absent, beginning on 21 February half a dozen emissaries from Walloon Flanders joined their counterparts from Artois and Hainaut for discussions, held largely at Arras though partly at Mons. Among them were two men from Douai and one of the bailiffs of the castellany – all of them men who had formerly represented the province at the Estates-General – as well as Willerval and Floris van der Haer, canon and treasurer of St. Pierre, Lille, and, like Willerval, a man who had the Magistrat's ear.[116] Doubtless their reports and contacts strongly influenced the Loi, but other factors must also have played a significant role in provoking Lille's eventual break with the Estates-General.

For one thing, the duke of Anjou, who had previously seemed to offer a Catholic third way between Spain and the increasingly Protestant-

---

[113] *RSG*, 2:599, late January 1579.
[114] The Walloon provinces' letter is in *Actes des Etats-Généraux*, 2:462–4; the reply by the Estates-General, dated 3 March 1579, is ibid., pp. 465–76.
[115] Van der Essen, *Alexandre Farnèse*, 2:118–19. The troops numbered some seven thousand men.

controlled Estates-General, tried in late December 1578 to imitate the ill-starred Don John by seizing Mons to use as a power base from which to restore his sagging position. Having failed, however, he recognized his isolation and went back to France. Then, on 23 February 1579, Farnese read letters just received from Philip. In them, the king pledged to ratify the Pacification of Ghent, the Union of Brussels, and the Perpetual Edict, thereby speaking directly to Lille's expressed concern.

At the same time as these events were pulling Lille toward a settlement with Farnese, other incidents were pushing it away from the Estates-General. Boats bound for Lille – along with Tournai and towns in Artois and Hainaut – once more began to be stopped and merchandise seized as rumors of a reconciliation spread. Although the Estates-General ordered the city governments of Antwerp, Ypres, and Ghent – which had taken this action under pressure from the populace – to release the goods, its pleas were ineffective and even Matthias's demands ignored.[117] Further, persecution of Catholics in Ghent resumed after some months of quiet, again in apparent reaction to the negotiations between the Walloon provinces and Farnese.[118] By this point, Bauduin de Croix confided, the Magistrat was becoming weary of the prolonged conflict, for it seemed to bring no result other than the spread of Protestantism.[119]

Once talks got under way, the Walloon provinces rapidly distanced themselves from the Estates-General. As early as the end of February, they requested withdrawal of the national assembly's troops on the ground that they were performing no services of value but simply roaming around. By the first week of March, the general subsidy was no longer being collected in Walloon Flanders or in Hainaut, Valenciennes, and Tournai.[120] At some point before 23 March, Lille began to participate in the conference, for on that day Farnese was informed by his

---

116 For the representatives, see *Traicté de réconciliation faict en la ville d'Arras le XVIIe de may XVcLXXIX avec sa Majesté par les provinces d'Arthois, Haynault, Lille, Douai et Orchies* (Douai, 1579), unpaginated. For van der Haer, who subsequently wrote a history of the revolt, *De initiis tumultuum Belgicorum* (Douai, 1587) – a book that, unfortunately, has little information about Lille – see Hautcoeur, *Histoire de Saint-Pierre*, 2:415–16.

117 See Morillon to Granvelle, 27 February 1579, *CG*, 7:322; *RSG*, 2:775, 3, 6 and 7 March 1579; Matthias to Ypres, 10 March 1579, *Documents historiques inédits*, 1:197, no. cxviii.

118 Van der Essen, *Alexandre Farnèse*, 2:145.

119 "Mémoires de Bauduin de Croix," fol. 138.

120 *RSG*, 2:632, 776, 28 February and 7 March 1579. On 24 February, Lille, Douai, and Orchies had been asked for 70,000 liv. toward a subsidy of 776,000 liv., once again far over its usual quota; ibid., pp. 685–6 n. 4.

agents among the negotiators that the city's delegates were now strongly inclined to reconcile.[121] Because the other provinces represented at Arras were already leaning in that direction, an understanding was soon reached. On 30 March, the four bailiffs of the castellany, the aldermen and councillors of Lille, clergy, nobles, and officers from the Gouvernance and the Chamber of Accounts, along with the representatives of the provincial Estates, determined to join with Artois and Hainaut and come to terms with the king. They took this step, they averred, not only because efforts toward a general reconciliation had failed, but also because the king had accepted the Pacification of Ghent and promised to remove foreign soldiers from the Netherlands. A resolution embodying their decision was accepted and sent to the Estates-General the following day.[122]

The actual treaty was not signed for another month and a half. During that period, the Walloon provinces and the Estates-General traded charges and countercharges, though without any effect on either side's position. The former claimed that a settlement was justified in order to uphold Catholicism, avoid disorder, and prevent a break with the legitimate sovereign. Although a common peace on those terms would have been preferable, a separate one was justified once the provinces' original aims of respecting the Pacification of Ghent and expelling Spanish troops had been realized.[123] The Estates-General reminded the dissident provinces that earlier royal promises had been drowned in blood by Alba, mentioned the dangers attendant upon civil war, and inveighed against a settlement that permitted the Spanish to turn upon the remaining provinces with additional troops.[124] Such warnings and pleas proved unpersuasive, however. Condemnations of separate treaties sounded particularly hollow, because on 23 January Holland, Zeeland, Utrecht, Gelderland, Friesland, and the Ommelanden around Groningen had concluded the Union of Utrecht. This compact committed them to act together when waging war or arranging peace. But it neither mandated the maintenance of Catholicism nor called for reconciliation with Spain.

On 17 April, Willerval wrote the Estates-General that he still hoped

---

[121] Letter of 23 March 1579, *CP*, ed. Lefèvre, 1:546, no. 944.
[122] Printed in *Actes des Etats-Généraux*, 2:479–82.
[123] The declarations of the provinces are in ibid., pp. 485–6, 490–2, 508–9 (6, 9, and 15 April 1579).
[124] The Estates-General's statements are in ibid., pp. 487–90, 509–22 (8, 28, and 29 April 1579).

that Artois and Hainaut would stay in the Generality and reported that Lille refused to accept Farnese as governor-general of the Low Countries. Perhaps, he added, the negotiations at Arras would break down.[125] Willerval was certainly playing a double game, for he was a leading negotiator of the reconciliation. Still, his news about Lille may have been accurate. The city could well have agreed with the representatives of the provincial nobility, who had close ties to Malcontent leaders like Lalaing and Montigny, that the governor-generalship, as well as leading posts in the army and Council of State, should be reserved for Walloon nobles.[126] Lille did not, of course, get satisfaction on this point, but if nothing else its stance made a fine bargaining chip, used to ensure that the sale of the former royal citadel to the municipality was ratified in any agreement.[127] Finally, on 17 May 1579, Lille's representatives (its mayor, Jean Picaret, and Denis le Guillebert, its clerk for criminal matters and former Estates-General delegate) signed the Treaty of Arras. They joined their colleagues from Douai; Floris van der Haer, deputy of the clergy; Jacques de Hennin, seigneur of Ghislenghien and bailiff of Comines, for the four bailiffs; Adrien de Rebreviettes, for the provincial nobles; acting governor Willerval; and delegates from Artois and Hainaut.[128]

The treaty contained twenty-eight articles, designed to maintain as far as possible the gains made by the provinces during rule by the Estates-General, to rid the country of foreign troops, to restore privileges enjoyed under Charles V, to restrict the power of governors-general, and to enhance that of the Estates and the Council of State. In return, the full authority of the king and his deputy was recognized. Several clauses were of particular importance to Lille. A provision that no citadel torn down would be rebuilt without the express consent of the province in which it had been located appeared as clause 4. Clause 7 certified that

---

[125] *RSG*, 2:751.

[126] Moncheaux to Vargas, 18 and 23 April 1579, *CP*, ed. Lefèvre, 1:569, 572, nos. 984, 989.

[127] This condition is cited in Moncheaux's letter of 23 April (see previous note). Royal letters accepting the sale are in AML, Reg. 15,885, fols. 200v–1, 1 July 1579. Although the Estates-General had already granted the citadel to Lille in October 1577, the Magistrat clearly felt that it had to assure that the king would go along. The city also wanted to forestall endless litigation on the part of the former garrison, whose rights were, in March 1579, still at issue; *RSG*, 2:637. Only in 1588, however, did Lille obtain royal letters patent granting the town full and free ownership; BML, MS. 597, pp. 207–11 at end.

[128] The delegates from Walloon Flanders are listed in "Mémoires de Bauduin de Croix," fols. 139–40.

the Netherlands' army would be formed only of local troops. The city must have been especially pleased with clause 13, which stipulated that garrisons could be posted in a town only if the municipal authorities agreed and even then could only contain natives of the Low Countries. Also of great value to Lille were clauses 19 and 20. They obliged the king to guarantee all annuities issued and other debts contracted to pay the costs of the recent wars and mandated a return to the forms of taxation found in the reign of Charles V – before, that is, the Tenth and Twentieth Pennies.[129]

Neither the Treaty of Arras nor subsequent military conflicts ended contact between the Estates-General and the Walloon provinces. As late as November 1579, the national assembly appealed to its former members to rejoin the Generality, or at least to enter into negotiations.[130] Trade also continued between the Walloon and Flemish provinces, with Ghent in particular protesting vociferously against any measure that threatened to interrupt the flow of merchandise.[131] But the signatories of the Treaty made it clear that they had no intention of renouncing their action. In November 1579, for instance, Lille, Douai, and Orchies contributed 50,000 florins to Parma's war effort, and the other reconciled provinces voted similar sums.[132]

VII

As far as can be ascertained, the decision to make peace with Spain did not divide the current Magistrat, although certain members may have taken the lead in urging the step. But the city government does seem to have felt that the move was sufficiently unpopular to make it wise to exile influential men – some of whom may have already shown themselves opposed to the Loi during one or another incident in the recent past – rather than to allow resistance to coalesce around them. So on 25 May, fourteen townspeople were summoned before the Loi. Informed that for unspecified "good reasons and motives," and to uphold public order, they would have to leave Lille by three in the afternoon, they were forbidden to return without explicit permission of the aldermen on pain

---

[129] The text is published in Van der Essen, *Alexandre Farnèse*, p. 208–13.
[130] *RSG*, 2:752–3, 760 (1 and 2 July and 21 November 1579).
[131] Ibid., pp. 706, 724, 778 (13 July, 17 and 29 August, 17 September 1579).
[132] AML, Reg. 15,885, fols. 204–5.

of death or other severe punishment. Several asked that they be told the basis of the expulsion order but their requests were denied. Others were more defiant. David Bigode, for instance, declared that "the sun shines as brightly elsewhere as here." No matter what their attitude, however, all were forced to leave.[133]

Despite the officials' refusal to justify the banishments, the timing strongly suggests that the Magistrat wanted to get rid of important people who might have been able to give leadership to protests against the Treaty of Arras. Many in this first group of involuntary expatriates came from wealthy, well-known families and themselves worked as lawyers, government bureaucrats, and merchants; several were substantial landowners in the castellany as well.[134] Jean de Smerpont, for instance, member of a leading merchant and political clan, seems to have been the same man who had belonged to the inner circle of the Magistrat between 1551 and 1560, and Jean (de) Thieulaine had once been usher (*huissier*) at the Council of Flanders.

Objections to the settlement may have been founded on religious grounds. A contemporary charged that those banished were suspected of being Protestants,[135] and as we shall see a few people came from purported heretic families. By May 1579, however, distinctions had been eroded as the possibility of a third way, Catholic but independent, was fast disappearing, and support for the Estates-General or hostility to Spain was widely considered tantamount to sympathy for Protestantism if not adherence. Hence those among the banished who later applied for readmission were obliged to swear an oath binding them both to live according to the Catholic faith and to obey king and Magistrat.[136]

It is also possible that at least David Bigode and Jean de Flandres, former lieutenants of citizen militia companies, were expelled for par-

---

133 AML, Reg. 278, fols. 52–3, 25 May 1579. This list, and many of those cited subsequently, have recently been published in Alain Lottin, "Le bannissement des protestants de Lille après la paix d'Arras (1579–82)," *RN* 66 (1984):487–98. In a few instances my interpretation of orthography, and thus identifications of individuals, does not agree with Lottin's. I also see, in contrast to Lottin, no conclusive evidence that all, or even most, of the exiles were Protestants. Information about occupations comes in part from the lists, in part from BML, MS. 597, and in part from many scattered sources.

134 Francis Lecaë and Colette Thibault, "La répression du protestantisme à Lille à travers les comptes de confiscations de 1580 à 1600" (Mémoire de Maîtrise, Université de Lille III, 1981), as cited in Lottin, "Bannissement," pp. 483–4.

135 *Mémoires anonymes*, 4:125.

136 The terms of the oath – which along with caution money of between 1,200 and 2,000 liv. was to be required even for a short visit to the town – can be found in AML, Reg. 278, fols. 52–3.

ticipating in the protests during the previous summer. De Flandres perhaps suffered an additional handicap, for he was the son of Antoine, one of the merchants accused in 1572 of Orangist and Protestant sympathies and of contributing money to the rebel cause. Another man exiled, François Lecat, probably was related to Antoine Lecat, similarly denounced back in 1572.[137]

An ordinance enacted the same day suggests that the aldermen considered this preemptive strike critical to maintaining (in their words) the city's "peace and tranquility." Denouncing "false" tales that many Lillois were "inventing and spreading" to promote "sedition, grumbling, and excitement" among townspeople, the authorities decreed that no news was to be reported unless the speaker was certain of its truth and able to prove it if challenged. In addition, all meetings were canceled and dancing and street games forbidden.[138] The actions seem to have been effective: No similar enactments are to be encountered thereafter. Generally high levels of employment, wages, and bread distributions, along with declining grain prices (Tables 8.1 and 8.2), must also have undercut militancy. Just to make sure, Rassenghien, released from Ghent after being held for nearly twenty months, returned to Lille in June accompanied by a hundred mounted harquebusiers and a company of infantry to bolster the troops already brought into the city at the end of the previous year.[139]

Although Lille was calm, the troops saw service in the countryside, which remained rife with disorder. On 10 August, Rassenghien informed Philip that besides the many seditious people still to be found throughout Walloon Flanders, and the men favorable to Orange who remained in public office, the province was bedeviled by "freebooters" who roamed through the countryside pillaging churches, attacking Catholics, and terrorizing towns.[140] More dangerous, during the fall French, Scottish, and other troops under the command of the Estates-General opened a campaign aimed at cleaning the Malcontents out of the Lys valley. The Estates-General's troops quickly took the towns of Wervik, Halluin, Comines, and Warneton, as well as the citadel of Bas-

---

[137] See Chapter 7, section II.
[138] AML, Reg. 383, fols. 50–50v, 25 May 1579.
[139] See "Mémoires de Bauduin de Croix," fols. 144–7. For Willerval's letter of resignation, see *RSG*, 2:769.
[140] *CP*, ed. Lefèvre, 1:652–3, no. 1127.

Warneton. Next, they defeated the Walloons in engagements at Bondues, Roncq, Wambrechies, Linselles, and Quesnoy-sur-Deûle – all of
them weaving villages as close as seven kilometers to Lille and active
Protestant centers from the 1560s. Finally, on 20 October the citadel of
Menen, where the Malcontents had initially established themselves, was
taken by surprise, opening the whole of Walloon Flanders to attack.[141]

Apart from two men exiled upon Rassenghien's return,[142] banishments had ceased from May until late October. But the capture of
nearby towns by troops of the Estates-General triggered expulsions once
again, suggesting that the aldermen believed there to be a continuing
danger from Lillois opposed to the break who now might coordinate a
rising with an attack from outside. Only a few days after Menen was
taken, fifty-four townspeople were exiled, four more following them by
the end of the year.[143] One of the schoolmasters whose orthodoxy was
impugned in 1569 was among those banished, as was a bookseller in
whose shop suspect works had been found at that time.[144]

A few prominent individuals were among the group, including perhaps five belonging to magisterial families, along with Helie Desplancques, reported in 1572 to have Orangist and Protestant sympathies, his
son, and the son and namesake of Maître Charles de Calonne, one of
the first fourteen to be banished.[145] This first mass expulsion struck
mainly at modest people, however, apparently mostly of artisan status,
because among the eighteen whose occupations can be established were
seven sayetteurs, three goldsmiths, two shopkeepers, a hotelkeeper, and
an artilleryman, as well as two merchants and two schoolmasters (plus
the wife of one of them). Perhaps on this occasion the Magistrat was
trying to rid the city of the rank and file of suspected Estates-General,
Protestant, or Orangist advocates.

Or perhaps the authorities were overreacting in the course of attempting to smash once and for all any possibility of a challenge to themselves

---

141 See the descriptions in *Mémoires anonymes*, 5:11–14, and the letter from Lalaing to Granvelle,
26 October 1579, *CG*, 7:486. Monnoier, "Journal," fols. [55–5v], lists most of the encounters,
ascribing them to the "Beggars."
142 AML, Reg. 278, fol. 54.
143 AML, Reg. 278, fols. 55v–8; Reg. 383, fol. 78, for one additional person.
144 See Chapter 7, section I.
145 See Chapter 7, section II, for Desplancques. An ambiguous marginal note suggests that he
finally did not have to go into exile, or returned very quickly, and he was not named in the
Magistrat's decree of 12 August 1580 (AML, Reg. 383, fols. 78–9) that recapitulated most of
the expulsions up to that time.

and their policies, no matter what the cost to individuals. According to depositions taken from six sayetteurs and three say combers, for example, Clement du Rot, a master comber living in St. Sauveur parish who was turned out several months later, had always lived peacefully, never saying anything that could be considered either scandalous or seditious. No one had ever considered him anything but a good Catholic and citizen, for he had attended the parish church regularly on Sundays and feast days, had performed his guard duty conscientiously, and had been steadily employed for years by the same man.[146] As far as these neighbors and fellow workers were concerned, du Rot was not the type of man to get involved in conspiracies against the Magistrat. Du Rot may have been marked by his occupation, membership in a specific militia company, or his circle of friends and acquaintances, rather than anything he had said or done. But no matter what the reason for his exile, he was forced to leave. His case may well not have been unique, although the survival of sources about him is.

One chronicler informs us that the militia companies came out in arms and prevented Rassenghien from bringing Walloon soldiers into Lille – ostensibly for guard duty – once they had been driven from Menen and their other strongholds. They justified their action, he noted, on the grounds that the citizens had guarded the city perfectly well while the governor had been imprisoned and would continue to do so.[147] This report does suggest abiding enmity toward the Malcontents. But whether or not the incident actually occurred – the story sounds suspiciously like a garbled account of what had happened a year before, and it has left no trace in municipal records – mercenary troops had already been in Lille for several months. Furthermore, as time went on the Magistrat no longer showed any hesitation in publicly supporting the Malcontents. Townspeople were ordered to send them foodstuffs, while the aldermen dispatched military supplies purchased with municipal funds.[148] It was at this time, too, that the city fathers fired the long-time municipal pensionary Antoine Muyssart, who had also been a delegate to the Estates-General. In a display of symmetrical symbolism, he was

---

146 *ADN*, Tab. 3308, fols. 121–3v, 26 September 1580, for the testimony; AML, Reg. 278, fol. 59v, for the expulsion.

147 *Mémoires anonymes*, 5:19.

148 AML, Reg. 383, fol. 61v, 13 December 1579; Schoonheere, *Histoire de vieux Comines*, pp. 161–2.

replaced by Claude Miroul, who had represented Lille at the negotiations leading up to the Treaty of Arras.[149]

Over the next year the dialectic of perceived external threat and banishment persisted, albeit on a reduced scale. When on New Year's Day 1580 a raiding party from Menen attacked Bondues and Marcq, concluding by burning down buildings in Lille's suburbs (including five or six windmills near the town walls), two men were driven out of the city.[150] An apparently frustrated assault on the city mounted from Flanders in April 1580, which resulted in the destruction of the village of Croix north of Lille, caused three more Lillois to be expelled immediately, and another twenty-two were sent away in May.[151] From June through August, an additional five men were exiled in the aftermath of raids on neighborhoods just outside Lille.[152] During the next nine months, military activity died down, and so did banishments: Only three were recorded between September 1580 and May 1581.[153]

Although apparently not initiated because of central government pressure, the policy of expulsions pursued by the magistrates of Lille, as well as their counterparts in Douai, Arras, Valenciennes, St. Omer, and elsewhere, won praise from Parma and Philip II. Both expressed the hope that it would forestall rebellions of the kind that had brought insurgents to power in other areas.[154] The authorities could also be pleased by the extent to which the reconciled provinces loosened their pursestrings. Walloon Flanders, for instance, voted an aide of 80,000 livres in September 1580, and another 30,000 livres in December.[155] Not that the province's wealth was readily forthcoming on every occasion. In July and August Parma found it very difficult to raise a loan of 50,000 livres to fight French troops – perhaps because the conflict was in Brabant – despite the fact that 200,000 livres had been contributed by

---

149 BML., MS. 597, at 1579; *Traicté de réconciliation*, unpaginated. Miroul came from a family that subsequently placed several men on the Magistrat.
150 "Mémoires de Bauduin de Croix," fol. 167; *Mémoires anonymes*, 5:82; Monnoier, "Journal," fol. [55v]; AML, Reg. 278, fol. 58, 15 January 1580.
151 *Mémoires anonymes*, 5:206; Monnoier, "Journal," fol. [55v]; AML, Reg. 278, fols. 59v–60v, 18, 21, and 22 April, 2, 6, and 9 May 1580.
152 AML, Reg. 278, fols. 61v (28 June), 62v (26 and 28 July), 63; Monnoier, "Journal," fol. [55v].
153 AML, Reg. 278, fols. 65 (24 November 1580), 66v (31 January 1581), 68 (14 March 1581).
154 See Parma's report to Philip on the expulsion of suspects, *CP*, ed. Lefèvre, 2:79, no. 154, 7 October 1580; the king's approving reply, ibid., p. 117, no. 226, 13 January 1581; and Parma's note that he would convey the royal satisfaction: ibid., p. 139, no. 275, 13 March 1581.
155 AML, Reg. 15,885, fols. 212v–17.

Artois, Hainaut, and Valenciennes.[156] But when local security was at stake, the Estates of Lille, Douai, and Orchies were much more obliging. On 25 August, while applauding the return of Margaret of Parma to the governor-generalship (the removal of Alexander Farnese from this post belatedly fulfilled one of Lille's demands at Arras), they commended Philip's decision to retain Parma as military commander. This step, the provincial assembly wrote, would enable the country to be rid once and for all of "the false beliefs that the sectaries and heretics have imprinted on the minds of the poor people." Soon thereafter, the delegates offered 40,000 florins (later raised to 50,000 florins and provisions) if Parma would recapture Menen and end its garrison's harassment of the countryside.[157]

Early in May 1581 emerged what turned out to be the final serious threat of attack on Lille, followed by a wave of expulsions that also was the last of significance. On 3 May came a rumor that an army from Flanders, Brabant, and especially Tournai (which had remained within the Estates-General and had dispatched numerous raiding parties into the castellany of Lille)[158] intended to descend upon Lille. In response, the Magistrat placed the citizen militia on armed alert the entire night, though in the event nothing happened. The aldermen were convinced, however, that the tale was true and that the governor of Tournai was plotting an assault in conjunction with some bourgeois of Lille. Two days later its suspicions were confirmed when a young woman from Tournai reported to her brother, a canon at St. Pierre, that preparations were indeed being made. Forewarned, the Magistrat rounded up over fifty townspeople suspected of complicity in the planned rising or of Protestantism and instituted day and night militia patrols. Then, apparently on a tip from the apaiseur Wallerand de Bailloeulx (or de Bapalmes), the aldermen arrested one of the leading conspirators, who, under threat of torture, revealed the plans and the names of his fellows. With the collaborators within the city thus neutralized and the guard

---

156 See letters of Parma to Philip, *CP*, ed. Lefèvre, 2:48, 68, nos. 91, 133, 3 July and 30 August 1580.
157 Walloon Flanders to Parma, ibid., pp. 65–6, no. 129; Parma to Philip, ibid., pp. 68, 80, nos. 133, 155, 30 August and 7 October 1580.
158 On 1 March 1580, Lille had ordered all Tournaisiens to leave the city at once (AML, Reg. 383, fol. 70) and on 28 July 1580 had expelled at least one citizen of that town; AML, Reg. 278, fol. 62v. Attacks on Lille's suburbs in August 1580 had allegedly been mounted from Tournai; Monnoier, "Journal," fol. [55v].

reinforced, an attack just before dawn on 10 May was doomed to fail. Not a signal from within but the massed and armed citizenry greeted the troops from Tournai when they gathered in the village of Lezennes, within sight of Lille. After a desultory attack, they rode off.[159]

Charged with treason, the four chief plotters were tried by a panel consisting of several aldermen and two special commissioners sent by Parma. The tribunal's composition suggests that the prince skillfully used the occasion to appeal to magisterial ambitions and solidify loyalties, because treason was a crime explicitly reserved to the sovereign's courts. After conviction, the two who were citizens were beheaded, the other two hung. All four corpses were drawn and quartered; then the parts were displayed throughout the town as a warning to other potential rebels. In strict accordance with Lille's privileges (recently codified in the Treaty of Arras), the conspirators' property located in the city and castellany was not confiscated.

Most prominent of the four was Jean Drumez, merchant and citizen of Lille, councillor in the Magistrat in 1561 and 1563, probably lieutenant in the same militia company as David Bigode in 1578, and married to Marguerite de Fourmestraux of the renowned merchant and at least partly Protestant family.[160] Because he told his interrogators that he had been promised 6,000 florins "or other large reward" for informing the attackers about the state of Lille's guard arrangements, Drumez may have joined for financial reasons. Another conspirator was Michel le Febvre, a dyer, citizen, and (since at least 1578) standardbearer of a militia company that was to be on duty at the time of the attack. His task was to inform the assailants of the correct password so they could enter the city by surprise.

A drap weaver originally from the village of Bondues but currently resident in Lille, Adrien le Plat had already been jailed on suspicion of being in contact with the forces of the Estates-General and of holding illegal (perhaps Protestant) meetings in his house. Although released in January 1580 after pledging to inform the authorities of anything he

---

159 "Mémoires de Bauduin de Croix," fols. 178–90. At the time, de Croix was rewart and thus commander in chief of the militia, so he played a central role in the events.

160 Jean de Croix called Drumez (only a very distant relation to Bauduin) was a lieutenant along with Bigode of the company captained by Michel Gommer in 1578 (AML, Reg. 15,924, fol. 82); for his Magistrat service see BML, MS. 597. For the appearances of two merchants named Jean Drumez in Antwerp between 1545 and 1584, see Coornaert, *Français à Anvers*, 1:359.

heard regarding the security of Lille, he was alleged to have immediately
plunged back into the conspiracy, passing on information about the
depth of moats to the attackers from Tournai. The final individual
executed was Beltremieu Mullier, a peasant from Baisieux, a village
between Lille and Tournai where Protestant meetings had been held at
least in 1566. Previously banished from the castellany for taking part in
that year's iconoclasm, he appears to have served as a message carrier.[161]

Ten other people were released from prison after posting bonds of at
least 300 florins and signing pledges binding them to do nothing
harmful to the security of Lille and to report any information about plots
against the city that they might hear. The group included Bauduin
Herreng, wine merchant, alderman and councillor between 1562 and
1568, and (at least in 1578) standardbearer in Jacques (le) Prevost's
militia company; Jacques Masurel, cloth merchant and apaiseur in 1577;
and Jean Morel, goldsmith and apaiseur in 1560.[162] Many more people
were forced to leave the city. The Magistrat summarily expelled 65
individuals in June, 4 in July, 1 in August, and 141 in September, for a
four-month total of 211 (177 men, 28 women, and 6 children).[163] It
appears that the authorities decided to oust anyone who conceivably
might have been involved in the past or might try anything in the future.
Perhaps, too, it was thought advisable to offset any possible repercussions of the Estates-General's Act of Abjuration of 26 July 1581, by
which Philip's authority was solemnly repudiated.

A handful of those exiled can probably be identified as having served
in the Magistrat at some time in the past, though only for short periods.
One man appears to have been an alderman in 1572, councillor in 1574,
and huit-homme in 1576; two other apaiseurs in 1565 and 1567 and

[161] The convictions are recorded in AML, Reg. 15,886, fols. 80–2 (7, 9, 13, and 28 June 1581). So
important was the privilege of nonconfiscation (as we have seen) that in May 1590 the Magistrat checked with the heirs of Drumez, le Febvre, and le Plat to make sure that they had
received their inheritances. No problems were reported; see ibid., fols. 82v–4. For Parma's
thanks to the Magistrat for foiling the plot, see ibid., fols. 82–2v. Records from the investigation
of the plot (ADN, Reg. B 2672, fol. 154) reveal that Charles de Boisot, who had been
spokesman for the opponents of the Zealots in 1577, had subsequently been promoted (as a
reward?) from the Gouvernance to the royal Privy Council, where he was currently councillor
and *maître aux requêtes ordinaire* as well as special deputy to Lille on this occasion.
[162] AML, Reg. 278, fols. 69v–70, 72v, 16 June and 1 July 1581. See further AML, Reg. 15,924,
fols. 82–2v; BML, MS. 597; Coornaert, *Français à Anvers*, 1:360. Betremieu Smerpont, also
released on 16 June, probably belonged to the wealthy de Smerpont clan, merchants and
(before 1560) members of the inner circle of the Magistrat, and he was probably related to
Jean, among the first to be banished in May 1579.
[163] AML, Reg. 278, fols. 70v–3v, 75–8v.

from 1572 through 1574; a fourth a huit-homme in 1577. More significant, at least four men who had served as militia officers in 1578 (and
perhaps more recently) were forced to leave the city. Jacques (le) Prevost, cloth merchant and the three-time member of the Loi just mentioned, had captained the company of which Bauduin Herreng had been
standardbearer. One of his lieutenants, Adrien Lallier, was expelled on
the same day as he (28 June). So was Michel de Fourmestraux, ensign
under Michel Gommer; with his departure, none of the subofficers of
that ill-starred company was left in Lille. Nicolas Bernard, exiled in
September with his wife, had been lieutenant under Mathias de le
Flye.[164]

At least nineteen married couples were banished, two of them with
children, and as many as a half a dozen people who had earlier witnessed
the expulsion of a husband, parent, child, or other relative. Among that
minority whose occupations were noted were eighteen light-cloth
weavers, eight combers, six merchants, three each of soldiers, mes-
sengers, servants, and tanners, two innkeepers, and nine other craftsmen and shopkeepers. With the exception of the soldiers and mes-
sengers – who occupied strategic roles for a rising – the social
composition of this small sample seems representative of the city as a
whole. Often artisans practicing the same trade or living in the same
street or courtyard are named together in the expulsion orders, suggesting the existence of nodules of suspicious talk or activity that caught the
authorities' attention (though perhaps reflecting nothing more than administrative convention or convenience).

Interestingly, most of the prominent people were exiled early, typically
in June. They may be assumed to have had some connection with or
leadership potential for the miscarried May foray, even if only in the
aldermen's minds. The September expatriates (about whose occupations we are much better informed) may thus have consisted not so
much of demonstrably dangerous people but of those, predominantly
artisans, whose political or religious loyalty was in doubt yet were only
considered menacing enough to expel in the presence of aggravating
circumstances. The sharp downturn in light-cloth output and rising
grain prices signaled by the last lines of Tables 8.1 and 8.2 – the effects

---

[164] In addition, Jean Beudart, banished on 28 June, may have been standard bearer in 1578 under
Henri de Preudhomme, seigneur of la Ghennerie. For the relevant data, see AML, Reg.
15,924, fols. 82–2v; BML, MS. 597.

of which were showing up by late summer but were unmatched by welfare increases until at least October – could well have constituted such circumstances.[165]

Parma praised the city's policies, telling the aldermen of Arras that "Lille's example . . . shows you sufficiently enough how you have to be alert and beware of deals, plots and betrayals by the sectaries and the ill-disposed," who dissimulate and await a fortuitous time to strike.[166] Philip, too, supported stern measures against all suspects, in the hope that anyone contemplating subversive activity would be frightened into submission.[167]

To be sure, raids around Lille did not cease until Parma had conquered Flanders and Tournai, and even then guerrilla sorties with attendant alarms and the resulting sense of insecurity continued sporadically until nearly the end of the century.[168] But once Lille's ruling class had thrown in its lot with reimposed Spanish rule, it did not hesitate to resort to expulsions to back up its decision. Three more people were exiled before the end of 1581, nineteen others in 1582. But then, as Parma's victories cleared the Estates-General's forces out of most of the southern Netherlands, only a handful: five in 1583, two the following year, and three in 1585.[169] The city also provided monetary aid, weapons, and provisions to Parma when he successfully besieged Tournai in the autumn of 1581.[170]

In December of that year, Parma, fresh from his victory, visited Lille and reported being greeted with many signs of affection and joy.[171] On 8 February 1582, the reconciled areas agreed to request the return of

---

[165] For monthly welfare outlays, see AASL, Reg. J611–13.

[166] Parma to Arras aldermen, 19 May 1581, in *Cartulaire de la commune d'Arras*, p. 416, no. cccxxxiii.

[167] See Philip to Parma, 27 September 1581, *CP*, ed. Lefèvre, 2:211, p. 412.

[168] For a brief list of the alarms during the last two decades of the century, see Saint-Léger, *Lille sous les dominations autrichienne et espagnole*, p. 115. For reports by Parma that the area around Lille remained a potential trouble spot, see *CP*, ed. Lefèvre, 2:289, 330–1, nos. 583, 671–2, (29 April and 16 September 1582). Granvelle's correspondent Morillon also reported that the rural districts were unsafe; see *CG*, 9:38, 272, 26 January and 9 August 1582. The monks of St. Christophe at Phalempin south of Lille, who to avoid marauding bands spent much of the 1570s and early 1580s in their refuge in the city, only returned to their abbey for good at the end of 1584; Théodore Leuridan, *Notice historique sur l'abbaye de Saint-Christophe de Phalempin* (Roubaix, 1905), pp. 78–9.

[169] AML, Reg. 278, fols. 78v, 80–80v, 81v–2v, 83, 84, 85, 89, 91, 92, 93, 101, 102v, 112; Reg. 383, fols. 100–1v (incomplete summary list).

[170] AML, Reg. 15,885, fols. 225–6, 229; Reg. 15,886, fols. 46v–7 (letter of thanks from Philip II).

[171] Letter to Philip, 16 December 1581, *CP*, ed. Lefèvre, 2:231, no. 461.

foreign troops for defense and reconquest. Even though this step represented an abrogation of the Treaty of Arras, these provinces had come to accept Parma's argument that it was the only way to deliver them from a drawn-out war and the heretic threat.[172] Early in August 1582, the first detachments of Spanish infantry marched into Lille with drums rolling and banners flying.[173] At Lille, the revolt of the Netherlands was over.

---

[172] See letters from Farnese and Estates of Lille, Douai, and Orchies, 8 February and 2 March 1582, ibid., pp. 258–9, 268, nos. 520, 539 (on the latter occasion the Estates of Walloon Flanders also offered an aide of 50,000 fl.).

[173] Parma to Philip, 15 August 1582, ibid., p. 326, no. 660.

Conclusion

~~~~~~

Stability in revolution

> The right of revolution is the obverse of the duty of obedience;
> the explanation of revolution the obverse of the explanation of
> stability.[1]

Repeated mass violence directed against the institutions and personnel
of the established church, armed insurrection designed to topple the
existing government, experiments with new political and religious forms
– all this and much more suggests that the Dutch Revolt lends itself well
to analysis informed by the scholarship on collective action. To be sure,
this literature was developed to explain change by investigation of the
behavior of determinate groups in pursuit of common goals. But for the
reasons alluded to in Freeman's observation just quoted, it can also help
the student of stability account for the weakness or absence of such
behavior. What follows draws upon this body of concepts, first to identify
the critical factors inhibiting collective action in Lille, and then to specify the conditions that fostered it in other cities.[2]

Before examining the various urban histories, it will be useful to
define and briefly outline the elements in collective action analysis relevant to this study. *Common interests* are the basis on which groups form to
take action. They may be oriented either toward gaining new benefits or
toward defending long-accepted rights and privileges. *Organization* is
the process of increasing the common identity – the consciousness –

---

[1] Michael Freeman, "Review Article: Theories of Revolution," *British Journal of Political Science 2*
(1972):339.
[2] I have found most helpful Tilly, *From Mobilization to Revolution*, and Rod Aya, "Theories of
Revolution Reconsidered: Contrasting Models of Collective Violence," *Theory and Society 8*
(1979):1–38.

and unifying structure among members of a group so it can act on its interests. Through *mobilization,* a group comes to control resources that will enable it to implement its members' common interests. *Opportunities* or *threats* are perceptions by groups that encourage or impel them to act, whereas *facilitation* and *repression,* measures taken by those in power, contribute to or prevent groups from acting.

Social relations arising from economic pursuits often create common interests, consciousness, and structures. But scholars of collective action argue that interest groups also form on the basis of religion, politics, residence – anything, in short, that generates both a shared situation perceived as such by its protagonists and a shared understanding of rights and responsibilities that mandate action. Thus collective action is frequently – and most successfully – undertaken not by single groups but by coalitions. In these alliances, the links among groups powerfully affect the ways in which common interests are construed and articulated, the forms of organization devised, the possibilities for mobilizing, and the environment in which any undertaking occurs.

Fissures within the existing government are crucial for the development of all components of collective action. Splits of this sort can, in particular, lead to alliances between contenders and a faction of the government; they can make the authorities unwilling or unable to use sufficient force to crush challenges; or they can be accompanied by the breakdown of normal forms of legitimation. Any manner of specific issue can provoke such breaches. But they are often grounded in social and economic change, and this at the same time tends to weaken the controls that help preserve the existing order in normal times. Finally, collective action is not, according to most scholars, predicated upon the existence of conscious revolutionary groups pursuing new or expanded interests. On the contrary, an intent to implement forward-looking radical change is rarely present at, nor is it necessary for, the outbreak of revolt. Much more common are conservative, reactive, defensive movements. Typically, they aim to protect existing interests against changes caused or condoned by the political authorities.

I

The policing measures taken by successive Magistrats and governors in response to immediate crises have understandably loomed large in Part

Two, where the atypicality and weakness of viable collective action has been a dominant theme of the analysis. These steps were successful in stabilizing Lille during the revolt, however, only because of arrangements – examined in Part One – that had been instituted over the previous decades and elaborated as needed thereafter. Begun piecemeal in response to currently pressing needs and demands, over time these arrangements came to constitute the crucial elements of a social and political order that served to dampen rather than promote disruption and rebellion. They did not, of course, predetermine the city's behavior, but they endowed Lille with a structural tendency to stability. Not only was there little pressure for religious or political change, but movements that did emerge lacked effective means for realizing their objectives. In particular, artisans and Protestants, who mounted significant challenges in other cities, were denied the resources needed to play a similar role in Lille.

Small commodity production and the municipal welfare system were of central importance to Lille's stability. Taken together, they channeled the growth of the light-textile industry to the advantage of a large group of petty masters with a firm stake in the developing social and economic structure. They also curbed the potentially destabilizing emergence of either a polarized class structure or intractable material grievances. Because, moreover, the municipal ruling class dominated corporate and charitable institutions and repeatedly intervened in the urban social economy, artisan interests were shaped by and mediated through the political elite. Hence ideas and practices that questioned the existing order not only lacked a viable social base but faced the hostility of both the great majority of artisans and the ruling group. Innovation could therefore be stigmatized as economically unjustified, socially disruptive, and morally indefensible.

At the same time that the structures of Lille's economy hindered the growth of an oppositional identity among urban masters, they also divided key groups of artisans in the city from their counterparts in the countryside. The social and economic experiences of textile artisans in Lille differed sharply from those of their counterparts in villages. Whereas urban weavers operated within the small commodity system, rural producers were much more likely to be dependent wage earners, typically employed in some sort of putting-out arrangement. In addition, a shared antagonism toward the development of rural textiles bound together ruling class and artisans in the city. The large body of urban weavers in particular objected to the emergence of competition in the countryside. After all, they benefited from the existing asymmetrical regional division of labor that assigned less remunerative preparatory work to rural areas, while reserving more lucrative jobs to the city. Not surprisingly, then, the urban monopolies that underlay this unequal distribution of tasks joined the interests of Magistrat and craftsman.

Besides foreclosing the emergence of autonomous artisan consciousness, organization, and mobilization within Lille and on a regional basis, small commodity production and the Common Fund also restricted the urban audience for Protestantism. They perpetuated viable corporate and civic institutions and ideology on the one hand, and they minimized change and hardship on the other. To be sure, an organized Reformed community did arise in sixteenth-century Lille, and local threats combined with opportunities created by national and regional incidents to stimulate some mobilization. But Lille's Protestants were unable to profit even when a broad political, religious, social, and economic crisis enveloped the Netherlands. Once their merchant element withdrew or fell silent, the Reformed were cut off from any access to urban political resources that might have eased the repression visited upon them.

Finally, Lille's social and economic structures discouraged rural and urban dissenters from forging strong common interests and viable coalitions. As it evolved, of course, the Protestant movement emphasized cooperation among fellow believers no matter where their place of residence. What is more, Reformed religion took root most firmly in the rural cloth communities of northern Walloon Flanders. Yet the continuing development of small commodity relations of production and welfare services meant that the life experiences of most Lillois remained consonant with the beliefs and practices of the traditional faith. So during the summer of 1566, when Reformers were pulling down the symbols of the old church and raising the new throughout Walloon Flanders, "the common people" (*la commune*) of Lille were "very agitated" about religion, the Magistrat reported.[3] But their activities were designed to stop heretics, not assist them.

---

[3] Response to Tournai's Protestants, printed in Verheyden, "Chronique de Gaiffier," pp. 81–2.

Over the long term, sustained economic growth provided a favorable environment for stability. As we have seen, however, it was the magistrates who enacted the arrangements that hobbled the emergence and mobilization of contending groups and then uniformly and effectively crushed any that managed to appear. There were a number of reasons why Lille's ruling class was able to intervene decisively over many tumultuous decades and indeed to redouble its efforts as the economic cycle became more erratic, inflation more pressing, and Protestant agitation more extensive after midcentury. To begin with, the city's political and economic elites overlapped considerably, the result of homogeneous social composition enhanced by intermarriage and dense networks of business relationships. The cohesion of the magistracy was further strengthened by rotation in office and the constitution of an informal inner circle, both of which encouraged unity founded on a community of interests as well as long acquaintanceship. In addition, the formation of factions that might have entered alliances with challengers from outside the government was discouraged by the absence of an entrenched patriciate and the consequent newness of the ruling class. Like the merchant class that provided the bulk of its members, Lille's governing group remained open to those who acquired the proper social and economic credentials. At the same time, the frustration of artisan entrepreneurial efforts removed the possibility that a wealthy and strategic group might emerge to contest not merely specific policies but the entire distribution of political power that bred them.

Conversely, the lack of corporate participation in city government meant that artisans had no political space of their own in which they might have formulated and enunciated demands distinct from, and perhaps in conflict with, those of the governing elite. Thus when direct challenges to the Magistrat were voiced in the late 1570s, they evoked no response within this solidary ruling class or for that matter among any other organized group of townspeople, save, on one occasion, some militia officers. In this instance, moreover, the fact that the municipal government rather than guilds or some other body controlled the civic companies allowed the authorities to nip the protest in the bud and regain the initiative. So lacking any politically significant resources – such as divisions among the authorities, allies for a coalition, or armed force – the contenders were quickly isolated and defeated. Even the

Estates-General, to whom the insurgents appealed for aid, quickly recognized that the balance of power overwhelmingly favored the established authorities.

The municipal government could also act effectively because its members remained closely attuned to urban society. On the one hand, very few of the merchants who dominated the Magistrat abandoned trade. On the other, aldermen and councillors – many of them drawn from the inner circle of the ruling class – sat on the bodies administering the textile crafts and the Bourse commune, where they learned at first hand about important issues. Probably it was this experience that made a merchant-controlled municipal government willing not merely to countenance but to construct and enforce small commodity production, sacrificing probable economic gain for social and political purposes. In turn, successful measures legitimated the Magistrat's rule while extending its control.

The same features that promoted the Loi's cohesion and secured its local hegemony likewise permitted it to retain a substantial degree of autonomy from successive central governments. The Magistrat was not a policy innovator and indeed usually sought to work with the regime in power, particularly in order to secure or extend economic and jurisdictional benefits. At the same time, however, it is clear that Lille's magistrates were consistently and firmly resolved to defend municipal privileges, the established faith, and their own authority, and would resist central-state measures that threatened any of these. These commitments explain not only their stubborn resistance to confiscation and rejection of the Tenth and Twentieth Pennies, but also their eventual break with the Estates-General.

On occasion, of course, the Magistrat did face challenges, whether from would-be entrepreneurs, Protestants, or Zealots. But in consequence of arrangements implemented largely by the ruling class, contenders never managed to assemble the resources needed to mobilize successfully and capitalize on dissidence. Only intervention from the outside promised any real breakthrough for the proponents of collective action for change in sixteenth-century Lille. Yet in the absence of any viable popular movement within the city, such attempts were doomed to rapid failure. In fact, as the popular vigilantism of summer 1566 intimated, and the crowds that greeted insurgent initiatives in 1578 strikingly demonstrated, it was the ruling class, not a rebellion, that could summon citizens into the streets and squares of Lille to enforce its program.

II

Lille's magistrates were scarcely the only ones who actively sought the stability that would preserve their rule and what they construed as their city's best interests. But to judge by the available studies – which to be sure have focused on towns where some sort of significant collective action did occur – the environment accounting for Lille's situation was rarely matched. The scholarly literature reveals the existence of two groups of towns, which may be called revolutionary centers and coup cities. Each exhibited a different pattern of interaction among material conditions, social and economic structure, religious ferment, political institutions, and magisterial conduct, and each was subject to distinct forms of mobilization for collective action.

Revolutionary centers lay mainly in the southern provinces of the Netherlands. Here broadly based, prolonged collective action effected political and/or religious change for a significant period of time, though never permanently. Among these centers were to be found the major light-cloth towns – apart from Lille. But it was the great cities of Brabant, notably Antwerp and Brussels, as well as Ghent in Flanders, that saw the most sustained and far-reaching revolutionary developments.[4]

With the partial exception of Ghent, these towns underwent rapid economic growth across the early sixteenth century. In all of them, too, the long period of expansion terminated soon after midcentury in a decade or more of stagnation ending in harsh crises. But if their economic and material histories resembled Lille's in these respects, the absence of viable protective structures or adequate ameliorative and regulative institutions crucially distinguished them. Ghent was further

---

[4] The following draws on Hocquet, *Tournai et le Tournaisis au XVIe siècle;* Paul Rolland, *Histoire de Tournai* (Tournai and Paris, 1957); *Histoire de Valenciennes,* ed. Henri Platelle (Lille, 1982); Clark, "An Urban Study during the Revolt of the Netherlands"; Van der Wee, *Rise of the Antwerp Market;* idem, "The Economy as a Factor in the Start of the Revolt"; *Antwerpen in de XVIde eeuw;* Hugo Soly, "Nijverheid en kapitalisme te Antwerpen in de 16de eeuw," in *Album Charles Verlinden* (Ghent, 1975); idem, "Economische vernieuwing en sociale weerstand. De betekenis en aspiraties der Antwerpse middenklasse in de 16de eeuw," *Tijdschrift voor Geschiedenis* 83 (1970):520– 35; idem, *Urbanisme en Kapitalisme te Antwerpen in de 16de eeuw* (Brussels, 1977); *Histoire de Bruxelles,* ed. Mina Martens (Toulouse, 1979); Alexandre Henne and Alphonse Wauters, *Histoire de Bruxelles,* 3 vols. (Brussels, 1845); Hans Van Werveke, *Gand, esquisse d'histoire sociale* (Brussels, 1946); Victor Fris, *Histoire de Gand,* 2nd ed. (Brussels, 1930).

set apart by a combination of commercial growth – principally in grain and linens – and industrial decline, strikingly evident in woolen drapery. But in the social results of economic development, Ghent did resemble the other revolutionary centers. A substantial middling artisanry suddenly faced the end of its accustomed prosperity in the 1560s, while impoverished wage earners became increasingly desperate. To be sure, even in new and less regulated crafts most enterprises were small, and even in Antwerp there is some evidence of support for masters' demands for safeguards against innovators.

Nevertheless, it was clear that the traditional social and economic order was under attack. Particularly disturbing to those threatened by such developments, the magistracies typically failed to act or even took the capitalists' side. Complaints against entrepreneurs and authorities alike began to stir artisans – already in 1554, riots in Antwerp revealed deep dissatisfaction – and led them to countenance joint action with the wage earners they normally despised.[5]

These processes of change and the grievances to which they gave rise had the added result of making artisans and wage earners more receptive to Protestantism, especially when religious dissenters offered charity that municipalities were unable or unwilling to extend. The groupings thus formed also found indispensable coalition partners among political contenders. The magistracies that held sway over these cities were closed oligarchies consisting largely of rentiers, nobles, and professionals – a social composition that may explain their unimaginative responses to artisan concerns. What is more, the ruling strata were widely, if not always accurately, perceived as doing the bidding of the central government to the detriment of municipal privileges and finances.

Among those challenging the city governments were groups excluded from decision making yet at the same time enjoying access to significant institutional and coercive resources that fostered mobilization while helping parry repression. In Brussels, for instance, both the patrician *lignages* and the guild and citizen elite, grouped into *nations*, had had

---

[5] Cf. the situation in the great West Flanders say-cloth center of Hondschoote. After coming to dominate local government, from about 1540 merchant entrepreneurs were allowed both to ignore previously enforced limits on loom ownership and to move in the direction of vertical concentration by taking over several stages of production. All this helped generate animosity that contributed to broad participation in iconoclastic riots. See Emile Coornaert, *Un centre industriel d'autrefois. La draperie-sayetterie d'Hondschoote (XIVe–XVIIIe siècles)* (Rennes, 1930).

their authority curbed by princely officials while nonetheless remaining part of municipal government. The guilds at Antwerp, which had become increasingly conscious of their rising economic importance, were strongly represented on the supervisory Broad and Monday Councils. The *Conseil particulier* of Valenciennes, established in 1497 in response to merchant complaints about the corruption of the Magistrat, conducted biweekly reviews of the aldermen's activities, and it controlled the civic militia. Named in principle by the sovereign, in practice the members of the council were coopted and served repeatedly, endowing the body with a great deal of unity and solidarity. At Tournai, the *bannières* (organizations that included every guild as well as all other citizens), and at Ghent the "members" (three bodies dominated by guilds, in particular the drap weavers) had within recent memory lost power to paid oligarchies of the rich, appointed and closely supervised by the central government. The corporate groups continued, however, to have charge of the militia.

Under these conditions, central-government policies – preeminently though not exclusively the persecution of Protestants – not only failed utterly but laid bare fissures within the local political order that were quickly exploited by insurgents. Common interests – largely defensive though also, in the case of religious reformers, innovative in nature – thus engendered organized groups that allied into mobilized coalitions. Armed with strategic ideological, social, and material resources, these alliances responded forcefully to threats and took full advantage of the distinctive opportunities arising in each city. At the same time, however, significant differences in constituency, goals, and resources existed among the various partners in these coalitions. Over time, these divergences generated a process of radicalization, as each group attempted to dominate the new regime. But they ended in internecine strife, mutual exhaustion, and acceptance of Spanish rule, whether achieved by military defeat or by negotiation.

In coup cities, collective action to effect religious and/or political change occurred but was less broadly based and intense than in the revolutionary centers. Thus success came only with aid from outside. Coups occurred principally during the second phase of revolt, when Beggar assaults with the assistance of accomplices within took over towns, most durably in Holland and Zeeland. But they also took place

315

during the period of Estates-General rule, when exiled Protestants and partisans of William of Orange patronized or provoked risings that they then helped to carry through.[6]

Most cities that underwent coups were experiencing economic decline, considerably sharpened in the period just preceding the risings, and this process caused bitter social tensions. Admittedly, in some towns attempts had been made to establish new industries (Ypres, for example, tried says and other light cloth), but most of these efforts had miscarried. At Bruges, a recently created fustian industry initially met with success, but after midcentury its output was characterized by substantial oscillations superimposed on a stagnant or even downward trend. In order to stimulate economic growth, moreover, urban authorities usually dismantled existing regulations that protected small producers or, as at Douai, vacillated so much that in the end they managed to satisfy neither masters nor entrepreneurs. Worse, none of the towns had adequate welfare systems to cope with widespread downward mobility and impoverishment. Clerical or corporate opposition derailed projects similar to Lille's Common Fund in several cities; continued economic decay bankrupted reforms that had been implemented elsewhere. The resulting misery provided Orangists and Protestants with a constituency and an issue that they were not slow to exploit.

Exclusive, ingrown oligarchies, city magistracies were also perceived as all too accommodating to central government pressures – notably, in Holland and Zeeland at least, in regard to Alba's taxes – even though

---

[6] The following discussion is based on J. C. Boogman, "De overgang van Gouda, Dordrecht, Leiden en Delft in de zomer van het jaar 1572," *Tijdschrift voor Geschiedenis* 57 (1942):81–112; T. S. Jansma, "De betekenis van Dordrecht en Rotterdam omstreeks het midden der zestiende eeuw," *De Economist* 92 (1943):212–50; N. W. Posthumus, *Geschiedenis van de Leidsche Lakenindustrie*, 2 vols. in 3 parts (The Hague, 1908–39); P. J. Blok, *Geschiedenis eener Hollandsche Stad*, 4 vols. (The Hague, 1910–18) [on Leiden]; C. C. Hibben, *Gouda in Revolt. Particularism and Pacifism in the Revolt of the Netherlands 1572–1588* (Utrecht, 1983); DuPlessis, "Urban Stability in the Netherlands Revolution" [on Douai]; J. A. Van Houtte, *Bruges. Essai d'histoire urbaine* (Brussels, 1967); idem, *De geschiedenis van Brugge* (Tielt, 1982); J. Vermaut, "Structural Transformation in a Textile Centre: Bruges from the Sixteenth to the Nineteenth Century," in *The Rise and Decline of Urban Industries in Italy and in the Low Countries (Late Middle Ages – Early Modern Times)*, ed. Herman Van der Wee (Leuven, 1988), pp. 187–205; J. De Mey, "De 'mislukte' anapassingen van de nieuwe draperie, de saainijverheid en de lichte draperie te Ieper," *Tijdschrift voor geschiedenis* 63 (1950):222–35; Raymond Van Uytven, *Stadsfinanciën en Stadsekonomie te Leuven van de XIIe tot het einde der XVIe eeuw* (Brussels, 1961); Offermans, *Arbeid en Levensstandaard;* Rudolf Kolman, *De Reductie van Nijmegen (1591), voor- en naspel* (Groningen, 1952); Pirenne, *'s-Hertogenbosch;* Decavele, *Dageraad van de Reformatie.* Cf. A. J. M. Beenakker, *Breda in de eerste storm van de opstand. Van Ketterij tot beeldenstorm 1545–1569* (Tilburg, 1971).

they tended to drag their feet on the issue of persecuting heretics. Corporations had no institutional presence in Holland and Zeeland municipalities, although elsewhere they had some voice in town affairs. But no matter what the reigning institutional arrangements, militias were generally independent of the town government, even when not under guild control, and they drew their membership largely from artisans. Additionally, the civic companies began to take a keener interest in their traditional role as guarantors of urban privileges now that magistracies were perceived to be laggard in this regard.

In coup towns, then, opposition groups had urgent dissatisfactions, and resources existed that would facilitate collective action. But both individually and even in coalition the contenders were too small in number and too divided in interests to win on their own. Because many artisans in these towns produced for local and regional markets, social and economic change affected or threatened only a minority. Even in the luxury drapery trades in the Flemish cities, in fact, corporations had retained most of their traditional religious and social attributes as well as protective rules, so new ideas and practices had made few inroads among the artisans.

Hence outside aid was essential for challengers to prevail. It might come from Beggars and exiles, as in Holland and Zeeland, from Ghent Calvinists and revolutionaries, as in Flanders, or from the troops of the Estates-General, as in Brabant. Hence, too, radical political experiments did not follow coups. Admittedly, many individual magistrates were purged on grounds of religion or hostility to Orangism, but neither the social composition nor the structure of the municipal regimes was altered. It was the weaknesses of the city governments, and their reliance on external support, that made successful coups possible; it was the weaknesses of contenders, and their reliance on external force, that limited the coups' effects. Even in the northern towns, where a new state and religious order were introduced, the dominant groups perpetuated their hegemony by exchanging Habsburg for Orangist tutelage.

Amsterdam formed something of an exception to other coup centers in that it had experienced rapid economic growth during the first two-thirds of the sixteenth century.[7] Yet the results of its development re-

---

[7] See A. J. M. Brouwer Ancher and Joh. C. Breen, "De Doleantie van een deel der burgerij van Amsterdam tegen den Magistraat dier stad in 1564 en 1565," *Bijdragen en Mededeelingen van het Historisch Genootschap* 24 (1902):59–200; H. Brugmans, *Opkomst en Bloei van Amsterdam* (Amster-

sembled those prevailing in the other towns in which coups took place. On the one side, traditional artisan crafts organized in guilds subordinate to and excluded from the city government remained dominant; on the other, harbingers of structural change were beginning to appear in some industrial sectors. In addition, during the 1560s opposition to the long-entrenched, resolutely Catholic "Dirkist" oligarchy emerged in the form of the "Doleanten" party. Resentful of their exclusion from the seats of municipal power despite possessing comparable if not greater wealth than the incumbents, the Doleanten also suspected the Dirkists of failing adequately to protect the vitally important grain trade. Further, the Doleanten found the current magistracy too subservient to Brussels's dictates on religious matters and insufficiently heedful of municipal privileges.

To be sure, despite serious iconoclasm in 1566, and a near-revolt by several thousand townspeople early the next year, the insurgent movement lacked sufficient common interests to prevail at the time. But a decade of severe depression, which the Dirkists failed to manage satisfactorily, corroded loyalties to the point that the citizen militia refused to defend the government during its final climacteric. Even then, however, Amsterdam's old regime retained substantial human, ideological, and repressive resources, and it was only overthrown in 1578 thanks to assistance provided by returning exiles.

III

Although well aware of the defensive aspects of the Dutch Revolt, Henri Pirenne presented it as essentially progressive in nature, the clash of protagonists pursuing forward-looking interests. He depicted a royal government bent on centralizing and unifying a nation; capitalist classes driven to overcome their alienation from the existing order through political, social, religious, and ideological innovation; and a bold new faith willing to employ novel forms of organization and discipline to break sharply with established belief and practice. Scholars of collective

dam, 1911); J. E. Elias, *Geschiedenis van het Amsterdamse Regentenpatriciaat* (The Hague, 1923); J. G. van Dillen, *Amsterdam in 1585* (Amsterdam, 1941); Henk F. K. van Nierop, *Beeldenstorm en burgerlijk verzet in Amsterdam 1566–1567* (Nijmegen, 1978); James D. Tracy, "A Premature Counter-Reformation: The Dirkist Government of Amsterdam, 1538–1578," *Journal of Religious History* 13 (1984):150–67.

action, in contrast, maintain that much radical and even revolutionary action occurs in order to prevent change, not to promote it.

The evidence presented in this book indicates that it was the interaction of both forward-looking and defensive forces that gave rise to the Dutch Revolt, at least in the cities. Some central government policies, most notably those directed toward building a more integrated state, were innovatory. Yet the Habsburgs – like their Protestant adversaries – clung stubbornly to the long-established belief that a single church must enjoy a religious monopoly in their domains. On their side, many municipal governments were devising new institutions or subordinating existing ones, thereby enhancing their control over urban populations. Almost without exception, however, they struggled to protect existing rights and privileges against Brussels's religious and financial policies. Those that failed to do so faced a risky loss of legitimacy at home, if not rebellion or even overthrow.

Again, it was neither the frustrated expectations nor the absolute impoverishment of social classes newly generated by capitalist development that alone gave strength to urban protest in the Netherlands. Rather, it was these in tandem with portents of structural change troubling small and medium producers at a time when steep inflation, market instability, and insufficient ameliorative systems increased this pivotal group's vulnerability to entrepreneurial initiatives. What mattered was less the presence of proletarians than the threat of proletarianization. Finally, Protestant demands for and steps toward the open exercise of their faith represented a break with rather than a continuation of the status quo. Yet if some people may have harkened to the new message because of unsettling changes in their work or social experiences, many others found the Reformed religion appealing because it expressed their fear of change. For their part, Protestants resembled not so much a mass movement – or even a disciplined revolutionary vanguard – as a heterogeneous alliance responding to a constantly shifting constellation of threats and opportunities. In and of themselves, the Reformed contributed to the outbreak of the revolt by exposing and exploiting weak points in the political system and its repressive apparatus. But to succeed in attaining their goals, even in part, Protestants had to form coalitions with groups with an essentially reactive orientation.

This book also maintains that it was a combination of defensive and forward-looking measures that permitted the achievement of stability in sixteenth-century Lille. Artisan mobilization was not inhibited because the city fathers acquiesced in extensive innovation or because they attempted to maintain a static social order. Instead, it was blocked because the Magistrat had recourse to selective adaptation, psychological as well as material. More generally, this book claims that while powerful economic, social, and religious currents created the potential for revolt in the mid-sixteenth-century Netherlands, it was the political response of the local ruling class that determined whether such an outcome would in fact be realized. As the example of Lille shows, even an oligarchic magistracy pursuing the repressive policy favored by an increasingly unpopular central government could stay firmly in control. What it had to do – and what few other urban governments apparently managed to accomplish – was at once resolutely to address the perceived sources of discontent and to tighten controls over the populace.

Lille's ruling class did not make its history entirely, or even largely, under conditions of its own choosing. The city's economic growth was – and this became painfully obvious during recurrent crises – dependent on conditions within a competitive international market over which its people, even its greatest merchants, had very little control. Similarly, the diffusion of religious dissent was a function of commercial routes, technological developments, and cultural evolution that the Magistrat could not interrupt. Even such favorable factors as electoral procedures or the recent formation of the urban political class were legacies that the Loi could turn to its benefit but had not created. What Lille's political leadership must be credited with is the ability to recognize that it could reproduce both stability and its own hegemony through discriminating intervention, particularly in social and economic affairs, that balanced economic considerations with broadly based cultural traditions and ideological commitments.

In the literature on the Dutch Revolt – indeed, in the scholarship on revolution as a whole – Lille thus continues to stand out as singular, a stark contrast to the centers of iconoclasm, resistance, and rebellion that have understandably received most attention. But its example suggests the advisability of studying locations where mobilization was checked, insurgency contained, and collective action blocked, if we wish to understand both revolution and its counterpart stability.

320

Appendix A

~~~~~~

The population of Lille in the sixteenth century

Both the absolute population figures and the demographic trends in sixteenth-century Lille are matters of controversy. One contemporary document survives: AML, Aff. gén., C. 241, d. 3, "Mémoire que en l'an 1566 fut trouve que a l'enclos de la ville ne avoit que iiiim maisson." This single sheet of paper summarizes information, very likely from a survey taken in April 1566, designed to ascertain the number of people available to bear arms in an emergency. It cites a total of 3,890 houses (not 4,000, as its title promises) in the five intramural parishes; 1,030 in St. Sauveur, 1,060 in St. Maurice, 1,100 in St. Etienne, 400 in Ste. Catherine, and 300 in St. Pierre. The parishes of St. André and La Madeleine, which lay outside the town walls, are not mentioned, although they were considered part of the city for purposes of law, taxation, welfare, and religious affairs.[1] At the bottom of the list, the anonymous scribe has written that each house is to be considered as containing 10 people, both adults and children ("Et a prendre a chascune maison dix personnes . . . et petis et grands . . ."), for a total of 40,000 people [sic]. What precisely the word "takes" (prendre) connotes and why the number 10 was chosen, is nowhere stated.

Many historians of Lille have used this figure of 40,000 as a valid approximation of the city's population in 1566. Besides the document itself, they point to evidence that Lille was overcrowded. In 1539, the Magistrat petitioned Charles V for permission to enlarge the city walls, and projects were drawn up in 1541 and again in 1556. In the event, however, nothing was done until 1603–4, when the seventeen hectares of the faubourg Notre-Dame were added on the southwestern flank of

---

[1] See Introduction, Chapter 4, section II, and Platelle, "La vie religieuse à Lille," p. 394.

the town, and again in 1617–22, when the annexation of the faubourgs of Courtrai and Reigneaux incorporated another thirty hectares to the northeast.[2] Scholars who accept the reliability of the 1566 figure thus consider the first accurate count, which found 32,604 people in the five intramural parishes in 1617, to indicate decline, attributable to emigration consequent upon the revolt.[3]

For several reasons, however, I conclude that the supposed 1566 population total is exaggerated.[4] In addition to the uncertainties already mentioned in regard to the document itself, the uniformly applied multiplier of 10 seems excessive. To be sure, tax documents, rent rolls, and banishment lists attest that Lillois (especially those in St. Sauveur parish) dwelt in cellars, attics, and courtyards throughout the early modern period, and indeed on up to the present day. Many times, too, several households also lived in one building. Even in 1625, for instance, when enlargement should have reduced crowding, we are told of houses containing 2 or 3 families.[5] In addition, the growth of the textile crafts (see Chapter 3) was accompanied by migration.

Other evidence, however, makes me reluctant to translate this testimony into so high a multiplier as 10 people per house. For one thing, a census taken in 1686, which counted 53,050 people in 11,284 families living in 7,769 houses, yields a mean of 1.45 families or 6.83 people in each house.[6] Perhaps more telling, in 1566 Antwerp, also a lively, growing, and crowded city, had an average of 7.4 inhabitants per house.[7] On its side, a figure of 40,000 seems too high for 1565 Lille. Recent estimates based on registration of new citizens, urban area calculations, and fiscal, church, and guild records place Lille's population at between 13,500 and 15,000 around 1455, rising to perhaps 20,000 at the beginning of the sixteenth century.[8] There can be little doubt that the city

2 Jules Houdoy, *La joyeuse entrée d'Albert et d'Isabelle. Lille au XVIe siècle d'après des documents inédits* (Lille, 1873), p. 12; *Saint-Léger, Lille sous les dominations autrichienne et espagnole*, p. 37; idem, "Le développement topographique de la ville de Lille," *Bulletin de la Société de Géographie de Lille* 70 (1928):211; J. Dilly, "La structure de l'agglomération lilloise," *RN* 37 (1955):31*.

3 Cf. Henri Platelle, *Les Chrétiens face au miracle, Lille au XVIIe siècle* (Paris, 1968), p. 16; Dilly, "Structure de l'agglomération lilloise," p. 31*; Saint-Léger, "Développement topographique," p. 211.

4 Sivéry, "Histoire économique et sociale," p. 202, also expresses reservations about this figure.

5 Buzelin, *Gallo-Flandria sacra et profana*, p. 10.

6 Reported in Lottin, *Vie et mentalité d'un Lillois*, p. 10.

7 Offermans, *Arbeid en Levensstandaard*, p. 50 n. 12.

8 See Sivéry, "Histoire économique et sociale," pp. 198–202, 261–2; Platelle, "La vie religieuse à

grew even more in the course of that century, but I am not convinced that it would have doubled or more in six decades. What is more, textile growth and immigration continued at least until the 1620s, time of the first census, casting doubt on any notion of population decline, even when emigration and exile caused by the revolt are figured in. Finally, if Lille's population diminished after 1566, why were two enlargements, which between them increased the city's land area nearly 50 percent, undertaken in the early seventeenth century?

My own estimate is based on a multiplier of seven, which yields an intramural total of some 27,000 townspeople in 1566, to which should be added another 2,000 to 3,000 people to account for residents of St. André and La Madeleine, clergy, and those living in hospices, orphanages, and other institutions. Hence the 1617 figure (which, it should be recalled, does not include either of the extramural parishes) would have represented an increase from the mid-sixteenth century rather than a diminution. Despite some emigration consequent upon the revolt, departures were probably more than compensated for by arrivals, as noted previously. Scattered baptismal records seem to bear out this supposition about the demographic trend. St. Maurice, which averaged 328.7 baptisms a year during the 1580s, had means of 364.1 (1590s), 388.1 (1600s), and 432.0 (1611–20); St. Pierre's annual mean was 71.5 between 1566 and 1575 but 92.7 between 1611 and 1620; St. André counted 51.3 baptisms each year from 1593 through 1600, 74.6 during the next decade, and 81.6 from 1611 through 1620.[9]

Lille," p. 392; Derville, "De 1300 à 1500," p. 152; idem, "Le nombre d'habitants des villes de l'Artois et de la Flandre Wallonne (1300–1450)," *RN* 65 (1983):287.

[9] AML, Reg. 14,448 and 14,460 (St. Maurice), 14,456 (St. Pierre), 14,409 (St. André).

Appendix B.

Marriage portions in sixteenth-century Lille (1544–1600) (amounts in livres)

Occupation	0–99	100–199	200–499	500–999	1000–1999	2000–2999	3000–4999	5000–9999	10,000 and up	Undeterminable
Servant	1	2	2	1						200 and property
Textile artisan (sayetteur, bourgetteur, shearer, drap weaver)	3	5	9	3	3	1				Land and personal property Tools
Food preparing and selling	1		2	3	4	1				
Capital-intensive trade (cloth retailer, tanner, crassier, dyer, apothecary, goldsmith, merchant draper)		2	2	3	7	1	1			600 and property 600 and property

Occupation							Small amount of land
Other artisan (clothing, metal, transport, saddlery, cooperage, construction)			2	3	4	1	Small amount of land
Lawyer; doctor			1		2	1	1,700 and land
Official (Chambre des Comptes, Gouvernance)				4	1	1	7,920 and land 7,200 and land
Noble or landowner calling himself *sieur*		1	1	1		2	400 and two fiefs of 23 ha. each
Merchant	1	9	12	5	10	7	1860 and 17 ha. land Cash, goods, 12 ha. land 23 ha. land 2,500 and land 5,000 and land

Sources: AML, Reg. 15434, 15435, 15435bis; ADN, Tab. 1146–8, 2828, 3308, 3851–5, 3857–9, 4165, 4168, 4237, 4250; Denis du Péage, *Recueil de généalogies lilloises*, 4:1435–8; Fremaux, *De Fourmestraux*, pp. 210–11 n. 5, 214 n. 1.

Appendix C

Assessments for Hundredth Penny tax, 1569 (amounts in livres)

Category	Mean tax	Median tax	Range of assessment
Merchants (N = 78)	14.53	8.00	1.1–142.5
Landowners (N = 18)	8.73	7.15	3.0–29.5
Clergy of collegiate church of St. Pierre (N = 24)	5.36	5.00	1.1–12.8
Government officials[a] (N = 29)	4.13	3.90	1.5–8.5
Lawyers (N = 13)	2.45	2.00	1.1–7.3
Shopkeepers and artisans in capital-intensive trades[b] (N = 38)	4.99	4.00	1.1–22.0
Textile artisans (N = 12)	2.39	1.50	1.3–6.3
Other artisans and shopkeepers (N = 35)	2.34	1.50	1.1–8.5

Note: N = number of taxpayers in category.
[a]Includes officials in Chambre des Comptes, Gouvernance, and municipal government.
[b]Includes crassiers, tanners, apothecaries, dyers, cloth retailers, *espessiers* (sellers of candles, oil, butter, and other similar items), mercers, goldsmiths.
Source: AML, Reg. 966.

Appendix D

Immigration to Lille of families of sixteenth-century merchants

Family name	Date of arrival[a]	Former residence[b]	Sources[c]
Drumez	1420	Village (WF)	*Familles*, p. 74
Castellain	1420s, 1430s	Lezennes (WF)	*Recueil*, 3:919
Deliot	1430	?	Ibid., 1:37
Bridoul	1438	Normandy	Ibid., 2:651
De Flandres	1440s, 1460s, 1480s	Lezennes (WF)	Ibid., 3:977
De Thieffries	Mid-15th century[d]	Emmerin (WF)	"Mélanges," 17:231–2
Le Boucq	1453	Hulst (Flanders)	Ibid., 16:189
De Smerpont (Semerpont)	1464	Artois	Ibid., 19:72–3
Delobel	1474	Flers (?) (WF)	*Recueil*, 4:1560
De Fourmestraux	1480, 1493	Sainghin-en Mélantois (WF)	Fremaux, pp. 194, 196
Dragon	1486	Merville (Flanders)	*Recueil*, 4:1452
Poulle	Ca. 1493[e]	?	Ibid., 1:131–2
Fasse	1497, 1499	Fleurbaix(?) (WF)	Ibid., 1:51
Miroul	Early 16th century[f]	Roubaix (WF)	Ibid., 2:766
De la Chapelle	1507	Tournai	Fremaux, p. 257

(*continued*)

327

Appendix D (*Continued*)

Family name	Date of arrival[a]	Former residence[b]	Sources[c]
Muette	1510	Arras (Artois)	*Recueil*, 3:1250
Le Pippre	1510	Armentières (WF)	Ibid., 3:1014
De Sailly	1511	La Madeleine (WF)	Ibid., 1:151
Levasseur	1512	?	Fremaux, p. 206
Desbuissons (du Buisson)	1519, 1520	Prémesques (WF)	*Recueil*, 1:43
De Vendeville	1520, 1559	Camphin-en-Pévèle (WF)	Ibid., 2:623
Coene	1521	Bruges (Flanders)	Fremaux, p. 262
Cambier	1529	Ennetières (WF)	"Mélanges," 16:164
Delecousture	1536	Marcq-en-Baroeul (WF)	Fremaux, p. 261
Tesson	1537	St. Omer (Artois)	*Recueil*, 2:600
Delannoy	1544, 1545, 1552	Cysoing (WF)	*Recueil*, 1:103
De Beaumont	Ca. 1549	Valenciennes (Hainaut)	Ibid., 1:207
Percourt	Mid-16th century	Tournai	Ibid., 1:381
Du Retz	1554	Armentières (WF)	Ibid., 3:1070

Du Beron	1556	Seclin (WF)	Ibid., 2:456
Du Forest	1557	Roncq (WF)	Ibid., 2:517
Van der Leure	1557–8	Courtrai (Flanders)	Coornaert, 1:163
Imbert	1564	Arras (Artois)	Fremaux, p. 258 n.1
Cambier	1571, 1577	Valenciennes (Hainaut)	"Mélanges," 16:161
Rouvroy	Ca. 1584	Poperinghe (Flanders)	*Recueil*, 1:409
Fruict	1588	Douai (WF)	Ibid., 4:1467
Wacrenier	Late 16th century	Armentières (WF)	Ibid., 1:185

[a] This is usually the date when citizenship was purchased; unless otherwise noted, it corresponded closely with date of arrival.

[b] Village or town if known, with province in parenthesis; otherwise, province only. WF = Walloon Flanders.

[c] *Familles* = Paul Denis du Péage, *Familles de Flandre* (Bruges, 1951); *Recueil* = Idem, *Recueil de généalogies lilloises*, 4 vols. (Mémoires de la Société d'Etudes de la province de Cambrai, vols. 12–15, Lille, 1906–8); "Mélanges" = Idem, "Mélanges généalogiques," *BSEPC*, vols. 16 (1911), 17 (1912), 19 (1914); Fremaux = Henri Fremaux, *Histoire généalogique de la famille De Fourmestraux* (Lille, 1907); Coornaert = Emile Coornaert, *Les Français et le commerce international à Anvers, fin du XVe–XVIe siècle*, 2 vols. (Paris, 1961).

[d] Citizenship bought from early fourteenth century.

[e] Date of immigration; citizenship bought from fourteenth century.

[f] First acquired citizenship in 1435.

Appendix E

The wealth of leading commercial families in Lille during the sixteenth century
(all amounts in livres)

Family name	Names of those participating in Antwerp trade, with dates[a]	Loans granted (names and amounts)				
		1537 (99)[b]	1543 (230)[b]	1552 (423)[b]	1556–7 (434)[b]	1562 (89)[b]
Du Bosquiel	Girard, 1554, 1560, 1561, 1568 Mahieu, 1545, 1563, 1564, 1569–71 Robert, 1546, 1569 Nicolas, 1559 Alard, 1560 Godefroyt, 1568 Jacques, 1569	Robert 200 Girard 100		Nicolas 240 Girard 200	Godefroyt, Paul and Mahieu 400	Nicolas 200 Girard 200 Mahieu 100 François 50 Godefroyt 50
Castellain	Jean, 1520 Jacques, 1562 Jean, 1553, 1571, 1573, 1575	Guillaume 300 Paul 200 Mahieu 72 Jacques 36	Guillaume and co. 700	Guillaume Sr. 1,600 Paul 1,00 Guillaume Jr. 400 Mahieu 400	Guillaume Sr. and co. 2,000 Paul and son 1,000 Mahieu 200	Gilles 100 Mahieu 100
Coene	Michel, 1521 Jaspart, 1550, 1564 Behoudt, 1553 Jacques, 1553, 1555, 1562 Pauwels, 1560, 1562	Jaspart 200	Jaspart 240	Jaspart 600	Jaspart and co. 1,200	Jacques 120 Pauwels 80
Deliot	Hubert, 1536, 1554, 1555, 1559 Wallerand 1552, 1553	Hubert 400	Hubert and co. 1,200	Hubert 2,000 Pierre 600	Hubert and co. 4,000	Guillaume 100

Bonds purchased		Hundredth Penny	
1555 (181)[c]	1557 (637)[c]	Assessments 1569[d]	Marriage portions[d]
Girard 600	Nicolas 1,050	Girard 142.5	
Alard 200		Robert 20.0	
Robert 200		Mahieu 12.0	
François 100		François 10.3	
Guillaume 1,500	Guillaume 1,600		
Paul 650	Paul 600		
Mahieu 200	Hugues 400		
Jean 100	Mahieu 300		
Jaspart 1,600	Jaspart 1,600		Jaspart, for son Paul 8,000 10 October 1550
Hubert 3,400			
Wallerand 400			

(*continued*)

Family name	Names of those participating in Antwerp trade, with dates[a]	1537 (99)[b]	1543 (230)[b]	1552 (423)[b]	1556–7 (434)[b]	1562 (89)[b]
	Pierre, 1554, 1576					
	Guillaume, 1568					
Delobel	Jean, 1542, 1545, 1570	Jean 200	Jean and co. 600		Jacques and co. (with Marie de Fourmestraux, widow of Jean Delobel) 1,800 Hugues 400	Jacques 100 Alard 100 Bauduin 100 Hugues 50
	Gerard, 1544, 1547, 1567					
	Hugues, 1545, 1556					
	Jacques, 1545, 1559, 1561, 1563, 1564, 1570, 1571					
	François, 1562, 1563, 1573, 1580					
	Paul, 1581					
Drumez	Jean, 1545, 1561, 1562, 1570	Jean 100			Pierre and co. (with Jean de Smerpont) 600	Jean 100 Pierre 100 Guillaume 50
	Pierre, 1561–2	Pierre 24				
	Jean, 1561, 1574, 1584					
	Antoine, 1562					
	Michel, 1572					
Fasse	Hugues, 1560, 1569	François 100	François 160	François 1,200	François and co. 1,600	François 200 Jacques 100 Hugues 50
	Jacques, 1560, 1569					
	François, 1560, 1569					
	Etienne, 1580					
	Pierre, 1580					

Bonds purchased		Hundredth Penny	
1555 (181)[c]	1557 (637)[c]	Assessments 1569[d]	Marriage portions[d]
	Gerard 1,064	Jacques 12.0	Hugues, for son Hubert
Hugues, son of Hugues 200		Paul 10.0 Allard 2.3	800; 1.3 ha. land = 600 (1,400) 21 July 1574
Hugues, son of Oste 100			
Pierre 200	Guillaume 800	Claude 15.0	
François 1,200	François 1,200	Jacques 36.3 Hugues 27.5	

(*continued*)

Family name	Names of those participating in Antwerp trade, with dates[a]	Loans granted (names and amounts)				
		1537 (99)[b]	1543 (230)[b]	1552 (423)[b]	1556–7 (434)[b]	1562 (89)[b]
De Fourmes-traux	Nicolas, 1531, 1540, 1545, 1550, 1554, 1557, 1558, 1571, 1575 (three men)	Nicolas 300	Nicolas and co. 1,000		Nicolas, Jean and co. (with Antoine de Thief-fries) 4,000	Nicolas 100 Jean 100 Georges 100 Mahieu 50 Robert 50
	Jacques, 1545, 1550, 1554, 1573, 1575					
	Jean, 1545, 1551, 1568, 1571					
	Gilles, 1546, 1562					
	Georges, 1552, 1557, 1568, 1569					
	Thierry, 1563					
	André, 1573					
	Robert, 1573, 1575					
	Mahieu, 1575					
	Toussaint, 1584					
	Guillaume, 1587					
Henniart	Noel, 1553, 1561–8, 1570	Jean 100 Adrien 24 Antoine 30		Adrien 200	Adrien 400 Antoine 100	Adrien 100 Antoine 100 Jean 50
	Antoine, 1563					
	Adrien, 1567					
	Charles, 1579					
	Gerard fils, 1580					
	Jean, 1580					

Bonds purchased		Hundredth Penny	
1555 (181)[c]	1557 (637)[c]	Assessments 1569[d]	Marriage portions[d]
	Bernard 800	Mahieu 23.8	Nicolas, for daughter Madeleine
	Jacques 776	Thierry 20.5	7,200 10 October
	Thierry 416		1550
Georges 200	Georges 216		Robert, for son Mahieu
Gilles 200			6,000; fief of
Jean 200	Jean 216	Jean 13.3	9 ha. in
Nicolas 200		Nicolas Jr. 8.0	Bondues 16 May 1587
			Robert, for daughter Marguerite 23,986.8 14 December 1598
Antoine 100	Antoine 100	Adrien 21.3	

(continued)

Family name	Names of those participating in Antwerp trade, with dates[a]	Loans granted (names and amounts)				
		1537 (99)[b]	1543 (230)[b]	1552 (423)[b]	1556–7 (434)[b]	1562 (89)[b]
(le) Mahieu	Colart, 1527, 1552, 1553 Gerard, 1550, 1557, 1562–4 Nicolas, 1559, 1560, 1565 Mahieu, 1559, 1563, 1572 Jean, 1562, 1563, 1565	Jean 200 Colart 150	Jean and co. 600	Jean 400	Nicolas and co. (with son and Mar- guerite Deliot, widow of Jean Ma- hieu) 1,200	Nicolas 100 Jean 100 Toussaint 100 Mahieu 100 Philippe 50
De Smerpont	Arnoul, 1545, 1551 Jean, 1556, 1560, 1561, 1564	Arnoul 100 Jean 50 Philippe 84	Arnoul 400		Arnoul 400 Jean and co. (with Pierre Drum- ez) 600 Wallerand 200	Jean Sr. 100 Wallerand 100

Bonds purchased		Hundredth Penny	
1555 (181)[c]	1557 (637)[c]	Assessments 1569[d]	Marriage portions[d]
Jean 400 Guillaume 200 Nicolas 200			Philippe, for daughter Jeanne 2,400; free room and board for couple for a year 13 October 1560 Philippe, for daughter Barbe 2,400 12 September 1570 Nicolas, for daughter Catherine 8,000 19 October 1560
Arnoul 200	Jean 864 Wallerand 600	Wallerand 16.88	Amery, for daughter Marguerite 2,674; share of real estate, 900; bonds, 3,250; bit of land (6,824 plus land) 9 February 1597

(*continued*)

Family name	Names of those participating in Antwerp trade, with dates[a]	Loans granted (names and amounts)				
		1537 (99)[b]	1543 (230)[b]	1552 (423)[b]	1556–7 (434)[b]	1562 (89)[b]
De Thieffries	Antoine, 1531, 1545 Guillaume, 1546, 1562, 1566 Jacques, 1551 Gerard, 1553 Laurent, 1573	Guillaume 40		Guillaume 200	Antoine and co. (with Nicolas and Jean de Fourmestraux) 4,000	Guillaume 300 Antoine 100

[a]Taken from Coornaert, *Français à Anvers*, 1:358–62.

[b]Number in parentheses equals average loan at this time.

[c]Number in parentheses equals average purchase at this time.

[d]Data are incomplete.

Sources: AML, Reg. 902, fols. 86v–92v; Reg. 15,884, fols. 23v–6; Pièce 146/2765–7; Reg. 15,885, fols. 3–16v; Reg. 16,289, fols. 70v–110; Reg. 16,291, fols. 65–86; Reg. 15,435–5bis; Reg. 966; ADN, Tab. 1148, 3852; Lottin, "Liste des riches lillois," pp. 68–72; Fremaux, *De Fourmestraux*, pp. 210–11 n. 5, 214 n. 1.

Bonds purchased		Hundredth Penny Assessments 1569[d]	Marriage portions[d]
1555 (181)[c]	1557 (637)[c]		
Antoine 400 Nicolas 200 Guillaume 200	Antoine 600		Jacques, merchant living in Antwerp, 1860 in company of Jacques, Antoine le Moisne, Jean de Smerpont, Jean Drumez and others; about 17.5 ha. land in five fiefs, one manor, and one other holding 11 April 1550

Appendix F

~~~~~~

Sources for the standard of living: problems and attempted solutions

The plentiful data available for Lille suffer from several defects. To begin with, although grains formed the largest single expenditure in every budget, Lille's sources are mute concerning the cost of rye. Most historians, however, consider rye to have been the principal cereal consumed by the early modern European population, especially its poorer strata.[1] Furthermore, the annual wheat price given in Lille's priserie is an average of those prevailing on the Wednesday markets just before and after the feast of St. Rémy (1 October).[2] Suitable for providing a standard for rent conversion, this procedure can be less satisfactory for understanding the experience of consumers, for it omits the often dramatic price movements occurring throughout the year. From literary evidence, for example, we know that in May 1546 the price of a rasière[3] of wheat rose from 6 livres early in the month to 8 livres on 21 May before falling back to 5 livres a week later. By August, the cost was down to 2 livres. The prices in the priserie around 1 October 1545 (4.2 livres) and 1 October 1546 (2.45) fail to capture these oscillations. Even more divergent were the levels reached in June 1557 (12 livres) and June 1558 (14) as compared with the official prices of 5.35, 3.05, and 2.6 livres in October 1556, 1557, and 1558 respectively.[4] In short, the priserie is a

---

[1] See Verlinden, Craeybeckx, and Scholliers, "Price and Wage Movements," pp. 59, 62; Scholliers, *Levensstandaard,* appendixes XI, XII, XIV.

[2] For an explanation of the mechanisms of price determination around St. Rémy, see Alain Derville, "Le marché lillois du blé à l'époque bourguignonne," *RN* 59 (1977):45–62.

[3] The capacity of Lille's rasière of wheat is variously given. Most commonly and, it appears, most accurately, it is said to have contained 70.14 liters, though several authors cite a figure of 72.2 liters. See Lottin, *Vie et mentalité d'un Lillois,* p. 384, and Van Hende, *Lille et ses institutions communales,* p. 115.

[4] For the various figures, see BN, Nouvelles acquisitions françaises, MS. 24,089, fols. 34–4v, 41v–2, published in *Chronique de Manteau,* pp. 22–4, 30; AML, Reg. 797.

once-yearly figure rather than an annual average and thus cannot necessarily be taken as the summary expression of a year's price history.

Most price data suffer from an additional shortcoming: The sources
give the cost of raw foodstuffs such as grain or cattle, not the price of
consumer products like a loaf of bread or a cut of meat. Yet the cost of an
end product included a significant wage component, and wage adjust-
ments in both directions nearly always lagged behind price movements.
Hence the data exaggerate decreases in purchasing power in periods
when prices rose more quickly than wages. Conversely, figures derived
from years when prices declined faster than wages convey too rosy a
picture of consumers' situation.[5] Historically, moreover, wholesale
prices have risen and fallen more often and more abruptly than retail
prices, which to a certain extent are smoothed out by small traders and
shopkeepers.[6]

Use of the available wage information presents other difficulties.[7] The
data pertain to craftsmen and manual laborers in the construction trades
employed for a wage by the city government. Further, the information
takes the form of per diem rates, although income was equally determined by the level of employment, which in turn depended on a variety
of factors including the municipality's demand for labor, the health of
the employee, and the weather. Because these trades were subject to a
number of highly specific conditions, in short, figures derived from
them cannot be assumed necessarily to reflect the experience of Lillois
employed in other occupations, each with its own particular situation.
Even less should construction wages be accepted without question as
indicating the incomes of the many townspeople who were self-employed or piece workers.

Translating these disparate figures concerning prices and wages into
usable estimates about the evolution of living standards constitutes the
most problematic task of all. Not only do we know little about the

---

[5] For discussions of these issues, see Herman Van der Wee, "Prices and Wages as Development Variables: A Comparison between England and the Southern Netherlands, 1400–1700," *Acta Historiae Neerlandicae* 10 (1978):62, and E. H. Phelps Brown and S. V. Hopkins, "Wage-Rates and Prices: Evidence for Population Pressure in the Sixteenth Century," *Economica* new ser. 24 (1957):292–3.

[6] E. H. Phelps Brown and S. V. Hopkins, "Seven Centuries of the Prices of Consumables Compared with Builders' Wage-Rates," *Economica* new ser. 23 (1956):304.

[7] For a fine recent warning about pitfalls in wage studies, see Denis Morsa, "Salaire et salariat dans les économies préindustrielles (XVIe–XVIIIe siècle). Quelques considérations critiques," *RBPH* 65 (1987):751–84.

composition of actual sixteenth-century budgets, but there is no consensus about the size of the average family. Taken together, these uncertainties make it difficult either to define typical patterns of consumption or to determine the income levels needed to support them. The paucity of information about the labor-force participation of family members further complicates matters. The construction workers hired by the municipality were all men, yet occupations like doubling, embroidering, and knitting were staffed almost exclusively by women. Women also became mistresses or workers in crafts such as say combing and weaving, operated inns, and carried on various kinds of retail trade.[8] Many of these women were married and, as we have seen in the textile trades, children also worked, so it is certain that family incomes frequently exceeded the wages earned by the men about whom we have data.

Information about the standard of living is, in short, frequently partial and interpreting it fraught with complications. Nonetheless, many of the deficiencies can be compensated for, if not wholly remedied, and several pathbreaking studies afford methodological guidance and results with which conclusions reached for Lille can be collated.[9] The existence of a series, albeit incomplete, of average annual wheat prices derived from purchases by the Hôpital Comtesse all across the year makes it possible both to extend analysis back to 1501 and to check the priserie figures. At times, it turns out, the annual average substantially exceeds the October price and on other occasions it is significantly below; these divergences are noted where relevant. More commonly, however, the two series yield very close results. They are identical, for instance, for 1545–6, despite the extremely high prices registered in May of the latter year and noted previously. Studies of other cities in the Low Countries reach the same conclusion: October cereal prices were near the annual mean, customarily lying only a few percentage points beneath.[10] So while figures derived from the priserie must not be attributed too great a degree of precision, they can be accepted as generally fair depictions of both the level and the trend of wheat prices from year to year.

[8] For a superb study demonstrating the wide variety of occupations in which women participated in the sixteenth-century Netherlands, see Martha C. Howell, *Women, Production and Patriarchy in Late Medieval Cities* (Chicago, 1986).

[9] Most helpful are Scholliers, *Levensstandaard;* Verlinden, Craeybeckx, and Scholliers, "Price and Wage Movements"; and the articles by Phelps Brown and Hopkins cited in nn. 5 and 6. See also P. H. M. G. Offermans, *Arbeid en Levensstandaard in Nijmegen omstreeks de Reductie (1550–1600)* (Zutphen, 1972).

[10] See Verlinden, Craeybeckx, and Scholliers, "Price and Wage Movements," fig. 5, p. 64.

There are, however, no rye prices at all from Lille or from nearby Douai, the largest market in the Low Countries for domestically raised grain.[11] This absence may well indicate that Lillois normally ate wheaten bread, rye being regarded as a stopgap to be avoided whenever possible.[12] After all, hospital records do not mention rye purchases. Even during periods of shortage, moreover, when prices were very high, the municipal government resolutely sought wheat for the poor, accepting rye only as a last resort.[13] But in light of the Netherlands' growing dependence on imported rye,[14] the lack of price data may be accidental, the product of idiosyncrasies of the distribution system, rather than a reflection of the actual eating habits of Lillois. The cereal-raising areas of Walloon Flanders, Artois, and northern France that supplied Douai's staple, and where the seigneuries served by Lille's priserie were located, specialized in wheat, which gave a higher yield per acre and brought a better price than rye.[15] Rye, in contrast, which was imported from the Baltic, then had to be shipped to Lille up the Scheldt, Lys, and Deûle, would have been priced neither at the Douai market nor for the priserie. Whatever the explanation for this apparent deficiency in the data, we do have evidence of rye consumption in Lille, if only in times of dearth. I have therefore included rye prices drawn from Ghent, the closest source, in an attempt to present as complete a picture as feasible of the cost of the grains likely to have been part of townspeople's diet.

What of the possible distortions introduced by using wholesale prices, or prices of unprocessed foodstuffs, to ascertain the cost of living for consumers who usually bought at retail? No general solution to this issue

---

[11] See the Douai price lists published by Monique Mestayer, "Les prix du blé et de l'avoine de 1329 à 1793," *RN* 45 (1963):157–76.

[12] Cf. Van der Wee, *Growth of the Antwerp Market,* 2:215, who asserts that people eschewed rye whenever they could.

[13] See, for example, AML, Reg. 277, fol. 153v, 3 October 1562; or ADN, Reg. B 1635–6, passim (mid-1590s).

[14] Verlinden, Craeybeckx, and Scholliers, "Price and Wage Movements," pp. 59–60, calculate that by the 1560s, 13% to 14% of domestic consumption in the Low Countries was supplied by Baltic imports, over 90% of which was rye. On the basis of different assumptions, Scholliers, *Levensstandaard,* pp. 61, 267, has raised his estimate of the level of dependency on Baltic supplies, contending that such imports constituted 23% of the Netherlands' requirements.

[15] See Blanchard, *La Flandre,* p. 361: In the area around Lille, "wheat has always formed the basis of cultivation." A list of seventy-four suppliers from which grain was obtained in 1557 (AML, Reg. 16,291, fols. 310–10v) shows that all but a handful were in Walloon Flanders, the rest being in Artois. Parish charities (*pauvretés*), which received in-kind payments of wheat and oats as part of their income from property they owned, never record receiving rye; see the accounts in AASL. See also Derville, "Marché lillois du blé."

has so far been discovered, yet several historians have found that the anticipated discrepancy between grain and bread prices was inconsequential. On the basis of formulas devised by Scholliers, it can be determined that the costs per calorie of unprocessed grain and of bread were virtually identical. Labrousse, in his massive study of prices and wages in eighteenth-century France, concluded that "the price of the pound of bread is that of the pound of wheat."[16] Consequently, it appears reasonable to consider that the available information discloses tolerably well the cost of city residents' basic foodstuff.

As already noted, the wage data, too, have serious limitations. Not only do they refer exclusively to that minority of the urban population dependent on money wages, but the people concerned worked for the municipal government. Barring the discovery of additional records, it will remain impossible to extend our knowledge of incomes to other groups in the population. But if wage information is occupationally restricted, comparisons indicate that it is valid beyond the specific employer whose continuous records have survived – that, in other words, the municipal government's pay rates corresponded to some sort of prevailing scale. Between 1520 and 1553, a period during which the Hôpital Comtesse repeatedly hired building-trades workers, skilled artisans received exactly the same wages from the hospital as from the town. Slight differences obtained for the laborers hired by the two institutions, but only in terms of the timing of raises. It appears, in other words, that at least a rudimentary labor market functioned in sixteenth-century Lille and that the wages paid by the aldermen can be considered an approximate reflection of the standard rate set by it. Indeed, the city, as probably the largest single employer, must have strongly influenced if not actually established the going pay scale.[17]

Converting daily wage rates into measures of annual income involves selecting among categories of employees and determining an average work year. Masons have been chosen to represent master artisans both because of the quality of records and because masons' pay seems to have

16 Scholliers, *Levensstandaard*, pp. 25–33, 210 (appendix XVII), 264 and 27 n. 11 (quotation from Labrousse).
17 Offermans, *Arbeid en Levensstandaard*, pp. 139, 141, shows that in the half-dozen cities he examined for comparative purposes the wages paid by the municipal governments set the local norms. The approved wage rates listed in the two sixteenth-century redactions of the Lille masons' guild statutes are also the same as what the municipal government was paying at the time; see AML, Reg. 16,002, fols. 43v–4 (1530); Reg. 16,003, fol. 18v (1577).

been typical of other building craftsmen's. Day laborers (*mainouvriers*) mark the lower end of the income scale: Their wages ordinarily stood at about 50 percent of masters'.[18] Establishing the length of the average work year is rather trickier. Although it is widely accepted that a year in the sixteenth century contained 270 potential working days, the true length of the normal work year is a subject of debate. Based on data from Antwerp, Scholliers judged that an average year contained 264 days. Of these, 189 were "summer" (which in Lille as elsewhere extended from early March to early November), when the hours of work were longer and the pay, as indicated previously, was correspondingly better. The remaining 75 days were remunerated at "winter" rates, commonly between a sixth and a quarter below summer.[19] Employing data that Van der Wee has gathered, however, Prevenier and Blockmans claim that Antwerpers worked a maximum of 252 to 260 days during the 1540s, up from an average of 200 to 220 days during most of the fifteenth and early sixteenth centuries. They contend, too, that Antwerp was exceptional and that in less-prosperous cities people were employed for a shorter part of the year.[20]

The archives in Lille provide insufficient evidence to decide confidently among these assertions. Yet as Guicciardini reported, and Chapters 2 and 3 have confirmed, Lille was an active, expanding town in the first half of the sixteenth century, resembling nowhere so much as Antwerp. It seems safe to expect, too, that demand for labor was high. When computing putative annual income, however, I conservatively assume a customary work year of 250 days (175 summer, 75 winter), a figure that at least one other scholar of the early modern standard of living has endorsed on the basis of investigation of several Netherlands cities.[21] I do not, however, invariably use this representative year, but correct it by reference to the general curve of economic activity, insofar as that can be

---

[18] The same proportion prevailed in most cities of the Low Countries during the first half of the sixteenth century; see Scholliers, "Pouvoir d'achat," table 3, p. 316.

[19] Scholliers, *Levensstandaard*, pp. 84–92.

[20] Blockmans and Prevenier, "Poverty in Flanders and Brabant," p. 24, using figures from Van der Wee, *Antwerp Market*, 1:540–4, appendix 48.

[21] Offermans, *Arbeid en Levensstandaard*, p. 144. After reviewing archival sources and printed materials, Leo Noordegraaf, *Hollands welvaren? Levensstandaard in Holland 1450–1650* (Bergen, North Holland, 1985), pp. 58–61, figures the average work year in Holland at 245 days before 1540, 260 days between 1540 and 1575, and 275 days thereafter. He also observes that workers employed by municipal governments for shorter periods than these averages were not necessarily jobless on the rest of the available workdays.

Appendix F

Table F.1. *Estimated budgets of urban wage earners in preindustrial Europe (% of total expenses)*

	France and Alsace 1401–1700	Antwerp 15th–16th centuries	Lyon 16th century
Bread	30	Ca. 30	50
All food and drink	80	70–80	80
Rent	—	5–15	10
Heat and light	7.5	5–10	5
Clothing; other finished goods	12.5	5–10	5

Sources: France and Alsace: Phelps Brown and Hopkins, "Wage-rates and Prices," esp. table I, p. 293. Antwerp: Scholliers, *Levensstandaard*, pp. 158–67, 277–8; App. XI–XVI. Lyon: Gascon, *Grand commerce et vie urbaine*, 1:402–3.

discovered. One additional qualification needs to be made. As previously noted, we have no way of finding out whether more than one person in each family unit worked, though this seems likely in many cases. But in order to bias results as conservatively as possible, all estimates of earnings discussed in Chapter 4 are premised on just one breadwinner per family.

Whether the presumptive yearly income would be sufficient to attain at least the level of subsistence depended on several other factors, notably the proportion of earnings devoted to various items of consumption – in other words, the composition of the budget – and the number of people who had to be supported, which entails the issue of family size. Neither is easy to discover. A number of historians have studied the living expenses of European populations; the conclusions of three investigations having greatest relevance for our purposes are summarized in Table F.1.

Although a large measure of agreement obtains, there is clearly an important divergence of opinion about the relative significance of bread, by far the leading foodstuff and source of between 50 and 80 percent of caloric intake.[22] Most scholars concur that the lower the income, the

[22] For estimates, see the material presented in Scholliers, *Levensstandaard*, appendixes XI–XVI, and in Blockmans and Prevenier, "Poverty in Flanders and Brabant," p. 22.

higher the proportion spent on bread; conversely, the more affluent would have had more money with which to purchase meat, wine, and better housing and clothing. What remains contentious is what figure to use for per capita consumption of grain. Scholliers puts the daily norm at 470 grams of bread plus the grain in 1.5 liters of beer, for a yearly total of about 200 kilograms of grains, the equivalent of about 2.85 Lille rasières. Annual per capita consumption of cereals is estimated at 250 liters, about 3.5 rasières in Lille, by Jan de Vries. Regulations governing the distribution of bread, drawn up by the city government of Douai in 1554, suggested that 3 rasières a year per person might suffice, but that 4 were preferable. Blockmans and Prevenier argue for a figure of about 300 kilograms (approximately 4.25 rasières), as do Verlinden, Craeybeckx, and Scholliers.[23] Lacking direct evidence for Lille bearing on this matter, I have made calculations based on per capita annual consumption of both 3 and 4 rasières of grain.

Trying to compute the proportion of family income spent on other items is even more difficult, and arriving at a typical budget impossible. What can be done is to examine the price histories of major categories of expenditure for which there is information and then compare them with wage rates. Ascertaining housing costs is problematic because many Lillois appear to have owned their dwellings, yet few sales contracts have survived and none of these permit the same property to be tracked across time.[24] The hospital archives do contain rent records of many houses in the possession of these institutions, but most were built, rebuilt, burned down, divided, or otherwise altered at some time in the course of the period under investigation. As a result, information about them is unusable for our purposes.

For a total of thirty-two dwellings, however, rents can be followed continuously during nearly the entire six and a half decades. Eleven were small houses in the rue d'Houdain donated in 1508 to the asylum of the Bonnes Filles by Gerard le Drut, treasurer of the municipal government and member of a family prominent in Lille's legal and

---

23 Scholliers, *Levensstandaard*, pp. 60–1, 267; de Vries, *Economy of Europe in an Age of Crisis*, p. 35; Eugène Tailliar, *Chroniques de Douai*, 2 vols. (Douai, 1875–7), 2:149–50; Blockmans and Prevenier, "Poverty in Flanders and Brabant," p. 22; Verlinden, Craeybeckx, and Scholliers, "Price and Wage Movements," p. 60.

24 A fragmentary tax list dating from 1569 (AML, Aff. gén., C. 889, d. 1) shows that houses were owned by masons, tilers, brewers, sayetteurs, and other artisans, as well as by merchants, lawyers, and physicians. Marriage contracts also suggest widespread homeownership in the artisanal strata.

political affairs in the first half of the sixteenth century. The other twen-ty-one were medium-sized residences in the rue de Fives and the place Saint-Martin that belonged to the Hôpital Comtesse. All were inhabited by weavers, basket makers, roofers, shoemakers, wine measurers, and other artisans. Because of differing specific circumstances, of course, the rent for each individual house changed at varying times and tempos. Nevertheless, all followed the same trends and thus a composite index can be constructed.

No data from sixteenth-century Lille furnish guidance on the crucial subject of the number of people for whom subsistence had to be pro-vided in an average family, and the evidence from studies of other cities is inconclusive. On the basis of a survey dating from 1586, Scholliers estimated that the typical family in Antwerp contained five people, in-cluding three children. Davis found that the average and median number of children in families assisted by Lyon's municipal welfare system was also three. Frequently, however, the characteristic urban family of the time is said to have been composed of four people. Even Scholliers, who discovered families of this size to have been the norm in poor neighborhoods, and Davis, who determined that most poor people had only two children, can be cited in support of the lower figure.[25] Once again, in order not to bias the discussion in favor of either the poorer or the better-off elements of the population, I have carried out calculations for mean family sizes of both four and five persons.

25 Scholliers, *Levensstandaard,* pp. 158–9, 277, and appendix VIII (p. 198); Natalie Davis, "Poor Relief, Humanism, and Heresy," in her *Society and Culture in Early Modern France* (Stanford, 1975), p. 22; Blockmans and Prevenier, "Poverty in Flanders and Brabant," pp. 21, 22, 24. The recent synthesis by A. M. van der Woude, "Demografische ontwikkeling van de Noordelijke Nederlanden 1500–1800," in *Algemene Geschiedenis der Nederlanden,* 15 vols. (Haarlem, 1977–83), 5:162–5, describes a mean family size of less than four. On the other side, Lille's census of 1686, which yields a mean family size of 4.7 people (cited in Lottin, *Vie et mentalité d'un Lillois,* p. 10) supports the larger estimate. An overview of the southern Low Countries, which finds eighteenth-century Flemish cities to have had 4.3 to 4.7 persons in each family, and the early modern urban mean to have been "often lower" than the rural average of about 5, can support a figure of either four or five; see E. Hélin, "Demografische ontwikkeling van de Zuidelijke Nederlanden 1500–1800," in *Algemene Geschiedenis der Nederlanden,* 5:189.

Appendix G

Monetary payments disbursed by Lille's Common Fund,
1536–1582 (amounts in livres)

Year[a]	November–April	May–October	Yearly total
1536	4,991.8	—	—
1537	5,717.5	—	—
1542	4,759.8	—	—
1546	—	9,469.9	—
1549	—	3,691.45	—
1551	—	5,453.85	—
1552	—	7,421.5	—
1553	—	7,281.25	—
1554	9,603.2	—	—
1558	—	4,003.9	—
1559	—	3,489.15	—
1560	3,485.55	—	—
1561	3,400.9	2,974.3	6,375.2
1562	3,482.2	3,356.85	6,839.05
1563	6,113.6	4,929	11,042.6
1564	6,723.35	5,223.45	11,946.8
1565	6,031.8	4,552.2	10,584
1566	10,566.55	7,419.9	17,986.45
1567	8,086	6,181	14,267
1568	6,875	5,342	12,217
1569	8,157	5,383	13,540
1570	6,713.5	5,914	12,627.5
1571	6,516	3,484.75	10,000.75
1572	6,490.5	4,006.5	10,497
1573	6,381	5,256	11,637
1574	6,870	3,801	10,671
1575	6,699.8	8,508.5	15,208.3
1576	8,574	6,502	15,076

(continued)

Appendix G   (*Continued*)

Year[a]	November–April	May–October	Yearly total
1577	8,160	5,829	13,989
1578	5,814	5,053.5	10,867.5
1579	3,497.35	3,174	6,671.35
1580	3,967	3,601	7,568
1581	3,923.5	3,010	6,933.5
1582	5,993.5	5,248	11,241.5

[a]Accounts were kept by aldermanic year, 1 November–31 October. Thus, e.g., 1536 extended from 1 November 1535 through 31 October 1536.
Source: AASL, Reg. J558–614.

Note on primary sources

This study is based in large part on unpublished documents found principally in archives in Lille. By far the largest proportion comes from the city archives (Archives municipales de Lille). The virtually unbroken series of annual financial accounts (those in Reg. 895, 16,237–337 cover the sixteenth century) were particularly valuable for studying commerce, textile output, annuity purchases, wages, and taxes. Along with the registers of aldermanic ordinances or *bans de police* (Reg. 32, 380–3), they also revealed much about the operation of the Magistrat. No transcripts of discussions at the Magistrat's meetings have survived, but the *Registres aux résolutions* (Reg. 277–80) summarize the decisions taken on those occasions. Substantial collections of fiscal and juridical documents (notably the *Registres aux titres*, Reg. 15,884–5, and the *Registre aux mandements de la Gouvernance*, Reg. 16,980) illuminated relations between sovereign and city. Scores of dossiers and loose pieces in dozens of boxes labeled *Affaires générales* furnished a wealth of information on Lille's urban economy and society, as well as scattered documentation on religious, military, and political matters. Social, economic, and political conditions were also clarified by data from the listings of new citizens (Reg. 414–19, 955–7); miscellaneous papers and reports of the Loi (Reg. 429–30, 15, 922–4); the grain priserie (Reg. 797); the fragmentary Hundredth Penny Tax roll (Reg. 966); and guild statutes (Reg. 16,002–3).

Welfare records (Archives de l'aide sociale de Lille, now housed in the municipal archives) made possible the detailed examination of the income and expenditures of the Common Fund presented in Chapter 4. Before 1560, the semestrial accounts (Reg. J558ff.) are incomplete, but from that point on there are few gaps. Like the other holdings of the

Archives municipales, most of the surviving welfare documentation is concerned with business conducted or directly supervised by the Magistrat. The records of the parish poor commissioners, who administered the Common Fund on a day-to-day basis and compiled lists of the poor receiving assistance, have disappeared, while as noted in the text the papers of the parish *pauvretés* are very sparse.

The *Registres des chartes* and the *Lettres missives* in Series B (the Chambre des Comptes collection) in the departmental archives (Archives départementales du Nord) contributed information on fiscal and legal matters, while some of the sixteenth-century notarial registers (*tabellions*) housed in the ADN yielded data on wealth and investments supplementing those drawn from the handful of similar volumes in the city archives (AML, Reg. 15,434–5bis). But for the purposes of this study the Archives hospitalières were the most important resource in the departmental archives. In this collection, the accounts of the Hôpital Comtesse (Reg. 4443–539) and the girls' orphanage of the Conception of Our Lady or *Bonnes Filles* (Reg. E3–10) proved especially helpful in determining the prices and wages discussed most extensively in Chapter 4 but repeatedly referred to in Part Two. In the Lille Public Library (Bibliothèque municipale), MS. 597, the register in which the names of the members of the municipal government were inscribed, along with information on their occupations and spouses, was indispensable to analysis of the urban ruling class.

Part One (and to a lesser degree Part Two) also draws repeatedly on three collections of printed documents: the second volume of Maurice Vanhaeck's *Histoire de la sayetterie à Lille* (1910), a broad selection concerning the textile trades, taken largely from the *Affaires générales;* Paul Denis du Péage's numerous genealogies and listings of seigneurial landholdings published in the *Bulletin* and *Mémoires* of the *Société d'Etudes de la Province de Cambrai* in the early twentieth century; and Jean Crespin's Calvinist martyrologies, *Actes des martyrs déduits en sept livres* (1564) and *Histoire des vrays tesmoins de la vérité de l'Evangile* (1570).

Although facilitated by an abundance of laws, rules, and data of a quantitative or quantifiable nature, investigation of prerevolt Lille is complicated by a paucity of contemporary literary documents. Beginning in the mid-1560s, however, the continuing profusion of archival sources of the kinds available for the previous decades is complemented by a much greater volume and variety of discursive material: memoirs, correspondence, reports and proceedings of official bodies, registers of the provincial Estates of Walloon Flanders, and the acts and resolutions of the Estates-General from the time of its convocation in 1576. Welcome as these sources are, however, they have to be used with care. Most obviously, while each provides important information – much of it absent from other documents – each also contains significant biases. Most of these sources emanated from members of the dominant classes, established institutions, and victorious parties; furthermore, Catholic voices far outnumber Protestant. Because the sources typically embody official or quasi-official perspectives, the interests, attitudes, and objectives of subordinate individuals, groups, and classes can, for the most part, be discovered only indirectly, intermittently, and partially. Furthermore, although such documents make it possible to create something of a narrative of the years 1566–82, each has its own at least implicit story to tell, which must be decoded rather than simply synthesized.

Three of the numerous chronicles that mention Lille were essential to this study. One, in the Archives de l'Etat at Namur, Belgium (Fonds de Gaiffier-de-Lévignen, MS. 399), is attributed to Pierre Gaiffier, alderman and burgomaster of that city. Most useful for our purposes are several letters, dating from the summer of 1566, written by and on behalf of Lille's Calvinists, along with a reply from the Magistrat. The "Recueil de plusieurs choses mémorables" by Toussaint Carette, a chaplain at the church of St. Pierre in Lille, mainly furnishes factual data, but it also allows us to glimpse attitudes toward Protestants. This account exists in two unfoliated eighteenth-century versions. The most complete (and the one most often employed in this book) comprises fols. [1–127] of BML, MS. 727. A very condensed version is found in BML, MS. 725, fols. [23–27], under the title "Journal de la ville et chatellenie [*sic*] de Lille et autres lieux circonvoisins."

By far the richest of the chronicles are the "Mémoires" of Bauduin de Croix, knight and seigneur of Wayembourg, which extend from 1566 to 1592. The extant manuscript (Bibliothèque municipale de Douai, MS. 1526) is a nineteenth- or early twentieth-century copy, with notes from other manuscripts and published works, translated anonymously into French from the Latin version of Jean Buzelin – who based much of his *Annales Gallo-Flandriae* (Douai, 1624) on it – which in turn was a rendition of de Croix's original Walloon. Because none of the Magistrat's deliberations have come down to us, this account is of singular

353

importance. De Croix belonged to a family of some consequence in Lille's sixteenth-century municipal government. His father Wallerand, a jurist and seigneur, served fourteen terms in the Magistrat, dying in office when rewart in 1560, and at least one brother (four terms), two sons (four and nine), and four other agnates (one, four, seven, and nine terms) were selected all across this period and into the early seventeenth century. Bauduin himself was chosen fourteen times between 1573 and 1592: four as rewart, another four as councillor, and two each as alderman, mayor, and huit-homme. He might well have enjoyed even longer tenure had he not been commissioned the bailiff of the castellany of Lille, upon which he was forced to relinquish his post as rewart. Besides the social attitudes typical of his class – he is apt to refer to the lower orders as "rabble" (*canaille*) – de Croix represents a religiously orthodox and normally progovernment current of opinion, but he also describes occasions on which the municipal ruling class opposed central-state policies.

A great deal of the correspondence that passed between government officials, advisors, and informants has been published in several imposing collections. First in importance are six volumes of letters and memorandums dating from Margaret of Parma's regency (1559–67), published in *Correspondance de Marguerite d'Autriche, duchesse de Parme, avec Philippe II*, edited by Louis-Prosper Gachard (1867–81), and in *Correspondance française de Marguerite d'Autriche, duchesse de Parme, avec Philippe II*, edited by H. A. Enno van Gelder in 1925–42. Although the communications concerning Lille inevitably emphasize the actions and perceptions, and therefore magnify the role, of Maximilian Vilain, baron of Rassenghien, governor of the province (author or recipient of most of them), they are indispensable for understanding the events of 1566–7. The originals of documents that have not been published in these collections, or that have only been excerpted or abstracted, have been consulted at the Belgian national archives (Archives Générales du Royaume) in Brussels, in the collection Papiers d'Etat et d'Audience, mainly Reg. 282, Correspondance de Flandre, Artois, Lille et Tournay [*sic*], 1565–7. The twelve volumes of the *Correspondance du Cardinal de Granvelle, 1565–1586*, edited by Edmond Poullet and Charles Piot (1877–96), contain missives and reports sent to Philip's most trusted counsellor, Antoine Perrenot, Cardinal de Granvelle. Despite his banishment from the Low Countries in 1564 in a vain effort to restore peace, Granvelle remained a careful and informed observer of the situation there, so his papers contain significant information, even if his intelligence about Lille typically came at second or even third hand.

Philip's informants in the Netherlands likewise usually lived outside Walloon Flanders, but their dispatches do present in summary form the knowledge available to officials in Brussels and become especially valuable after for the period after 1572, when other central government reports are scanty. Two collections, totaling ten volumes, have been published: *Correspondance de Philippe II sur les affaires des Pays-Bas*, edited by Louis-Prosper Gachard (1848–79, 1936), and *Correspondance de Philippe II sur les affaires des Pays-Bas, deuxième partie*, edited by Joseph Lefèvre (1940—60). The *Correspondance secrète de Jean Sarrazin, Grand-prieur de Saint-Vaast, avec la cour de Namur (1578)*, edited by Charles Hirschauer in 1912, provides useful intelligence on affairs during 1578, when Sarrazin, prior of the wealthy abbey of St. Vaast near Arras and champion of orthodoxy and monarchy, was actively engaged in the negotiations for a reconciliation between the Walloon provinces and the king.

More directly based on local testimony are the dossiers assembled in autumn 1567 by investigators delegated by the Council of Troubles established by the duke of Alba to ferret out and punish those responsible for the iconoclasm and armed revolt of the previous year. Informers' statements to that body during the next few years also contain items of value, along with wild rumors. All were consulted in the AGR, collection Raad van Beroerte, especially MS. 65. The responses of Lille's Magistrat to the investigators' queries (recorded in BML, MS. 699, fols. 572–82, "Les grands devoirs, diligences et bonz offices faits par Messieurs de la loy de la ville de Lille, ès années 1566 et 67") reveal the city fathers' understanding of the events of the preceding eighteen months of tumult and of their role during them. These records are based, of course, largely on retrospective testimony, and they tend to special pleading. Often, however, they can be checked against other sources. In any event, they are admirably indicative of attitudes current in the early period of Alba's reign, a time for which there exist few other documents.

Two registers of the provincial Estates dating from 1566–73 (AML, Reg. 137, 145) allow changes and continuities in opinions to be followed as opposition to the duke of Alba began to mount. The papers of the Estates-General, finally, record Lille's participation in, and growing disenchantment with, the de facto central government after the collapse of the royal regime. A two-volume selection edited by the indefatigable Louis-Prosper Gachard in 1861–6, *Actes des Etats-Généraux des Pays-Bas. 1576–1585*, has been completed by N. Japikse's multivolume *Resolutiën der Staten-Generaal van 1576 tot 1609*, the first three volumes of which (published in 1915–18) cover the years from 1576 through 1582.

Index

absolute deprivation thesis, 119, 131–2, 314, 319

Aerschot, Philippe de Croy, duke of, 37, 230, 256, 257, 266, 267, 271, 274, 279n71

aged: charity for, 151; institutions for, 137; work opportunities for, 101, 112

aides, 41, 44, 49, 100, 247; Walloon Flanders's share of, 48n102, 244

Alba, Fernando Alvarez de Toledo, duke of, 244, 247, 254, 263, 355; military actions of, 235, 267, 279, 293; new taxes under, 233–4, 241–2, 316

aldermanic bench, *see* aldermen

aldermen, 258, 278, 290, 293; authority of, 18–19, 20, 47, 90, 109, 138, 140, 141, 302, 312; membership of, 25, 29, 30n39, 289; selection of, 19, 21; *see also* Magistrat of Lille

Aleander, Jerome, 171

Alençon, Francis Hercules, duke of, 268, 278, 291

Alleu, 177, 209, 236, 250; Protestants in, 205, 207, 219, 227

Amiens, 60, 182, 190

Amsterdam, 5n12, 8, 70, 71; revolt in, 317–18; trade of, 1–2, 54, 55, 82

Anabaptists, 173–4, 208

Anjou, *see* Alençon

annuities, 147, 155, 245, 295, 351; artisan purchases of, 100, 103; Estates-General sale of, 43–5, 100, 259–60, 264; merchant purchases of, 75–9, 80–1, 102, 331, 333, 335, 337, 339

Antwerp, 8, 11, 57, 65, 68, 71, 74, 79n119, 80n125, 139, 170n38, 235, 244, 263, 265, 277n64, 287, 315, 345; Estates-General at, 274, 281, 284, 291; Lillois at, 174, 339; merchants of, 81n127, 246, 250; population of, 5n12, 322; Protestants in, 187, 227, 229, 254; revolutionary activity at, 313–14; Spanish fury in, 257, 260; trade at, 1, 22, 23, 50, 54, 68, 82, 89

apaiseurs, 19, 25, 29, 30n39; *see also* Magistrat of Lille

apothecaries, 26, 27, 29, 69, 245, 324, 326

Armentières, 3n10, 11n15, 61, 177, 210, 235, 245; Protestants in, 182, 207, 208, 211, 219, 227, 229

Arras, 55, 85, 89–90, 174, 193, 246, 280, 289, 305; negotiations at, 290, 291, 294, 301; relations with Lille, 49, 273n43; Treaty of, 293–5, 296, 300, 302, 306

artisans, 9, 64, 71, 304, 317, 347n24, 348; commercial activities of, 64–5; in Lille Magistrat, 25–6, 29; religious choices of, 183, 184, 186, 188–91; wealth of, 66, 325, 326

357

Index

Artois, 51, 218, 247, 251, 264, 343;
  governor of, 37, 274; industry in, 52,
  105, 108; Protestantism in, 171n45,
  183, 190; reconciliation with Spain
  of, 283, 289, 291–4
Assézat, Pierre, 70

Baillet, Denis, 57–8; family, 23, 68, 71,
  74
Bailloeulx (Bapalmes), de, Wallerand,
  301
Baisieux, 77, 81, 303
Baltic area, 2, 41, 91, 135, 343
Barge, Nicolas, 54
Bassee, Wouter, 190n118
Bave family, 31, 63, 80
Beaumont, de, family, 328
Becque, de le, Loys, 76n113
Beggars, 210, 227, 237, 248, 250, 251,
  315, 317; see also Sea Beggars
beggars, 134, 141, 182
begging, 34, 127, 140, 141, 152, 252
Berghes, de, Cornille, 166
Berlaymont, de, Charles, 264; Claude,
  seigneur of Haultpenne, 264
Bernard, family, 74; Nicolas, 304
Beron, du, family, 329
Bertault, de, Antoine and Jean, see Hol-
  lande, de, Jean
Béthune, 63, 265
Beudart, Jean, 304n164
Bigode, David, 296, 302
bishoprics, reorganization of, 45, 166–7,
  233
Boisot, de, Charles, 282, 287, 303n161
bonds, see annuities
Bondues, 302, 334; fighting at, 298,
  300; presches at, 205–6, 213–14;
  Protestants at, 182, 207, 254
booksellers, 170, 298; suspect books at,
  238, 239
Bordeaux, 53, 54, 57, 68, 70
Bosquiel, du, Alard, 330–1; family, 23,
  27, 56, 63, 68, 73, 80, 330; François,

330–1; Gerard (Girard), 24, 330–1;
  Godefroyt, 330; Jacques, 330; Mahieu, 24, 330–1; Nicolas, 24, 29,
  330–1; Paul, 330; Robert, 59, 330–1
Boucq, le, family, 327
bourgeoisie, see Lille, citizenry of; Lille,
  citizenship of
bourgetterie: free workers in, 98,
  112n109, 115; guild in, 90, 97; masters in, 89, 101, 112n109, 115; output of, 94–6, 130, 213, 238n15, 245,
  249; products of, 91, 92, 96, 249;
  religious choices in, 188, 191; wealth
  in, 324; see also changéants; light
  woolens industry in Lille; velveteens
Bournel, de, Hugues, seigneur of Steenbecque, see Steenbecque
Bourse commune, see Common Fund for
  the Poor
Bouvy, Simon, 56
Brabant, 86, 183, 204, 247, 259, 273,
  278, 301, 316; aides of, 48n102,
  289n106; cities of, 1, 49, 313; Estates
  of, 1, 254, 256–7, 267
Brès (Bray), de, Guy, 179; at Lille, 176,
  177, 188, 192
Breucq, du, François de Hennin, seigneur: commissioner for selection of
  Lille Magistrat, 285, 287; delegate to
  Estates-General, 259, 264, 268; Malcontent conspirator, 284n87, 286;
  military leader, 278, 280; see also
  Hennin (Haynin)
Bridoul, family, 327; Jean, 81
broadcloth, see drapery
brotherhoods, see confraternities
Bruges, 5n12, 49, 142, 170n38, 244,
  269; Lille's trade with, 53, 70–1, 86;
  textiles of, 38, 316; wool staple, 82–
  3n134
Brully, Pierre, 174, 185
Brussels, 5n12, 244, 246, 313; Alba at,
  233, 242–3; Estates-General at, 257,
  274; government at, 314–15; revolu-

tionary committee at, 267, 269;
Union of, 277, 292; *see also* Habsburg
government
Bucerian reform, 170, 174, 186
budget, 346–7; *see also* cost of living
Bus, de, Louis, 111, 112, 118, 253
Bus, du, Catherine, 66; family, 63

Calonne, de, Charles, 298
Calvinism, 11, 156, 170, 319; at Lille,
171, 175, 176, 179, 185, 189, 192–3,
214, 281, 285, 310; in Holland and
Zeeland, 257, 262; synods, 183, 254,
277; *see also* Protestantism in Lille
Cambe, de le, Denis, seigneur of la
Haye, 37, 126–7
Cambier family, 328–9
Cambrai, 58, 190
capitalism, 50; conditions promoting, 97,
104, 314, 319; hindered in Lille, 107,
110, 114–16, 118, 155, 272; Pirenne's account of, 10, 11, 84, 97,
104, 114–15, 118, 186, 318; *see also*
entrepreneurs; proletarians
Carette, Toussaint, 218, 219n71, 353
Carlier, Georges, 69; Marguerite, 69
Casimir, John, 283, 284
Casteckre, Gilles, 66
Castellain, family, 23, 24, 27, 68, 73, 74,
327, 330; François, 80; Gilles, 80,
330; Guillaume, 28, 80, 187n112,
330–1; Hugues, 331; Jacques, 330;
Jean, 28, 57–8, 269, 270, 330–1;
Mahieu, 28, 330–1; Paul, 80, 139,
330–1
castellany of Lille, 46, 48n103, 134; bailiffs of, 47, 211n33, 241, 246n46,
291, 293; iconoclasm in, 209–10,
218, 232, 303; insecurity in, 251,
297, 301; presches in, 277–8; Protestants in, 226, 298
Castiel (Catel), Jean, 181
Catholic Church, 158; attitudes toward,
169, 192–4, 199, 226, 237, 281;

clergy's attraction to Protestantism,
184, 185, 281; clerical problems in,
164–6, 169; clerical support for Don
John in, 275; horistes, 34, 159, 165–
6, 185n103, 194; popular devotions,
160–3, 164–5, 169, 172, 186
Catholicism: fears about, 280, 283–5,
290; under Pacification of Ghent,
257–8, 259, 262, 264, 291
Cauwet, Antoine, 29
Chamber of Accounts, *see* Chambre des
Comptes
chambers of rhetoric, 2, 162, 180; *see
also* Notre-Dame du Puy
Chambre des Comptes, 8; officials of,
19, 25, 63, 241n22, 266, 275, 293,
325–6; relations with Magistrat of
Lille, 36, 37n71, 109
Champagne, fairs of, 51, 55
changéants: weaving of, 90, 91, 93, 108,
110, 130, 271; output of, 94, 96, 213,
238–9, 249; *see also* bourgetterie;
light woolens industry in Lille
Chapelle, de la, family, 327; Jacques, 69;
Jean, 64; Jeanne, 69
charitable institutions, 138, 309, 313,
316; *see also* Common Fund for the
Poor
Charles V, 35, 44, 131, 152n75, 167,
174, 321; relations with Lille, 34, 46,
85, 169, 172, 178, 198, 321; state-
building, 10, 32, 283, 294; *see also*
Habsburg government
Château de Courtrai, 7, 218, 223, 265–
6, 290, 294
Chausses, aux, Gilles, 166n24
Chevalier, Paul, 39, 171n44, 180–1,
188n113, 194
children: welfare for, 147; work of, 127,
272
civic privileges, 46, 314, 317–18
Clichtove, Josse, 167
Closer Union, 273
cloth retailers, 69, 245, 324, 326

coalitions, 308, 311, 314–15, 320
Coene, Behoudt, 330; family, 23, 68, 71, 74, 328, 330; Jacques, 330; Jaspart, 24, 330–1; Michel, 330; Pauwels, 330; Pierre, 236n4
collective action: analysis of, 12, 307–8, 318–19, 320; occurrences of, 312, 313; weakness of at Lille, 309
Cologne, 51, 55, 236
combers, 89, 106, 206, 245, 299, 304; Protestants among, 171, 175, 189, 191
combing, 104–5n83, 106, 107, 188, 342
Comines, 37n69, 81, 245, 297; bailiff of, 264, 294; Protestantism at, 206, 207n12, 211, 230
Common Fund for the Poor: clergy's reaction to, 143–4; disbursements by, 146–50, 153–4, 224, 238, 248, 249, 252–3, 254, 261, 271, 272, 297, 305, 349–51; foundation of, 35, 143; ideology of, 140–1, 151; Magistrat's power over, 32–4, 140, 141, 312; parish commissioners of, 33, 142, 143, 144, 153; regulatory aspects of, 156; revenues of, 144–6, 153, 245, 252, 351; role in crises of, 151, 154, 191, 224–5; structure of, 33–4, 143–4, 352
Compromise of the Nobility, 203, 204, 205n2, 208n17; signatories, 181n90, 210n26, 227, 228, 229, 230, 234, 242
Confederates, *see* Compromise of the Nobility, signatories
confiscation of property, 312; of exiles, 241; of heretics, 174, 178, 181, 247; *see also* privilege of nonconfiscation
confraternities: activities of, 97, 136n36, 143, 163–4, 197; and religion, 169, 179, 187, 190, 199; craft, 97, 163; new foundations of, 162–3; Notre-Dame de la Treille, 161

consumption: conspicuous, 135; limits on, 136; per capita grain, 120, 132, 347
contagious disease, 126; *see also* influenza; plague
Coornaert, Emile, 80, 115
Coppin, 173
Cornette, Jean, 53
corporative spirit, 84, 115
cost of living, 149; *see also* budget; prices
Council of Flanders, 38, 296; appeals to, 34, 37n67, 45, 166n24
council of Lille, 18, 28, 29, 30, 109, 312; *see also* Magistrat of Lille
Council of State, 263, 284, 286; arrest of, 257, 258; members of, 274, 276n62, 289, 294; rule by, 235, 256
Council of Trent, 166
Council of Troubles, 255; investigations by, 205n2, 225; officials of, 240, 241n22, 271, 355; prosecutions by, 233, 235–6
councillors, 19, 21, 30n39, 47, 289, 293; *see also* Magistrat of Lille
coup cities, 313, 315–18
Courtrai, 56, 64, 269, 283
crassiers, 180, 184, 324, 326
Craeybeckx, Jan, 128, 156, 347
Crespin, Jean, 175, 176, 177, 178, 179, 181, 194, 352
Croix, de, Bauduin, seigneur of Wayembourg: delegate to Estates-General, 259, 287; in Magistrat, 271, 278, 284, 354; memoirs cited, 207, 209, 213, 216, 219n71, 240, 265, 279, 280–2, 284, 285–6, 288, 290, 292, 353; military captain, 286; Oste, sieur of Drumez, 64; Wallerand, 354
Croy, de, Adrien, Count of Roeulx, 36–7; Charles, 167; *see also* Aerschot
curriers, 89, 109, 184
Cuvillon, Baude, 37n70, 40, 204

Dale, van, Pauwels, 70

Dancoisne, family, 63, 68, 71, 73–4, 80; Guillaume, 59, 73; Hugues, 76n113

Danzig, 55, 134

Delannoy, Alart, 236n4; family, 68, 328; Pierre, 236n4

De la Barre, Guillaume, 69; Pol, 69

Delecluse, family, 23

Delecousture, family, 328; Gilles, 269, 270; Gilles junior, 269n33

Delesalle (Deledalle), Jean, 58; Pierre, 54

Delft, 55, 70

Deliot, family, 23, 68, 79, 327, 330; Guillaume, 75, 152, 269, 270, 330, 332; Hubert, 23, 145n62, 152, 330–1; Jeanne, 73; Marguerite, 336; Marie, 187n111; Pierre, 330, 332; Wallerand, 330–1

Delobel, Allard, 332–3; Bauduin, 332; family, 23, 24, 58, 59, 68, 73n99, 74, 80, 327, 332; François, 250, 332; Gerard, 187, 332–3; Hubert, 333; Hughes (Hugues), 59, 332–3; Jacques, 59, 332–3; Jean, 58, 332; Mathieu, 187n112; Paul, 332–3; Robert, 269

Delplace (de le Place), Gervais, 218, 225

Den Bosc, *see* 's Hertogenbosch

Denis, Etienne, 60, 71–2; family, 63; Jean, 72

deputies, *see* ministres généraux

Desbarbieux, family, 80; Symphorien, 176

Desbucquois, family, 23; Jean, 24; Pierre, 24

Desbuisson (du Buisson) family, 80, 328

Descamps, Bauduin, 100; Marie, 100

Desmaistres, Allard, 64

Despretz, Antoine, 69; Charles, 69

Desmuliers, family, 23

Desplancques, Helie, 54, 59, 250, 298

Deûle River, 51, 210, 343

Dominicans, 158, 161n9, 172n47

Dommessent, seigneurs of Boisgrenier, 25

Don John of Austria, 268, 283; and Spanish troops, 260, 264; appointment as governor-general, 257–8, 262; attack by feared, 273, 278; measures against, 265, 266, 275; military actions of, 274, 276, 292; seizure of Namur, 262–4

Douai, 45n94, 47n99, 79, 170n38, 294, 300, 316, 347; delegates to Estates-General, 48n103, 259; delegates to provincial Estates, 47, 241; Franciscans, 180, 193; grain market at, 52–3, 134, 343; heresy at, 174, 179n78; reconciliation by, 289, 291; trade of, 55, 246

doublers, *see* thread doubling

Douchet, Antoine, 250

dowries, 26, 65, 77n115, 82, 100; *see also* marriage portions

Dragon, family, 23, 327

drapery, 98, 324; new, 86, 88n15, 104; old (traditional), 86, 88n15, 90–1; output of, 86–8, 94, 155, 213, 238, 239, 245, 249, 253, 261, 272, 282; religious choices in, 184, 188; structure of, 97–8; types of, 9, 86–8, 96; wage labor in, 98, 188; wool sources of, 86, 245

Drumez, Allard, 53; Antoine, 332; Claude, 333; family, 68, 73, 327, 332; Guillaume, 64, 332–3; Jean, 73, 302, 303n161, 332, 339; Michel, 332; Pierre, 332–3, 336

Drut, le, Gerard, 347

Dubois, family, 68; Jean, 59, 73

Dupont, family, 23, 68, 73n99, 74; Guillaume, 24; Jean, 24, 187n112; Jeanne, 59; Pierre, 24, 59, 73

Dutch Revolt: causes of, 3, 7, 156, 198, 318–20; study of, 10, 13, 307

Index

Dutch Revolt (*cont'd*)
dyeing, 26, 98, 184, 245; and rural
cloth, 93n38, 249n57; guild in, 97,
109; wealth in, 65, 69, 324, 326

échevins, *see* aldermen
economic activity, indexes of, 129–31
Eighty Years' War, *see* Dutch Revolt
Egmont, Lamoral, count of, 37, 211,
242
emigration, 247; *see also* exiles
employment, *see* work, availability of
England: exiles from Lille at, 236;
Lille's trade with, 51, 53, 56, 86;
Protestant communities in, 176
English Channel, ports of, 55, 82
entrepreneurial liberty, 252, 254
entrepreneurs, 314, 316, 319; artisan,
104, 110, 115, 311; in light textiles,
104, 108, 118, 190, 271; industrial,
10, 31; merchant, 83, 102, 104, 110,
115; obstacles to, 113, 118, 311; potential, 117, 198, 311–12; *see also*
capitalism; proletarians
epidemic, *see* contagious disease; influenza; plague
episcopal reorganization, *see* bishoprics,
reorganization of
Escaubecque, seigneur of, 211n33, 227,
228
Escaut River, *see* Scheldt River
Estates-General, 1, 257, 267, 298; and
reconciliation with Spain, 275, 285,
289, 295, 303; deputies to, 48, 259;
financial demands of, 257, 259–60,
264, 289n106; involvement in Lille
elections by, 267–70, 271, 273, 286–
7, 312; Lillois at, 48–9; rule of, 258,
275, 277, 289, 295, 316, 353;
troops of, 257, 259, 261, 276, 292,
297, 317
Estates of Lille, Douai, and Orchies:
aide grants by, 244, 260, 276; religious declarations by, 40, 169n35,
212, 277; delegates to, 47, 241; dele-

gates to Estates-General from, 263–
4, 267, 270, 274n46, 294, 299;
grants to Farnese by, 295, 300–1,
306n172; loans to Lille by, 44, 47;
meeting place of, 3, 47, 241; relations
with Estates-General of, 258, 260,
276, 278, 282; reconciliation with
Spain by, 274, 293; response to
Alba's tax proposals by, 48, 246, 255;
structure of, 46–7, 48
Estaires, 205, 291
exiles, 317; from Lille, 232, 236, 323;
from Walloon Flanders, 178, 232;
return of, 203, 207; *see also* Lille,
expulsions from

family size, 120, 132, 342, 346, 348
Farnese, Alexander, prince of Parma:
and reconciliation, 283, 289–92; relations with Lille, 270, 294, 300, 305,
306
Fasse, Etienne, 332; family, 68, 74, 80,
327, 332; François, 23, 269, 332–3;
Hugues, 332–3; Jacques, 332–3;
Pierre, 332
Feast of Fools, 195–6
Feast of the Holy Innocents, 195–6,
232, 240, 251
Febvre, le, Julien, 68; Michel, 302,
303n161
Fives, 225, 237
Flanders, 1, 37, 48n102, 52, 247, 251,
259, 283; attacks on Lille from, 300,
301, 305; Estates of, 255, 267; heresy
hunting in, 177, 179, 181; iconoclasm
in, 204, 218; Protestants in, 183, 215,
219, 317; West Quarter of, 209, 228,
229, 231
Flandres, de, Antoine, 65, 250, 297;
family, 327; Jean, 65, 296–7
Flory, François, 61
Flye, de le, Mathias, 304
Forest, du, family, 80, 329
Fortrie, de le, Catherine, 69; François,
287; Jean, 69, 212n36; Marie, 69

Fourmestraux, de, André, 236n4, 334; Bernard, 335; Collard, 59, 73; commerce of, 14, 27, 58, 59, 68, 70, 72–3; family, 76n111, 79, 334–5; Gaspard, 236n4; Georges, 334–5; Gilles, 59, 334–5; Guillaume, 236n4, 334; Jacques, 58, 59, 334–5; Jean, 54, 60, 269, 270, 334–5, 338; Madeleine, 335; Mahieu, 334–5; Marguerite, 73, 302, 335; Marie, 58, 73, 332; marriages of, 74, 174–5n56; Mathieu, 64; Michel, 304; Michelle, 73; Nicolas, 54, 59–60, 64, 70, 73, 334–5, 338; Nicolas junior, 59, 334–5; origins of, 71, 327; Pierre, 58; Protestantism of, 14, 187, 228n104; Robert, 334–5; Thierry, 334–5; Toussaint, 236n4, 334
France, 41, 51, 91, 170, 236, 343; Lille's trade with, 51, 53–4, 55, 56, 60, 82, 86, 89; Protestants from, 182, 207, 227, 237
Frankfurt, 55, 178n76
Frelin, de, Jean, 172n47
Fremault, Alexandre, 194; family, 27, 63n64; Georges, 54; Jean, 174, 187; Philippe, 227n101
French Flanders, *see* Walloon Flanders
Friesland, 91, 287, 293
Fruict, family, 329
frustrated expectations thesis, 119, 130–2, 314, 319
fulling, 89, 91, 93n38, 97–8, 109, 110, 184, 245

Gaiffier, Pierre, 221, 353
Galliot, Bauduin, 78, 80n125
gard-orphènes, 18–20, 21n22, 29, 30n39
Gardin (Jardin), (du), family, 23
Gay, le, Jean, 100
Gelderland, 25, 289n106, 293
general secretaries, *see* ministres généraux
Generality, 294–5

Geneva, 33, 86, 174, 236
Gerard, Jacques, 81
German states, *see* Germany
Germany, 53, 56, 70, 82, 89, 226, 236
Ghent, 5n12, 38, 236n2, 244, 265, 283, 315; alleged threats to Lille from, 277–8; grain staple of, 134, 343; Lille's relations with, 49, 292, 295; Protestants at, 178, 227, 317; revolt at, 267, 269, 280, 313; trade of, 54, 295
Gobau, Alexandre, 60; family, 23; Jean, 60; Jean junior, 60
goldsmiths, 64, 188; expulsions of, 298, 303; in Magistrat, 26, 29; wealth of, 69, 324, 326
Gommer, Michel, 271, 274n46, 279n71, 284n89, 304
governor-general, 257, 258, 262, 267, 270, 273, 294, 301; *see also* Don John; Farnese; Margaret of Parma; Matthias
Gouvernance, 8; authority of, 39, 40, 168, 173–4n54, 174; officials of, 79, 180, 205n2, 266, 282, 287, 293, 303n161, 325, 326
Granvelle, de, Antoine Perrenot, Cardinal, 209, 288, 289, 354
Great Council at Mechelen, 39, 79, 174
Guicciardini, Lodovico, 3, 6, 8, 90, 345
guilds, *see* Lille, craft guilds in
Guillard (Guillart), Louis, 167
Guillebert, le, Denis, 290, 294

Habsburg government, 7, 35, 256, 318; financial problems of, 41–2, 44–5, 49, 82; fiscal policy of, 41–5; military forces of, 203, 217–18, 235, 248; religious policy of, 38, 212, 319; relations with Lille Magistrat, 35–46, 312; troops of, 256, 258, 273; *see also* Charles V; Margaret of Parma; Philip II; Privy council
Habsburg Netherlands, *see* Netherlands

Haer, van der, Floris, 291, 292n116, 294

Hainaut, 183, 246, 251, 277n64, 301; deputies to Estates-General of, 257, 259, 268; Estates of, 256, 274n48; iconoclasm in, 204, 218; industry in, 52, 105; reconciliation with Spain by, 283, 285, 289, 291–4

Halluin, 3n10, 37n69, 297

Hamburg, 54, 82

Hangouart, family, 25n31, 63; Guillaume, 63; Philippe, 63, 241n22; Rogier, 63; Wallerand, 63

Has, de, family, 23, 68, 73n99; Jean, 54; Jeanne, 73

Havet, Antoine, 180n85

hedge preachers, 206, 210

Hellin, de Jacques, 232n123

Henniart, Adrien, 23, 81, 334–5; Antoine, 334–5; Charles, 334; family, 68, 334; Gerard fils, 334; Jean, 334; Noel, 334

Hennin (Haynin), de, family, 266; Catherine, 286n96; François, seigneur du Breucq, *see* Breucq; Guislain, seigneur du Breucq, 278n69; Jacques, seigneur of Ghislinghien, 263–4, 294; Maximilien, count of Bossu, 263

heresy, 164; jurisdictional conflicts over, 34, 39–40, 45, 172; *see also* Calvinism; Lille, relations with central government; Lutheranism; Protestantism

heretics: executions of, 172, 178–8; *see also* confiscation of property

Herreng, Bauduin, 54, 303, 304

Heyden, van der, Cornelis, 185n101

Holland, 91, 204, 256; cities of, 1, 11, 49, 234; military action in, 234, 251, 255; peace negotiations with, 235, 259; relations with Estates-General of, 257, 259, 262, 273, 289n106; religion in, 262, 276–7; revolt in, 315–17; rumored league of, 283, 293

Hollande (Bertault), de Antoine, 269–70; Jean, 23, 77–8, 79, 80n125, 81

Hondschoote, 11n15, 61, 88, 228, 314n5

Hôpital Comtesse, 124n14, 185, 344, 348, 352

Hot, du, family, 80

Hove, de, Zegre, 205n2

Hove, van den, family, 58; Jacques, 59

huit-hommes, 29, 30n39; functions of, 18, 19, 47, 303; selection of, 20, 21; *see also* Magistrat of Lille

Hundredth Penny, 80n125, 252; Estates of Lille, Douai, and Orchies and, 241–2, 244; individual assessments for, 72, 250n62, 331, 333, 335, 337, 339; new ones proposed, 255, 260; wealth calculated from, 65–6, 100, 326

"hunger year" (1565–6), 135, 203

Iberian peninsula, 55, 86; *see also* Portugal; Spain

iconoclasm: in Netherlands in 1566, 128, 199, 204, 225, 228, 236n2, 314n5, 318, 320; near Lille in 1566, 209–11, 217–20, 231, 303, 355; suspected in Lille in 1566, 186, 218–20

Imbert, family, 329

Immeloot (Ymmelot), Joris, 177n72

immigration, 122, 130, 252, 323; and religion, 190; and wages, 125, 127; of merchants, 63–4, 71, 72

impoverishment, 119, 128, 131, 314

inflation: chronic, 10, 41, 119, 126, 165, 198, 212; in Lille, 122, 135; in 1520s, 139; in 1573–4, 252, 254; in 1576–7, 271; on eve of revolt, 96, 135; *see also* price revolution

influenza, 134, 253; *see also* contagious disease; plague

innkeepers, 65, 304, 342

inquisitor, 172n47, 181

Italy, 51, 52, 53, 55, 56, 82, 86, 89

Index

Jeanne, Countess of Flanders, 17, 196
Jovenel, Gilles, 180, 227n102, 237
jurés, see councillors
justices of the peace, see apaiseurs

La Bassée, 51, 190
labor market, 97, 344
Laigniel, Lievin, 65, 69; Marie, 65, 69;
    Nicaise, 69
Lalaing, de, Antoine, Count Hoog-
    straten, 37n69; Philippe, Count, 260,
    279n71, 284, 294; see also Montigny
Lallier, Adrien, 304
Laman, Jean, 173
Lannoy, 229, 232n118, 290
Lannoy, de, Philippe, 95n44
La Rochelle, 54, 57, 68, 70
Latin schools, 34, 168
Lattre, de, Jean, sayetteur, 100; Jean,
    seigneur of le Vichte, 144
lawyers, 79, 347n24; in Magistrat, 21,
    22, 25, 27, 29; wealth of, 325, 326
Lecat, Antoine, 250, 297; François, 297
Leers, 95n44, 105
Lempereur, Cornille, 69; Jean, 69
Leure, van der, family, 64, 68, 329
Levasseur, family, 23, 68, 328; Jacques,
    73; Jean, 73
light drapery, see light woolens industry
    in Lille
light woolens industry in Lille: appren-
    ticeship in, 98, 104, 110, 136n37,
    252n76; children's work in, 101, 112,
    272; costs in, 91n31, 92, 101n68,
    104–5n83; development of, 88–90;
    guilds in, 98, 102, 115, 163; ideology
    about, 111–14, 117; investments in,
    83, 103; loom limits in, 108–9, 110–
    11, 225, 249, 250, 253, 254; Mag-
    istrat's role in, 32, 89–90, 106, 108,
    115, 117, 271–2, 312; mastership in,
    98, 99, 104, 109, 190n118, 252n76;
    output of, 122, 129–30, 136, 139,
    155, 190, 213, 238, 239, 252, 253,
    254, 261, 271, 272, 282, 304; profit

margins in, 103; putting out in, 98,
    102, 103–4, 106, 108, 109, 110, 111,
    113, 190, 225, 249, 253, 254; rela-
    tions with rural industry of, 93, 105,
    310; religious preferences in, 179–
    80, 184; small producers in, 100–1,
    106, 107; social relations in, 107,
    112–14, 190; structure of, 98–102,
    111–12, 115; thread market of, 103,
    105–7, 110–11, 252; thread supplies
    of, 104–7, 109–10, 190, 253; types
    of cloth in, 90–1; upward mobility in,
    112–13; wage labor in, 98, 104, 107,
    112–14, 272; wealth of producers in,
    99–101, 103, 115; wool sources of,
    91; see also, bourgetterie; changéants,
    ostades; satins; sayetterie; says;
    velveteens
Lille: asylums in, 5, 120, 137, 347; ban-
    ishments from, see Lille, expulsions
    from; citadel of, see Château de
    Courtrai; citizen guard, 251, 254,
    275, 299 (see also Lille, militia of);
    citizenry of, 20, 21, 25, 230n112;
    citizenship of, 20–1, 230, 231, 329;
    civic ritual in, see Lille, processions
    in; cloth industry of, see bourgetterie;
    drapery; light woolens industry in
    Lille; linens; sayetterie; tapestries;
    commerce of, 9, 50–7, 170, 292, 351
    (see also merchants of Lille); condi-
    tions in late 1560s in, 237–40, 243;
    craft guilds in, 31, 96–7, 169, 309,
    351; description of, 3, 5–8; education
    at, see Latin schools; parishes of Lille,
    schools in; entry to restricted, 135;
    expulsions from, 135, 136, 140, 141,
    232, 279n71, 290, 295–301, 303–5;
    garrisons in, 45, 243–4, 248, 278–9,
    285, 287, 288, 295; grain supplies at,
    135, 136, 154, 213, 223–4, 253, 343;
    hospices in, 5, 120, 137, 323; hospi-
    tals in, 5, 120, 137, 143; iconoclastic
    scare in, 218–20; immigrants to, 97,
    189, 232; leprosarium of, 6, 145;

Lille (*cont'd*)
mercenaries at, 217, 222, 223, 248, 251, 278, 279, 280, 290, 297, 299; military defense of, 216–20, 222–3, 258, 265, 275; militia of, 20n14, 218, 222, 230, 231, 254, 258, 265, 269, 282, 304; militia officers of, 269, 270, 277, 279, 302, 303, 311; morality at, 151–2, 165; municipal finances of, 19, 36, 42–5, 351; municipal welfare system of, 32, 136, 199, 309 (*see also* Common Fund for the Poor); orphanages in, 5, 6, 25, 137, 141, 323, 352; passports in, 135, 231; pensionaries of, 17n4, 246n46, 259, 267, 270; pilgrims at, 141, 161–2; plot against in 1581, 301–3; policing measures in, 33, 136, 156, 215, 221, 239–40, 262, 297, 309; political and religious slogans at, 215, 226, 262, 275, 280n74, 297; poor commissioners in, 139 (*see also* Common Fund for the Poor); population of, 5, 137, 153, 321–3; processions in, 49, 135, 163, 196–7, 212, 232, 239, 243, 255; provost of, 35, 63, 178; relations with royal government, 35–49, 351; routes at, 50–1; schoolteachers at, 184, 238, 239, 298; sworn military companies of, 39, 40, 162, 197, 216, 218; taxes, *see* municipal taxes; vigilantism at, 225–6, 312
linens, 85n1, 90
Linselles, 76, 213, 298
Lo, de, Jacques, 171, 175, 176, 179, 186n106, 191, 192, 193
loans, 100, 259–60, 300; by Lille merchants, 67, 71–2, 76, 78, 79, 330, 332, 334, 336, 338; forced, 29, 65, 66, 72, 100; to central government, 41, 44
Loi, *see* Magistrat of Lille
Lomme, 210, 225
London, 70, 82, 152n75
Longastre, sieur of, 286, 287

Longueval, de, Maximilien, seigneur of Vaux, 274–5, 279
Loos, 209, 210, 237
Low Countries, *see* Netherlands
Lutheranism, 2, 171, 172, 177n72; *see also* Protestantism
Lyon, 33n52, 55, 70, 151
Lys River, 3n10, 283; transport on, 50, 51, 226, 343
Lys River valley: Malcontents in, 297; Protestantism in, 205–6, 214, 227; weaving area in, 3n10, 173, 177, 214, 231

Maastricht, 260, 265n24
Magistrat of Lille: cohesion of, 30–2, 49, 199, 221, 295, 311–12; composition of, 22–26, 117, 187, 199, 221, 280, 311–12, 352; delayed selection in 1577 of, 267–73, 278; heresy jurisdiction of, 39–40, 172n47, 180; in summer 1566, 220–3; inner circle of, 28–30, 221, 296, 303n162, 311–12; intermarriage within, 30, 311, 352; policy towards popular festivities of, 195–7; price regulations of, 123–4; prosecution of Protestants by, 181, 191–2, 212, 277; reaction to Alba's new taxes by, 243–4; relations with church of, 34, 144, 165–8; origins of, 17; selection in 1578 of, 285–9; selection procedures for, 19–20, 267; structure of, 17–18; subsidies to preachers by, 193–4; terms in office of, 27–8, 221–2, 289; *see also* aldermen, apaiseurs, councillors, gardorphènes, huit-hommes, mayor, rewart
Mahieu, (le), Barbe, 337; Catherine, 73, 337; Colart, 336; family, 23, 27, 68, 73n99, 74, 336; Gerard, 24, 59, 73, 336; Guillaume, 337; Jean, 336–7; Jeanne, 337; Mahieu, 336; Nicolas, 24, 336–7; Philippe, 336–7; Toussaint, 24, 336

Malcontents, 283, 286, 290, 291, 294, 297–8, 299

Mallatrie, Marie, 78n115

manans, 20, 266

Marchiennes, 210, 258

Marcq, 213, 300

Margaret of Parma, 23, 233, 283, 301; in 1566, 203–4, 211–12, 217–18, 223, 228, 230; relations with Lille, 35, 40, 45, 220; *see also* Habsburg government; Moderation

Marquette, 209, 213, 225, 237

marriage portions, 72, 81, 101, 324–5; *see also* dowries; merchants, of Lille, marriage portions of; sayetterie, marriage portions in

Mary, duchess of Burgundy, 89

Mary of Hungary, 95n44, 174, 180n85

Masquelier, family, 23

Masurel, Jacques, cloth merchant, 303; Jacques, sayetteur, 249

Matthias, Archduke of Austria, 266, 267, 273, 292; and Lille, 281, 286, 287, 288

Maximilian, duke of Burgundy, 89

mayor, 18, 19, 21, 29, 259n4, 294, 354

Melantois, Nicolas, 250

Melun, de, François, 166

Menen, 251, 283, 286, 291, 298, 300–1

mercers, 184, 245, 326

merchants of Lille: Antwerp trade of, 52, 55, 56, 57, 65, 70, 72, 77, 213, 238, 248–9, 252–3, 272, 330, 332, 334, 336, 338; business practices of, 57–62; elite among, 68–74; expulsions of, 298, 304; foreigners among, 71; immigration of, 63–4, 70, 72; intermarriage among, 27, 59, 73–4; internal stratification of, 64–74; investments of, 74–82, 102–3; marriage portions of, 65, 66, 68, 78, 325, 331, 333, 335, 337, 339; partnerships of, 58–60, 62; political dominance of, 22–4, 28; profits of, 103; relation to light-cloth industry of, 102–3, 114;

reports about, 23, 215n55, 246; religious preferences of, 23–4, 83, 186–8, 250, 269; social mobility of, 72, 186; social origins of, 64, 70; wealth of, 65–8, 71–2, 100, 326, 330–9; *see also* Lille, commerce of

Mesre, le, family, 31; Jean, 26, 69; Jeanne, 69

Middelburg, 54, 55, 58, 269

ministres généraux, 141–3, 146, 149, 152, 154, 224; *see also* Common Fund for the Poor

Miroul, Claude, 300; family, 327

mobilization, 14, 308, 315; at Lille, 156, 183, 218, 288, 310–13, 320

Moderation, 203, 205n2, 208n17, 211, 212, 228

Moisne, le, Antoine, 73, 339; family, 23, 68

Mons, 140, 176, 189n117, 247n50, 248, 250, 278, 291, 292

Mont, du, Gilles, 229

Montigny, Emanuel-Philibert de Lalaing, baron of, 283–4, 286, 290, 294

Montmorency, de, François, 259; Jean, seigneur of Courrières, 37, 179n78, 180n85; Philippe, seigneur of Hachicourt, 37n69

Morel, Jean, 303

Motte, de la, seigneur, 279, 290

Muette, family, 328; Françis, 81n127; Martin, 61

Mullier, Beltremieu, 303

municipal government of Lille, *see* Magistrat of Lille

municipal taxes, 45, 79n117, 146, 262; sales, 42–3, 44; special, 223n88, 243, 253, 261, 266, 276n61

Muyssart; Antoine, 14, 259, 267–73, 286n96, 299; Toussaint, 286, 287, 289n103

Namur, 262, 264, 266

Netherlands, 2n7, 10, 48; *see also* Dutch Revolt

Index

New World, 56, 89, 94, 96

nobles, 21, 45, 66, 325; as forebears of merchants, 64, 71; commercial ties of, 79, 80; in Magistrat, 24–5; of Walloon Flanders, 19, 47n98, 77, 78, 79, 293–4; social origins of, 62–3

Noircarmes, Philippe of St. Aldegonde, baron of, 229

Notre-Dame du Puy, 162, 168, 180

Noyelles, de, Adrien, 211n33, 227

Nuremberg, 55, 190n118

Oguier, Baudichon, 173, 175–6, 192, 193, 194; family, 175, 178; Jeanne, 175, 186n106; Robert, 171, 175, 189n117, 191; Robert junior, 178n76

Oignies, d', Adrien, seigneur of Willerval, see Willerval; Gilbert, 166–7, 199

Olivier, Bernard, 194

Orange, William of, 255, 266, 289; effective chief of state, 273, 286, 287; leader of revolt, 234, 250, 262

Orangism, 248, 251, 269, 316–17; at Estates-General, 263, 267, 271, 274; at Lille, 14, 250, 268, 270, 273, 282, 285, 297, 298

Orchies, 47, 48n103, 210, 241, 246, 259

Order for the poor of Lille, 140–1, 151–2; see also Common Fund for the Poor

orphans' guardians, see gard-orphènes

ostades, 90–1, 93, 94n42, 108, 111, 130

Oudenaarde, 51, 269

outdoor preaching, see presches

Pacification of Ghent, 258, 264; terms of, 257, 276–7; implementation of, 262, 276–7; Lille and, 280, 290–1; Philip II's acceptance of, 292, 293

Paris, 53, 170n38

parishes of Lille, 34, 66n76; chapels in, 161, 162, 163; charities of, 137–9, 148, 245, 343n15, 352; clergy of, 19, 165, 185n103; description of, 5, 6; fabric of, 159–60, 169; population of,

321, 322, 323; relations with Common Fund of, 141–2, 144, 148–9; schools in, 152, 168, 238n14; sermons in, 193, 194

Parma, prince of, see Farnese, Alexander

particularism, 2, 47, 263

patrie, 49, 207, 258

pauvretés, see parishes of Lille, charities of

Percourt, family, 328

Perpetual Edict, 258, 260, 262, 263, 292

Philip II, 203, 257, 262, 263, 292; and causes of revolt, 10, 198; and Tenth and Twentieth Pennies, 247, 254; new policies under Alba, 233, 241; relations with Lille, 44, 45, 46, 49, 169, 178, 220, 300–1, 305

physicians, 21, 184, 325, 347n24; in Magistrat, 22, 25, 29

Picaret, Jean, 294

Pippre, le, family, 328

Pirenne, Henri, 10–11, 32, 36, 48, 83, 98, 104, 114, 115, 118, 186, 189, 193, 318

plague, 134, 148, 234, 253, 272

Plat, le, Adrien, 302, 303n161

Pocquet, Antoine, 173n51

Pollet, Jean, canon of St. Pierre, 177; Jean, fuller, 65

Poullain, Valerand, 174, 185

Poulle, Dominique, 236n4; family, 64, 68, 71, 327

Pragmatic Sanction of 1549, 257

presches, 177, 182; in summer 1566, 203, 205–8, 212, 214–15, 221, 223, 226–7, 230; in 1578, 277, 278

Preudhomme, (de), seigneurs of Coisne, 25, 27, 63n64; Henri, seigneur of la Ghennerie, 304n164

Prevost, le, Jacques, 304; Sebastien, 241n22, 243, 271

price revolution, see inflation

prices, 119–25, 129, 131, 155, 340–4; beer, 120, 123–4; bread, 341, 344, 346; grain, 119, 128, 132, 149–50,

212, 224, 238, 240, 249, 252, 254, 282, 297, 304, 340, 344; rye, 122, 124–5, 130, 134, 154, 248, 253, 261, 272, 343; salt, 120, 122, 248n55; trends in, 120–5, 136, 341; wheat, 122–5, 130, 134, 154, 248, 252–3, 261, 272, 342, 343

printing, 1, 170, 171

priserie, 119, 340, 342, 343

privilege of nonconfiscation, 20n14, 39–41, 45, 254, 302; *see also* confiscation of property

Privy Council, 40, 79, 111, 254, 272, 303n161

professionals, 25, 29, 185; *see also* lawyers; physicians

proletarianization, 11n15, 319

proletarians, 10, 11, 84, 115, 319; *see also* capitalism

Protestantism in Lille, 31, 226, 254; and material difficulties, 118, 198; appeals for toleration of, 214, 319, 353; before Dutch Revolt, 170–93; in 1566, 213–14, 227; social composition of, 183–9; under Estates-General, 273, 277, 279, 281–2, 287–8, 296

Protestantism in Lille area, 205, 215, 236, 254, 310

psalm singing, 171, 182

purchasing power, 125, 128, 131–4, 155

Quemble, de, Jean, 241n22

Quesnoy, du, Eustache, 174

Quesnoy-sur-Deûle, 207, 254, 298

Radical Reformation, 172–4; *see also* Anabaptists; Spiritual Libertines

Rassenghien, Maximilien Vilain, baron of: activities during 1566–7 of, 208, 217, 219, 220, 222–3, 228–30, 278; appointment as governor, 37, 207; during Estates-General rule, 259n3, 260, 265, 299; imprisonment at Ghent of, 267, 269, 274, 276n62; reports in summer 1566 by, 199,

205n5, 206, 211, 215, 217; return from Ghent of, 297–8; role in Tenth and Twentieth Penny struggle of, 242, 243, 244

Rebreviettes, de, Adrien, 274, 284, 294; Marguerite, 286n96; Martin, seigneur of Thibauville, 274n46

reconciliation with Spain, 270, 284, 289, 290, 294–5

Reformed Religion, *see* Calvinism; Protestantism in Lille

regent, *see* Margaret of Parma, Mary of Hungary

reimbursements by royal government, 43–4

religious freedom, Protestant project for, 70, 187

Religious Peace, 277

Remy, Mathias, 180, 192

Renault, Jean, 65

rentes, *see* annuities

rents: house, 80n125, 347–8; trends in, 121, 122

Requesens, de Don Luis, 235, 254, 255, 256, 264

Retz, du, family, 328; Louis, 60; Thomas, 60

revolutionary centers, 275, 277, 313–15

rewart, 17, 18, 19, 21, 22, 25, 30n39; *see also* Magistrat of Lille

Riez de Canteleu, 6, 20n14, 148, 253

Riviere, de la, Philippe, seigneur of Warnes, 222n83, 281

Rogier, Guillaume, 101

Ronsee, seigneurs of Rabecque, François, 24; Jacques, 24

Rosimbos, de, François, 166

Rot, du, Clement, 299

Rotewe, Adrien, 81

Roubaix, 95n44, 105, 206

Rouen, 53, 55, 56, 70, 82

Rouvroy, family, 329

royal government, *see* Habsburg government

Ruffault, de, Jean, 159n6, 161

rural textiles, 38, 92, 95n44, 102, 105, 106, 107, 127, 309, 310

Sailly, de, Antoine, 65; family, 328; Michelle, 65
St. Omer, 64, 82–3n134, 300
St. Pierre, collegiate church of, 158, 159, 195, 275n54; canons of, 63, 79, 144, 158, 177, 266, 291, 301; chaplains of, 158, 162, 195; chapter of, 34, 165, 166, 168, 193n128; in 1566–7, 218, 223n88, 232
Sallengre, Pierre, 54
Sarrazin, Jean, 280, 284, 285n92, 287, 288, 355
satins, 90, 93, 94n42, 108–9, 111
Savereulx, Georges, 172
sayetterie: guild of, 90, 97, 109, 163; importance of, 88–9; marriage portions in, 100, 324; master (free) workers in, 99, 112; masters in, 99, 101n69, 103, 109, 114, 272; origins of, 89–90; output of, 92–4, 213, 238, 239, 245, 248, 249; products of, 91, 92, 271, 342; religious indifference in, 237; religious preferences in, 179, 188–91; stratification in, 99, 107–8, 111; Vingtaine, 99, 101, 107, 108, 110, 111, 113–16, 272
says, 38, 90–1, 109
Scheldt River, 3n10, 50, 56, 343
Scholliers, Etienne, 128, 156, 344, 345, 347
Sea Beggars, 234, 247, 248n55; *see also* Beggars
Seclin, 210, 286
seigneuries, 75, 80
seigneurs, 22, 24–5, 29, 185
Sellier, le, Philippe, 178
Seville, 57, 89n20
shearers, 91, 97n49, 324
's Hertogenbosch, 5n12, 268n30
shopkeepers, 298, 304, 326
small commodity production: definition of, 115–16; effects of, 225, 309, 310;

implementation of, 116–18, 191, 198, 272, 312
small producers, 31, 194
Smerpont (Semerpont), de, Amery, 337; Arnold (Arnoul), 22, 336–7; Betremieu, 303n162; family, 64, 68, 71, 74, 327, 336; Jean, 73, 296, 303n162, 332, 336–7, 339; Marguerite, 337; Philippe, 336; Wallerand, 336–7
Smit, J. W., 31, 47
Spain, 53, 60, 82, 89
Spanish America, *see* New World
Spanish fury, *see* Antwerp
Spanish troops, 258, 259, 260, 262, 263, 264, 291, 293; *see also* Habsburg government, troops of
spinners, 89, 103, 106, 245
spinning, 104, 104–5n83, 106, 107
Spiritual Libertines, 173
spoolers, 89, 101
stability, 11–12, 14, 156, 213, 225, 309, 311, 319–20
standard of living, 10, 118, 119–20, 198, 340–8
Steenbecque (Estaimbeke), Hugues de Bournel, seigneur of, 269n32, 274, 276n62
Strasbourg, 140, 174
subsistence, 120, 130, 132, 133, 136, 248–9, 253
Sunday schools, 152
Surbise, van, Bussaert, 281, 282

Tack, Antoine, 170n38
tanners, 65, 69, 304, 324, 326
tapestries, 85
Tenth and Twentieth Pennies, 241, 243–8, 254–5, 295, 312
Tenremonde, de, Jacques, seigneur of Blanche Maille, 24
Tesson, family, 328; Nicolas, 61, 64
Thiebreghien, Jean, 26
Thieffries, de, Antoine, 54, 59, 60, 73, 334, 338–9; family, 68, 71, 73, 74,

79, 327, 338; Gerard, 338;
Guillaume, 338–9; Hugues, 64;
Jacques, 64, 73, 81, 338–9; Laurent,
338; Nicolas, 339
Thieulaine, de, Jean, 296
thread doubling, 89, 101, 112, 342
Tilly, Charles, 13, 156
Titelmans, Pieter, 177–8, 181, 182
Touart, Guillaume, 175
Toufflers, 95n44, 105
Toulouse, 53, 55, 57, 70
Tourcoing, 95n44, 105, 182, 206–7,
254
trimming makers, 180, 184, 188–9
Tournai, 5n12, 11n15, 64, 180n85, 193,
235, 244, 250, 274n48, 292, 305,
315; and reconciliation with Spain,
283n83, 289; at Estates-General,
259, 264, 287; bishops of, 38n75, 79,
166, 205n5, 208, 238 (*see also* Croy,
Charles de; Guillard, Louis; Oignies,
Gilbert d'); episcopal court of, 38n75,
172, 180; iconoclasts from, 210n25,
218, 219; military threats to Lille
from, 301–3; Protestants in, 173n51,
174, 176, 179, 182, 189n117,
190n118, 192, 213–14, 226, 227,
229; Protestants in neighborhood of,
174, 205, 208; relations with Lille of,
49, 56; revolt at, 228–9
Tournésis, 208, 241, 264, 283n83

unemployment, 136, 234
Utrecht, 5n12, 234, 265, 268; Union of,
293

vagabonds, 127, 134
Valenciennes, 11, 55, 215n55, 235, 244,
265, 269, 315; Protestants in,
173n51, 174, 176, 182, 190n118,
226, 227; reconciliation of, 292, 300,
301; relations with Lille of, 49, 51;
revolt in, 228–9, 231, 232
Vanderlinde, Jean, 69

Van der Wee, Herman, 122, 128, 156,
345
Vaux, *see* Longueval
velveteens, 90, 91, 93, 130; output of,
94, 95–6, 213, 238n15, 239, 249,
261; *see also* bourgetterie; light wool-
ens industry in Lille
Vendeville, de, Antoine, 79; family, 64,
68, 71, 73, 74, 79, 328; Guillaume,
79; Jacques, 54, 68, 79; Jean, 79
Venice, 12n18, 82, 142, 146
Verlinden, Charles, 128, 156, 347
Vertbois, seigneurie of, 205, 213
Vicq, de, Roland, seigneur of Northoven,
260
Vigneron, Pierre, 53
Vilain, Maximilien, baron of
Rassenghien, *see* Rassenghien
Villain, Albin, 61
Vincent, Jean, 101
Vingtaine, *see* sayetterie
Vlieghe, le, Jean, seigneur of la Grurie,
259n4
voir-jurés, *see* councillors

Wacrenier, family, 329
wages, 41, 128, 248, 272, 344, 351;
controversy over, 126–7; grain equivalents of, 133, 249; masters', *see* skilled artisans; rates, 125–6, 347; skilled
artisans', 126, 132, 136, 198, 212,
252, 341, 344–5; trends, 122, 128,
134, 136, 252–3, 297, 341; unskilled
laborers', 126, 132, 136, 198, 212,
341, 345
Walloon Flanders, 228, 251; and Estates-General, 258, 260–1, 264, 273,
274, 276, 277n67, 289n106, 292; description of, 3n10, 8, 52; disaffection
among political elites of, 276, 282,
284, 289; Estates of, *see* Estates of
Lille, Douai, and Orchies; governors
of, 19, 36, 37n67 (*see also* Croy,
Adrien de; Montmorency, Jean de;
Rassenghien; Steenbecque); lieuten-

Walloon Flanders (*cont'd*)
  ant governors of, 19, 37, 63, 204 (*see
  also* Cambe, de le, Denis; Cuvillon,
  Baude); Protestantism in, 176, 182,
  204–9, 236, 251, 277, 298; *see also*
  aides; castellany; nobles
Wambrechies, 76, 182, 207, 210–11,
  254, 298
Warenghien, de, Jean, 241n22
Warnes, *see* Riviere
Wattrelos, 228–9, 232n118
Wicart, Mahieu, 69; Pierre, 69
Willerval, Adrien d'Oignies, seigneur of,
  276n62, 297n139; as promoter of
  reconciliation with Spain, 283, 290,
  291, 294; in 1578, 278–82, 286–8;
  relations with Estates-General, 284,
  289, 293–4
Wittman, Tibor, 1, 30–1, 36, 80
women: and citizenship, 20; commercial
  activities of, 58–9; employment of,
  100–1, 112, 189n116, 342; mastership open to, 99; religious choices of,
  186

woolens industries, *see* bourgetterie;
  drapery; light woolens industry in
  Lille; rural textiles; sayetterie
work, availability of, 128–30, 136, 150,
  252, 261, 282, 297, 341
work year, length of, 132, 344–5

Ypres, 206, 236, 278, 283, 316; radical
  regime at, 283, 285, 292; welfare
  reform at, 140, 141, 142, 143, 144

Zealots for the public weal, 281–2, 287–
  8, 303n161, 312
Zeeland, 204, 235, 256, 283, 293; cities
  of, 1, 234; military activity in, 251,
  255; relations with Estates-General
  of, 257, 259, 262, 273, 289n106;
  religion in, 262, 276–7; revolt in,
  315–17
Zegre, Cornille, 100; Evonne, 100
Zenne (De Lesenne), de le, Cornille,
  205, 206, 208, 210, 213, 227n103

CAMBRIDGE STUDIES IN EARLY MODERN HISTORY

*Edited by Professor J. H. Elliott, Regius Professor of Modern History,
Oxford University; Professor Olwen Hufton, Harvard University;
Professor H. G. Koenigsberger*

Society and Religious Toleration in Hamburg 1529–1819
JOACHIM WHALEY

*Absolutism and Society in Seventeenth-Century France: State Power and Provincial Aristocracy
in Languedoc*
WILLIAM BEIK

Turning Swiss: Cities and Empire 1450–1550
THOMAS A. BRADY JR

The Duke of Anjou and the Politique Struggle during the Wars of Religion
MACK P. HOLT

Neighbourhood and Community in Paris 1740–1790
DAVID GARRIOCH

Renaissance and Revolt: Essays in the Intellectual and Social History of Early Modern France
J. H. M. SALMON

The Princes of Orange: the Stadholders in the Dutch Republic
HERBERT H. ROWEN

The Changing Face of Empire: Charles V, Philip II and Habsburg Authority, 1551–1559
M. J. RODRIGUEZ-SALGADO

Louis XIV and the Origins of the Dutch War
PAUL SONNINO